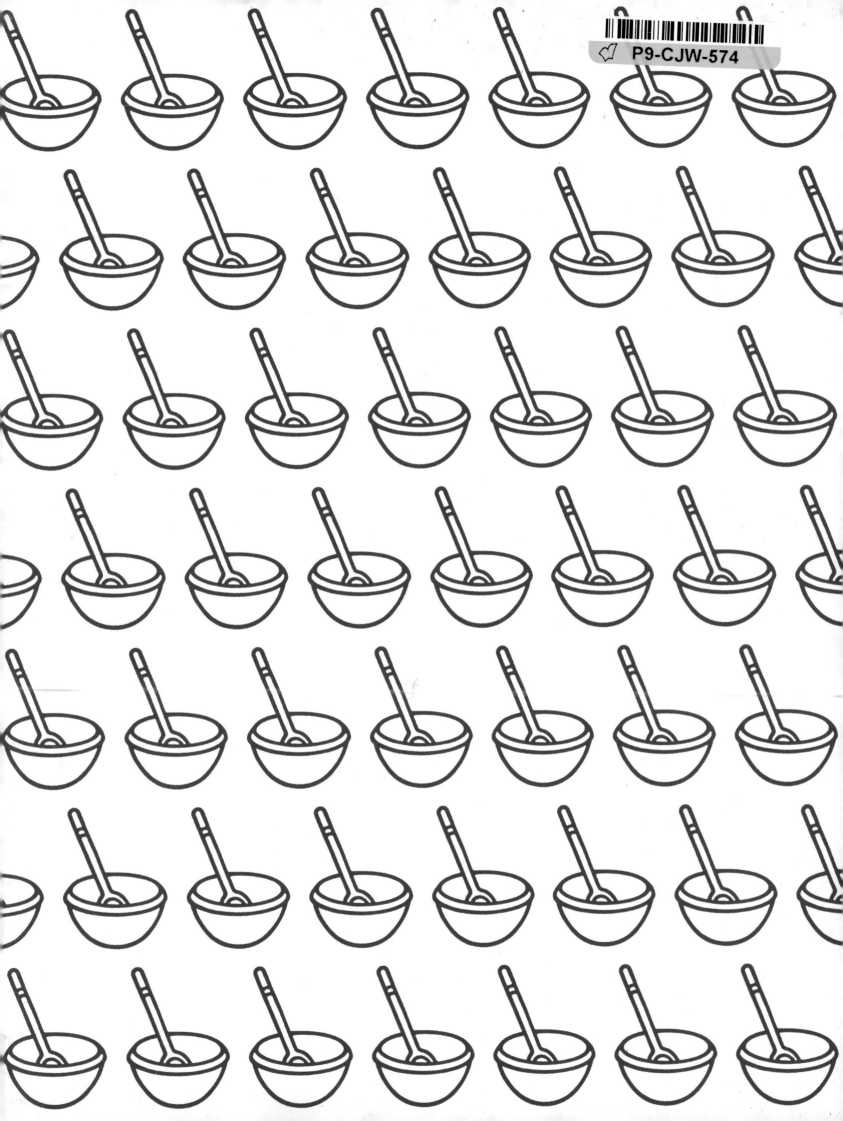

THE ULTIMATE
COOKING
COURSE

THE ULTIMATE
COOKING
COURSE

AND KITCHEN ENCYCLOPEDIA

CONSULTANT EDITOR: CAROLE CLEMENTS

HERMES
HOUSE

This edition published by Hermes House
Anness Publishing Inc.
27 West 20th Street
New York
NY 10011

ISBN 1 84038 108 6

Publisher: Joanna Lorenz
Authors: Norma MacMillan and Frances Cleary
Project Editor: Carole Clements
Designer: Sheila Volpe
Jacket Designer: Bobbie Colgate Stone
Photography: Amanda Heywood
Food Styling: Frances Cleary, Carole Handslip, Elizabeth Wolf-Cohen
Steps: Marilyn Forbes, Cara Hobday and Nicola Fowler

The author would like to thank Jill Eggleton
for her help in testing recipes

The publishers wish to thank Cuisinarts Corporation,
1 Cummings Point Road, Stamford, Connecticut 06904

Printed and bound in Hong Kong / China

1 3 5 7 9 10 8 6 4 2

~ CONTENTS ~

~

THE COOK'S KITCHEN BIBLE

AMERICAN HOME COOKING

~ INTRODUCTION ~

Whether you are a complete novice, an experienced cook, or an occasional dabbler, there are times when everyone longs for basic techniques and methods to be laid out clearly and simply. This book does just that.

In addition, there are lots of recipes and recipe ideas, too, so you can try out the skills you are learning or brushing up. The recipes are designed to illustrate a particular technique. When you read these recipes, take a moment to assess any additional techniques required. Look them up in the index, if you want to review.

USEFUL EQUIPMENT
To be able to cook efficiently and with pleasure, you need good equipment. That is not to say that you should invest in an extensive collection of pots, pans, tools, and gadgets, but a basic range of cookware is essential.

In addition, buy the best equipment you can afford, adding more as your budget allows. Well made equipment lasts and is a sound investment; inexpensive cookware is likely to dent, break, or develop "hot spots" where food will stick and burn, so will need replacing. Flimsy tools will make food preparation more time consuming and frustrating.

For the Rangetop
When choosing pots and pans, look for those with heavy bases, sturdy insulated handles and knobs, and tight-fitting lids. Bear in mind, too, how much the pan will weigh when full – a large pot for pasta or stock must not be too heavy for you to lift.

Copper conducts heat best, but is hard to care for. Aluminum is good, as is cast iron, although the latter needs scrupulous care to prevent rust. Enamel- or porcelain-coated cast iron is a good compromise. Stainless steel is lightweight and durable, but it conducts heat unevenly. A composite or clad bottom containing another metal can improve heat conduction.

- **Rangetop essentials:** 3 saucepans with lids (1-, 2-, and 3-quart), 6- or 8-inch skillet, 12-inch skillet with lid, flameproof casserole or Dutch oven with lid (4- or 6-quart), kettle or stockpot with lid (8-quart).
- **Helpful equipment:** Double boiler, wok, omelette pan, crêpe pan, sauté pan, ridged grill pan, steamer.

For the Oven
Cake and muffin pans and baking sheets should be made of shiny metal (aluminum, tin, or stainless steel) for even heat distribution. Pie plates should be dull metal, ceramic, or glass. Roasting pans can be made of any material, but they must be sturdy, as should all bakeware.

- **Baking and roasting essentials:** 9-inch round cake pans, 8- or 9-inch square cake pans, 9- × 13-inch baking pan, loaf pan (8- × 4-inch or 9- × 5-inch, or both), muffin pan, 9-inch pie plate, 9-inch removable bottom tart pan, 9-inch springform pan, 10- × 15-inch jelly roll pan, 2 baking sheets, roasting pan with rack, wire rack, large soufflé dish, shallow and deep baking dishes, broiler pan with rack, pot holders or oven mitts, oven and meat thermometers.

- **Helpful bakeware:** 2 layer cake pans (8- or 9-inch), 10-inch tube pan, round and square pans, pie plates, tart pans, and springform pans of various sizes, individual soufflé dishes, gratin dishes, metal skewers.

Cutting Tools
A good set of knives is the most important tool in food preparation. Yet so many cooks make do with flimsy, dull, or nicked knives, which can turn even the chopping of onions into an arduous task.

Knives made of carbon steel can be given the sharpest edge, but they rust and discolor easily so must be washed and dried immediately after use. High-carbon stainless steel knives will take a sharp edge and they resist discoloration, but are more expensive. Ordinary stainless steel knives are very difficult to sharpen efficiently.

Whatever knives you choose, keep them sharp. More accidents occur with blunt knives than sharp ones.

- **Cutting essentials:** Chef's knife with rigid 10-inch blade, paring knife with rigid 3-inch blade, flexible vegetable knife with serrated edge and pointed tip, rigid serrated knife with 10- to 12-inch blade, sturdy kitchen scissors, knife block or magnetized bar, several cutting boards in different sizes and reserved for different uses.
- **Helpful cutting tools:** Filleting knife with thin flexible 7-inch blade and sharp point, boning knife with thin rigid 6-inch blade, utility knife with rigid 6-inch blade, grapefruit knife with curved serrated blade, poultry shears, carving knife and fork.

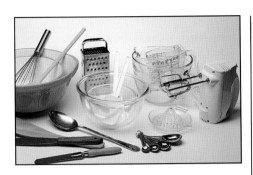

Preparation Tools
You can do a lot with just a big bowl and a sturdy spoon, but there are many tools that make cooking easier.

● **Preparation essentials**: 4 mixing bowls in varying sizes, wooden spoons, long-handled slotted spoon, ladle, wooden spatula, rubber spatulas, narrow metal spatula with flexible 10-inch blade, slotted spatula/pancake turner, tongs, 12-inch wire balloon whisk, handheld electric mixer, citrus press, colander, measuring cups (liquid and dry) and spoons, vegetable peeler, grater, 2 strainers (1 metal, 1 nylon), 2-pronged fork, rolling pin, pastry brush, can and bottle openers, corkscrew, kitchen timer, paper towels, wraps, string.

● **Helpful equipment**: Salad spinner, food processor and/or blender, potato ricer, meat pounder, rotary grater, nutmeg grater, citrus zester, channeling knife, apple corer, melon baller, pastry blender, pastry scraper, trussing needle, cherry pitter, pasta machine, countertop electric mixer, parchment paper.

BUYING AND STORING FOOD
A well-stocked kitchen makes meal preparation easy. The key is planning – planning menus for the next few days or the week ahead, then making a shopping list that includes fresh foods as well as those frequently-used foods whose stocks are running low or that are near or past their expiration date. Allow yourself to be a little flexible, though. When shopping, take advantage of fresh seasonal foods and special offers.

Knowing how and where to store food – both fresh and preserved – and how long to keep it will be a great help in shopping to stock the kitchen.

In the Refrigerator
All foods in the refrigerator or freezer should be well wrapped or stored in sealed containers. This preserves flavor and moisture, and prevents the flavors and odors of other, stronger foods being transferred. It is essential to keep raw meat and poultry well wrapped as their drippings can transfer bacteria to other foods.

Perishable fresh foods, such as meats, poultry, fish and seafood, eggs, cheese and other dairy products, and many fruits and vegetables, must be kept refrigerated at a temperature of 35–40°F. For longer storage, many can also be frozen at 0°F or lower. Cooked leftovers must also be refrigerated or frozen. Check the refrigerator and freezer temperatures with a special thermometer. If temperatures are too high, food will spoil rapidly.

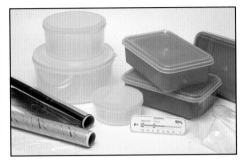

Storing Fresh Fruits
Those fruits that can be kept at room temperature while still unripe include apricots, kiwi fruits, mangoes, nectarines, papayas, peaches, pears, pineapples, and plums. Once ripe, all these should be refrigerated and eaten within 2–3 days.

Fruits that can be stored at cool room temperature include apples (although they will be crisper if refrigerated), bananas, dates, lemons, limes, grapefruit, and oranges. Apples can be kept at room temperature for a few days, dates for several weeks, and citrus fruit up to a week; beyond that, refrigerate them.

Unless you intend to eat them on the day of purchase, refrigerate fully ripe and perishable fresh fruits. These include berries, cherries, figs, grapes, melons, pomegranates, and tangerines. They can be kept refrigerated for 2–3 days.

Storing Fresh Vegetables
Like fruits, there are some vegetables that can be stored at room temperature. A dark, cool place (about 50°F) with good ventilation is ideal. Suitable vegetables are chayotes, garlic, onions, potatoes and sweet potatoes, rutabaga, and winter squash. All can be kept about 2 months. Store tomatoes at room temperature until they are ripe. After that, refrigerate.

Perishable vegetables should be refrigerated. Some, such as peas or corn should be used quickly, while others, like carrots or cabbage, can be kept for a longer period. In most cases, do not wash the vegetable until just before using. Celery, curly endive, escarole, hearty greens, herbs, lettuce, spinach and watercress should be washed before storage.

Storing Canned and Dry Foods

Full pantry shelves are a boon for a busy cook, but canned and dry foods can deteriorate if not stored properly or if left too long on the shelf. Kitchen cabinets should be cool (no more than 65°F) and dry. Staples such as flour, salt, sugar, pasta, and grains are best stored in moistureproof containers. If necessary remove them from their wrappings and decant them into canisters or jars. Whole-grain products (whole-wheat flour and pasta, brown rice, etc.) cannot be kept as long as refined ones.

Dried herbs and spices will keep their flavor and scent best if stored in sealed jars. Light is their enemy; store in a cabinet or drawer, rather than on an open spice rack. Oil, too, should be stored in a cool dark place, in an airtight container. Refrigerate nut oils to preserve them longer.

Herbs and Spices

The judicious use of an herb or spice, or both, can transform a dish. It's fun to experiment, once you know what you like and which seasonings go well with what foods.

Whenever possible, use fresh herbs, for their wonderful flavor, scent, and color. They're widely available in supermarkets and are also easy to grow, even in pots on a windowsill. Fresh herbs impart their flavor very quickly, so chop just before using, and add to hot dishes towards the end of cooking. If fresh herbs are not available, you can, of course, substitute dried. Use them in a ratio of 1 teaspoon dried to 1 tablespoon fresh.

Most spices, both whole and ground, need time to impart their aroma and flavor to a dish. Some are pungent and spicy-hot, others are sweet and fragrant. If you can, grind spices freshly, using a spice mill, nutmeg grater, or mortar and pestle. The difference in flavor and aroma between pre-ground and freshly ground is amazing.

GETTING THE TIMING RIGHT

Successful meal preparation is as much dependent on organization as on culinary skills. The initial planning of a menu – whether for the family supper or a company dinner – must give consideration to many things: a good range of flavors, colors, and textures, as well as a balance in protein, fat, fiber, and other healthy considerations.

That done, it then becomes a question of what you can prepare ahead, and what remains to do at the last minute so that all is ready at the same time. For the beginner, this can be daunting.

The first step is to read all the recipes before making a final choice. The main dish, with simple accompaniments such as vegetables or a salad and bread, is a good starting point. Surround that with a cold first course (if there is to be one) and a cold dessert that can be made ahead of time. This way you can concentrate your efforts at each stage.

If you do choose two or more hot dishes, consider their cooking times and oven temperatures. If you have only one oven, and the temperatures required for the two dishes are different, this will present difficulties.

Next, make a shopping list. Check that you have all the equipment you require. Once you have everything on hand, you can start the preparation.

Read each recipe through again so you know what lies ahead and try to estimate how long each preparation stage will take. Review techniques in the preparation that are unfamiliar, using the index to locate them, if necessary. Set the time you want to serve the meal, and work back from there so you know when to start the preparation. It's not a bad idea to write down all these times, as if you were planning military strategy.

If you are serving a first course, you will need to plan what can be left unattended while you are at the table. If your chosen dessert is frozen, it may need some time out of the freezer before serving, so decide at what point to transfer it to the refrigerator.

Remember to allow time for the final draining of vegetables, or carving of meat, or seasoning of a sauce. It is usually the case that all of these need to be done at the same time – but you only have one pair of hands. So decide what can wait and what will keep hot. Also allow time for plates to be cleared from the table if you are serving more than one course.

If any recipe requires the oven to be preheated or pans to be prepared, do this first. Pots of boiling salted water for cooking vegetables or pasta can be brought to the boil while you are doing the chopping and slicing.

Set out all the ingredients required and prepare them according to recipe directions. If more than one dish calls for the same ingredients, say chopped onion or parsley, you can prepare the total amount at the same time.

Now start cooking, following your timetable. Check the recipe as you work, and don't be distracted. Keep tasting and sniffing the food as you go – that's much of the fun!

MEASURING TECHNIQUES

Cooks with years of experience, preparing familiar recipes, may not need to measure ingredients, but if you are a beginning cook or are trying a new recipe for the first time, it is a good idea to follow instructions carefully. Also, measuring all the ingredients precisely will insure consistent results.

The recipes in this book have been tested using a conventional, not fan assisted, oven. Unless specified otherwise, flour is all-purpose, sugar is granulated, and eggs are USDA size large.

SOME USEFUL EQUIVALENTS

3 teaspoons = 1 tablespoon = ½ fluid ounce = 14.79 milliliters

4 tablespoons = ¼ cup = 2 fluid ounces

5 tablespoons + 1 teaspoon = ⅓ cup

8 tablespoons = ½ cup = 4 fluid ounces

10 tablespoons + 2 teaspoons = ⅔ cup

12 tablespoons = ¾ cup = 6 fluid ounces

16 tablespoons = 1 cup = 8 fluid ounces = 236.6 milliliters

2 cups = 1 pint = 16 fluid ounces

4 cups or 2 pints = 1 quart = 32 fluid ounces

1.06 quarts = 1 liter

4 quarts = 1 gallon = 128 fluid ounces

1 ounce = 28.35 grams

16 ounces = 1 pound = 453.59 grams

2.205 pounds = 1 kilogram

1 inch = 2.5 centimeters

12 inches = 1 foot = 30 centimeters/.305 meter

40 inches = 3.28 feet = 1 meter

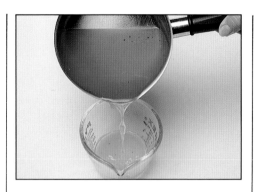

1 ▲ For liquids measured in cups: Use a glass or clear plastic measuring cup. Put the cup on a flat surface and pour in the liquid. Bend down and check that the liquid is exactly level with the marking on the cup, as specified in the recipe.

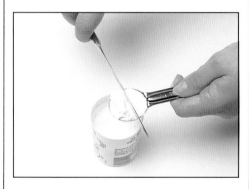

3 ▲ For measuring dry ingredients in a cup or spoon: Fill the cup or spoon. Level the surface even with the rim of the cup or spoon, using the straight edge of a knife.

5 ▲ For measuring brown sugar in a cup or spoon: If the recipe specifies firmly packed brown sugar, scoop the sugar and press it firmly into the cup or spoon. Level the surface.

2 ▲ For liquids measured in spoons: Pour the liquid into the measuring spoon, to the brim, and then pour it into the mixing bowl. Do not hold the spoon over the bowl when measuring because liquid may overflow.

4 ▲ For measuring flour in a cup or spoon: Scoop the flour from the canister in the measuring cup or spoon. Hold it over the canister and level the surface.

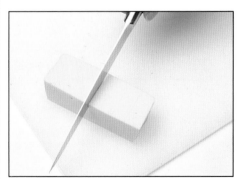

6 ▲ For measuring butter: With a sharp knife, cut off the specified amount following the markings on the wrapper.

POULTRY

~

With chicken and other birds a mainstay of weekday meals and holiday gatherings, knowing how to handle poultry helps you make the most of it. It is simple to make your own stock for great gravy and economical to cut up or bone poultry yourself.

TRUSSING POULTRY

Trussing holds a bird together during cooking so that it keeps a neat, attractive shape. If the bird is stuffed, trussing prevents the stuffing from falling out. You can truss with strong string or with poultry skewers or lacers as shown here.

Alternatively, use a long trussing needle and string. Pass the needle through the body from one side to the other near where the legs are attached, then through both wings and tie the string. Pass the needle through the tail and tie the string around the ends of the drumsticks.

Remove all trussing before serving.

1 ▲ For an unstuffed bird: Set it breast down and pull the flap of neck skin over the neck opening. Turn the bird onto its back. Fold each wing tip back, over the neck skin, to secure firmly behind the shoulder.

2 ▲ Cross the ends of the drumsticks and press the legs firmly down and into the breast.

3 ▲ If there is a band of skin across the tail, tuck the ends of the drumsticks under the skin. Otherwise, loop a length of string several times around the drumstick ends, then tie a knot and trim off excess string.

4 ▲ For a stuffed bird: Fold the wing tips back as above. If the bird has been stuffed in the neck end, first fold the flap of skin over the opening and secure it with a skewer, then fold over the wing tips.

5 ▲ Put any stuffing or flavorings (herbs, lemon halves, apple or onion quarters, etc.) in the body cavity, then secure the ends of the drumsticks as above, tying in the tail end, too.

6 ▲ Alternatively, the cavity opening can be closed with skewers: Insert 2 or more skewers across the opening, threading them through the skin several times.

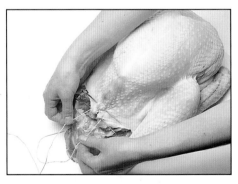

7 ▲ Lace the skewers together with string. Tie the drumsticks together over the skewers.

Stuffing Tips
- Stuffing should be cool, not hot or chilled when put into the bird.
- Pack it loosely in the bird because it expands during cooking. Cook any leftover stuffing separately in a baking dish.
- Do not stuff poultry until just before cooking.
- If stuffing the body cavity of a large bird, use maximum roasting times (page 14) because the stuffing could inhibit heat penetration, and thus not kill all harmful bacteria.

Pot-Roast Chicken with Sausage Stuffing

SERVES 6

2 2½-pound chickens

2 tablespoons vegetable oil

1½ cups chicken stock or half wine and half stock

1 bay leaf

FOR THE STUFFING

1 pound bulk pork sausage

½ cup chopped onion

1–2 garlic cloves, minced

1 teaspoon hot paprika

½ teaspoon hot pepper flakes (optional)

½ teaspoon dried thyme

¼ teaspoon ground allspice

1 cup coarse fresh bread crumbs or crumbled cornbread

1 egg, beaten to mix

salt and pepper

1 Preheat the oven to 350°F.

2 ▲ For the stuffing, put the sausage, onion, and garlic in a frying pan and fry over medium heat until the sausage is lightly browned and crumbly, stirring and turning so it cooks evenly. Remove from the heat and mix in the remaining stuffing ingredients with salt and pepper to taste.

3 Divide the stuffing between the chickens, packing it loosely into the body cavities (or, if preferred, stuff the neck end and bake leftover stuffing separately). Truss the birds.

4 ▼ Heat the oil in a Dutch oven that is just large enough to hold the chickens. Brown the birds all over.

~ VARIATION ~

For Pot-Roast Guinea Hen, use guinea hens instead of chickens.

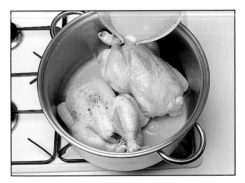

5 ▲ Add the stock and bay leaf and season. Cover and bring to a boil, then transfer to the oven. Pot-roast until the birds are cooked (the juices will run clear), about 1¼ hours.

6 Untruss the chickens and spoon the stuffing onto a serving platter. Arrange the birds and serve with the strained cooking liquid.

ROASTING POULTRY

Where would family gatherings be without the time-honored roasted bird? But beyond the favorite chicken, all types of poultry can be roasted – from small Cornish hens to large turkeys. However, older, tougher birds are better pot-roasted.

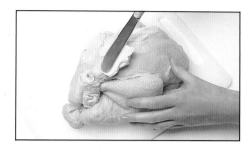

Protect and Flavor

Before roasting, loosen the skin on the breast by gently easing it away from the flesh with your fingers. Press in softened butter – mixed with herbs or garlic for extra flavor – and smooth back the skin.

1 ▲ Wipe the bird inside and out with damp paper towels. Stuff the bird, if the recipe directs, and truss it. Spread the breast of chicken with melted or softened butter or oil; bard the breast of a lean game bird; prick the skin of duck and goose.

2 ▲ Set the bird breast-up on a rack in a small roasting pan or shallow baking dish. If you are roasting a lean game bird, set the bird in the pan breast down.

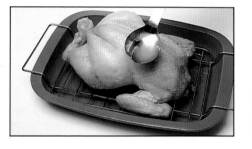

3 ▲ Roast the bird, basting it every 10 minutes after the first ½ hour with the juices and fat in the pan. Turn it if the recipe directs. If it is browning too quickly, cover loosely with foil.

4 ▲ Transfer the bird to a carving board and let it rest at least 15 minutes. If desired, deglaze for a simple pan sauce (page 48) or make gravy with the pan juices (page 38).

Simple Roast Chicken

Squeeze the juice from a halved lemon over a 3- to 3½-pound chicken, then push the lemon halves into the body cavity. Smear 1 tablespoon softened butter over the breast. Roast in a preheated 375°F oven until done, about 1¼ hours. Skim all fat from the roasting juices, then add ½ cup water and bring to a boil, stirring well to mix in the browned bits. Season with salt and pepper, and pass this sauce with the chicken. *Serves 4.*

ROASTING TIMES FOR POULTRY

Note: Cooking times given here are for unstuffed birds. For stuffed birds, add 20 minutes to the total roasting time.

Cornish hen	1–1½ pounds	1–1¼ hours at 350°F
Chicken (broiler-fryer or roaster)	2½–3 pounds	1–1¼ hours at 375°F
	3½–4 pounds	1¼–1¾ hours at 375°F
	4½–5 pounds	1½–2 hours at 375°F
	5–6 pounds	1¾–2½ hours at 375°F
Capon	5–7 pounds	1¾–2 hours at 325°F
Duck (domestic)	3–5 pounds	1¾–2¼ hours at 400°F
Goose	8–10 pounds	2½–3 hours at 350°F
	10–12 pounds	3–3½ hours at 350°F
Turkey (whole bird)	6–8 pounds	3–3½ pounds at 325°F
	8–12 pounds	3–4 hours at 325°F
	12–16 pounds	4–5 hours at 325°F
Turkey (whole breast)	4–6 pounds	1½–2¼ hours at 325°F
	6–8 pounds	2¼–3¼ hours at 325°F

Cornish Hens Waldorf

SERVES 6

6 Cornish hens, each weighing about
   1¼ pounds

3–4 tablespoons melted butter

FOR THE STUFFING

2 tablespoons butter

1 onion, minced

2 cups cooked rice

2 celery stalks, minced

2 red-skinned apples, cored and finely
   diced

½ cup chopped walnuts

⅓ cup cream sherry or apple cider

2 tablespoons lemon juice

salt and pepper

1 Preheat the oven to 350°F.

2 For the stuffing, melt the butter in a small frying pan and fry the onion, stirring occasionally, until soft. Turn the onion and butter into a bowl and add the remaining stuffing ingredients. Season with salt and pepper and mix well.

3 ◄ Divide the stuffing among the hens, stuffing the body cavities. Truss the hens. Arrange in a roasting pan. Sprinkle with salt and pepper and drizzle over the melted butter.

4 Roast until cooked through, 1¼– 1½ hours. Untruss before serving.

CARVING POULTRY

Carving a bird neatly for serving makes the presentation attractive. You will need a sharp, long-bladed knife, or an electric knife, plus a long, 2-pronged fork and a carving board with a well to catch the juices.

   Cut away any trussing string. For a stuffed bird, spoon the stuffing from the cavity into a serving bowl. For easier carving, remove the wishbone.

   Insert the fork into one breast to hold the bird steady. Cut through the skin to the leg joint on that side of the body, then slice through the joint to sever the leg from the body. Repeat on the other side.

1 ▲ Slice through the joint in each leg to sever the thigh and drumstick. If carving turkey, slice the meat off the thigh and drumstick, parallel to the bone, turning to get even slices; leave thighs and drumsticks of chicken whole.

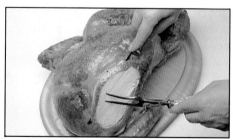

2 ▲ To carve the breast meat of a turkey or chicken, cut ⅛–¼-inch thick slices at an angle, slicing down on both sides of the breastbone. For smaller birds, remove the meat on each side of the breastbone in a single piece, then slice across.

PREPARING DUCK AND GOOSE FOR ROASTING

Duck and goose are bony birds, with most of their rich meat in the breast. There is a thick layer of fat under the skin which could make the birds greasy if it is not removed before cooking or melted out during cooking.

Lean By Nature
Wild duck and geese are not as fatty as domestic ducks, and should be prepared as you would a game bird so the meat doesn't dry out: bard the breast with slices of bacon or pork fatback.

1 ▲ Pull out any fat from the body and neck cavities. With a skewer or toothpick, prick the skin all over the breast of the bird. This will allow the melted fat to run out while the bird is being cooked.

2 ▲ Tie the ends of the drumsticks together with string as for a chicken.

Duck with Peach Sauce

SERVES 4

5- to 6-pound duck, prepared for roasting

salt and pepper

5 ripe but firm peaches

1 cup orange juice

¼ cup Southern Comfort, peach brandy, or additional orange juice

1 teaspoon cornstarch

2 teaspoons water

2 teaspoons Dijon-style mustard

fresh parsley or watercress, for garnishing

1 Preheat the oven to 400°F.

2 Rub the duck all over with salt and pepper. Set it on a rack in a roasting pan and roast 1¼ hours.

3 Meanwhile, peel the peaches: dip in boiling water for 30 seconds, then in ice water to remove the skin. Cut them in half and remove the pits. Purée 2 peach halves with the orange juice in a blender or food processor.

4 Put the remaining peach halves in a saucepan and sprinkle with the alcohol or additional orange juice. Set aside.

5 ▲ Pour all the duck fat from the roasting pan. Place the duck in the pan, without the rack, and pour the orange and peach mixture over it. Roast, basting occasionally with the sauce in the pan, for about 15 minutes longer, or until the duck is cooked (lift it with a long 2-pronged fork: the juices that run out of the cavity should be clear).

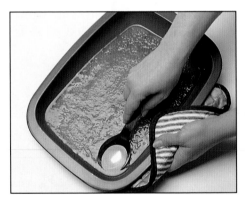

6 ▲ Transfer the duck to a carving board and keep warm. Skim all the fat from the sauce, then set the pan over medium heat and bring to a boil. Blend the cornstarch with the water and stir into the sauce. Simmer, stirring, until thickened.

7 Quarter the duck. Warm the peach halves, then remove with a slotted spoon. Add the mustard to the pan and mix well. Stir this mixture into the sauce and taste. Serve the duck with the peaches and garnish with parsley or watercress. Pass the peach sauce separately.

BUTTERFLYING POULTRY

Whole chickens, Cornish hens, guinea hens, and game birds can be split open in half and opened up flat like a book, to resemble the wings of a butterfly. They will then cook evenly under the broiler or on a charcoal grill. A heavy chef's knife can be used to split the bird, but kitchen scissors or poultry shears are easier to handle.

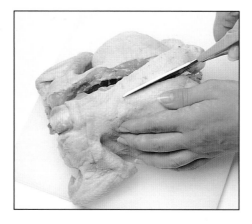

1 ▲ Set the bird breast down. Cut through the skin and rib cage along one side of the backbone, working from the tail to the neck. Repeat on the other side of the backbone to cut it free. Keep the backbone for stock, if desired.

2 ▲ Turn the bird breast up. With the heel of your hand, press firmly on the breastbone to break it and flatten the breast. Fold the wing tips back behind the shoulders.

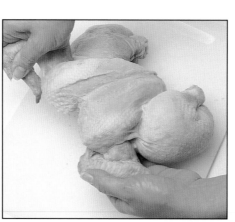

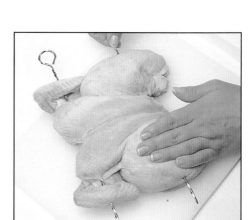

3 ▲ Thread a long metal skewer across the neck end of the bird, through one wing and the top of the breast halves and out the other wing.

4 ▲ Thread a second skewer through the thighs and bottom of the breast halves. These skewers will keep the bird flat while it is being cooked, and will make it easy to turn over.

Testing For Doneness
Overcooked poultry is dry, tough, and tasteless, so knowing when a bird is done is critical. The most reliable test for a whole bird is to insert an instant-read thermometer deep into the thigh meat (the internal temperature should be about 175°F). Without a thermometer, you can test by piercing the thigh with a skewer or the tip of a knife: the juices that run out should be clear, not pink. Or lift the bird with a long 2-pronged fork and tilt it so that you can check the color of the juices that run out of the cavity into the roasting tin. Pieces of poultry, particularly breast halves, can be tested by pressing with a finger: the meat should be firm but still slightly springy.

BROILING TIMES FOR POULTRY

Note: Cook 4–6 inches from the heat, with thinner pieces (less than 1 inch) nearer the heat. If the poultry seems to be browning too quickly, move it farther away from the heat.

Chicken	
squab chicken, butterflied	20–25 minutes
broiler-fryer, split in half or butterflied	25–30 minutes
breast half, drumstick, thigh	30–35 minutes
breast half, skinless boneless	10–12 minutes
Cornish hen, split in half	25–30 minutes

Broiled Butterflied Squab Chickens

SERVES 4

4 squab chickens or Cornish hens, each weighing about 1 pound, butterflied

olive oil

salt and pepper

FOR THE SAUCE

2 tablespoons dry sherry wine

2 tablespoons lemon juice

2 tablespoons olive oil

½ cup minced scallions

1 garlic clove, minced

¼ cup chopped mixed fresh herbs such as tarragon, parsley, thyme, marjoram, lemon balm

4 ▲ Meanwhile, for the sauce, whisk together the wine, lemon juice, olive oil, scallions, and garlic. Season with salt and pepper.

5 ▼ When the birds are done, transfer them to a deep serving platter. Whisk the herbs into the sauce, then spoon it over the chickens. Cover tightly with another platter or with foil and let rest 15 minutes before serving.

1 Preheat the broiler, or prepare a charcoal fire.

2 ▲ Brush the birds with some of the olive oil and season them. Set them on the rack in the broiler pan, about 4 inches from the heat, or on the grill 6 inches above the coals.

3 ▲ Cook until tender, 20–25 minutes. Turn and brush with more oil halfway through the cooking.

CUTTING UP POULTRY

Although chickens and other poultry are sold already cut up, sometimes it makes sense to buy a whole bird and to disjoint it yourself. That way you can prepare 4 larger pieces or 8 smaller ones, depending on the recipe, and you can cut the pieces so that the backbone and other bony bits (which can be saved for stock) are not included. Also a whole bird is cheaper to buy than pieces.

A sharp knife and sturdy kitchen scissors or poultry shears make the job of cutting up a chicken very easy.

Safe Handling of Raw Poultry
Raw poultry may harbor potentially harmful organisms, such as salmonella bacteria, so it is important to take care in its preparation. Always wash your hands, the chopping board, knife, and poultry shears in hot soapy water before and after handling the poultry. It is best to use a chopping board that can be washed at high temperature in a dishwasher and, if possible, to keep the chopping board just for the preparation of raw poultry. Also, make sure to thaw frozen poultry completely before cooking.

1 ▲ With a knife, cut through the skin on one side of the body down to the leg joint. Bend the leg out away from the body and twist it to break the hip joint.

2 ▲ Hold the leg out away from the body and cut through the joint, taking the "oyster" meat from the backbone with the leg. Repeat the same procedure on the other side to remove the other leg.

3 ▲ To separate the breast from the back, cut through the flap of skin just below the rib cage, cutting toward the neck. Pull the breast and back apart and cut through the joints that connect them on each side. Reserve the back for stock.

4 ▲ Turn the whole breast over, skin side down. Take one side of the breast in each hand and bend back firmly so the breastbone pops free. Loosen the bone on both sides with your fingers and, with the help of the knife, remove it.

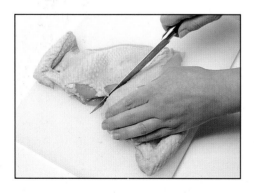

5 ▲ Cut the breast lengthwise in half, cutting through the wishbone. You now have 2 breast halves with wings attached and 2 leg portions.

6 ▲ For 8 pieces, cut each breast half in half at an angle so that some breast meat is included with a wing portion. Trim off any protruding bones.

7 ▲ With the knife, cut each leg portion through the joint to separate the thigh and drumstick.

Country Captain

SERVES 4

2 tablespoons vegetable oil

1 onion, chopped

1 green or red bell pepper, seeded and diced

1 garlic clove, minced

1½ tablespoons mild curry powder

½ teaspoon dried thyme

2 cups peeled, seeded, and chopped
    tomatoes or canned crushed tomatoes

2 tablespoons lemon juice

½ cup water

⅓ cup dried currants or raisins

salt and pepper

3½-pound chicken, cut into 8 pieces
    and the pieces skinned

⅓ cup toasted sliced almonds (optional)

cooked rice, for serving

1 Preheat the oven to 350°F.

2 Heat the oil in a wide, deep frying pan that has an ovenproof handle or in a flameproof casserole. Add the onion, diced bell pepper, and garlic. Cook, stirring occasionally, until the vegetables are soft.

3 ▲ Stir in the curry powder and thyme, then add the tomatoes, lemon juice, and water. Bring the sauce to a boil, stirring well. Stir in the dried currants or raisins. Season to taste with salt and pepper.

4 ▲ Put the chicken pieces in the frying pan, arranging them in one layer, and turn to coat them with the sauce. Cover the pan and transfer to the oven. Cook until the chicken is tender, about 40 minutes. Turn the chicken pieces halfway through cooking.

5 Remove the chicken and sauce to a warmed serving platter. Sprinkle with almonds, if desired, and serve with freshly cooked rice.

~ VARIATION ~

For Chicken Curry, omit the bell pepper; cook 1½ tablespoons minced fresh ginger and 1 small green chili pepper, seeded and minced, with the onion and garlic in a flameproof casserole. In step 3, stir in the curry and thyme with 2 cups plain yogurt; omit the tomatoes, lemon juice, and water. Add the chicken, cover, and cook in a preheated 325°F oven until tender, about 1–1¼ hours.

PAN-BRAISING POULTRY

Pan-braising combines frying and braising, producing particularly succulent results. It is a method suitable for pieces of poultry as well as for small whole birds such as quails, squab chickens, and Cornish hens.

As with frying, the poultry should be dried thoroughly with paper towels before cooking to ensure that it browns quickly and evenly.

1 ▲ Heat a little oil, a mixture of oil and butter, or clarified butter in a heavy frying pan or sauté pan.

2 ▲ Add the poultry and fry it over medium-high heat until it is deep golden brown all over.

3 ▲ Add liquid and flavorings as directed in the recipe. Bring to a boil, then cover and reduce the heat to medium-low. Continue cooking gently until the poultry is done, turning the pieces or birds once or twice for even cooking.

4 ▲ If the recipe directs, remove the poultry from the pan and keep it warm while finishing the sauce. This can be as simple as boiling the cooking juices to reduce them, or adding butter or cream for a richer result.

Pan-Braised Chicken with Bacon and Mushrooms
Chop 6 slices bacon and cook over medium heat until lightly colored. Remove and reserve. Pour off most of the fat. Dredge a 3½-pound chicken, cut in 8 pieces, in seasoned flour. Fry in the remaining fat, turning, until golden. Add 3 tablespoons dry white wine and 1 cup poultry stock. Bring to a boil. Add 6 ounces mushrooms, quartered and browned in 1 tablespoon butter, and the bacon. Cover and cook over low heat until tender, 20–25 minutes. *Serves 4.*

5 ▲ **To thicken cooking juices**: Mash equal parts of butter and flour to a paste (called "beurre manié"). Use 1 tablespoon each of butter and flour to thicken 1 cup of liquid. Whisk small pieces gradually into the boiling sauce until it is smooth and silky.

6 ▲ Another method of thickening cooking juices is to add a mixture of cornstarch and water (2 teaspoons cornstarch diluted with 1 tablespoon water per cup of cooking liquid). Boil for 2–3 minutes, whisking constantly, until the sauce is syrupy.

Stuffed Chicken Breasts with Cream Sauce

SERVES 4

4 large skinless boneless chicken breast halves

4 tablespoons butter

3 large leeks, white and pale green parts only, thinly sliced

1 teaspoon grated lime rind

salt and pepper

1 cup chicken stock or half stock and half dry white wine

½ cup whipping cream

1 tablespoon lime juice

1 ▼ Cut horizontally into the thickest part of each breast half to make a deep, wide pocket. Take care to cut into the center and not all the way through. Set the breasts aside.

2 Melt half the butter in a large heavy frying pan over low heat. Add the leeks and lime rind and cook, stirring occasionally, until the leeks are very soft but have not colored, 15–20 minutes.

3 Turn the leeks into a bowl and season with salt and pepper. Let cool. Clean the frying pan.

~ **VARIATION** ~

For Onion-Stuffed Chicken Breasts, use 2 sweet onions, halved and thinly sliced, instead of leeks.

4 ▲ Divide the leeks among the chicken breasts, packing the pockets full. Secure the openings with wooden toothpicks.

5 Melt the remaining butter in the frying pan over medium-high heat. Add the stuffed breasts and brown lightly on both sides.

6 Add the stock and bring to a boil. Cover and simmer until the chicken is cooked through, about 10 minutes. Turn the breasts over halfway through the cooking.

7 With a slotted spatula, remove the breasts from the pan and keep warm. Boil the cooking liquid until it is reduced by half.

8 ▼ Stir the cream into the cooking liquid and boil until reduced by about half again. Stir in the lime juice and season with salt and pepper.

9 Remove the toothpicks from the breasts. Cut each breast on the diagonal into ⅜-inch slices. Pour the sauce over them and serve.

FRYING CHICKEN

Fried chicken is justifiably popular – crisp and brown outside and tender and juicy within. It's a quick and easy cooking method that can be applied to pieces of rabbit and hare and small pieces of turkey, too.

Dry the pieces thoroughly with paper towels before frying. If they are at all wet, they will not brown properly. If the recipe directs, lightly coat or bread the pieces.

Succulent Fried Chicken
Lightly mix 1 cup milk with 1 beaten egg in a shallow dish. On a sheet of wax paper or in a plastic bag, combine 1 cup flour, 1 teaspoon paprika, salt, and pepper. One at a time, dip 8 chicken pieces in the egg mixture and turn them to coat all over. Then dip in the seasoned flour and shake off any excess. Deep-fry 25–30 minutes, turning the pieces so they brown and cook evenly. Drain on paper towels and serve very hot. *Serves 4.*

1 ▲ For pan-frying: Heat oil, a mixture of oil and butter, or clarified butter in a large, heavy-based frying pan over medium-high heat. When the oil is very hot, put in the chicken pieces, skin side down. Do not crowd them or they will not brown evenly; cook in batches if necessary.

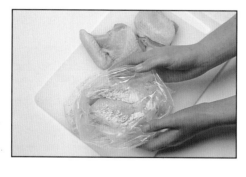

3 ▲ For deep-frying: Dip the pieces into a mixture of milk and beaten egg, then coat lightly with seasoned flour; let the coating set 20 minutes before frying. (Or, coat them with a batter just before frying.)

5 ▲ With a slotted metal spatula or tongs, lower the chicken pieces into the oil, a few at a time, without crowding them. Deep-fry until they are golden brown all over and cooked. Turn them so they color evenly.

2 ▲ Fry until deep golden brown all over, turning the pieces so they color evenly. Fry until all the chicken pieces are thoroughly cooked. Remove pieces of breast before drumsticks and thighs (dark meat takes longer to cook than white meat). Drain on paper towels.

4 ▲ Half fill a deep pan with vegetable oil and heat it to 365°F. You can also test the temperature with a cube of bread. Drop in the bread; if it takes 50 seconds to brown, the oil is at the right temperature.

6 ▲ Drain on paper towels and serve hot. If you want to keep a batch of fried chicken hot while you fry the rest, put it into a low oven, but don't cover it or it will become soggy.

Chicken with Cajun Sauce

SERVES 4

3½-pound chicken, cut into 8 pieces

¾ cup flour

salt and pepper

1 cup buttermilk or milk

vegetable oil, for frying

chopped scallions, for garnishing

FOR THE SAUCE

½ cup lard or vegetable oil

½ cup flour

1½ cups chopped onions

1 cup chopped celery

1 cup chopped green bell pepper

2 garlic cloves, minced

1 cup tomato purée

2 cups red wine or chicken stock

1 cup peeled, seeded, and chopped tomatoes

2 bay leaves

1 tablespoon brown sugar

1 teaspoon grated orange rind

½ teaspoon cayenne

1 For the sauce, heat the lard or oil in a large, heavy pan (preferably cast iron) and stir in the flour. Cook over medium-low heat, stirring constantly, until the mixture (called a "roux") has darkened to the color of hazelnut shells, 15–20 minutes.

2 ▲ Add the onions, celery, bell pepper, and garlic and cook, stirring, until the vegetables are softened.

3 Stir in the remaining sauce ingredients, with salt and pepper to taste. Bring to a boil, then let simmer until the sauce is rich and thick, about 1 hour. Stir from time to time.

4 Meanwhile, prepare the chicken. Put the flour in a plastic bag and season with salt and pepper. Dip each piece of chicken in buttermilk, then dredge in the flour to coat lightly all over. Shake off excess flour. Set the chicken aside for 20 minutes to let the coating set before frying.

5 Heat oil 1-inch deep in a large frying pan until it is very hot and starting to sizzle. Fry the chicken pieces, turning them once, until deep golden brown all over and cooked through, about 30 minutes.

6 ▼ Drain the chicken pieces on paper towels. Add them to the sauce and sprinkle, with scallions.

~ **VARIATION** ~

For Pork Chops with Cajun Sauce, substitute 4 large loin chops. The Cajun sauce is also good with steak, jumbo shrimp, or fish fillets.

BONING CHICKEN AND TURKEY BREASTS

Boneless poultry breasts, both whole and halves, are widely available, but they tend to be more expensive than bone-in breasts. It is much more economical to bone the breasts yourself, and it is very easy to do. A thin-bladed boning knife is the best tool to use for this.

Stockpiling Bones
Save chicken and other poultry bones in the freezer until you are ready to make stock. Store them up until you have enough to make a good rich stock.

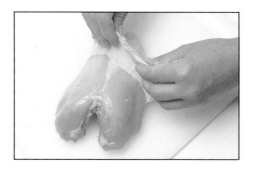

1 ▲ To take 2 boneless breast halves from a whole breast: First pull off the skin and any loose fat. Then, with the knife, cut through the breast meat along both sides of the ridged top of the breastbone.

2 ▲ With the knife at an angle, scrape the meat away from the bone down one side of the rib cage. Do this carefully so the breast meat comes away in one neat piece. Repeat on the other side. You now have 2 skinless boneless breast halves.

3 ▲ To remove the meat from breast halves: If the wing is attached, cut through the joint between the wing and breast to separate them. (Keep the wings for stock or another use.) Pull off the skin, if desired.

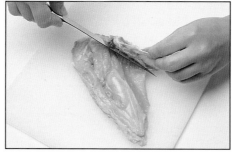

4 ▲ Turn the breast over and scrape the meat from the bone, using short strokes and lifting away the bone as it is freed.

5 ▲ Before cooking, remove the tendon next to the long flap or fillet on the underside of the breast. Cut it free of the meat at one end and pull it away, scraping it gently with the knife to remove it neatly.

6 ▲ Trim any fat from the breast halves. If desired, put them between 2 sheets of plastic wrap or wax paper and pound lightly with a meat pounder, the base of a pan, or a rolling pin to flatten the breast slightly.

7 ▲ To bone a whole breast for stuffing: You must keep the skin intact. Set the breast skin-side down and scrape the meat away from the ribcage, starting at one side and working up to the ridged top of the breastbone. Repeat on the other side.

8 ▲ When the meat has been freed on both sides, lift up the ribcage and scrape the skin gently away from both sides of the top of the breastbone, taking care not to cut through the skin. The whole breast is now boned in one piece.

Stuffed Turkey Breast

SERVES 8

4½- to 5-pound whole turkey breast, skin on, boned

salt and pepper

4 tablespoons butter, melted

¼ cup dry Madeira wine or dry white wine

1½ cups turkey or chicken stock or water

FOR THE STUFFING

2 tablespoons butter

1 onion, minced

½ pound smoked ham, ground or very finely chopped

1⅓ cups fresh bread crumbs

2 tablespoons chopped fresh parsley

½ teaspoon dried thyme

½ cup coarsely chopped almonds

1 egg, beaten to mix

1 Preheat the oven to 325°F.

2 ▲ For the stuffing, melt the butter in a frying pan and fry the onion, stirring occasionally, until soft. Turn the onion and butter into a bowl and add the remaining stuffing ingredients. Season to taste with salt and pepper and mix well.

3 Lay the boned turkey breast flat, skin side down. Season with salt and pepper. Spread the stuffing over it in an even layer.

4 ▲ Roll up the breast neatly and tie in several places with string. Use poultry pins to secure the ends.

5 Place the turkey roast on a rack in a roasting pan. Brush on half the melted butter. Mix the remaining butter with the wine. Roast 2–2½ hours, basting three or four times with the butter-wine mixture, until done: a meat thermometer should register 170°F.

6 Remove the turkey roast to a carving board. Set aside in a warm place to rest for at least 15 minutes.

7 ▼ Meanwhile, set the roasting pan over high heat. Add the stock or water, bring to a boil, and stir to scrape up all the browned bits. Boil 3–4 minutes. Strain and check the seasoning. Untie the roast and carve into neat slices. Serve with the sauce.

PREPARING TURKEY CUTLETS

Cutlets are slices cut crosswise from the turkey breast. Economical and extremely versatile, they are a lean meat that cooks quickly and can be substituted in most recipes that call for veal scaloppine. Turkey cutlets can also be treated in much the same way as thin beef or pork steaks, or used in place of chicken breast fillets.

Slicing across the grain insures that the cutlet won't shrink or curl when it is cooked, and cutting on the diagonal gives good-sized slices.

1 ▲ With a large sharp knife, cut the boned breast half across the grain, at a slight angle, into ⅜-inch slices.

2 ▲ Put each slice between 2 sheets of plastic wrap or wax paper and pound lightly with the base of a pan, a meat pounder, or a rolling pin to flatten to ⅛–¼-inch thickness. Be careful not to make holes in the meat.

Turkey Rolls with Cranberries

SERVES 4

4 turkey cutlets, prepared for cooking

salt and pepper

2 tablespoons vegetable oil

½ cup cranberry juice or fruity red wine

½ teaspoon each arrowroot and water, mixed

FOR THE STUFFING

1 cup fresh or thawed frozen cranberries

1 cup seedless red grapes

1 large red-skinned apple, quartered and cored

1 tablespoon honey

2 teaspoons minced fresh ginger

½ teaspoon ground allspice

1 For the stuffing, combine the cranberries, grapes, and apple in a food processor. Chop until coarse-fine.

2 Put into a strainer placed in a bowl and drain, pressing the fruit to extract the juice. Reserve the juice. Mix the fruit with the honey, ginger, and allspice.

3 Season the turkey cutlets with salt and pepper. Divide the stuffing among them and spread it over them evenly, almost to the edges.

4 ▲ Roll up each cutlet, tucking in the sides, and tie in 2 or 3 places with string, or secure with toothpicks.

5 Heat the oil in a frying pan just large enough to accommodate the turkey rolls. Add the rolls and brown them on all sides over medium-high heat, 5–7 minutes.

6 ▲ Add the reserved fruit juice and the cranberry juice or wine to the pan and bring to a boil. Cover and simmer until the turkey is tender and cooked through, about 20 minutes. Turn the rolls halfway through the cooking.

7 Remove the turkey rolls from the pan and keep warm. Boil the cooking liquid until it has reduced to about ¾ cup. To thicken the liquid, stir in the arrowroot mixture and boil 2 minutes. Remove the string or toothpicks from the turkey rolls and cut into slices. Serve the cooking liquid as a sauce.

MAKING POULTRY STOCK

A good homemade poultry stock is invaluable in the kitchen. It is simple and economical to make, and can be stored in the freezer up to 6 months. If poultry giblets are available, add them (except the livers) with the wings.

MAKES ABOUT 2½ QUARTS

2½–3 pounds poultry wings, backs, and necks (from chicken, turkey, etc.)

2 onions, unpeeled, quartered

4 quarts cold water

2 carrots, roughly chopped

2 celery stalks, with leaves if possible, roughly chopped

a small handful of fresh parsley

a few fresh thyme sprigs, or ¾ teaspoon dried thyme

1 or 2 bay leaves

10 black peppercorns, lightly crushed

A Frugal Stock

Stock can be made from the bones and carcasses of roasted poultry, cooked with vegetables and flavorings. Save the carcasses in a plastic bag in the freezer until you have 3 or 4, then make stock. It may not have quite as rich a flavor as stock made from a whole bird or fresh wings, backs, and necks, but it will still taste fresher and less salty than canned broth or bouillon cube stock.

1 ▲ Combine the poultry wings, backs, and necks and onions in a stockpot. Cook over medium heat, stirring occasionally so they color evenly, until the poultry and onion pieces are lightly browned.

3 ▲ Add the remaining ingredients. Partly cover the pan and barely simmer the stock about 3 hours.

5 ▲ When cold, remove the layer of fat that will have set on the surface.

2 ▲ Add the water and stir well to mix in the sediment on the bottom of the pot. Bring to a boil, skimming off the impurities that rise to the surface.

4 ▲ Strain the stock into a bowl and let cool, then refrigerate.

Stock Tips

● Instead of wings, backs, and necks, use a whole bird for stock, preferably an older stewing chicken, which will give a wonderful flavor, and you will have chicken meat to use in salads, sandwiches, soups, and casseroles.

● No salt is added to stock because as the stock reduces the flavor becomes concentrated and saltiness increases. Add salt to the dish in which you use the stock.

Scallion Cream Soup

SERVES 4–6

2 tablespoons butter
1 small onion, chopped
1½ cups chopped scallions, white parts only
½ pound potatoes (2 medium-sized), peeled and chopped
2½ cups chicken stock
1½ cups light cream
2 tablespoons lemon juice
salt and white pepper
chopped scallion greens or fresh chives, for garnishing

1 ▲ Melt the butter in a saucepan. Add the onion and scallions. Cover and cook over very low heat until soft but not browned, about 10 minutes.

2 ▲ Add the potatoes and the stock. Bring to a boil, then cover again and simmer over medium-low heat about 30 minutes. Let cool slightly.

3 Purée the soup in a blender or in a food processor.

4 ▼ If serving the soup hot, pour it back into the pan and add the cream. Reheat gently, stirring frequently. Stir in the lemon juice and season with salt and pepper to taste.

5 ▲ If serving the soup cold, pour it into a bowl. Stir in the cream and lemon juice, and season to taste with salt and pepper. Cover the bowl and chill at least 1 hour.

6 Sprinkle with green scallion tops or chives before serving.

MEAT

~

Whether quickly broiled or stir-fried, or long-simmered for rich
flavor, meat lends itself to endless variety. With the basic
cooking methods that follow, you can choose to suit the time
available and your own preferences.

PREPARING MEAT FOR COOKING

You can buy meat ready for cooking from butchers and most good supermarkets. However, some cuts need further preparation, depending on how they are to be cooked – removing excess fat or adding protective fat, for example, or tying a roast after stuffing.

How Much to Buy
As a general guide, when buying boneless meat that has little or no fat, allow 5–7 ounces per serving. For bone-in meat that has a little fat at the edge, allow about ½ pound per serving. Very bony cuts such as shank and spareribs have proportionally little meat so you will need 1 pound per serving.

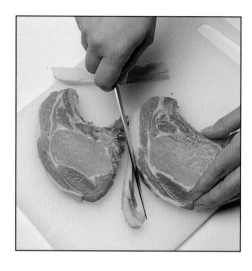

1 ▲ To trim: If a recipe directs, use a sharp knife to trim all fat from the surface. Leave a little fat on steaks to be grilled, and slash this fat at regular intervals to prevent the steak curling up during cooking. Meat cuts to be roasted should retain a thin layer of fat (⅛–¼ inch). Cut away the sinews and tough connective tissue.

2 ▲ If you like, cut and scrape all fat and gristle from the ends of protruding bones (such as on chops or roasts that contain rib bones); this is called "frenching."

3 ▲ To chine a roast: For large cuts of meat that contain rib bones, such as beef rib roast, pork loin, and rack of lamb, it is a good idea to cut the chine bone (backbone) where it is joined to the rib bones, to loosen it, or to remove it completely before cooking. Do this with a meat saw and sharp knife. Without the chine bone, the roast will be easy to carve.

4 ▲ To bard a roast: If a very lean cut of meat is to be roasted without a protective crust (a spice mixture, oil and crumbs, or pastry, for example), it is a good idea to bard it to keep it moist. Wrap very thin slices of beef fat, pork fatback, or blanched bacon around the roast and tie them in place. Discard the fat before serving but keep the bacon, if desired.

5 ▲ To tie a boned roast: Cuts that have been boned should be tied into a neat shape for roasting or pot roasting. The butcher will do this, but if you want to add a stuffing or seasoning, you will need to retie the roast yourself. Reshape it into a neat roll that is even in circumference. Use butcher's twine to make ties around the circumference at 1-inch intervals.

Boned Pork Loin with Apple Cream Sauce

SERVES 6

3-pound boned pork loin roast, barded, rolled, and tied

1 tablespoon fresh thyme leaves, or 1 teaspoon dried thyme

salt and pepper

fresh thyme sprigs, watercress, and sliced apples, for garnishing

FOR THE SAUCE

1½ tablespoons butter

1 onion, chopped

2 apples, such as Granny Smiths, peeled, cored, and chopped

½ cup whipping cream

½ tablespoon Dijon-style mustard

1 tablespoon cream-style horseradish

1 Preheat the oven to 375°F.

2 ▲ Untie the pork loin and set the barding fat aside. Lay the pork out flat. Sprinkle it with the thyme, salt, and pepper and pat on.

~ **COOK'S TIP** ~

A boned roast will take longer to cook than the same weight roast with bone. This is because the bone conducts heat more readily than the flesh.

3 Reroll the loin and tie it into a neat shape, with the barding fat.

4 Put the pork loin on a rack in a small roasting pan. Roast until well cooked, about 1¼–1½ hours.

5 ▼ Meanwhile, for the sauce, melt the butter in a saucepan and add the onion and apples. Cook over low heat, stirring occasionally, until very soft, 20–25 minutes.

6 ▲ Let the apple mixture cool slightly, then transfer it to a food processor. Add the cream, mustard, and horseradish. Blend until smooth. Season with salt and pepper. Return the sauce to the pan and reheat just before serving.

7 When the pork is cooked, remove it from the oven and let it rest about 10 minutes before carving. Garnish with thyme, watercress, and apples.

ROASTING MEAT

The dry heat of oven-roasting is best suited to tender cuts of meat. If they don't have a natural marbling of fat, bard them. Alternatively, marinate the meat or baste it frequently with the roasting juices during cooking.

Meat for roasting should be at room temperature. Roast on a rack in a pan that is just a little larger than the roast. Without a rack, the base of the roast would stew and not become crisp.

There are two methods of roasting meat. For the first, the roast is seared at a high temperature and then the heat is reduced for the remainder of the cooking time. For the second method, the meat is roasted at a constant temperature throughout. Scientific studies have shown that both methods produce good results, and that it is prolonged cooking, not the method, that affects juiciness and shrinkage. So use whichever method you prefer or follow recipe directions.

Suggested Roasting Times
Following the second roasting method, in a 350°F oven, approximate timings in minutes per pound:
   Beef, rare, 20 + 20 extra*
      medium, 25 + 25 extra
      well done, 30 + 30 extra
   Veal, 25 + 25 extra
   Lamb, 25 + 25 extra
   Pork, 35 + 35 extra
(*Prime cuts such as rib of beef and tenderloin need less time.)

1 ▲ According to recipe directions, rub the roast with oil or butter and season. If desired, with the tip of a sharp knife, make little slits in the meat all over the surface. Insert flavorings such as herbs, slivers of garlic, olive slices, shards of fresh ginger, and so on.

3 ▲ Transfer the meat to a carving board and let it rest before carving. If desired, deglaze for a simple pan sauce (page 48) or make gravy with the roasting juices (page 38).

2 ▲ Insert a meat thermometer in the thickest part, not touching a bone. (An instant-read thermometer is sometimes inserted toward the end of roasting.) Roast for the suggested time, basting if necessary, until the meat has reached the desired degree of doneness.

Roast Leg of Lamb
Trim a 6-pound bone-in leg of lamb, removing almost all the fat. Cut 2–3 garlic cloves into very thin slices. Pull the leaves from 3 sprigs of fresh rosemary. Insert the garlic slices and rosemary leaves in the slits in the lamb. Rub the lamb with olive oil and season with salt and pepper. Roast to the desired degree of doneness. *Serves 8.*

MEAT THERMOMETER READINGS

Beef		Lamb	
rare	125–130°F	rare	130–135°F
medium-rare	135°F	medium	140–145°F
medium	140–145°F	well done	160°F
well done	160°F		
		Pork	
Veal		medium	150°F
well done	160°F	well done	160–165°F

Testing for Doneness

The cooking times given in a recipe are intended to be a guideline. The shape of a cut can affect how long it takes to cook, and people have different preferences for how well cooked they like meat to be. So testing is essential.

Natural Law of Roasting

A roast will continue to cook in its own retained heat for 5–10 minutes after being removed from oven or pot, so it is a good idea to take it out when it has reached 5° short of the desired thermometer reading.

1 ▲ Large cuts of meat that are roasted or pot roasted can be tested with a metal skewer. Insert the skewer into the thickest part and leave it 30 seconds. Withdraw the skewer and feel it. If it is warm, the meat is rare; if it is hot, the meat is well cooked.

2 ▲ The most reliable test for doneness is with a meat thermometer, inserted in the center of the roast, away from bones. Some instant-read thermometers are inserted at the end of cooking. Follow manufacturer's instructions. See the chart on page 36 for the internal temperatures.

Cooking Methods and Choice of Meat Cuts

Roasting

Beef: chuck eye roast, rib roast, rib eye roast, back ribs, tenderloin roast, top sirloin roast, sirloin tip roast, bottom round roast, top round roast, round tip roast, eye round roast

Veal: rib roast, shoulder roast, loin roast, breast roast

Pork: blade roast, loin roast, top loin roast, tenderloin, rib crown roast, spareribs, country-style ribs, back ribs, smoked picnic, smoked shoulder roll, smoked ham, country ham, smoked loin chop, Canadian bacon

Lamb: shoulder roast, rib roast, loin roast, leg, leg roast, spareribs

Pot-roasting, braising, and stewing

Beef: mock tender roast (chuck), top blade roast, shoulder pot roast, arm pot roast, short ribs, back ribs, round steak, bottom round roast, round tip roast, eye round roast, brisket (fresh and corned), shanks, flank steak, skirt steak

Veal: blade steak, shoulder steak and roast, rib chop, loin chop, sirloin steak, top round steak, cutlet, riblet, breast roast, shanks

Pork: shoulder roast, blade steak and roast, loin chop, top loin chop, rib chop, sirloin chop, spareribs, country-style ribs, back ribs, smoked picnic, smoked hock, smoked shoulder roll

Lamb: arm chop, shoulder roast, blade chop, sirloin chop, spareribs, shanks, riblets

Pan-frying

Beef: rib eye steak, top loin steak, tenderloin steak (filet mignon), T-bone steak, porterhouse steak, shell steak (Delmonico steak), sirloin steak, round tip steak, round steak, flank steak, skirt steak

Veal: blade steak, shoulder steak, rib chop, loin chop, sirloin steak, top round steak, cutlet

Pork: blade steak, loin chop, top loin chop, rib chop, sirloin chop, ham slice, smoked loin chop, Canadian bacon, bacon

Lamb: arm chop, blade chop, rib chop, loin chop, sirloin chop

Broiling and grilling

Beef: chuck steak, blade steak, rib steak, rib eye steak, top loin steak, tenderloin steak (filet mignon), T-bone steak, porterhouse steak, shell steak (Delmonico steak), sirloin steak, round tip steak, round steak, flank steak, skirt steak

Veal: rib chop, loin chop, sirloin steak, cutlet

Pork: blade steak, loin chop, top loin chop, rib chop, sirloin chop, spareribs, country-style ribs, back ribs, ham slice, smoked loin chop, Canadian bacon, bacon

Lamb: arm chop, blade chop, rib chop, loin chop, sirloin chop, butterflied leg, leg steaks, spareribs, riblets

Stir-frying

Beef: flank steak, skirt steak, mock tender (chuck)

Veal: top round steak, cutlet

Pork: tenderloin

Lamb: sirloin, leg

MAKING GRAVY

Gravy made from the roasting juices is rich in flavor and color. It is a traditional accompaniment for roast meat and poultry.

For a thinner sauce, an alternative method to that explained here is deglazing, where liquid is added to skimmed pan juices and boiled to reduce. This is explained on page 48.

> **Resting a Roast Before Carving**
> Once a roast is removed from the oven or pot, it should be left in a warm place to "rest" 10–15 minutes. During this time, the temperature of the roast evens out, and the flesh reabsorbs most of the juices. Thus, the juices won't leak during carving.

1 ▲ Spoon off most of the fat from the roasting pan. Set the pan over medium-high heat on top of the stove. When the roasting juices begin to sizzle, whisk or stir in flour.

2 ▲ Cook, scraping the pan well to mix in all the browned bits from the bottom, until the mixture forms a smooth, brown paste. Add stock or another liquid, as specified in the recipe, and bring to a boil, stirring or whisking constantly. Simmer until the gravy has the right consistency, then season with salt and pepper.

Prime Rib of Beef with Shallots

SERVES 8

1 beef prime rib roast (4 ribs), weighing about 10 pounds, chined

vegetable oil

salt and pepper

1 pound plump shallots, unpeeled

1½ tablespoons flour

1½ cups beef stock, or 1 cup beef stock and ½ cup red wine

1 Preheat the oven to 350°F.

2 If the ends of the rib bones have been left on the roast you can scrape them clean, if desired. Rub any exposed bone ends with oil. Season the beef with salt and pepper. Set the beef in a roasting pan, fat side up.

3 Roast the beef until cooked to the desired degree of doneness, about 2 hours, basting often with the juices in the pan.

4 ▲ Meanwhile, peel off the outer, papery layers of skin from the shallots, leaving at least 2 layers. Trim the root and stem ends, if necessary.

5 About 30 minutes before the beef has finished cooking, put the shallots into the roasting pan around the beef.

6 When the beef is ready, transfer it to a carving board and set aside to rest at least 15 minutes. Remove the shallots from the pan and keep warm.

7 ▼ Spoon off all but 2 tablespoons of fat from the roasting pan. Mix in the flour, then add the stock and boil, stirring, until thickened.

8 Carve the beef. Serve with the gravy, the shallots still in their skins (they slip out easily), and roasted potatoes, if desired.

BONING A LEG OF LAMB

A boned leg of lamb is much easier to carve than a roast with bone. By removing the bones, you can also stuff the pocket left before tying the roast into a neat shape with string.

Boning a leg of lamb and leaving the meat opened up flat (which is called butterflying it), shortens the cooking time by about a third. A butterflied leg can be roasted, broiled, or charcoal-grilled.

Before boning, trim off all fat from the surface of the leg.

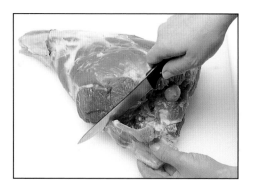

1 ▲ Set the leg hip bone upward. Working from the wide cut end, cut around the ball joint between the hip bone and the main leg bone to release it from the meat. Cut around the hip bone to separate it from the meat, then remove it.

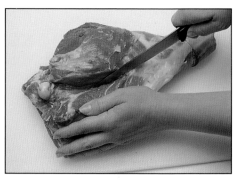

2 ▲ Cut through the meat straight down the length of the leg bone, from the hip to the knee.

3 ▲ Using short strokes, cut and scrape the meat away from the bone all around. Cut off the white chip of bone (the knee cap), if it is there.

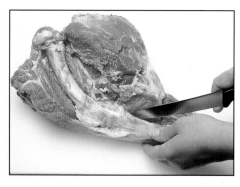

4 ▲ Continue cutting down the length of the leg bone below the knee (the shank bone). Cut and scrape the meat away from the bone as before to free the bone.

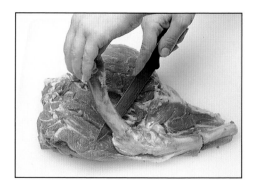

5 ▲ Lift the end of the leg bone and cut around the knee to detach it from the meat. To avoid tough meat, cut out the tendons from the meat at the shank end.

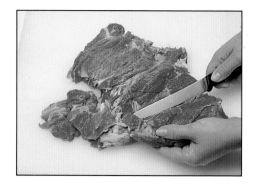

6 ▲ To butterfly: Lay the boned leg out flat. Trim off all visible fat, then slash the thick portions of meat and open them so that the whole leg is reasonably even in thickness.

7 ▲ Thread 2 skewers crosswise through the meat at its widest part. These will keep the butterflied leg flat during cooking.

Broiling and Grilling Meat
These dry-heat methods of cooking are most suitable for naturally tender cuts of meat or those that have been tenderized. In broiling, meat is cooked under direct heat, usually in an electric or gas range; in grilling, meat is cooked on a barbecue grill over hot coals. The cooking time is mainly determined by the distance the meat is from the heat source – normally 3 inches below the broiler or 4–6 inches above the coals.

Mustard-Glazed Butterflied Leg of Lamb

SERVES 6–8

½ cup Dijon-style mustard

1–2 garlic cloves, minced

2 tablespoons olive oil

2 tablespoons lemon juice

2 tablespoons chopped fresh rosemary, or 1 tablespoon crumbled dried rosemary

salt and pepper

a 5- to 5½-pound leg of lamb, boned and butterflied

1 ▲ Combine the mustard, garlic, oil, lemon juice, rosemary, salt, and pepper in a shallow glass or ceramic dish. Mix well together.

2 ▲ Add the leg of lamb, secured with skewers, and rub the mustard mixture all over it. Cover the dish and let marinate at least 3 hours. (If the lamb is marinated in the refrigerator, let it return to room temperature before cooking.)

3 Preheat the broiler or prepare a charcoal fire.

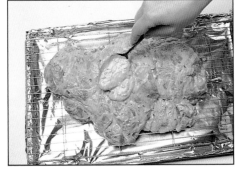

4 ▲ Place the lamb flat on the rack in the broiler pan (lined with foil) or on the grill over the charcoal fire. Spread with any mustard mixture remaining in the dish.

5 If broiling, set the lamb 4–5 inches from the heat. Cook under the broiler or over charcoal until the lamb is crusty and golden brown on the outside, 10–15 minutes on each side for rare meat, 20 minutes for medium, and 25 minutes for well done.

6 Transfer the lamb to a carving board and let it rest for at least 10 minutes before carving into slices (not too thin) for serving.

SEARING MEAT FOR POT-ROASTING OR ROASTING

Large cuts and pieces of meat to be roasted or pot-roasted are sometimes seared as the initial step in cooking. This may be done either by roasting briefly at a high temperature and then reducing the heat, or by frying. The result is a browned crust that adds delicious flavor.

Pot-Roasting or Braising
This method of cooking tenderizes even the toughest cuts of meat. Prime cuts can also be pot-roasted, but cooking times are cut short – just long enough to reach the degree of doneness you like. Depending on the desired result, meat to be pot-roasted or braised may or may not have an initial searing.

1 ▲ To sear by frying: Dry the meat well with paper towels. Heat a little oil in a frying pan, flameproof casserole, or roasting pan until it is very hot. Put in the meat and fry over high heat until it is well browned on all surfaces. Turn the meat using two spatulas or spoons. (Piercing with a fork would let juices escape, which would be boiled away.)

2 ▲ If roasting, transfer the meat, in its roasting pan, to the oven. If pot-roasting, add a small amount of liquid and cover the pot tightly. If a frying pan has been used for searing, be sure to deglaze it: add some of the liquid called for in the recipe and bring to a boil, scraping up the browned bits from the bottom. Add this flavorful mixture to the pot.

Veal Pot Roast with Herbs

SERVES 6

1 tablespoon vegetable oil

3-pound boned veal shoulder roast, rolled and tied

4 medium onions, quartered

½ cup chicken stock or water

a few sprigs each of fresh thyme, marjoram, and rosemary, or ¾ teaspoon each dried thyme, oregano, and rosemary

salt and pepper

1 Preheat the oven to 300°F.

2 Heat the oil in a Dutch oven or other flameproof casserole over high heat (choose a casserole not much larger than the veal roast). Put in the veal roast and brown it, turning frequently to color it evenly on all sides.

3 ▼ Add the onions, stock, and herbs. Season with salt and pepper. Cover and transfer to the oven. Cook until well done, 2½–3 hours.

Other Cuts for Pot-Roasting
Other large roasts can be pot-roasted in the same way as the veal. For instance, use pork shoulder arm or butt roasts.

4 ▲ Transfer the veal roast to a carving board. Remove the onions and keep warm. Let the veal rest at least 10 minutes. Discard the strings before carving.

5 Skim the cooking juices to remove all fat. Bring to a boil, then strain. Taste for seasoning. Serve with the veal and onions.

Lamb Shanks Braised with Carrots

SERVES 4

4 lamb shanks, weighing 3½–4 pounds, cracked

4 small onions, halved

2 large celery stalks, cut into chunks

1 bay leaf

1 cup chicken stock

2 tablespoons tomato paste

1 teaspoon Worcestershire sauce

1 tablespoon chopped fresh parsley

salt and pepper

½ pound small carrots, halved lengthwise

Emphasizing Natural Flavor
To emphasize the natural flavors of the ingredients rather than those that result from browning, the initial searing stage is omitted.

---

1 Preheat the oven to 350°F.

2 Arrange the lamb shanks in a flameproof casserole, in one layer or slightly overlapping. Tuck the onions, celery, and bay leaf around the lamb.

3 ▼ Combine the stock, tomato paste, Worcestershire sauce, parsley, salt, and pepper. Pour into the casserole. Cover and braise in the oven 1 hour.

4 Add the carrots and cover the pot again. Braise until the lamb is very tender and is pulling away from the bones, about 1 hour longer.

5 ▲ With a slotted spoon, transfer the lamb shanks and vegetables to a serving platter. Skim all the fat from the cooking liquid and discard the bay leaf, then spoon it over the lamb and vegetables. Serve hot.

Veal Pot Roast with Herbs (left), Lamb Shanks Braised with Carrots

STEWING WITH A FRY-START

Fry-start stews have a wonderful rich flavor, due greatly to the initial searing – or browning – of the meat and vegetables. The long cooking period, in a seasoned liquid, produces a very tender and flavorful result. Be sure to use a heavy-based pan or casserole, such as a Dutch oven.

Saving the Flavor

If a different pan is used for searing the meat and vegetables, deglaze it: Add wine, stock, or water and bring to a boil, scraping up the browned bits from the bottom of the pan. Then add the resulting liquid to the stewpot.

1 ▲ Cut the meat into equal-sized cubes and dry it thoroughly with paper towels. Coat lightly with flour if the recipe directs.

2 ▲ Heat a little oil in a frying pan or flameproof casserole until it is very hot. Add a few cubes of meat – just enough to cover the bottom of the pan without touching each other. Do not crowd the meat in the pan. If the temperature drops too much, a crisp brown crust will not form.

3 ▲ Fry over medium-high heat until well browned on all sides. Turn the cubes so they brown evenly, and remove them as they are done.

4 ▲ Add the vegetables and cook, stirring occasionally, until they are well browned. Discard excess oil if directed in the recipe.

5 ▲ Return the meat to the pan. If flour is added now, sprinkle it over the meat and vegetables and let it brown, stirring well.

6 ▲ Add liquid barely to cover and stir to mix. Add any flavorings. Bring the liquid to a boil, then reduce the heat to a gentle simmer and complete the cooking as directed.

7 ▲ If flour hasn't been used already, the liquid may be thickened at the end of cooking. One method is butter and flour paste (1 tablespoon each per cup of liquid), stirred in gradually (page 22).

8 ▲ Or thicken with cornstarch (2 teaspoons diluted with 1 tablespoon water per cup of liquid); boil for 2–3 minutes, stirring (page 22). Or, simply boil the liquid to reduce it.

Beef Stew with Dumplings

SERVES 4

¼ cup flour

salt and pepper

1½ pounds boneless beef for stew, such as chuck or round, cut into 1½-inch cubes

3 tablespoons vegetable oil

2 large onions, chopped

2 celery stalks, coarsely chopped

2 large carrots, thickly sliced

2 turnips, cut into cubes

1½ cups cubed rutabaga

2 cups beef stock

1 tablespoon soy sauce

1 bay leaf

1½ teaspoons fresh thyme leaves, or ½ teaspoon dried thyme

FOR THE DUMPLINGS

1 cup flour

2 teaspoons baking powder

½ teaspoon salt

¼ teaspoon English mustard powder

⅔ cup milk

2 tablespoons vegetable oil

1 Put the flour in a plastic bag and season. Add the beef cubes, a few at a time, and toss to coat. Remove them, shaking off excess flour.

2 ▲ Heat the oil in a Dutch oven or other flameproof casserole over medium-high heat. Add the cubes of beef, in batches, and brown them well on all sides. Remove them from the casserole as they are browned.

3 Add the onions, celery, carrots, turnips, and rutabaga. Brown them all over, stirring frequently.

4 ▲ Return the beef cubes to the casserole. Add the stock, soy sauce, bay leaf, and thyme. Bring to a boil, stirring well to mix in the browned bits from the bottom of the pan.

5 Cover tightly, then reduce the heat to very low. Simmer until the beef is very tender, about 2 hours.

6 For the dumplings, sift the dry ingredients into a bowl. Add the milk and oil and stir just until the dry ingredients are bound into a soft, batter-like dough.

7 ▲ Uncover the casserole and bring the stew liquid back to a boil. Drop the dumpling dough onto the surface of the stew, in 8–10 dollops.

8 Cover again and simmer over low heat until the dumplings are just set and fluffy, 12–15 minutes. Serve hot, directly from the casserole.

~ **VARIATION** ~

For Beef Pot Pie, omit dumplings and put the stew in a baking dish. Cover with pie pastry (page 222) and bake at 400°F for 25 minutes.

STEWING WITH A RAW-START OR A SWEAT-START

In stews and pot-roasts where you want to emphasize the natural flavors of the ingredients rather than the flavors that result from browning, the initial searing stage is omitted. For a raw-start, the ingredients are simply put in the cooking dish.

Sweat-start stewing is similar to fry-start stewing, but doesn't use added oil or fat, relying instead on the fat naturally present in the meat.

1 ▲ Raw-start stewing: Put the meat in a casserole or other pot. Add vegetables, liquid, and seasonings as directed in the recipe.

2 ▲ If the recipe directs, bring the liquid to a boil, then cover the pot. Continue cooking on top of the stove, or transfer to the oven.

3 ▲ Sweat-start stewing: Combine the meat and a little liquid in the stewpot. Cover and cook gently to draw out the meat juices.

4 ▲ Uncover and boil the juices to reduce them to a sticky brown glaze. Continue cooking briskly to brown the meat, then remove it.

5 ▲ Add liquid to deglaze the pot. Add vegetables, flavorings, and more liquid, then return the meat to the pot and complete the cooking.

Pork Hotch-Potch with Apples

SERVES 4

2 tablespoons butter

4 large pork loin chops, well trimmed

1 small onion, thinly sliced

2 apples, peeled and thinly sliced

1 teaspoon sweet paprika

½ tablespoon chopped fresh sage, or ½ teaspoon dried sage

salt and pepper

¼ cup apple cider

1¼–1½ pounds sweet potatoes, thickly sliced

1 Preheat the oven to 350°F.

2 ▼ Grease a baking dish with 1½ teaspoons of the butter. Arrange the chops in the dish in one layer.

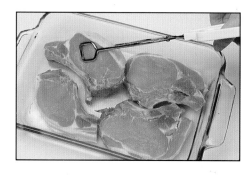

3 Scatter the onion and apples on top and sprinkle with paprika, sage, salt, and pepper. Pour over the cider.

4 ▲ Lay the potato slices over the surface, slightly overlapping them. Cover with foil or a lid. Bake about 1½ hours. Uncover and dot with the remaining butter. Continue baking, uncovered, until the potatoes are lightly browned, 20–30 minutes more.

Lamb Stew with Green Peas

SERVES 4–6

2–2½ pounds boneless lamb shoulder, trimmed of excess fat and cut into 1½-inch cubes

2 cups lamb or chicken stock

1 onion, chopped

1 tablespoon minced fresh rosemary, or 1 teaspoon crumbled dried rosemary

salt and pepper

2 cups frozen green peas, thawed and drained

1 tablespoon mint jelly

1 Put the lamb cubes and ½ cup stock in a Dutch oven or other flameproof casserole. Cover and cook over medium-low heat to draw out the juices, about 30 minutes.

2 Remove the lid and boil the juices, stirring occasionally, until they reduce to a sticky, brown glaze.

3 ▼ Continue cooking to brown the meat well on all sides, turning the cubes of lamb so that they color evenly. Using a slotted spoon, remove the lamb cubes from the casserole and set aside.

4 Skim off as much fat as possible from the juices remaining in the casserole, then add another ½ cup stock. Bring to a boil, stirring to mix in all the browned bits from the bottom of the casserole.

5 ▲ Add the onion and rosemary and cook until the onion is soft, stirring occasionally. Return the lamb to the casserole with the remaining stock and season. Bring to a boil. Cover and simmer gently over low heat until the lamb is tender, about 1 hour, adding more stock if needed.

6 Remove the lamb from the casserole and keep warm. Skim all fat from the cooking liquid. Add the peas; simmer 2 minutes. Stir in the mint jelly until melted. Add the lamb and serve hot.

Pork Hotch-Potch with Apples (left), Lamb Stew with Green Peas

PAN-FRYING AND SAUTÉING

Tender cuts of meat, such as steaks and chops, slices of calf's liver, and hamburgers are ideal for cooking quickly in a heavy frying pan. And the juices left in the pan can be turned into an easy sauce.

Before pan-frying and sautéing, trim excess fat from steaks, chops, scaloppine, etc., then dry thoroughly with paper towels.

For cooking, use a fat that can be heated to a high temperature. If using butter, adding an equal amount of vegetable oil will help prevent burning, or use clarified butter.

1 ▲ Heat the fat in the pan over high heat until very hot but not browning. Put in the meat, in one layer, without crowding.

2 ▲ Fry until browned on both sides and done to your taste. If pan-frying pork or veal chops, reduce the heat to medium once they are in the pan.

Testing Steak for Doneness
A reliable way to test steak is by pressing it with your finger. When raw, it is soft and can be squashed. When cooked rare, it will be only slightly springy. When cooked medium, it will offer more resistance and drops of red juice will appear on the surface. When well done, it will be firm to the touch.

Pan-Fried Teriyaki Steak
Combine 3 tablespoons vegetable oil, 1 tablespoon each soy sauce, honey, red wine vinegar, and minced onion, 1 minced garlic clove, and ½ teaspoon ground ginger in a heavy-duty plastic bag. Add 4 boneless sirloin steaks and turn so they are well coated. Let marinate 2 hours. Drain the steaks and pat dry, then pan-fry to the desired degree of doneness. The steaks can also be broiled or grilled. *Serves 4.*

DEGLAZING FOR A PAN SAUCE

After pan-frying or sautéing, a simple yet delicious sauce can be made in the pan. The same method can be used to make gravy for roasted meat. Deglazing is also a good way to maximize flavor when making stews and casseroles.

Before deglazing, remove the meat and keep it warm. Pour or spoon off all the fat from the pan, unless the recipe calls for shallots, garlic, etc. to be softened. In that case, leave 1–2 teaspoons of fat and cook the vegetables in it.

1 ▲ Pour in the liquid called for in the recipe (wine, stock, vinegar, etc.). Bring to a boil, stirring well to scrape up all the browned bits from the bottom of the pan and dissolve them in the liquid.

2 ▲ Boil over high heat until the liquid is almost syrupy. (The time needed to reduce the liquid depends on the amount used.) If the recipe directs, enrich the sauce with cream or butter. Season with salt and pepper and serve.

Pepper Steak with Mushrooms

SERVES 4

2 tablespoons black peppercorns, coarsely crushed
½ teaspoon hot pepper flakes (optional)
4 boneless sirloin or filet mignon steaks, 6–8 ounces each, well trimmed
3 tablespoons vegetable oil
1 tablespoon butter
2 cups sliced mushrooms
2 tablespoons Cognac, bourbon, Scotch, or beef stock
½ cup whipping cream
salt

1 ▲ Combine the peppercorns and hot pepper flakes and press onto both sides of the steaks.

2 ▲ Heat 1 tablespoon of the oil with the butter in a heavy frying pan that is large enough to accommodate the steaks in one layer. Add the mushrooms and cook over medium heat, stirring and turning them occasionally, until they are wilted, about 5 minutes.

3 Increase the heat to medium-high and continue cooking until the liquid from the mushrooms has evaporated and they are lightly browned. With a slotted spoon, remove them from the pan and reserve.

4 Add the remaining oil to the frying pan. When it is very hot, add the steaks. Fry until well browned, about 2 minutes on each side. Continue cooking to the desired degree of doneness. (Test by pressing with your finger.) Remove the steaks from the pan and keep hot.

5 ▲ Pour off all the fat from the pan. Add the alcohol or stock and bring to a boil, stirring and scraping to mix in the browned bits from the bottom of the pan. Add the cream and bring back to a boil. Boil 1 minute.

6 Stir in the mushrooms and reheat them. Check the seasoning, then pour this sauce over the steaks.

STIR-FRYING

The preparation of ingredients for stir-frying often takes longer than the cooking itself. This is because all ingredients must be cut to uniform sizes so that the cooking can be accomplished quickly and evenly.

A wok is excellent for stir-frying because its high sides let you stir and toss the ingredients briskly. Use long cooking chopsticks or a wooden spatula to keep the ingredients moving around the wok.

1 ▲ Prepare all the ingredients following recipe directions.

2 ▲ Heat a wok or large, deep skillet over medium-high heat. Dribble in the oil down the sides.

Stir-Fried Beef with Snow Peas
Cut 1 pound lean, boneless, tender beef into very thin strips. Combine 3 tablespoons soy sauce, 2 tablespoons dry sherry, 1 tablespoon brown sugar, and ½ teaspoon cornstarch in a bowl. Heat 1 tablespoon vegetable oil in the hot wok. Add 1 tablespoon each minced fresh ginger and minced garlic and stir-fry 30 seconds. Add the beef and stir-fry until well browned, about 2 minutes. Add ½ pound snow peas and stir-fry 3 minutes longer. Stir the soy sauce mixture until smooth, then add to the wok. Bring to a boil, stirring and tossing, and simmer the mixture until just thickened and smooth. Serve immediately, accompanied by freshly cooked rice. *Serves 4.*

3 ▲ When the oil is hot (a piece of vegetable should sizzle on contact), add the ingredients in the order directed in the recipe. (Those that take longer to cook are added first.) Do not add too much to the wok at a time or the ingredients will start to steam rather than fry.

4 ▲ Fry, stirring and tossing constantly with chopsticks or a spatula, until the ingredients are just cooked: vegetables should be crisp-tender and meat and poultry tender and juicy.

5 ◄ Push the ingredients to the side of the wok, or remove them. Pour liquid or sauce, as specified in the recipe, into the bottom. Cook and stir, then mix in the ingredients from the sides. Serve immediately.

Pork Chop Suey

SERVES 4

¾ pound pork tenderloin or boneless pork shoulder steak

1½ tablespoons cornstarch

¼ cup soy sauce

1 tablespoon minced fresh ginger

½ cup beef or chicken stock

¼ cup dry sherry wine

½ teaspoon sugar

salt and pepper

3 tablespoons peanut or vegetable oil

1 celery stalk, thinly sliced

½ green bell pepper, seeded and thinly sliced

8 medium-size mushrooms, thinly sliced

1 garlic clove, minced

1 zucchini, thinly sliced

½ cup sliced canned water chestnuts

1 cup bean sprouts

1 Trim any fat from the pork, then cut it across the grain into very thin slices. (If you freeze the pork 20–30 minutes, it will be easier to slice.)

2 ▲ Combine 1 tablespoon cornstarch, half the soy sauce, and the ginger in a bowl. Add the pork and mix. Cover and let stand 30 minutes.

3 In another bowl, mix together the remaining cornstarch and soy sauce with the stock, sherry, sugar, salt, and pepper. Set aside.

4 ▼ Heat the wok, then add half the oil. When it is hot, add the pork mixture and stir-fry over high heat until all the slices of pork have changed color, 1–2 minutes. Turn the pork onto a plate.

5 Add the remaining oil to the wok. When hot, add the celery, bell pepper, mushrooms, and garlic. Stir-fry 1 minute.

6 ▲ Add the zucchini, water chestnuts, and bean sprouts. Stir-fry until the vegetables are crisp-tender, 1–2 minutes longer.

7 Return the pork to the wok and add the sherry mixture. Cook, stirring, until the sauce boils and thickens. Serve immediately.

PREPARING MEAT SCALLOPS

Scallops, or scaloppine, are slices of veal top or bottom round, cut ⅜-inch thick. They need to be pounded before cooking, to break the fibers. This tenderizes them and helps to keep them flat during cooking.

Slices of other meat or poultry may also be prepared in the same way as veal, such as turkey cutlets or beef slices, cut from the round, to be rolled and braised.

Pounding It Out
You can also use the base of a heavy saucepan or skillet to pound and flatten meat scallops. Choose a pan with a smooth base.

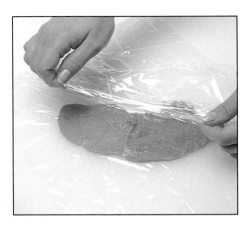

1 ▲ Trim any fat and gristle from around the edge of each scallop. Lay flat between two sheets of plastic wrap or wax paper.

2 ▲ Using the smooth side of a meat pounder or the long side of a rolling pin, pound gently but firmly all over the scallop to flatten it to ⅛- to ¼-inch thickness. It will spread out to almost twice its original size.

Veal Scaloppine with Tomato Sauce

SERVES 4

½ cup flour
2 tablespoons freshly grated Parmesan cheese, plus additional Parmesan for serving
salt and pepper
1 egg
2 tablespoons milk or water
1¼–1½ cups fine fresh bread crumbs
1 garlic clove, halved (optional)
8 small veal scallops, weighing 1–1¼ pounds in total, prepared for cooking
1 tablespoon butter
3–4 tablespoons olive oil
1 cup tomato-herb sauce (page 172)

1 Combine the flour, cheese, salt, and pepper on a large sheet of wax paper. Lightly beat the egg with the milk or water in a shallow bowl. Spread the bread crumbs on another large sheet of wax paper.

2 If using the garlic, rub the cut sides over the veal scallops.

3 ▼ One at a time, dip a veal scallop in the flour mixture to coat both sides lightly; shake off excess flour. Then dip the scallop in the egg mixture. Finally, coat on both sides with bread crumbs and press them on lightly to help them adhere.

4 ▲ Heat half the butter and oil in a large frying pan over medium-high heat. Add 4 of the prepared veal scallops and fry until golden brown on both sides and cooked through, about 1½ minutes on each side. Remove from the pan and keep hot while you fry the remaining veal scallops.

5 Top each scaloppine with heated tomato sauce. Serve with additional Parmesan cheese and pasta, if desired.

Beef Rolls with Mustard

SERVES 4

8 thin slices of beef top round, weighing about 1¾ pounds, prepared for cooking

3 tablespoons spicy brown mustard

salt and pepper

4 large dill pickles, halved lengthwise, or 8 medium-size pickles

2 tablespoons vegetable oil

2 onions, thinly sliced

1 cup dark beer or beef stock

1 bay leaf

1 Preheat the oven to 350°F. Have ready a frying pan with an ovenproof handle or a flameproof casserole.

2 Lay the slices of beef (pounded to a thickness of about ¼ inch) flat on a work surface. Spread each slice with mustard, almost to the edges. Season with salt and pepper.

3 ▼ Place a piece of pickle along one end of each slice and roll up neatly. Tie the rolls with string or secure them with wooden toothpicks.

4 Heat the oil in the frying pan or casserole. Add the beef rolls and fry over medium-high heat until they are browned on all sides. Remove them from the pan and set aside.

5 Add the onions to the pan and fry until soft and beginning to brown, stirring frequently.

6 ▲ Return the beef rolls to the pan and add the beer and bay leaf. Bring to a boil over high heat.

7 Cover the pan tightly and transfer it to the oven. Cook until the beef rolls are very tender, about 1 hour. Turn them over halfway through cooking to insure even cooking.

8 Remove the string or toothpicks and discard the bay leaf before serving. If desired, serve rice or potatoes with the beef rolls.

Veal Scaloppine with Tomato Sauce (left), Beef Rolls with Mustard

GRINDING MEAT

Ground meats of all kinds are easily obtainable, but when you want something more unusual for a pâté or you want to use a particular cut of meat, well trimmed of gristle and tendons, you will grind it yourself. Also, if ground meat is to be served raw, as in steak tartare, it must be freshly prepared.

1 ◄ **With a meat grinder**: This produces the most uniform ground meat, and you can choose coarse or fine grinds, according to recipe use. Trim the meat well and cut it into 1½-inch cubes or strips, then feed through the machine.

2 ▲ **With a food processor**: Trim the meat carefully (be sure to remove all gristle because a food processor will chop gristle, too) and cut it into cubes. Place in the machine fitted with the steel blade and pulse.

3 ▲ In between turning the machine on and off, stir the meat around a few times so that it is evenly ground. Care must be taken not to overprocess meat to a paste, particularly if making hamburgers (they would be tough).

4 ▲ **By hand**: Trim the meat well. Using a large chef's knife, first cut the meat into cubes, then chop into smaller and smaller cubes. Continue chopping until you have the consistency you want, coarse or fine.

Meat Loaf with Mushroom Stuffing

SERVES 6

½ pound mushrooms, coarsely chopped

1 small onion, minced

2 tablespoons butter

3 cups fresh bread crumbs

2 teaspoons steak sauce

3 tablespoons minced fresh parsley

1 teaspoon dried thyme

salt and pepper

1½ pounds ground beef chuck

½ pound ground lean pork

⅓ cup ketchup

2 eggs, beaten

1 Preheat the oven to 375°F.

2 Cook the mushrooms and onion in the butter over medium heat until soft. Turn the mushrooms into a bowl.

3 ▲ Add the bread crumbs, steak sauce, parsley, thyme, salt, and pepper. Mix well.

4 In another bowl, combine the beef, pork, ketchup, and eggs. Mix well.

5 ▲ Pack half of the meat mixture into a large loaf pan, pressing it into an even layer. Pack the mushroom mixture on top, then cover with the rest of the meat. Bake 1¼ hours.

6 Remove from the oven and let the meat loaf stand 15 minutes. Pour off the juices, then unmold the meat loaf onto a serving plate. Serve hot.

Lamb Burgers with Cucumber Sauce

SERVES 4

1½ pounds lean ground lamb

1 small onion, minced

8 dried apricot halves, finely chopped

¼ cup pine nuts

¼ cup fine dry bread crumbs

2 teaspoons mild curry powder

1 egg

salt and pepper

4 pita (pocket) breads

FOR THE SAUCE

½ hothouse cucumber, peeled and grated

1 cup plain yogurt

2 tablespoons chopped fresh mint

1 ▼ Combine the lamb, onion, apricots, pine nuts, bread crumbs, curry powder, egg, salt, and pepper in a bowl. Mix together with your fingers until well blended.

2 ▲ Divide into 8 portions and shape each into a small patty. Cover and refrigerate 30 minutes.

3 Meanwhile, for the sauce, squeeze the grated cucumber in a double thickness of paper towels to extract excess water.

4 ▲ Mix together the cucumber, yogurt, and mint. Season with salt and pepper.

5 Preheat the broiler or prepare a charcoal fire.

6 Broil or grill the burgers until they are cooked to your taste, about 10 minutes for medium. Turn them halfway through cooking to insure that they brown and cook evenly.

7 Warm the pita breads and cut in half. Serve the burgers in the pita halves, with the cucumber sauce.

Beef and Mashed Potato Pie

SERVES 4

4 tablespoons butter
1 large onion, minced
1 celery stalk, finely diced
1 large carrot, finely diced
1 pound ground round
1 tablespoon flour
1 cup hot beef stock
2 tablespoons minced fresh parsley
1 tablespoon tomato paste
salt and pepper
2 pounds baking potatoes, peeled
3–4 tablespoons milk
2 teaspoons spicy brown mustard

1 Melt 1 tablespoon of the butter in a frying pan over medium heat. Add the onion, celery, and carrot and cook until the onion is soft, stirring the vegetables occasionally.

2 ▲ Add the beef and fry, stirring, until it is brown and crumbly.

3 ▲ Sprinkle the flour over the surface and stir it into the meat and vegetables.

4 ▲ Gradually add the stock, stirring well. Stir in the parsley and tomato paste. Season with salt and pepper.

5 Bring to a simmer, then cover and cook over very low heat, stirring occasionally, about 45 minutes.

6 Meanwhile, cook the potatoes in boiling salted water until they are tender. Drain well.

7 Press the potatoes through a ricer into a bowl, or mash them. Add the remaining butter and just enough milk to make a soft, fluffy texture. Season with salt and pepper.

8 Preheat the oven to 400°F.

9 Stir the mustard into the beef mixture, then turn it into a baking dish. Cover with a neat layer of potatoes and seal to the sides of the dish. Decorate with tines of a fork. Bake 20–25 minutes. Serve hot.

COOKING BACON AND SAUSAGE

Bacon is cured and smoked meat from the fatty side (or belly) of a hog. Canadian bacon, cut from the loin, in the middle of the back, is very lean and tender, more like ham. While ordinary bacon has to be cooked, Canadian bacon is precooked and can either be reheated for serving or used directly from the package.

Uncooked sausage – fresh or smoked – must be thoroughly cooked before eating. Test for doneness by piercing with a skewer: the juices that run out should be clear. Many precooked sausages are heated to serving temperature by poaching, braising, frying, broiling, or grilling.

1 ▲ To fry Canadian bacon slices: Grease a heavy frying pan with a little oil. Arrange the slices in the pan in one layer and cook over medium-low heat, turning often, until hot and lightly golden. This will take 5–8 minutes, according to the thickness of the slices.

2 ▲ To fry bacon slices: Arrange them in a heavy unheated frying pan in one layer. Set the pan over medium-low heat. Cook the bacon, turning it occasionally, until crisp and golden brown, 8–10 minutes, according to the thickness of the slices. Drain on paper towels.

3 ▲ To bake or broil bacon slices: Arrange them side by side on a rack in a baking pan. Bake in a preheated 400°F oven, turning once, until crisp and golden brown, 10–15 minutes. Or, broil 3–4 inches from the heat, turning once, until crisp and brown on both sides, 3–8 minutes.

4 ▲ To fry uncooked sausage patties: Arrange in a heavy, unheated frying pan in one layer. Cook over medium-low heat until done (test with a skewer), 10–12 minutes. Turn once during cooking.

5 ▲ To pan-braise uncooked sausage links: Arrange in one layer in a heavy, unheated frying pan with 3 tablespoons water. Bring to a boil. Cover and simmer over low heat until cooked through (test with a skewer), 5–15 minutes according to thickness. Drain. Uncover and cook until brown.

6 ▲ To bake or broil uncooked sausage: Arrange links or patties on a rack in a shallow baking pan. Bake in a preheated 400°F oven until cooked (test with a skewer), about 20 minutes. Or, broil 3–4 inches from the heat until browned on all sides.

7 ▲ To fry bulk sausage meat: Cook in a frying pan over medium heat until golden brown and crumbly. Stir constantly while cooking and break up with the side of a spoon or fork. Drain off excess fat.

8 ▲ To poach frankfurters and cooked sausages: Add them to a saucepan of boiling water. Reduce the heat, cover, and simmer until heated through, 5–10 minutes. To brown poached sausages, broil 3–4 inches from the heat, or fry gently.

Sausage and Bean Casserole

SERVES 4–6

2 cups dried navy or Great Northern beans, soaked overnight
½ cup firmly packed light brown sugar
2 teaspoons dry English mustard
⅓ cup light molasses
1 large onion, chopped
salt and pepper
12 frankfurters or other cooked sausages, cut into 1-inch pieces

1 Drain the beans and put them in a large saucepan. Cover with plenty of fresh cold water. Bring to a boil, then simmer over low heat about 1 hour. Drain the beans and reserve the cooking liquid.

2 Preheat the oven to 300°F.

3 ▲ Mix 2 cups of the reserved cooking liquid with the sugar, mustard, and molasses.

4 ▲ Put the beans and onion in a casserole. Add the molasses mixture and season. Cover and bake 3 hours, stirring occasionally, and adding more cooking liquid if necessary.

5 ◀ Stir in the sausage pieces. If the beans seem dry, add more of the reserved cooking liquid so they are well moistened.

6 Cover again and continue baking 1 hour longer, stirring occasionally. Serve hot, from the casserole.

A Look at Sausage

Sausage is available in many forms. Some are ready to eat, but fresh sausages must be cooked thoroughly and those sold as cooked are often heated before serving. All kinds of meats are used and each country has its sausage traditions.

Uncooked sausage includes fresh links, patties, bulk sausage meat (fry, pan-braise, broil, or bake); bockwurst and bratwurst (poach and then fry, broil, or grill); chorizo, may be smoked (broil or grill, or remove from casings and fry); Italian sausages, sweet or hot (fry, pan-braise, broil, grill, oven-braise, or remove from casings and cook).

Fully cooked sausage includes blood sausage (fry, broil, or grill); bologna, lightly smoked (ready to eat cold); braunschweiger, smoked, and liverwurst (ready to eat cold); frankfurter (poach, broil, or grill); kielbasa/Polish sausage, smoked (ready to eat cold, or add to soups and stews); knockwurst (poach, broil, grill).

Semi-dry and dry sausage includes cervelas/summer sausage, smoked (ready to eat cold, or add to soups or bean dishes); mortadella, smoked (ready to eat cold); pepperoni (ready to eat cold, or hot on pizza); salami (ready to eat cold).

MAKING MEAT STOCK

The most delicious meat soups, stews, casseroles, gravies, and sauces rely on a good homemade stock for success. Neither a bouillon cube nor a canned bouillon or broth will do if you want the best flavor. Once made, meat stock can be kept in the refrigerator 4–5 days, or frozen for longer storage (up to 6 months).

On the Light Side
For a light meat stock, use veal bones and do not roast the bones or vegetables. Put in the pot with cold water and cook as described.

MAKES ABOUT 2 QUARTS

4 pounds beef, veal, or lamb bones, such as shank, knuckle, leg, and neck, cut into 2½-inch pieces
2 onions, unpeeled, quartered
2 carrots, roughly chopped
2 celery stalks, with leaves if possible, roughly chopped
2 tomatoes, coarsely chopped
4½ quarts cold water
a handful of parsley stems
a few fresh thyme sprigs, or ¾ teaspoon dried thyme
2 bay leaves
10 black peppercorns, lightly crushed

1 ▲ Preheat the oven to 450°F. Put the bones in a roasting pan or flameproof casserole and roast, turning occasionally, until they start to brown, about 30 minutes.

2 ▲ Add the onions, carrots, celery, and tomatoes and baste with the fat in the pan. Roast until the bones are browned, about 30 minutes longer. Stir and baste from time to time.

3 ▲ Transfer the bones and vegetables to a stockpot. Spoon off the fat from the roasting pan.

4 ▲ Add a little of the water to the roasting pan and bring to a boil on top of the stove, stirring well to scrape up any browned bits. Pour this liquid into the stockpot.

5 ▲ Add the remaining water. Bring just to a boil, skimming frequently to remove all the foam from the surface. Add the herbs and peppercorns.

6 ▲ Partly cover the pot and simmer the stock 4–6 hours. The bones and vegetables should always be covered with liquid, so add a little boiling water from time to time if necessary.

7 ▲ Strain the stock through a strainer. Skim as much fat as possible from the surface. To remove all the fat, let the stock cool, then refrigerate it; the fat will rise to the top and set in a layer that can be removed easily.

Hearty Beef and Vegetable Soup

SERVES 6

½ pound beef chuck, cut into ½-inch cubes

½ pound lean boneless pork shoulder butt, cut into ½-inch cubes

2 quarts beef stock

1 bay leaf

1½ cups peeled, seeded, and chopped tomatoes

1 small red bell pepper, seeded and chopped

1 small onion, chopped

2 carrots, chopped

1 large boiling potato, peeled and diced

1 cup fresh or thawed frozen corn kernels

1 tablespoon Worcestershire sauce

salt and pepper

1 ▲ Put the beef and pork in a large, heavy kettle and add the stock. Bring to a boil, skimming off all the froth that rises to the surface.

2 ▲ When the liquid is free of froth, add the bay leaf. Partly cover the pan and barely simmer over very low heat about 1 hour.

3 ▼ Add the tomatoes, bell pepper, onion, carrots, and potato. Bring back to a boil. Continue simmering, partly covered, for about 45 minutes. Stir from time to time.

4 Add the corn and simmer until all the vegetables and meat are very tender, 20–30 minutes longer.

5 Discard the bay leaf. Stir in the Worcestershire sauce. Taste and adjust the seasoning before serving.

~ COOK'S TIP ~

This soup can be made 2 or 3 days ahead. The flavor will improve.

FISH & SEAFOOD

~

*No need to be wary of preparing fish and seafood. It is lean,
tasty, and quick to cook – a good weeknight solution as well as
a celebration treat. Just keep in the natural moisture and don't
overcook. You can even cut your own fish steaks or fillets.*

PREPARING WHOLE FISH FOR COOKING

Most fish have scales and these should be removed before cooking unless the fish is to be filleted or the skin is to be removed before serving. Fish sold in markets is normally scaled as well as cleaned (eviscerated or drawn), but you can do this yourself, if necessary. Trimming the tail gives a whole fish a neat appearance.

All fish preparation is best done in or near the sink, with cool water running. Salt your hands for a good grip on fish.

1 ▲ To scale: Grasp the tail firmly and scrape off the scales using a special fish scaler or a knife, working from the tail toward the head. Rinse the fish well. Repeat on the other side.

2 ▲ To trim: For flatfish to be cooked whole, use kitchen scissors to trim off the outer half of the small fin bones all around the fish.

3 ▲ For round fish, cut the flesh on both sides of the anal and dorsal (back) fins and pull them out; the small bones attached will come out, too. Trim off the other fins.

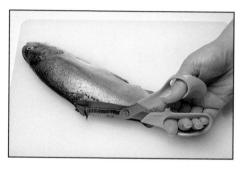

4 ▲ If the fish is to be cooked whole, leave the fins on, or just trim them, because they help keep the shape of the fish.

5 ▲ To trim the tail: If the tail is to be left on, cut a neat "V" in the center with scissors. The fish is now dressed for cooking.

A LOOK AT FISH

In terms of shape and structure, most fish fall into one of two general categories: round fish and flatfish.

Round fish have thicker bodies and many of their bones are attached to their fins. They can be filleted or cut into steaks, but both will contain small pin bones.

Flatfish have a flat central bone with a row of bones attached on either side. This simple bone structure makes flatfish easy to fillet. Most are too thin to cut into steaks.

Large fish such as tuna have a thick bone running down the center of their bodies; spiking out from this are four rows of bones that divide the flesh into quarters. These boneless "loins" are usually cut into slices called steaks.

The fat content of fish is an important consideration in deciding how to cook it. Lean fish can dry out at high temperatures, so a protective coating is a good idea when frying. When broiling, marinate or baste them. Lean and moderately lean fish are best cooked by moist methods such as steaming, poaching, or baking in a sauce. Oily fish, however, almost baste themselves during cooking, so

they are ideal for broiling, grilling, and pan-frying.

Texture and flavor are also important to consider in choosing how to prepare fish. If the flavor of the flesh is mild, it is important not to overwhelm it. But fish with rich, distinctively flavored flesh will stand up well to spicy, pungent seasonings.

Fish that are delicate in texture need careful cooking. Pan-frying with a flour coating, steaming, and gentle baking are best. However, fish with meaty, dense flesh can be cubed and put onto skewers.

Pan-Fried Trout with Olives and Capers

SERVES 4

4 whole trout, ¾–1 pound each, cleaned and trimmed

salt and pepper

flour, for coating

¼ cup vegetable oil

6–8 tablespoons butter

½ cup sliced black olives

3 tablespoons capers

2 tablespoons lemon juice

lemon wedges, for serving

1 ▲ Sprinkle the trout with salt and pepper. Coat them lightly with flour, shaking off any excess.

Terms Used in the Fish Market
Drawn: Whole fish that has had its internal organs removed. Other terms used are cleaned, gutted, and eviscerated. The gills may also have been removed.
Dressed: Whole fish that has been drawn and scaled. Another term for this is whole-dressed.
Pan-dressed: Whole fish that has been drawn and scaled and the head, tail, and fins removed.
Fillet: Boneless piece cut length-wise from the sides of the fish. May or may not be skinned.
Steak: Slice cut crosswise from a whole dressed fish.

2 ▲ Heat the oil in a large frying pan over medium heat. Add the trout and fry until golden brown on both sides and cooked through, 12–15 minutes.

3 Transfer the trout to a warmed serving platter and keep warm. Pour off all the oil from the pan.

4 ▼ Add the butter to the frying pan and melt it. When it starts to brown and smell nutty, stir in the olives, capers, and lemon juice. Cook 10 seconds, then pour this sauce over the fish. Serve immediately.

BAKING FISH

Most fish are suitable for baking – whole or in fillets or steaks. Lean fish, in particular, benefit from some protection so they don't dry out, such as a stuffing or coating, or baking them in a little liquid or sauce, which can also be served with the fish. All of these add extra flavor to the fish, too.

Cooking in foil or paper is suitable for many fish, both whole ones and fillets and steaks. This method seals in moisture, so is similar in effect to steaming. It's a good solution for fish too large to fit in a steamer or poacher.

A good rule of thumb for cooking time is 10 minutes in a hot oven (425°F) to each inch, calculated at the thickest part of the fish.

1 ▲ To bake fish with liquid: Pour over a small amount of stock, wine, water, or other liquid as directed, and add flavorings and seasonings.

2 ▲ To bake fish in foil or paper: Wrap tightly with seasonings and flavorings as directed and place the package on a baking sheet.

Baked Fish Steaks
Arrange 1½ pounds white fish steaks in a shallow baking dish. Sprinkle the fish with 2 tablespoons minced shallot or onion and 3 tablespoons lemon juice or dry white wine. Drizzle with 2 tablespoons melted butter and season with salt and pepper to taste. Bake in a preheated 425°F oven until the fish is done, about 10 minutes. Pour the cooking juices over the steaks before serving. *Serves 4.*

A SELECTION OF FISH VARIETIES

Choose the freshest fish you can find. If necessary, substitute another variety with similar qualities.

Lean Fish
Cod (Scrod, if young)
- round fish, saltwater
- flaky, tender texture; mild flavor
- broil, bake, steam, poach
- substitute haddock, halibut, lingcod

Flounder
- flatfish, saltwater
- fine texture; delicate flavor
- fry, broil, bake, steam
- substitute sole, whitefish, orange roughy

Grouper
- round fish, saltwater
- firm, medium-dense texture; mild flavor
- bake, fry
- substitute cod, monkfish, sea bass

Haddock
- round fish, saltwater
- soft, moist texture; mild flavor
- broil, bake, steam, poach
- substitute cod, halibut

Halibut
- flatfish, saltwater
- firm, moist texture; mild, sweet
- broil, bake, steam, poach
- substitute flounder, sole

Mahimahi (Dolphinfish)
- thick central bone, saltwater
- firm, medium-dense; mild, sweet
- bake, broil, fry
- substitute grouper, halibut

Perch
- round fish, freshwater
- firm, flaky texture; mild flavor
- fry, broil, bake
- substitute trout, Atlantic perch, catfish

Red snapper
- round fish, saltwater
- firm, moist texture; mild, sweet
- bake, broil, steam, poach
- substitute trout, whitefish

Rockfish (Striped bass)
- round fish, saltwater (spawns in freshwater)
- tender texture; slightly sweet
- bake, poach, fry
- substitute trout, grouper

TESTING FOR DONENESS

All seafood cooks quickly. If overcooked, it becomes dry and loses its succulent quality. In the case of meaty fish such as tuna and swordfish, it can be unpleasantly chewy. It is therefore worth knowing how to judge when fish is perfectly cooked.

The flesh of raw fish and crustaceans is translucent; it becomes opaque when it is cooked. However, as fish will continue cooking from residual heat, it should be removed from the heat source before it is entirely opaque.

1 ▲ To determine whether a fish is cooked, make a small slit in the thickest part. Lift with the knife to look into the opening.

2 ▲ The fish is ready when still very slightly translucent in the center or near the bone, but the rest of the flesh is opaque throughout.

Sea bass
- round fish, saltwater
- flaky or firm flesh; mild flavor
- broil, fry, bake
- substitute salmon

Sole
- flatfish, saltwater
- fine texture; delicate flavor
- fry, broil, bake, poach
- substitute flounder

Moderately Lean Fish
Catfish
- round fish, freshwater
- soft, moist texture; mild, sweet
- fry, steam, poach
- substitute trout

Orange roughy
- round fish, saltwater
- firm, moist texture; delicate, sweet flavor
- bake, steam, poach
- substitute cod

Porgy (Scup, Sea bream)
- round fish, saltwater
- firm, moist texture; mild, sweet
- fry, broil, bake, steam
- substitute perch, butterfish

Sea trout (Weakfish)
- round fish, saltwater
- moist, flaky texture; mild, sweet
- broil, bake, fry
- substitute cod, haddock, bluefish

Swordfish
- thick central bone, saltwater
- firm, meaty texture; mild
- broil, bake, steam, poach
- substitute shark, tuna

Trout
- round fish, freshwater
- tender, flaky texture; mild, rich
- fry, broil, bake
- substitute salmon, whitefish

Tuna
- thick central bone, saltwater
- meaty texture; mild to strong
- bake, steam, poach, broil
- substitute salmon, swordfish

Moderately Oily and Oily Fish
Bluefish
- round fish, saltwater
- fine, moist texture; mild flavor if small, more distinctive in larger fish
- bake, broil, fry
- substitute flounder, lake trout

Carp
- round fish, freshwater
- soft, flaky texture; mild flavor
- bake, broil, fry, steam
- substitute cod, haddock

Mackerel
- round fish, saltwater
- moist and tender or firm texture; rich, distinctive flavor
- broil, bake, steam, poach
- substitute tuna

Pompano
- round fish, saltwater
- firm, moist texture; sweet flavor
- broil, bake, fry
- substitute sole, bluefish, red snapper

Salmon
- round fish, freshwater/saltwater
- flaky, tender texture; mild to rich
- bake, broil, steam, poach
- substitute swordfish, tuna, trout

Whitefish
- round fish, freshwater
- tender, flaky texture; mild, sweet
- bake, broil, fry
- substitute haddock, lake trout

POACHING FISH

Whole fish, large and small, as well as fillets and steaks are excellent poached because the gentle cooking gives succulent results. Poached fish can be served hot or cold, with a wide variety of sauces. The poaching liquid may be used as the basis for a sauce.

Poaching Containers
A long rectangular fish poacher with a perforated rack enables you to lift the fish out of the liquid after cooking. You could also use a rack set in a deep roasting pan such as that for turkey.

1 ▲ To oven-poach small whole fish, fillets, or steaks: Place the fish in a buttered, flameproof dish that is large enough to hold the pieces comfortably. Pour in enough liquid to come two-thirds of the way up the side of the fish.

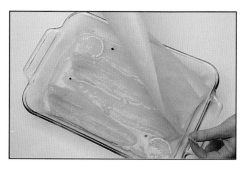

2 ▲ Add any flavorings called for in the recipe. Press a piece of buttered wax paper on top to keep in the moisture without sticking to the fish.

3 ▲ Set the dish over medium heat and bring the liquid just to a boil. Transfer the dish to a preheated 350°F oven and poach until the fish is just cooked. To test, with the tip of a sharp knife, make a small cut into the thickest part of the fish (ideally next to a bone): the flesh should be very slightly translucent in the center.

4 ▲ To poach whole fish, fillets, or steaks on the top of the stove: Put large whole fish on the rack in a fish poacher, or set it on a piece of cheesecloth that can be used like a hammock. Put small whole fish, fillets, and steaks on a rack, or set directly in a baking dish, wide saucepan, or frying pan.

5 ▲ Prepare the poaching liquid (salted water, milk, wine, stock, or court bouillon) in the fish poacher or in a large roasting pan (or a wide saucepan or frying pan for fillets and steaks). Set the rack in the poacher, or the cheesecloth hammock in the roasting pan. Add more liquid, if necessary, to cover the fish.

6 ▲ Cover the poacher or pan and bring the liquid just to a boil. Reduce the heat and simmer very gently until the fish is cooked.

Poached Sole Fillets
Oven-poach 8 skinless sole fillets, each ½-inch thick (about 1½ pounds). Use 1 cup dry white wine or fish stock, to almost cover, with ¼ cup minced scallions, 4–6 lemon slices, and a few allspice berries for flavoring. Simmer 3–5 minutes, then remove the fish. Boil the cooking liquid until reduced to about ¼ cup, then strain it. Season with salt and pepper. *Serves 4.*

Poached Whole Fish with Green Mayonnaise

SERVES 6 OR MORE

1 whole salmon, striped bass, sea bass, or grouper, weighing about 5 pounds, scaled if necessary, cleaned and trimmed

green mayonnaise (page 180), for serving

FOR THE COURT BOUILLON

2 cups dry white wine

about 3 quarts water

1 large onion, sliced

2 carrots, thinly sliced

1 celery stalk, thinly sliced

½ lemon, sliced

a few parsley sprigs

1 bay leaf

12 black peppercorns

4 allspice berries (optional)

salt

4 ▼ Remove the poacher from the heat and lift the fish, by means of the rack or cheesecloth hammock, out of the court bouillon. Drain well, then transfer it to a serving platter and let cool slightly.

5 ▲ Gently peel off the skin and pull out the fins. If salmon has been used, gently scrape off the thin layer of grayish flesh. Let cool completely.

6 Serve the cooled fish with the green mayonnaise.

1 ▲ Combine all the ingredients for the court bouillon in a fish poacher or in a large roasting pan. Bring to a boil, then cover and simmer 20 minutes.

2 Place the fish on the poacher rack, or set it on a piece of cheesecloth. Lower the fish into the court bouillon. The fish should be covered with liquid, so add more water if necessary.

3 Cover and bring back to boiling point, then simmer very gently until the fish is just cooked, 15–20 minutes.

STEAMING FISH

This simple, moist-heat method of cooking is ideal for fish and shellfish. If you don't have a steamer, it is easy to improvise.

Steamed Salmon with Herbs
Line a heatproof plate with fresh herb sprigs (dill, parsley, chives, etc.). Set 2 portions of seasoned salmon fillet, each 1-inch thick, on top. Steam Chinese-style about 10 minutes. If desired, top with flavored butter (page 174) or serve with a sauce such as Hollandaise (page 178). *Serves 2.*

1 ▲ Using a steamer: Arrange the fish on the rack in the steamer and set over boiling water. Cover and steam until done.

3 ▲ Steaming larger fish and fillets: Arrange the fish on a rack in a roasting pan of boiling water or on a plate set on the rack. Cover tightly with foil and steam until done.

2 ▲ Chinese-style steaming: Arrange the fish on a heatproof plate that will fit inside a bamboo steamer or wok. Put the plate on the rack in a steamer or wok; set over boiling water. Cover and steam until done.

4 ▲ Steaming in foil: Wrap the fish and seasonings in foil, sealing well, and set on a rack in the steamer or in a large roasting pan of boiling water. Steam until done.

CUTTING FISH STEAKS

Round fish, such as cod or salmon, and large flatfish, such as halibut or turbot, are often cut into steaks for cooking. The usual range of thickness for the steaks is 1–1½ inches. Steaks cut from the tail are smaller, but may contain fewer bones.

1 ▲ With a large, sharp knife, slice the fish crosswise, perpendicular to the backbone, into steaks of the desired thickness.

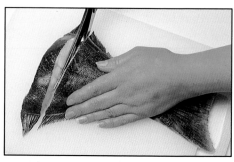

2 ▲ If necessary, cut through the backbone with kitchen scissors or a knife with a serrated blade.

Fish Steaks with Mustard Sauce

SERVES 4–6

4–6 halibut or turbot steaks, 1-inch thick

salt and pepper

3 tablespoons butter, melted

FOR THE SAUCE

¼ cup Dijon-style mustard

1 cup whipping cream

½ teaspoon sugar

1 tablespoon white wine vinegar or
   lemon juice

~ **VARIATION** ~

If preferred, steam the fish steaks
instead of broiling them.

1 Preheat the broiler. Season the fish steaks with salt and pepper. Arrange on an oiled rack in the broiler pan and brush the tops with melted butter.

2 ▼ Broil the steaks about 4 inches from the heat for 4–5 minutes. Turn them over and brush with more butter. Broil until the fish is cooked, 4–5 minutes longer.

3 ▲ Meanwhile, for the sauce, combine the ingredients in a saucepan and bring to a boil, whisking constantly. Simmer, whisking, until the sauce thickens. Remove from the heat and keep warm.

4 Transfer the fish to warmed plates. Spoon the sauce over them, and serve as soon as possible.

CUTTING FISH FILLETS

Fillets are boneless pieces of fish, and for this reason are very popular. A sharp filleting knife, with its thin, flexible blade, is the tool to use for removing the fillets. Be sure to keep all the bones and trimmings for making stock.

Round fish are easy to fillet and they produce a boneless piece from each side. Large flatfish are also easy to deal with, although they are filleted slightly differently from round fish and yield 4 narrow fillets – 2 from each side.

Filleting Small Flatfish

You can take 2 fillets from smaller flatfish (one from each side). Cut behind the head and down the sides of the fish as above, but do not make the central cut. Starting from the head end on one side and working down the fish, cut the flesh away from the rib bones until you reach the center (the backbone). Rotate the fish and repeat on the other side to cut away the whole fillet. Turn the fish over and repeat to cut away the second whole fillet.

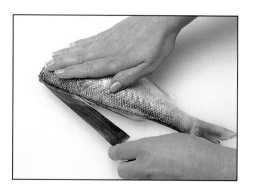

1 ▲ **To fillet a round fish**: First cut off the head. With the tip of the knife, cut through the skin all along the length of the backbone.

2 ▲ Working from head to tail and holding the knife almost parallel to the fish, use short strokes to cut 1 fillet off the rib bones in one piece. Follow the slit cut along the backbone.

3 ▲ When you reach the tail, cut across to release the fillet. Repeat the procedure on the other side to remove the other fillet.

4 ▲ Run your fingers over the flesh side of each fillet to locate any stray bones. Pull them out with tweezers.

5 ▲ **To fillet a flatfish**: Lay the fish on the work surface and make a curved cut behind the head, cutting down to but not through the backbone. With the tip of the knife, slit the skin down both sides of the fish where the fin bones meet the rib bones, "outlining" the fillets, and slit across the tail.

6 ▲ Slit straight down the center line of the fish, from head to tail, cutting down to the backbone. Working from the center at the head end, cut 1 fillet neatly away from the rib bones on one side. Hold the knife blade almost parallel to the fish and use short strokes.

7 ▲ Rotate the fish and cut away the second fillet. Turn the fish over and repeat to remove the 2 fillets on the other side. Pull out any stray bones with tweezers.

Fish Fillets with Peppers in Paper Packages

SERVES 4

2 tablespoons olive oil

1 onion, thinly sliced

1 garlic clove, minced

2 bell peppers, 1 green and 1 red, seeded and cut into thin strips

1 cup coarsely chopped tomatoes

1 tablespoon chopped fresh mint

2 teaspoons chopped fresh marjoram, or ½ teaspoon dried oregano

salt and pepper

4 skinless rockfish or orange roughy fillets

¼ pound feta cheese, crumbled

1 Preheat the oven to 350°F.

2 ▲ Heat the oil in a frying pan and cook the onion, stirring occasionally, until soft, 3–5 minutes. Add the garlic and bell peppers and fry until tender but not browned. Stir in the tomatoes and herbs. Season with salt and pepper. Remove from the heat.

3 ▲ Cut 4 rounds of parchment paper or foil, each the size to wrap a fillet comfortably.

4 ▲ Put a spoonful of the pepper mixture on one half of each piece of paper or foil and set a fish fillet on top. Spoon some of the remaining pepper mixture over each portion of fish. Scatter the cheese on top.

5 ▼ Fold the paper or foil over the fish and fold the edges over several times to seal. Set the packages on a baking sheet.

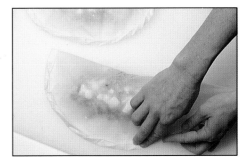

6 Bake until the fish is cooked, 20–25 minutes. If paper was used, you can serve the fish in the packages, but remove fish from foil for serving.

SKINNING FISH FILLETS

Before cooking, dark or tough skin is usually removed from fish fillets. However, if they are to be broiled, the skin helps keep the shape and should not be removed.

Getting a Grip on Fish
If you salt your fingers, you will get a better grip on the tail end so you can hold the skin taut as you cut. It is also a good way to hang on to fish while scaling.

1 ▲ Lay the fillet flat, skin side down, tail end toward you. Make a small crosswise cut through the flesh down to the skin at the tail end.

2 ▲ Grip the bit of skin firmly and insert the knife blade so it is almost parallel to the skin, then cut the fillet away. Use a gentle sawing motion and make one continuous cut.

Scalloped Fish

SERVES 6–8

3 cups milk

1 slice of onion

2–3 sprigs of fresh parsley

1 bay leaf

a few black peppercorns

6 tablespoons butter

5 tablespoons flour

½ teaspoon grated lemon rind

1 egg, beaten to mix

salt and pepper

1½ cups coarse cracker crumbs

1½ pounds skinless white fish fillets, finely diced

½ pound skinless finnan haddie or smoked whitefish fillet, cut into strips

1 Preheat the oven to 350°F.

2 Bring the milk to the boil with the onion, herbs, and peppercorns. Off the heat, let stand 20 minutes to infuse. Melt 5 tablespoons of the butter, stir in the flour, then strain in the milk. Bring to a boil, whisking constantly. Simmer until thickened.

3 ▲ Remove the pan from the heat. Add the lemon rind and egg and mix well. Season with salt and pepper.

4 ▲ Scatter about one-third of the cracker crumbs over the bottom of a buttered baking dish. Cover with a layer of half the diced fish. Spoon half the sauce over the fish and arrange the strips of finnan haddie on top. Repeat the layers of crumbs, fish, and sauce.

5 ▼ Scatter the remaining cracker crumbs over the surface. Dot the top with the remaining butter.

6 Bake until bubbling around the edges and lightly browned on top, about 35 minutes. Serve hot.

~ **VARIATION** ~

For Fish Pie, omit the cracker crumbs and egg. Fold the diced fish into the sauce. Put half in a buttered baking dish and cover with a layer of smoked fish strips. Top with the remaining fish mixture. Cover with mashed potatoes, dot with butter, and bake as above.

BONING FISH FOR STUFFING OR BUTTERFLYING

Round fish, such as trout, mackerel, and salmon, are normally cleaned by slitting open the belly. It is a simple step on from here to removing the backbone. This leaves a bone-free fish and a neat shape for stuffing.

When the boned fish is opened out, or butterflied, it is approximately the same thickness throughout for even, quick cooking.

Boning Through the Back

An alternative boning method to the one shown here is done from the back rather than the belly. Leave the head and tail on the fish. Set the fish belly down on the work surface and use a sharp knife to slit the skin along one side of the backbone, all the way from the head to the tail. Ease the knife through the slit and work it down the side of the rib cage to detach the bones completely from the flesh. Slit the skin on the other side of the backbone and ease the knife down the rib cage to detach the flesh on that side. With scissors, snip the backbone free at head and tail ends, then lift it out along with the gills and the stomach contents.

1 ▲ If the head has not already been removed, cut it off by slicing just behind the gills. Remove the tail completely, cutting straight across.

2 ▲ Enlarge the belly opening. Set the fish on a board, skin side up, with the belly flaps against the board. Press firmly along the backbone to loosen it. Turn the fish over.

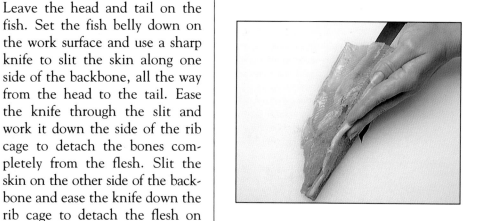

3 ▲ If it is possible, lift out the backbone and rib cage in one piece after freeing it with the knife. If it is necessary to cut the backbone out, slide the knife under the bones along one side of the rib cage.

4 ▲ Gently ease the knife outward under the rib bones, away from the backbone. Repeat on the other side.

5 ▲ Lift up the rib cage in one piece and slide the knife under the backbone, to free it from the skin.

6 ▲ Run your fingers over the flesh to locate any other bones and pull them out with tweezers.

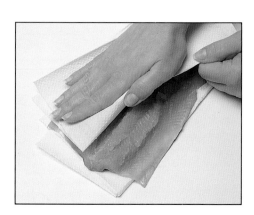

7 ▲ After boning, rinse the fish under cool running water and pat dry with paper towels.

Baked Fish Stuffed with Crab

SERVES 4

4 slices of bacon
½ cup chopped scallions
¼ cup diced celery
grated rind of 1 large lemon
1 tablespoon chopped fresh parsley
½ cup bread crumbs made from day-old French or Italian bread
salt and pepper
6–8 ounces lump crabmeat (about 1 cup)
1 egg, beaten to mix
4 whole fish such as trout or red snapper, ¾–1 pound each, scaled if necessary, cleaned and boned for stuffing

1 Preheat the oven to 375°F.

2 Fry the bacon slices in a frying pan until crisp and rendered of fat. Drain on paper towels. Crumble the bacon.

3 Pour off all but 1 tablespoon bacon fat from the frying pan into a small bowl and reserve. Brush a little reserved fat over the bottom of a baking dish or roasting pan that will accommodate the fish comfortably. Set aside.

4 ▲ Heat the fat still in the frying pan and cook the scallions and celery, stirring occasionally, until softened, 5–7 minutes.

5 Mix together the vegetables, lemon rind, parsley, crumbs, salt, and pepper. Fold in the crabmeat and bacon. Bind with the egg.

6 ▼ Open up each fish like a book, skin side down. Spread the stuffing over one half. Pack it down firmly, then fold over the other half and press down gently. Close the opening with wooden toothpicks, if desired.

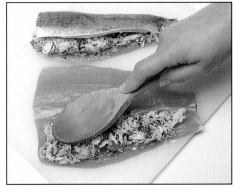

7 ▲ Set the fish in the prepared baking dish or roasting pan. Brush the tops of the fish with a little reserved bacon fat. Bake until the fish is cooked, 25–30 minutes.

8 Carefully transfer the fish to warmed serving plates and serve immediately.

BROILING FISH

The intense dry heat of this method of cooking is best used for fish with a lot of natural oil, such as salmon, mackerel, and tuna. However, leaner fish can also be broiled, as long as you baste them frequently to keep them moist or cook them in a little liquid.

Always preheat the broiler. If desired, line the broiler pan with foil to save on clean up.

Fish can also be very successfully grilled over charcoal. Choose full-flavored fish that will not be overwhelmed by the smoky taste. Thin pieces are easier to handle if placed in a hinged wire fish basket. Be sure to baste well during cooking to prevent the fish from drying out.

Fish Kabobs with Lemon Butter
Combine 2 tablespoons each melted butter and lemon juice with 1 teaspoon English mustard powder and 1 minced garlic clove. Cut 1½ pounds halibut, grouper, or sea bass steaks into 1-inch cubes. Thread onto skewers with pieces of red bell pepper. Brush with the butter mixture and broil, basting frequently and turning to cook evenly, until done. *Serves 4.*

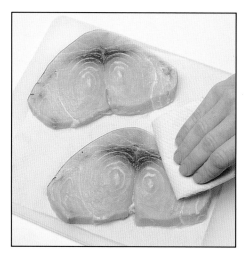

1 ▲ To broil oilier fish (small whole fish, boned and butterflied fish, fillets and steaks that are at least ½-inch thick, or cubes of fish on skewers): Rinse the fish and pat it dry with paper towels. Marinate the fish if the recipe directs.

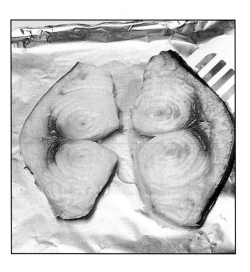

3 ▲ Set the fish under the broiler, 3–4 inches from the heat (thin pieces should be closer to the heat than thicker ones). Broil, basting once or twice and turning if the recipe directs, until the fish is done.

2 ▲ Preheat the broiler with the broiler pan in place. When hot, lightly brush the hot pan with oil or line with foil and then brush with oil. Arrange the fish in the pan, in one layer, skin-side down. Brush the fish with butter, oil, or a basting mixture, according to the recipe directions.

4 ▲ To broil leaner fish (small whole fish, and fish steaks and fillets that are at least ½-inch thick and prepared for cooking as above): Arrange in a buttered flameproof dish. Add a little liquid (wine, stock, etc.) just to cover the bottom of the dish. Brush the fish with butter, oil, or a basting mixture, according to the recipe directions. Broil the fish as above, without turning.

Broiled Butterflied Salmon

SERVES 6–8

| 1½ tablespoons dried juniper berries |
| 2 teaspoons dried green peppercorns |
| 1 teaspoon sugar |
| ⅛ teaspoon salt |
| 3 tablespoons vegetable oil |
| 2 tablespoons lemon juice |
| 1 5-pound salmon, scaled, cleaned, and boned for butterflying |
| lemon wedges, for serving |

1 Put the juniper berries and peppercorns in a spice grinder or mortar and pestle and grind coarsely. Turn the ground spices into a small bowl and stir in the sugar, salt, oil, and lemon juice.

2 ▲ Open the salmon like a book, skin side down. Spread the juniper mixture evenly over the flesh. Fold the salmon closed again and place on a large plate. Cover and let marinate in the refrigerator at least 1 hour.

3 Preheat the broiler.

4 ▼ Open up the salmon again and place it, skin side down, on an oiled baking sheet. Spoon any juniper mixture left on the plate over the fish.

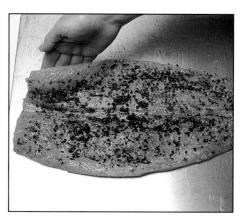

5 Broil about 4 inches from the heat until the fish is cooked, 8–10 minutes. Cut the fish into portions for serving, with lemon wedges.

BREADING AND FRYING FISH

Fish to be fried is often coated with crumbs, or with a batter. The coating keeps the fish moist and full of flavor as well as making a crisp or crunchy crust. Many other foods – boneless chicken breast halves, veal scaloppine, and vegetables, for example – are also breaded.

Deep-Fried Catfish
Bread 8 catfish fillets, using sea-soned flour, egg, and cornmeal. Pan-fry or deep-fry and serve with lemon wedges. *Serves 4.*

1 ▲ Lightly beat egg in a shallow dish. Spread flour on a plate or sheet of wax paper. Season it with salt and pepper (or as recipe directs). Spread crumbs (fine bread crumbs, crushed crackers, cornmeal, etc.) on another.

3 ▲ Next, dip the floured fish in the egg, turning to moisten both sides.

2 ▲ To bread large pieces of fish: Dip first in the flour, turning to coat both sides lightly and evenly. Shake or brush off the excess flour.

4 ▲ Dredge the fish in the crumbs, turning to coat evenly. Press to help the crumbs adhere. Shake or pat off excess crumbs. Refrigerate to set the coating, at least 20 minutes.

5 ▲ To bread small pieces of fish (strips of fish fillet, shrimp, etc.): Put the crumbs in a plastic bag. After dipping the fish in flour and egg, toss a few pieces at a time in the bag of crumbs to coat them.

6 ▲ To pan-fry: Heat oil or a mixture of oil and butter in a frying pan (enough fat to coat the bottom of the pan in a thin layer). When it is very hot, put the fish in the pan, in one layer. Fry until golden brown on both sides and the fish is done. Drain on paper towels before serving.

7 ▲ To deep-fry: Half fill a deep pan with oil and heat it to 375°F on a deep-frying thermometer. Gently lower the breaded pieces of fish into the hot oil (frying them only a few at a time). Fry until golden brown, turning them occasionally so that they cook evenly. Remove and drain on paper towels before serving.

Chinese-Spiced Breaded Fish Fillets

SERVES 4

½ cup flour

1 teaspoon Chinese five-spice powder

salt and pepper

8 skinless fillets of fish such as sole, flounder, or catfish (about 1¾ pounds)

1 egg, beaten to mix

1½–2 cups fine fresh bread crumbs

peanut oil, for frying

2 tablespoons butter

4 scallions, cut diagonally into thin slices

1½ cups seeded and diced tomatoes (peeled first, if preferred)

2 tablespoons soy sauce

3 ▼ Drain the fillets on paper towels, then transfer to plates or a serving platter and keep warm. Pour off all the oil from the pan and wipe out the pan with paper towels.

4 ▲ Melt the butter in the pan and add the scallions and tomatoes. Cook over medium heat, stirring, about 1 minute. Stir in the soy sauce.

5 Spoon the tomato mixture over the fish and serve immediately.

1 ▲ Sift the flour together with the Chinese five-spice, salt, and pepper onto a plate. Bread the fish fillets, dipping them first in the seasoned flour, then in beaten egg, and finally in bread crumbs.

2 Pour oil into a large frying pan to a depth of ½ inch. Heat until it is very hot and starting to sizzle. Add the breaded fillets, a few at a time, and fry until just cooked and golden brown on both sides, 2–3 minutes according to the thickness of the fillets. Do not crowd the pan or the temperature of the oil will drop and allow the fish to absorb too much oil.

MAKING FISH STOCK

Fish stock is much quicker to make than meat or poultry stock. You may have the basic ingredients, or ask your fish merchant for heads and bones.

MAKES ABOUT 1 QUART

1½ pounds heads, bones, and trimmings from white fish (not strong, oily fish)
1 onion, sliced
2 celery stalks with leaves, chopped
1 carrot, sliced
½ lemon, sliced (optional)
1 bay leaf
a few fresh parsley sprigs
6 black peppercorns
5½ cups water
½ cup dry white wine

1 ▲ Rinse the fish heads, bones, and trimmings well under cold running water. Put in a stockpot with the vegetables, lemon, if using, the herbs, peppercorns, water, and wine. Bring to a boil, skimming the surface frequently, then reduce the heat and simmer 25 minutes.

2 ▲ Strain the stock without pressing down on the ingredients in the strainer. If not using immediately, let cool and then refrigerate. Fish stock should be used within 2 days, or it can be frozen up to 3 months.

Fisherman's Stew

SERVES 4

6 slices of bacon, cut into strips
1 tablespoon butter
1 large onion, chopped
1 garlic clove, minced
2 tablespoons chopped fresh parsley
1 teaspoon fresh thyme leaves or ½ teaspoon dried thyme
2 cups peeled, seeded, and chopped tomatoes, or canned crushed tomatoes
½ cup dry vermouth or dry white wine
2 cups fish stock
2 cups diced potatoes
1½–2 pounds skinless white fish fillets, cut into large chunks
salt and pepper

1 Fry the bacon in a large saucepan over medium heat until lightly browned but not crisp, then remove and drain on paper towels. Pour off all but about 1 tablespoon of fat.

2 ▲ Add the butter to the pan and cook the onion, stirring occasionally, until soft, about 3–5 minutes. Add the garlic and herbs and continue cooking for 1 minute, stirring. Add the tomatoes, vermouth or wine, and stock and bring to a boil.

3 Reduce the heat, cover, and simmer the stew for 15 minutes. Add the potatoes, cover again, and simmer until they are almost tender, about 10–12 minutes.

4 ▼ Add the chunks of fish and the bacon. Simmer gently, uncovered, until the fish is just cooked and the potatoes are tender, about 5 minutes longer. Taste for seasoning and serve.

~ COOK'S TIP ~

For fish stock, use heads, bones, and trimmings only from mild, white-fleshed fish, not from strong-flavored oily fish.

PEELING AND DEVEINING SHRIMP

Shrimp can be cooked in their shells, but more often they are peeled first (the shells can be used to make an aromatic stock). The intestinal vein that runs down the back of the shrimp is removed mainly because of its appearance, although if the shrimp are large, the vein may contain grit. The deveining slit may be cut further to open out, or butterfly, the shrimp.

Shrimp are occasionally sold with their heads. These are easily pulled off, and will enhance the flavor of stock made with the shells.

1 ▲ Holding the shrimp firmly in one hand, pull off the legs with the fingers of the other hand.

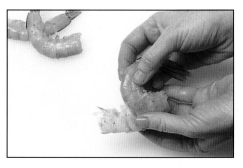

2 ▲ Peel the shell away from the body. When you reach the tail, hold the body and pull away the tail; the shell will come off with it. Or, you can leave the tail on the shrimp and just remove the body shell.

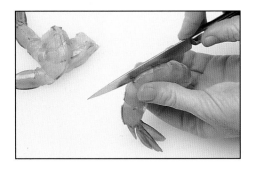

3 ▲ Make a shallow cut down the center of the curved back of the shrimp. Pull out the black vein with a toothpick or your fingers.

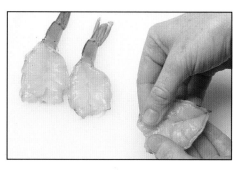

4 ▲ To butterfly shrimp: Cut along the deveining slit to split open the shrimp, without cutting all the way through. Open up the shrimp flat.

5 ▲ To devein shrimp in the shell: Insert a toothpick crosswise in several places along the back where the shell overlaps to lift out the vein.

Spicy Butterflied Shrimp

SERVES 4–6

6 tablespoons olive oil
1/3 cup orange juice
1/4 cup lime juice
1 large garlic clove, minced
1 teaspoon allspice berries, crushed
1/4 teaspoon hot pepper flakes
salt and pepper
2 pounds raw large or jumbo shrimp, peeled, deveined, and butterflied
lime wedges, for serving

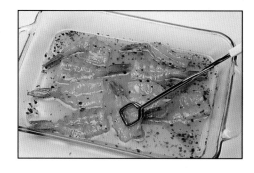

1 ▲ Combine the oil, fruit juices, garlic, allspice, pepper flakes, and seasoning in a large shallow baking dish. Add the shrimp and turn to coat completely with the spiced oil.

2 Cover the dish and let the shrimp marinate for 1 hour at room temperature or for at least 2 hours in the refrigerator.

3 Preheat the broiler.

4 Spread out the shrimp in one layer in the baking dish, arranging them cut side up as much as possible. Broil about 4 inches from the heat until the flesh becomes opaque, 6-8 minutes. There is no need to turn the shrimp.

5 Serve hot, with lime wedges.

Scallops Wrapped in Prosciutto

SERVES 4

24 medium sea scallops, prepared for cooking

lemon juice

8–12 slices of prosciutto, cut lengthwise into 2 or 3 strips

olive oil

pepper

lemon wedges, for serving

1 Preheat the broiler or prepare a charcoal fire.

2 Sprinkle the scallops with lemon juice. Wrap a strip of prosciutto around each scallop. Thread onto 8 skewers.

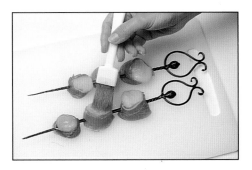

3 ▲ Brush with oil. Arrange on a baking sheet if broiling. Broil about 4 inches from the heat, or grill over charcoal, until the scallops are opaque, 4-5 minutes on each side.

4 Set 2 skewers on each plate. Sprinkle the scallops with freshly ground black pepper and serve with lemon wedges, if desired.

Preparing Scallops

Scallops are usually shucked at sea, and the shell and coral-colored roe are discarded. Only large sea scallops need further preparation.

Pull off and discard the small piece of gristle from the side of the scallop. Rinse the scallop well to remove any grit, and pat dry.

Spicy Butterflied Shrimp (left), Scallops Wrapped in Prosciutto

PREPARING CLAMS AND MUSSELS

Mollusks such as clams and mussels should be eaten very fresh and must be alive when you buy them and cook them (unless they have been shucked and frozen). They are alive if their shells are tightly closed; any shells that are open should close promptly when tapped. Dead clams or mussels, or any with broken shells, should be discarded.

If you have dug the clams yourself, let them stand in a bucket of sea water for several hours, changing the water once or twice. (Do not use fresh water because it will kill the clams.) Add a handful or two of cornmeal to the water to help clean the clams' stomachs. Clams bought in the fish market will have been purged of sand.

Sailor's Mussels
Prepare 2–3 quarts live mussels. Steam with 1 cup dry white wine or fish or chicken stock, 1 small onion, chopped, 1–2 minced garlic cloves, and ½ cup minced fresh parsley. With a slotted spoon, transfer the opened mussels to large bowls. Add 3 tablespoons butter to the cooking liquid and stir until melted, then add pepper. Pour this liquid over the mussels. *Serves 4.*

1 ▲ Scrub the shells of mussels with a stiff brush and rinse well. Scrub clams under cool running water.

3 ▲ **To steam**: Put a little dry white wine or water in a large pot, with flavorings as the recipe directs. Add the clams or mussels, cover tightly, and bring to a boil. Steam until the shells open, 5–10 minutes, shaking the pot occasionally.

5 ▲ **To shuck a live clam or mussel**: Hold it firmly in one hand, with the hinge in your palm. Insert the side of a clam or oyster knife blade between the shell halves and work it around to cut through the hinge muscle.

2 ▲ Before cooking mussels, pull off their "beards" (their anchor threads) with the help of a small knife. Rinse the mussels well.

4 ▲ Serve the clams or mussels in their shells, or shuck them before using. Strain the cooking liquid (which will include all the delicious liquor from the shells) and spoon it over the clams or mussels, or use it as the basis for a sauce.

6 ▲ Open the shell and cut the clam or mussel free of the shell. Do this over a bowl in order to catch all the liquor from the shell. (Clams are sometimes eaten raw, but mussels are always cooked.)

Phyllo Clam Puffs

MAKES ABOUT 4½ DOZEN

9 sheets phyllo pastry, each about 12 × 18 inches

¾ pound (1½ cups) cream cheese

1 egg, beaten to mix

1 cup coarsely chopped steamed clams or well drained canned clams

⅓ cup chopped scallions

2 tablespoons chopped fresh dill

a few drops of hot pepper sauce

salt and pepper

1½–2 sticks (12–16 tablespoons) butter, melted

1 Preheat the oven to 400°F.

2 Stack the sheets of phyllo pastry and cover with a sheet of plastic wrap.

3 ▲ Combine the cream cheese, egg, clams, scallions, dill, pepper sauce, and some salt and pepper in a bowl. Mix thoroughly.

~ **COOK'S TIP** ~

Phyllo (or filo) pastry dries out very quickly and then can become too brittle to use. So when working with phyllo pastry, keep the sheets you are not using covered with plastic wrap and a damp dish towel, and remove the sheets individually just before brushing with melted butter or oil.

4 Lay one sheet of phyllo pastry on the work surface and brush it lightly and evenly with melted butter. Lay another sheet of phyllo pastry neatly on top and brush it also with butter. Cover with a third sheet of phyllo pastry and brush with butter.

5 ▼ Spoon about one-third of the clam mixture in a line along one long side of the stacked phyllo pastry, about 1 inch in from the edge.

6 ▲ Fold the nearest long phyllo pastry edge over the clam filling and continue rolling up. Cut the roll across in half and put the two halves on a buttered baking sheet. Brush the rolls with melted butter.

7 Make two more rolls in the same way and put the halves on the baking sheet. Brush them all with melted butter. Bake until golden brown and crisp, about 20 minutes.

8 Using scissors, cut the rolls across into bite-size pieces. Serve as soon as possible, as an appetizer.

PASTA & GRAINS

~

Perfect for any occasion, simple to cook, and satisfying to eat,
pasta, rice, and other grains are now a mainstay of
everyone's diet. Here are plenty of ideas for cooking them.
And try making your own pasta — it's rewarding and fun.

COOKING PASTA

Both fresh and dried pasta are cooked in the same way. The golden rules for success are: use plenty of water and keep checking the pasta to be sure it does not overcook.

Fresh pasta will cook much more quickly than dried – in 1–4 minutes as opposed to 5 minutes or more.

Buttered Noodles
Cook 1 pound fettuccine or tagliatelle (fresh or dried) until "al dente." Drain well and return to the pot. Add 3–4 tablespoons butter and ⅛ teaspoon freshly grated nutmeg. Season with salt and pepper. Toss until the noodles are coated, then serve. *Serves 6.*

Buttered Noodles with Herbs
Omit the nutmeg and add ¼ cup minced fresh herbs such as parsley, dill, basil, or thyme – singly or a mixture.

Buttered Noodles with Cheese
Add 3 tablespoons freshly grated Parmesan cheese.

1 ▲ Bring a very large pot of salted water to a boil. (Use at least 4 quarts of water and 2 teaspoons salt to 1 pound of pasta.) Drop in the pasta all at once and stir to separate the shapes or strands.

3 ▲ Bring the water back to a boil, then reduce the heat slightly and boil until the pasta is just done. For dried pasta, follow the package directions, but start testing as soon as you reach the minimum time given. To test, lift a piece of pasta out on a wooden fork or slotted spoon. Cut it in half. There should be no sign of opaque, uncooked pasta in the center. Or bite it – it should be tender but still firm. In Italian, this is when it is "al dente," or to the tooth.

2 ▲ If you are cooking spaghetti, let the ends in the water soften slightly and then gently push in the rest as soon as you can.

4 ▲ Drain the pasta well in a colander, shaking it vigorously to remove all excess water. Serve immediately because the pasta will continue to cook in its own heat.

When to Undercook Pasta
If you are going to cook the pasta further, by baking it in a lasagne for example, undercook it slightly at this first stage. Pasta for a salad should also be a little undercooked, so that it will not become soggy when it is mixed with the dressing.

Pasta, Bean, and Vegetable Soup

SERVES 4–6

¾ cup dried cranberry or pinto beans, soaked overnight

5 cups vegetable or chicken stock or water

1 large onion, chopped

1 large garlic clove, minced

2 celery stalks, chopped

½ red bell pepper, seeded and chopped

1½ cups peeled, seeded, and chopped tomatoes or canned crushed tomatoes

½-pound piece of Canadian bacon

½ cup tiny pasta shapes for soup

2 zucchini, halved lengthwise and sliced

1 tablespoon tomato paste

salt and pepper

shredded fresh basil, for garnishing

1 Drain the beans and put them in a large pot. Cover with fresh cold water and bring to a boil. Boil 10 minutes, then drain and discard the water. Rinse the beans.

2 Return the beans to the rinsed pot, add the stock, and bring to a boil. Skim off the foam from the surface.

3 ▲ Add the onion, garlic, celery, bell pepper, tomatoes, and bacon. Bring back to a boil. Cover and simmer over low heat until the beans are just tender, about 1½ hours.

4 Lift out the bacon. Shred the meat coarsely with two forks and set aside.

5 ▼ Add the pasta shapes, zucchini, and tomato paste to the soup. Season to taste with salt and pepper. Simmer the soup, uncovered, 5–8 minutes longer, stirring occasionally. (Check the suggested pasta cooking time on the package.)

6 ▲ Stir in the shredded bacon. Taste and adjust the seasoning, then serve the soup hot, sprinkled with shredded fresh basil.

MAKING PASTA DOUGH

Pasta dough is very simple to make and, like most things, the more you do it the better the results will be. As in making pastry and bread doughs, the quantity of liquid needed can vary, according to how absorbent the flour is. The recipe here is for a basic egg pasta, with several variations.

MAKES ABOUT 1 POUND

| 1½ cups unbleached flour |
| 1 teaspoon salt |
| 2 extra large eggs, beaten to mix |

1 ▲ Put the flour and salt on a work surface and make a well in the center. Add the eggs to the well.

2 ▲ With fingertips, gradually incorporate the flour into the eggs. When all the flour is mixed in, you should be able to gather up a pliable dough; if too moist, add more flour.

Pasta Flavorings
- For *Green Pasta*: Blanch ¾ pound of spinach, Swiss chard, or other greens, then drain well and squeeze dry. Purée or mince very finely. Add with the eggs.
- For *Fresh Herb Pasta*: Mince 1 cup loosely packed fresh herb leaves, such as basil, flat-leaf (Italian) parsley, and coriander (cilantro). Add with the eggs.
- For *Tomato Pasta*: Add 1½ tablespoons tomato paste with the eggs.
- For *Lemon Pasta*: Add 1½ tablespoons grated lemon rind with the eggs.
- For *Herb and Garlic Pasta*: Add ¼ cup minced parsley and oregano or marjoram and 1–2 minced garlic cloves with the eggs.
- For *Saffron Pasta*: Add ½ teaspoon ground saffron to the flour and salt or dissolve ½ teaspoon saffron threads in 1 tablespoon very hot water and add with the eggs through a small strainer.
- For *Whole-Wheat Pasta*: Substitute ½–1 cup whole-wheat flour for the same quantity of all-purpose flour.

3 ▲ Flour the work surface. Knead the dough by pushing it away with the heel of your hand and then folding it back. Continue kneading until it is smooth and elastic, 8–10 minutes. (Or, use a pasta machine for kneading – see page 94.)

4 ▲ Shape the dough into a ball and put it in a bowl. Cover with plastic wrap. Let it rest at least 30 minutes before rolling and cutting.

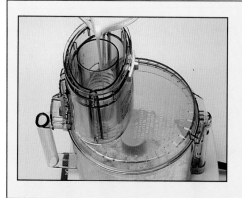

Food Processor Pasta Dough
To mix the pasta dough in a food processor, put the flour and salt in the container. Pulse to blend. With the machine running, gradually add the eggs through the feed tube. Continue processing until the dough comes together into a ball that is smooth and elastic, 3–5 minutes.

ROLLING AND CUTTING PASTA DOUGH BY HAND

You can roll pasta dough by hand, but it is hard work. So if you intend to make pasta frequently, it is worth buying a machine.

Divide the dough into 3 or 4 pieces. Roll and cut one piece at a time. Keep the remaining dough tightly wrapped in plastic to prevent it from drying out while you work.

Pasta with Ham and Peas

Cook 2 minced garlic cloves in 2 tablespoons of butter in a medium saucepan until softened, about 3 minutes. Add 1 cup thawed frozen peas, ½ pound cooked ham cut into matchstick strips, 1 cup whipping cream, and seasoning, and bring to a boil. Toss with 1 pound thinly cut fresh pasta, cooked and drained, and ½ cup freshly grated Parmesan cheese. Serve immediately, with more cheese if desired. *Serves 4.*

Keeping Fresh Pasta

If fresh noodles are not to be cooked the day they are made, allow them to dry completely. Then wrap loosely and store at room temperature for up to 4 days.

1 ▲ Put a piece of dough on a lightly floured surface and pat it into a flat disk. Using a long rolling pin, roll out the dough in all directions, starting from the center each time.

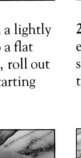

3 ▲ For stuffed pasta shapes, use the dough immediately, while it is still malleable. If cutting noodles, sprinkle the rolled-out dough with flour and let it dry 10–15 minutes.

5 ▲ Uncoil the noodles with your fingers and scatter them on a floured dish towel. Let dry about 5 minutes before cooking. Or, wrap in plastic wrap and refrigerate for later cooking.

2 ▲ Continue rolling, with long even strokes, until you have a large sheet of dough that is about ⅛-inch thick, or less for thinner noodles.

4 ▲ To cut, roll up the sheet of dough like a flat jelly roll. With a knife, cut across the roll into noodles of the required width (⅛ inch for fettuccine, ¼ inch for tagliatelle).

6 ▲ To dry, leave them on the floured towel, or hang them over a broom handle, and let dry 2–3 hours. Sprinkle them with cornmeal to prevent them sticking together and pack loosely in a plastic bag or in a box with each layer separated.

USING A PASTA MACHINE

A pasta machine – hand-cranked or electric – takes all the drudgery out of making fresh pasta. You are able to roll the dough paper-thin and to cut very fine noodles such as tagliolini and tagliarini (¹⁄₁₆-inch width).

The smooth rollers on a pasta machine can be set wide apart or very close together, normally with the use of a dial. You start at the widest setting to knead the dough and then reduce the space gradually until the dough reaches the right thickness. Then a roller with blades cuts noodles of the desired width.

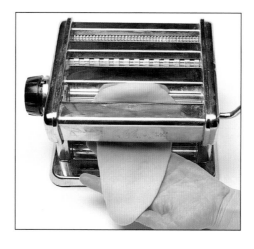

1 ▲ To knead dough: Flatten one piece of dough slightly and then feed it through the machine's rollers on their widest setting.

2 ▲ Fold the resulting strip of dough in half and feed it through again. Continue folding the dough and feeding it through until smooth and elastic, 8–10 times. (If it feels sticky, dust it with flour before continuing.)

Lemon Pasta with Clam Sauce
Cook 3 minced garlic cloves in 5 tablespoons of olive oil until softened, about 3 minutes. Add 1½ cups steamed shucked clams, chopped if large, with 3 tablespoons of their cooking liquid, or 2 (7-ounce) cans chopped cooked clams, drained. Heat the clams through; add ¼ cup chopped fresh parsley and 2–3 tablespoons lemon juice. Toss the sauce with 1 pound lemon pasta, cooked and drained, and plenty of freshly ground pepper. Serve immediately. *Serves 4.*

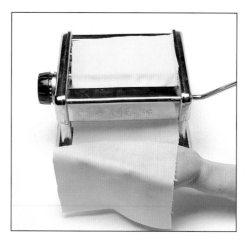

3 ▲ To roll dough: Adjust the rollers to the next narrower setting and feed the strip of dough through again, without folding it. Narrow the rollers again and feed the strip of dough through. Continue feeding the dough through the rollers at increasingly narrow settings until it is the desired thinness. Sprinkle with flour and let dry 10–15 minutes.

4 ▲ To cut noodles: Set the blades on the machine to the desired width. Feed the strip of dough through the blades, letting it fall onto a floured dish towel. Let dry about 5 minutes before cooking. (Or dry completely for longer storage; see page 93.)

Drying Before Cutting
It is important to let the pasta dough dry out a bit before cutting it into noodles, or they will tend to stick together. If the day is humid, this initial drying can take up to 30 minutes.

Noodles with Tomato and Mushroom Sauce

SERVES 3–4

1 ounce dried Italian mushrooms (porcini)
¾ cup warm water
4 cups peeled, seeded, and chopped tomatoes or drained canned tomatoes
¼ teaspoon dried hot pepper flakes
salt and pepper
3 tablespoons olive oil
4 slices of pancetta or Canadian bacon, cut into thin strips
1 large garlic clove, minced
¾ pound tagliatelle or fettuccine
freshly grated Parmesan cheese, for serving

1 Put the mushrooms in a bowl and cover them with the warm water. Let soak about 20 minutes.

2 Meanwhile, put the tomatoes in a saucepan with the pepper flakes, salt, and pepper. If using canned tomatoes, crush them with a fork or potato masher. Bring to a boil, then reduce the heat, and simmer until the mixture has reduced to about 3 cups, 30–40 minutes. Stir occasionally to prevent sticking.

3 ▲ When the mushrooms have finished soaking, lift them out and squeeze over the bowl; set aside. Carefully pour the soaking liquid into the tomatoes through a cheesecloth-lined strainer, leaving the sandy grit in the bottom of the bowl. Let the tomatoes simmer 15 minutes longer.

4 ▼ Meanwhile, heat 2 tablespoons of the oil in a frying pan. Add the strips of pancetta or bacon and fry until golden but not crisp. Add the garlic and mushrooms and fry about 3 minutes longer, stirring. Set aside.

5 Cook the pasta in a large pot of boiling salted water until it is just tender to the bite ("al dente").

6 ▲ Add the bacon and mushroom mixture to the tomato sauce and mix well. Season with salt and pepper.

7 Drain the pasta and return it to the pot. Add the remaining oil and toss to coat the strands. Divide among hot plates, spoon the sauce on top, and serve, with Parmesan cheese.

CUTTING FLAT PASTA SHAPES

For wide noodles like pappardelle, and pasta for layering or rolling up such as lasagne and cannelloni, roll the dough by hand or machine to about ⅛-inch thickness. Lay the rolled dough strip, which will be about 4–5 inches wide, on a lightly floured surface. Trim the sides to make them straight and square with a sharp knife, or, for pappardelle, with a fluted pastry wheel. Lasagne may also be cut with a wheel for a decorative fluted edge.

1 ▲ To make lasagne or cannelloni: For lasagne, cut the dough strip into rectangles that are about 10–12 inches long, or of a size to fit your baking dish. For cannelloni, cut into smaller rectangles, about 3- × 5-inches.

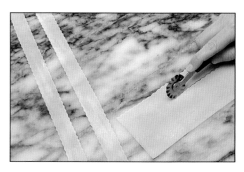

2 ▲ For pappardelle: Cut the strip of dough into long noodles about ⅝-inch wide. Pappardelle are traditionally cut with a fluted pastry wheel, and need not be uniform as they are meant to have a rustic quality.

Tuna Lasagne

SERVES 6

1 quantity fresh pasta dough (pages 92–94), cut for lasagne, or ¾ pound dry lasagne

1 tablespoon butter

1 small onion, minced

1 garlic clove, minced

¼ pound mushrooms, thinly sliced

¼ cup dry white wine (optional)

2½ cups white sauce (page 170)

½ cup heavy whipping cream

3 tablespoons minced parsley

salt and pepper

2 7-ounce cans tuna, drained and flaked

2 canned pimientos, well drained, seeded, and cut into strips

½ cup thawed frozen peas

¾ cup shredded mozzarella

⅓ cup freshly grated Parmesan cheese

1 Bring a large pot of salted water to a boil. Add one-third of the lasagne noodles, one at a time, and cook until almost tender to the bite. Lift the noodles out with a slotted spatula into a colander and rinse with cold water.

2 ▲ Lay them on a dish towel, in one layer, to drain. Cook remaining noodles the same way, in 2 batches.

3 Preheat the oven to 350°F.

4 ▲ Melt the butter in a saucepan. Cook the onion until soft. Add the garlic and mushrooms. Cook until they are soft, stirring occasionally.

5 Pour in the wine, if using. Boil 1 minute. Add the white sauce, cream, and parsley. Season to taste.

6 Spoon a thin layer of sauce over the bottom of a 9- × 12-inch baking dish. Cover with a layer of lasagne noodles. Scatter half of the tuna, pimientos, peas, and shredded mozzarella over the noodles. Spoon one-third of the remaining sauce evenly over the top and cover with another layer of lasagne noodles.

7 ▲ Repeat the layers, ending with noodles and sauce. Sprinkle with the Parmesan. Bake until bubbling hot and the top is lightly browned, 35–40 minutes. Cut into large squares and serve from the baking dish.

MAKING RAVIOLI

The variety of stuffings for these pasta shapes is endless, and they can be dressed simply with butter, oil, or cream, or with a rich sauce. Roll the dough, divided into 2 or 4 portions, very thinly – no more than 1/16 inch.

Making Individual Ravioli
If making ravioli with hand-rolled pasta, it is easier to cut out squares or rounds from the dough rather than making them in strips. Put a mound of stuffing in the center of each square or round, moisten the edges, and set another square or round on top. Or, fold rounds into half moons. Crimp ends to seal.

1 ▲ Lay the rolled strip of dough on a lightly floured surface. Spoon mounds of the stuffing, 1/2–3/4 teaspoon each, in neat rows over the dough, spacing the mounds evenly about 1 1/2-inches apart (or according to recipe directions).

2 ▲ Using your fingers or a pastry brush, moisten the dough around the mounds with cold water.

3 ▲ Lay another strip of dough carefully on top.

4 ▲ With your fingers, press the sheets of dough together between the mounds of stuffing.

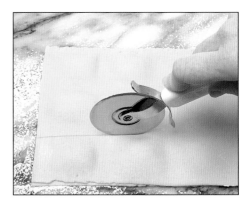

5 ▲ Using a pastry wheel, pizza cutter, or knife, cut neatly between the mounds to make squares.

6 ▲ Crimp the edges of each ravioli with a fork to insure they are completely sealed.

7 ▲ Alternatively, cut out ravioli with special cutters, which are available in different shapes, or with cookie cutters.

8 ▲ Sprinkle the ravioli with cornmeal or semolina, coating them all over, to prevent them from sticking together.

Ravioli with Cheese and Herbs

SERVES 4–6

1 cup cream cheese, softened

1 garlic clove, minced

½ cup minced fresh mixed herbs such as thyme, basil, chives, parsley

salt and pepper

1 quantity fresh pasta dough (pages 92–94), rolled by machine into 2 12-inch-long strips, or divided in 4 and rolled by hand as thinly as possible

cornmeal or flour

1 stick (8 tablespoons) butter

1 ▲ Mix together the cream cheese, garlic, and ⅓ cup of the herbs. Season with salt and pepper.

2 Make the ravioli, filling them with the cheese and herb mixture. Toss the ravioli in a little cornmeal or flour and let rest at room temperature about 15 minutes to dry out a little.

3 ▼ Bring a large pot of salted water to a boil. Drop in the ravioli and cook until they are just tender to the bite, 7–9 minutes. Drain well.

~ **VARIATION** ~

For Ravioli with Gorgonzola Cheese and Pine Nuts, fill the ravioli with a mixture of ½ cup cream cheese and ½ cup crumbled gorgonzola cheese; omit the garlic and herbs. Sprinkle the ravioli with ¼ cup toasted pine nuts instead of herbs.

4 ▲ Melt the butter. Toss the ravioli with the melted butter. Sprinkle with the remaining herbs and serve.

COOKING RICE

There are many different ways to cook rice, and each has its adherents. The simplest is to cook rice in a large quantity of boiling water, then drain. However, valuable nutrients will be discarded in the water. The ways given here retain the rice's nutrients. Timings are for long-grain rice (one part rice to two parts water).

Rice Salad
Steam or bake 1 cup long-grain rice. While hot, dress with 6 tablespoons vinaigrette (page 182). Let cool. Add ½ cup each chopped scallions, celery, radishes, cucumber, and quartered black olives with another ½ cup vinaigrette. Toss well and sprinkle with chopped parsley. *Serves 4–6.*

2 ▲ To sauté and steam rice (pilaf): Heat oil, butter, or a mixture of the two in a saucepan over medium heat. Add the rice and stir to coat the grains. Sauté 2–3 minutes, stirring constantly. Add the measured quantity of boiling salted water. Bring back to a boil, then cover and steam over very low heat until the water has been absorbed and the rice is tender.

1 ◄ To steam rice: Put the measured quantity of salted water in a saucepan and bring to a boil. Add the rice and stir. Bring back to a boil, then cover the pan and steam over very low heat until the rice has absorbed all the water and is tender, 15–18 minutes for white rice and 35–40 minutes for brown rice. Remove the pan from the heat and let stand 5 minutes. Before serving, fluff the rice with a fork.

3 ▲ To bake rice: Put the rice in a baking dish and add the measured quantity of boiling salted water. Cover tightly with foil or a lid and bake in a preheated 350°F oven until the water has been absorbed and the rice is tender, 20–30 minutes for white rice and 35–45 for brown. Cooking time depends on many factors, including the seal of the dish.

A LOOK AT RICE

There are thousands of varieties of rice grown all over the world, with differing flavors and aromas. But for the cook, the choice of which rice to use in a dish is based mainly on the length of the rice grain.

Long-grain rice has grains that are four to five times as long as they are wide. It is dry and fluffy after cooking, with the grains remaining separate. Examples of long-grain rice include: Basmati (aromatic, with a rich nutty flavor; much used in Indian cooking), brown long-grain rice (husk removed but nutritious bran layer left; texture is slightly chewy, mild nutty flavor), and white or polished long-grain rice (most widely used; mild in flavor). Long-grain rice is excellent steamed or baked, in pilafs, and salads.

Short-grain rice, with an almost round shape, is very starchy and tends to cling together after cooking. Examples of short-grain rice include: Arborio rice (it gives a creamy texture to dishes) and glutinous or sweet rice (very sticky after cooking; used in Asian desserts and snacks). Short-grain rice is the one to use for puddings, risotto, croquettes, sushi, stir-fried rice, and molded rice dishes.

Medium-grain rice, in between the other two, is more tender than long-grain rice but less moist than short-grain. It is fluffy and separate if served hot, but clumps as it cools.

Raisin and Almond Pilaf

SERVES 4

3 tablespoons butter

¼ cup sliced almonds

1 small onion, minced

⅓ cup firmly packed raisins

1¼ cups long-grain rice

2½ cups boiling chicken stock or water

salt and pepper

1 Melt the butter in a saucepan. Add the almonds and fry over medium heat, stirring, until they are golden brown. Remove the almonds with a slotted spoon, drain on paper towels, and set aside.

2 Add the onion to the saucepan and cook until soft, stirring occasionally.

3 ▼ Stir in the raisins and rice and sauté until the rice looks slightly translucent, 2–3 minutes.

4 ▲ Add the stock or water. Bring to a boil, then cover the pan and steam over very low heat until the rice is tender and all liquid has been absorbed, 20–25 minutes.

5 Season with salt and pepper. Fluff in the almonds with a fork and serve.

MAKING RISOTTO

This Italian favorite lends itself to so many variations, and, depending on the flavorings and additions, it can be served as a first course, a main dish, or an accompaniment.

If possible, use imported short-grain risotto rice such as Arborio because it retains its nutty texture while giving the essential creaminess to the risotto. For best results, use a well-flavored homemade stock.

Risotto with Parmesan
Make the risotto with 5 cups chicken stock, 2 tablespoons butter, 3 tablespoons minced onion, 1 minced garlic clove, and 1½ cups Arborio rice. Just before the risotto is ready, stir in another 2 tablespoons butter and ½ cup freshly grated Parmesan cheese. Season with salt and pepper, and serve. *Serves 6.*

Regulating the Temperature
During cooking, adjust the heat so that the risotto bubbles merrily, but don't let it boil fiercely or the stock will evaporate before it can be absorbed by the rice.

1 ▲ In a saucepan, bring the measured quantity of stock to a boil, then reduce the heat so the liquid is kept at a gentle simmer.

3 ▲ Add the rice and stir to coat it with the fat. Sauté 1–2 minutes over medium heat, stirring constantly.

2 ▲ Heat butter, oil, or a mixture of the two in a wide, heavy pan. Add chopped onion (plus garlic and/or other flavorings specified in the recipe) and cook over low heat until soft, stirring occasionally.

4 ▲ Add ½ cup of the simmering stock (or an initial quantity of wine, vermouth, etc., as the recipe directs) and stir well. Simmer, stirring frequently, until the rice has absorbed almost all the liquid.

5 ◄ Add another ½ cup of simmering stock and cook, stirring, until it is almost all absorbed. Continue adding the stock in this way until the grains of rice are tender but still firm to the bite ("al dente," like pasta) and the risotto is creamy but not runny. You may not need to add all the stock. Total cooking time will be about 30 minutes.

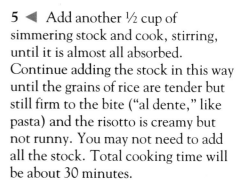

Risotto with Chicken

SERVES 4

2 tablespoons olive oil

½ pound skinless boneless chicken
   breast, cut into 1-inch cubes

1 onion, minced

1 garlic clove, minced

¼ teaspoon saffron stems

2 ounces prosciutto, cut into thin
   strips

2 cups short-grain risotto rice, preferably
   Arborio

½ cup dry white wine

5½ cups simmering chicken stock,
   preferably homemade

2 tablespoons butter (optional)

¼ cup freshly grated Parmesan cheese,
   plus more for serving

salt and pepper

1 ▲ Heat the oil in a wide, heavy-
based pan over medium-high heat.
Add the chicken cubes and cook,
stirring, until they start to turn white.

2 ▲ Reduce the heat to low and add
the onion, garlic, saffron, and
prosciutto. Cook, stirring, until the
onion is soft. Stir in the rice. Sauté
1–2 minutes, stirring constantly.

3 ▲ Add the wine and bring to a
boil. Simmer gently until almost all
the wine is absorbed.

4 Add the simmering stock, ½ cup or
so at a time, and cook until the rice is
just tender and the risotto creamy.

5 ▼ Add the butter, if using, and
Parmesan cheese and stir in well.
Season with salt and pepper to taste.
Serve the risotto hot, sprinkled with
more Parmesan cheese.

COOKING WILD RICE

Although called "rice," this is actually an aquatic grass. Its deliciously nutty flavor and firm, chewy texture make it a perfect complement to many meat and poultry dishes. It is also an excellent partner for vegetables such as winter squashes and mushrooms. It can be cooked like rice, by boiling or steaming, needing only a longer cooking time.

1 ▲ To boil wild rice: Add the rice to a large pot of boiling salted water (about 1 quart water to each cup of rice). Bring back to a gentle boil and cook until the rice is tender but still firm and has begun to split open, 45–50 minutes. Drain well.

2 ▲ To steam wild rice: Put the rice in a saucepan with the measured quantity of salted water. Bring to a boil, cover, and steam over very low heat until the rice is tender, 45–50 minutes. Cook uncovered for the last 5 minutes to evaporate excess water.

Wild Rice and Turkey Salad

SERVES 4

| 1 cup wild rice, boiled or steamed |
| 2 celery stalks, thinly sliced |
| ½ cup chopped scallions |
| ¼ pound small button mushrooms, quartered |
| 4 cups diced cooked turkey breast |
| ½ cup vinaigrette dressing, made with walnut oil (page 182) |
| 1 teaspoon fresh thyme leaves |
| 2 pears, peeled, halved, and cored |
| ¼ cup walnut pieces, toasted |

1 ▲ Combine the cooked wild rice, celery, scallions, mushrooms, and turkey in a bowl.

2 ◄ Add the dressing and thyme and toss to coat thoroughly.

3 Thinly slice the pear halves lengthwise, without cutting through the stem end, and spread the slices like a fan. Divide the salad among 4 plates. Garnish with fanned pear halves and walnuts.

PREPARING BULGUR WHEAT

Bulgur wheat, a nutritious grain, is made by steaming whole wheat berries and then drying and cracking them into very small pieces. Cook like rice, either steamed plain or as a pilaf, or soak it to rehydrate. Serve as an accompaniment or use in salads.

1 ▲ **To steam bulgur:** Use two parts water to one part bulgur. Put the bulgur in a saucepan with water or other liquid such as stock, add flavorings if directed, and bring to a boil. Cover and simmer over low heat until tender, 12–15 minutes.

2 ▲ **To soak bulgur:** Put the bulgur in a strainer and rinse under cold running water until the water runs clear. Put the bulgur in a bowl, cover with fresh cold water, and let soak 1 hour until plump. Drain well, pressing out all excess moisture.

Cooking Simple Bulgur Pilaf
Soften 1 small minced onion in 2 tablespoons butter. Add 1 cup bulgur wheat, 2 cups chicken stock, and a bay leaf. Cover and steam. To serve, season and stir in 2 tablespoons minced parsley.

Bulgur Wheat Salad with Herbs

SERVES 6

¾ cup bulgur wheat, soaked and drained
1 cup seeded and diced ripe tomatoes
½ cup chopped red onion
¼ cup chopped scallions
1 cup minced parsley
¼ cup chopped fresh mint
½ cup olive or salad oil
⅓ cup lemon juice
salt and pepper
black olives and mint leaves, for garnishing

1 ▲ Combine all the ingredients in a large bowl.

2 ◀ Stir to mix the ingredients thoroughly. Taste and adjust the seasoning, adding more salt and pepper if needed.

3 Serve the salad at room temperature, garnished with black olives and mint leaves, if desired.

PREPARING COUSCOUS

A staple in North-African cooking, couscous is a type of tiny pasta made from semolina (which is ground from durum wheat). Its mild taste makes it the perfect accompaniment for spicy dishes, in particular the Moroccan and Tunisian stew also called couscous. It is delicious in stuffings and baked casseroles and even as a breakfast cereal.

1 ▲ To prepare regular couscous: Put the couscous in a strainer and rinse under cold running water until the water runs clear. Put the couscous in a bowl, cover with plenty of fresh cold water, and let soak 30 minutes. Drain well in a fine strainer.

2 ▲ Rub the couscous in your fingers to be sure there are no lumps, then put it in a cheesecloth-lined colander. Set over a pan of boiling water (or over the pot containing the spicy stew) and steam, uncovered, until soft, about 30 minutes.

Couscous Stuffing
Prepare 1 cup quick-cooking couscous, using 2 cups chicken or turkey stock, 2 tablespoons butter, 1 teaspoon ground cinnamon, and ½ teaspoon each ground cumin and coriander. Season with salt and pepper, then stir in ½ cup each chopped dried apricots and golden raisins. Use to stuff Cornish hens, chicken, turkey, or boned chicken pieces before roasting or pot-roasting. Makes enough to stuff 1 chicken or 2 Cornish hens.

3 ▲ To cook quick-cooking couscous: Put the liquid (preferably stock) in a saucepan, with 2 tablespoons butter if desired, and bring to a boil. Off the heat, gradually add the couscous and stir. Return to a boil, then cover the pan, remove from the heat, and let stand about 10 minutes. Fluff the couscous with a fork before serving. Serve hot as an accompaniment, adding seasoning and other flavorings as required, or use as a stuffing for vegetables or poultry.

4 ▲ To soak quick-cooking couscous: Put the couscous in a bowl, cover with boiling water, and let soak 20–30 minutes until plump. Drain well. Use for salads.

Special Equipment
A special pot (called a "couscous-sière") is traditionally used for cooking this grain. The bottom part of the pot is filled with a spicy stew; the perforated top part holds the couscous, where it cooks in the fragrant steam.

Spicy Vegetable Stew with Couscous

SERVES 4

1½ tablespoons vegetable oil
2 large onions, cut into chunks
½ teaspoon ground cumin
½ teaspoon ground cinnamon
¼ teaspoon turmeric
¾ pound carrots, cut into chunks
¾ pound white turnips, cut into chunks
3½ cups vegetable or chicken stock or water
¾ pound zucchini or yellow summer squash, cut into chunks
1 red bell pepper, seeded and cut into large squares
¼ cup raisins
2 cups quick-cooking couscous
2 tablespoons butter
1 cup thawed frozen green peas
salt and pepper

1 Heat the oil in a large pot. Add the onions and cook until they begin to soften, stirring occasionally.

2 Stir in the spices and cook, stirring, for 1 minute.

3 ▲ Add the carrots, turnips, and ½ cup of the stock. Bring to a boil. Cover and cook 5 minutes.

4 ▲ Add the zucchini, bell pepper, and raisins. Cover again and simmer until the vegetables are almost tender, about 10 minutes longer.

5 Meanwhile, cook the couscous, using the remaining vegetable or chicken stock and the butter.

6 ▼ Add the peas to the vegetable stew. Cover and cook until all the vegetables are tender, 3–5 minutes longer. Season with salt and pepper.

7 Fluff the couscous with a fork and divide among hot bowls. Make a well in the center of each and spoon in the vegetable stew.

COOKING WITH CORNMEAL AND POLENTA

Cornmeal, finely ground from yellow or white corn, is used as an ingredient in many recipes – from breakfast porridge ("mush"), through muffins, breads, dumplings, and pancakes. It also serves as a coating for fried foods.

Polenta is a more coarsely ground cornmeal, much used in Italian cooking. It may be served plain or mixed with butter and cheese, to take the place of rice or potatoes, or it can be cooled until firm, sliced, and then fried or toasted.

1 ▲   For cornmeal "mush": Use four parts lightly salted water to one part cornmeal. Bring the liquid just to a boil in a saucepan. Gradually add the cornmeal in a steady stream, stirring constantly. Do not add it all at once or it will form lumps.

2 ▲   Cover the pan, reduce the heat, and cook gently, stirring occasionally, until very thick, about 10 minutes. Serve hot with butter, milk, or maple syrup. (The "mush" can also be molded, cooled, sliced, and fried like polenta.)

Cornmeal-Cheese Topping
Combine 1½ cups milk, 2 table-spoons butter, and ½ teaspoon salt in a saucepan. Bring just to a boil, then gradually add ½ cup cornmeal, stirring. Cook, unco-vered, until thick, 2–3 minutes, stirring constantly. Remove from the heat and stir in 2 beaten eggs and 1½ cups shredded Cheddar cheese. Spread over 3 cups chili (made with or without meat) in a baking dish, covering the chili completely. Bake in a pre-heated 375°F oven until set and lightly browned, 35–40 minutes. *Serves 4.*

3 ▲   For polenta: Add polenta gradually to boiling liquid as for cornmeal (see above). Reduce the heat to low and simmer, uncovered, until thick and pulling away from the sides of the pan, 10–20 minutes, stirring constantly. The polenta is now ready to be served or molded.

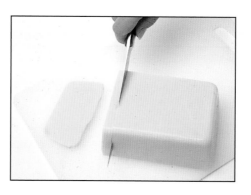

5 ▲   Cut the set polenta into shapes or slices about ½-inch thick.

4 ▲   If to be cooled and then later fried or toasted, pour the polenta into an oiled or buttered pan or dish and let it cool completely.

Polenta with Cheese
Toast polenta slices under the broiler until lightly browned on both sides. Top with slices of a strong cheese such as gorgonzola. Broil briefly until the cheese starts to melt, then serve.

Polenta with Chicken Livers

SERVES 4

3 cups chicken stock or salted water

¾ cup polenta

4 tablespoons butter

2 tablespoons olive oil

1 pound chicken livers, trimmed and cut in half

1–2 garlic cloves, minced

¼ cup minced parsley, preferably flat-leaf (Italian) parsley

1 teaspoon chopped fresh oregano, or ½ teaspoon dried oregano

squeeze of lemon juice

salt and pepper

1½ cups tomato sauce (page 172), heated

1 Bring the stock or salted water to a boil in a large saucepan. Gradually add the polenta, stirring constantly. Simmer over low heat until very thick while continuing to stir.

2 ▲ Pour the polenta into a buttered 8-inch round pan. Set aside to firm up, at least ½ hour.

~ VARIATION ~

For Polenta with Mushrooms, use 1 pound sliced mushrooms sautéed in 3 tablespoons of butter in place of the chicken livers and serve with tomato-wine sauce (page 172), if preferred.

3 ▼ Invert the block of polenta onto a board. Cut it into 8 wedges. Fry in 3 tablespoons of the butter until golden brown on both sides, turning once.

4 Heat the remaining butter and the oil in a frying pan over medium-high heat. Add the chicken livers and fry until they are starting to brown, 2–3 minutes, turning once.

5 ▲ Add the garlic, herbs, lemon juice, salt, and pepper. Continue cooking until the livers are lightly browned on both sides but still pink in the center, 1–2 minutes longer.

6 Put a wedge of polenta on each warmed plate. Spoon the tomato sauce over the polenta and arrange the chicken livers on top. Serve hot.

VEGETABLES

~

What an array of fresh vegetables we have today – good enough to be the star of the meal. Young seasonal vegetables need no dressing up, but this abundance offers the chance to try your hand at more creative preparations as well as simple ones.

PREPARING AND COOKING VEGETABLES

To enjoy their full flavor, fresh vegetables are often best prepared and served simply. The following guidelines for vegetable preparation and cooking will help you make the most of seasonal bounty.

Season all vegetables to taste. Suggested amounts of raw prepared vegetable per portion are found with Serving Ideas. Recipes serve 4.

ROOTS AND BULBS
Carrots
Naturally sweet, carrots are used in innumerable dishes, both hot and cold, raw and cooked.

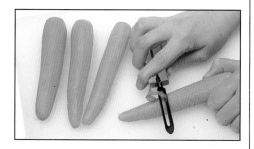

Preparation: If they are young, there is no need to peel them; just trim the ends and scrub well. Larger, older carrots should be peeled. Leave them whole or cut as directed. If carrots have a woody core, cut it out.

Cooking: *To boil,* drop into boiling salted water, then simmer until just tender: 8–10 minutes for whole baby carrots, 10–20 minutes for larger whole carrots, 4–10 minutes for sliced or grated carrots. *To steam,* cook whole baby carrots, covered, in a steamer over boiling water about 10 minutes. *To braise,* cook whole baby carrots or thinly sliced carrots with

3 tablespoons stock or water and 2 tablespoons butter per pound, tightly covered, for about 5 minutes. Boil, uncovered, to evaporate excess liquid before serving.

Serving Ideas (4 ounces per portion)
● Dress hot carrots with butter and chopped fresh herbs such as parsley, chives, thyme, or marjoram.
● Add a little sugar or honey and a squeeze of lemon or orange juice when braising. Or, try spices such as nutmeg, ginger, or curry powder.
● Serve raw carrot sticks with a dip.

Parsnips
Their sweet, nutty flavor makes a delicious addition to soups and stews or enjoy them on their own.

Preparation: Trim the ends and peel thinly. Leave small parsnips whole; cut up larger ones. If large parsnips have a woody core, cut it out.

Cooking: *To roast,* blanch in boiling salted water, then put in a roasting pan with butter or oil and cook in a preheated 400°F oven about 40 minutes. Baste occasionally. *To boil,* drop in boiling salted water, then simmer until just tender, 5–10 minutes. *To fry,* blanch in boiling

water 1–2 minutes and drain. Fry in butter until golden brown and tender, 10–12 minutes.

Serving Ideas (4–5 ounces per portion)
● Add 4 tablespoons butter and ¼ cup honey to 1¼ pounds boiled parsnips; cook, covered, 5 minutes.
● Sauté sliced parsnips with sliced carrots; sprinkle with minced herbs.
● Bake 1¼ pounds small parsnips with ½ cup orange juice and 3 tablespoons butter, covered, in a preheated 350°F oven for 1 hour.
● Roast blanched parsnips in the pan around a roast of beef or pork.

Turnips
Mildly piquant, turnips go well with both sweet and savory seasonings.

Preparation: Trim the ends and peel the turnips thinly.

Cooking: *To steam,* cook cubes, covered, in a steamer over boiling water until tender, about 15 minutes. *To boil,* drop into boiling salted water and simmer until tender: 20–30 minutes for small whole turnips, about 7 minutes for diced. *To braise,* cook thin slices with 2 tablespoons butter and ⅓ cup stock or water per pound, covered tightly, for 4–5 minutes.

Serving Ideas (4 ounces per portion)
● Mash boiled turnips with milk and butter; mix with an equal quantity of mashed carrots, parsnips, or potatoes.
● Cover 1 pound steamed turnips with 2 cups hot white sauce (page 170). Top with bread crumbs and shredded cheese; brown under the broiler.
● Add sugar (1 tablespoon per pound) when braising turnips; uncover and boil to evaporate excess liquid and to caramelize the turnips.

Rutabaga
The orangey-yellow flesh of this root vegetable is sweet and full of flavor.

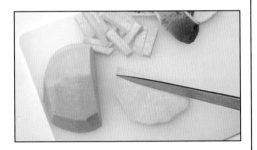

Preparation: Peel, removing all tough skin and roots. Cut as recipe directs.

Cooking: *To boil*, drop chunks into boiling salted water, then simmer until tender, 15 minutes. Do not overcook or the vegetable will be watery and mushy. *To steam*, cook slices or cubes, covered, in a steamer over boiling water until tender, about 10 minutes. *To braise*, cook with 2 tablespoons butter and ⅓ cup stock or water per pound, covered, for 5–7 minutes. *To roast*, put chunks or sticks around roasting meat and coat with the drippings. Roast at 400°F for about 45 minutes according to size.

Serving Ideas (5 ounces per portion)
● Braise 1¼ pounds grated rutabaga seasoned with 1 tablespoon brown sugar and 1 teaspoon soy sauce.
● Mash 1¼ pounds boiled rutabaga until smooth; beat in 2 eggs, ¼ cup whipping cream, 2 tablespoons flour, and ¼ teaspoon nutmeg until fluffy. Bake in a buttered dish in a preheated 350°F oven about 30 minutes.

Potatoes
Boiling potatoes are moist with a waxy texture so they keep their shape when cooked. Baking potatoes are dry and starchy and their texture is more mealy after cooking. In addition, there are orange-fleshed sweet potatoes, often called yams.

Preparation: If the potato skins will be eaten, scrub them well. Otherwise, peel potatoes.

Cooking: *To bake*, prick skins all over with a fork and bake in a preheated 400°F oven until tender, 1–1½ hours or 30–40 minutes for sweet potatoes. *To boil*, put in a pan of cold salted water, bring to a boil, then simmer until just tender, 10–20 minutes according to size. *To roast*, blanch peeled potatoes 1–2 minutes; drain and pat dry. Put in pan around

roasting meat and turn to coat with drippings; roast 1–1½ hours, turning occasionally. *To fry*, boil until partly cooked (unpeeled, if recipe directs), then fry slices or cubes in butter or oil until brown and crisp.

To deep fry (French fries), cut in sticks and soak in cold water at least 30 minutes; drain and pat dry. Fry (in small batches) in oil heated to 375°F until beginning to color, 3–7 minutes according to size. Drain on paper towels, then fry again until golden brown and crisp, about 3 minutes.

Stuffed Twice-Baked Potatoes
Cut baked potatoes in half lengthwise and scoop out the flesh, leaving a thin wall of flesh. Mash the scooped-out flesh with a little butter and 3 tablespoons each shredded Cheddar cheese and diced cooked ham per potato. Season to taste. Fill the potato shells with the mixture, mounding it. Sprinkle the tops with a little grated Cheddar, then bake at 400°F for 10–15 minutes.

Serving Ideas (6 ounces per portion)
● Dress boiled new potatoes with butter and minced mixed parsley and mint or toasted pine nuts.
● Mash boiled or baked sweet potatoes with an electric mixer. Add butter, salt and pepper to taste, orange juice to moisten, and a little ground cinnamon. Beat well.

Celery Root

The coarse knobby appearance of celery root, or celeriac, belies its delicate and delicious flavor.

Preparation: Peel off the thick skin. Do this just before cooking because celery root discolors when cut. If serving it raw, drop the peeled root or pieces into water acidulated with lemon juice or vinegar. Cut as directed in recipe.

Cooking: *To steam*, cook cubes, covered, in a steamer over boiling water until tender. *To boil*, drop cubes into boiling salted water, then simmer, covered, until just tender, 5–15 minutes according to size. *To braise*, cook grated celery root with 4 tablespoons butter and 2 tablespoons stock or water per pound, covered, for 5 minutes. Uncover and boil to evaporate excess liquid.

Serving Ideas (5 ounces per portion)
● Dress matchsticks of raw celery root with spicy mayonnaise (page 180) and sprinkle with shreds of salami.
● Boil slices of celery root in beef stock; drain. Sprinkle with grated Parmesan cheese and serve hot.

Onions

The onion is one of those ingredients basic to almost every savory dish. There are pungent round onions and sweet mild onions: flat ones, large spherical ones (Spanish-type), and elongated Italian red ones. In addition, there are small boiling and pearl onions, shallots, and scallions (also called green onions).

Preparation: Peel off the papery skin. Then slice, chop, mince, etc., as the recipe directs. For scallions, trim the root end and cut off any wilted or discolored green leaves. Cut as directed, using just the white bulbs or both white and green parts.

Cooking: *To fry*, cook chopped or sliced onions, uncovered, in butter and/or oil over medium heat, stirring occasionally, until translucent and soft, about 5 minutes. If directed, continue cooking until the onions are golden brown. *To slow-cook or sweat*,

cook sliced or chopped onions, covered, in butter and/or oil over low heat, stirring occasionally, until very soft and uniformly golden, about 30 minutes. *To boil* small onions, drop into boiling salted water, then simmer until tender, 15–20 minutes.

Serving Ideas
● Top hamburgers or hot dogs with slow-cooked sliced onions. (½ pound makes about ½ cup, cooked)
● Combine 1 pound boiled small onions with 3 tablespoons butter and ⅓ cup firmly packed light brown sugar; cook over low heat, stirring, until caramelized, about 10 minutes.
● Trim all but 2 inches of green from scallions. Stir-fry in hot oil and sprinkle with soy sauce.
● Use thin slices of sweet and red onions raw in salads.
● Bake whole onions in a 425°F oven until tender, about 45 minutes.

Leeks

This sweet and subtle member of the onion family has so many uses – both as a vegetable on its own and as a flavoring in soups, stews, and so on.

Preparation: Trim the root end and the dark green leaves, leaving just the pale green and white. (Save the dark green leaves for the stockpot.) Unless the leeks are to be cooked whole, slit them open lengthwise, to the center. Soak them in cold water for about 20 minutes. Drain well, shaking and squeezing out the excess water. If leeks are to be sliced or chopped, do this before rinsing them thoroughly in a colander under cold running water.

Cooking: *To braise,* cook with 2 tablespoons butter and ⅓ cup stock or water per pound, covered, until just tender. *To boil,* drop into boiling salted water or stock, then simmer until tender, 10–15 minutes. *To steam,* cook sliced or whole baby leeks, covered, in a steamer over boiling water until tender, 5–7 minutes.

Serving Ideas (6 ounces per portion)
● Boil whole leeks. Marinate while warm in a vinaigrette dressing (page 182); serve cool, not cold.
● Toss hot sliced leeks with butter and fresh herbs such as sage, tarragon, thyme, or parsley.
● Wrap whole boiled leeks in slices of ham. Cover with cheese sauce (page 170), sprinkle with grated cheese, and broil until the top is golden.

FRUITING VEGETABLES
Eggplant
The most familiar eggplants are the large ones with shiny purple skins, but there are also small round ones and long, thin ones, ranging in color from creamy white to deep violet. All can be used interchangeably.

Preparation: Trim off the stem end. Leave the eggplant whole or cut according to recipe directions.

Cooking: *To broil,* brush cut surfaces with oil. Broil, 3–4 inches from the heat, until tender and well browned, about 10 minutes total; turn once and brush with oil. *To fry,* coat slices or thick sticks with flour or dip in batter, if recipe directs, then pan-fry in hot oil or butter until golden, about 5 minutes on each side. *To braise,* brown slices or wedges in a little hot oil, add ¼ cup stock or water per pound, cover, and cook until tender, about 12 minutes total. Add more liquid if necessary. *To bake,* prick whole eggplant all over with a fork. Bake in a preheated 400°F oven until soft, about 20 minutes.

Serving Ideas (5 ounces per portion)
● Baste broiled or grilled eggplant with garlic- or herb-flavored olive oil.
● Braise eggplant, adding 2 peeled, chopped tomatoes and ¼ cup chopped fresh basil.
● Serve fried flour-coated eggplant with garlic mayonnaise (page 180).

Summer Squashes
Thin-skinned squashes, such as zucchini, pattypan, and crookneck, are completely edible, skin and all.

Preparation: Trim the ends from summer squash. Cut as directed.

Cooking: *To fry* sliced summer squash, cook in butter or oil until tender and golden brown, 5–10 minutes. *To boil,* drop in boiling salted water, then simmer until tender: 10–12 minutes if whole, 3–8 minutes if sliced. *To steam,* cook, covered, in a steamer over boiling water until tender. *To braise,* cook sliced squash, with 2 tablespoons butter and ⅓ cup stock or water per pound, tightly covered, until tender, 4–5 minutes.

Serving Ideas (5 ounces per portion)
● Sauté sliced summer squash with minced garlic and chopped fresh parsley and oregano.
● Cut small zucchini in half lengthwise and spread cut surfaces with grainy mustard. Broil about 4 inches from the heat until crisp-tender, about 5 minutes.

Winter squashes
Acorn, butternut, and hubbard squashes, and pumpkin have a hard rind and central seeds and fibers that should be removed before cooking.

Preparation: Unless baking in the skin, peel winter squash with a large, sturdy knife. Scrape away the seeds and stringy fibers.

Cooking: *To steam,* cook cubes, covered, in a steamer over boiling water until tender. *To bake,* cut in serving pieces, leaving on the rind, and score the flesh. Arrange cut-side up in greased baking dish, dot with butter, and bake in a preheated 375°F oven until tender, about 45 minutes. *To boil,* drop pieces in boiling salted water, then simmer until tender, 4–5 minutes. *To braise,* cook cubes of winter squash as for summer squash.

Serving Ideas (5–8 ounces per portion)
● Add 1 diced apple, a squeeze of lemon juice, and 2 tablespoons brown sugar when braising 1¼ pounds winter squash. If desired, spice with a little cinnamon, nutmeg, or curry powder.
● Bake acorn squash halves with 1 teaspoon maple syrup in each.

LEAFY, GREEN, AND OTHER VEGETABLES
Spinach
Small tender leaves have a delicate flavor and can be used raw in salads. Large, strongly flavored, darker leaves taste better cooked.

Preparation: Spinach can hide a lot of grit so needs careful rinsing. Immerse in cold water, swish around, and let

soak 3–4 minutes. Then lift out the spinach and immerse in fresh cold water. Repeat, then drain in a colander. Discard any damaged or yellowed leaves. Pull off tough stems.

Cooking: *To steam-boil,* put in a large pan (there should be sufficient water left on the leaves after rinsing so that no more is needed). Cook until just wilted, 5–7 minutes, stirring occasionally to help evaporate the liquid. Drain well and press the spinach between two plates or squeeze in your fist. *To braise,* cook with 2 tablespoons butter per pound, covered, until wilted. Uncover and boil to evaporate excess liquid. *To stir-fry,* cook small or shredded leaves in hot oil until just wilted, 3–5 minutes.

Serving Ideas (6 ounces per portion)
● Add ¼ cup whipping cream and ¼ teaspoon grated nutmeg to 1¼ pounds braised spinach.
● Stir-fry minced onion and garlic, then add spinach with halved cherry tomatoes and stir-fry 1 minute.
● Steam-boil spinach leaves; chop finely after draining. Fry in olive oil with minced garlic, stirring, until the garlic just starts to turn golden and the spinach is heated through.
● Combine equal parts of chopped cooked spinach and cooked rice with butter and seasoning to taste.

Greens
Hearty greens include those from the cabbage family – kale, collards, rape, mustard greens – as well as beet greens and Swiss chard. Serve alone, or add them to soups and stews.

Preparation: Discard damaged or yellowed leaves. Trim off root ends and large or coarse stems. Leave the leaves whole or shred, according to recipe directions. Cut leaves from stems of Swiss chard and cook separately (the stems take longer).

Cooking: *To braise,* put shredded leaves (or Swiss chard stems) in a pan with 2 tablespoons butter and 3 tablespoons stock per pound. Cook, covered, until just tender. Boil, uncovered, to evaporate excess liquid. *To steam-boil,* put in a large pan (there should be enough water left on the leaves after rinsing so no more is needed). Cover and cook until just wilted, 5–15 minutes according to variety. *To boil,* drop shredded leaves (or Swiss chard stems) in boiling salted water, then simmer until just tender.

Serving Ideas (6–8 ounces per portion)
● Toss hot braised greens with whipping cream or sour cream and grated nutmeg; heat gently.
● Mix boiled greens with mashed potato. Shape into patties, coat in fine bread crumbs, and fry in butter until golden brown on both sides.
● Top boiled or braised greens with crisply fried bacon and shredded Swiss cheese; broil to melt the cheese.

Green Beans

Crisp green beans are available in varying sizes, from tiny French ones ("haricots verts") to very large ones, often called pole beans. Yellow versions are known as wax beans. Green beans are also called string (or stringless) beans, runner beans, or snap beans; Chinese long beans are similar, but longer.

Preparation: Snip off both ends with scissors or use a knife. For string beans, snap off the ends, pulling the strings from the sides as you do so. Cut large beans diagonally or sliver.

Cooking: *To boil,* drop into boiling salted water, then simmer until just tender but still crisp and bright green, 3–15 minutes, according to size. *To steam,* cook, covered, in a steamer over boiling water until tender. *To braise,* cook with ⅓ cup stock or water and 2 tablespoons butter per pound, tightly covered, until tender. *To stir-fry,* blanch in boiling water for 2 minutes; drain, refresh, and pat dry. Stir-fry in hot oil 2–3 minutes.

Serving Ideas (4 ounces per portion)
- Dress boiled or steamed beans with melted butter, chopped herbs, and a squeeze of lemon juice.

- Add ⅓ cup whipping cream per pound to braised beans. Cook, stirring, until the liquid has reduced and the beans are glazed.
- Top hot beans with quickly fried shreads of prosciutto. Or, top with sliced almonds or pecans lightly browned in butter.

Peas

Snow peas and sugar peas are completely edible, pod and all. Green or garden peas are removed from their pods for cooking; the pods weigh as much as the peas, so you need to allow twice as much as edible pod peas.

Preparation: If green peas are in the pod, split it open and pop out the peas. Snap off both ends from snow and sugar peas, pulling any tough strings from the sides as you do so.

Cooking: *To steam,* cook, covered, in a steamer over boiling water until tender. *To boil,* drop into boiling salted water, then simmer until just tender: 5–10 minutes for green peas, 1–2 minutes for snow and sugar peas. *To braise,* cook, covered, with 2 tablespoons butter and ¼ cup stock or water per pound, until tender: 5–10 minutes for green peas, 2 minutes for snow and sugar peas.

Serving Ideas (4 ounces per portion)
- Add sliced scallions, shredded lettuce, and a generous pinch of sugar when braising green peas.
- Stir-fry snow peas with thinly sliced onion and mushrooms.
- Add ¼ cup whipping cream to braised sugar peas and cook uncovered, stirring, until almost all liquid has evaporated.

Broccoli

Serve this green vegetable hot or let it cool and use in salads. It is also excellent in stir-fries.

Preparation: Trim off the end of the stem. If the rest of the stem is to be used in the recipe, peel it. According to recipe directions, leave the head whole or cut off the florets, or flowers, taking a little stem with each one. Cut the remainder of the peeled stem across in thin slices.

Cooking: *To steam,* cook, covered, in a steamer over boiling water until tender. *To boil,* drop into boiling salted water, then simmer until just tender: 7–12 minutes for heads, 4–6 minutes for florets and thinly sliced stems. *To braise,* cook with ⅓ cup stock and 2 tablespoons butter per pound, covered, until tender.

Serving Ideas (5 ounces per portion)
• Toss hot broccoli with a flavored butter (page 174).
• Cover hot broccoli with cheese sauce (page 170), sprinkle with grated Parmesan, and brown under broiler.
• Blanch small broccoli florets about 1 minute; drain and refresh. Serve cold, dressed with vinaigrette (page 182) and sprinkled with toasted nuts.

Cauliflower

White or ivory cauliflower is the most widely available, although there are also green and purple varieties.

Preparation: Cut away the large green leaves, leaving only the tiny ones if desired. Trim the stem level and cut an "x" in the base or cut out the core. Leave the head whole, or break into florets before or after cooking.

Cooking: *To steam,* cook florets, covered, in a steamer over boiling water, 12–15 minutes. *To steam-boil,* put stem-down in a pan with about 1 inch boiling salted water and a bay leaf. Cover and cook until crisp-tender: 15–30 minutes for whole heads, 5–9 minutes for florets. Drain well. *To braise,* cook florets, with 3 tablespoons butter and ⅓ cup stock per pound, covered, for 5–7 minutes.

Serving Ideas (5–6 ounces per portion)
• Dress hot cauliflower with butter; sprinkle with chopped fresh chives or parsley, or toasted sliced almonds or chopped pecans.
• Top hot cauliflower with hollandaise sauce (page 178).
• Bread florets in egg and crumbs, then deep-fry and serve with garlic or spicy mayonnaise (page 180).

Cabbage

Rich in vitamins and very versatile, cabbage is good cooked or raw. Varieties include firm, round heads (green, white, and red), looser round heads (Savoy with its crinkly leaves), and long, loose heads (bok choy and Napa, Chinese, or celery cabbage).

Preparation: Discard any wilted or discolored outer leaves. Cut the heads into small wedges (or quarters for long, loose heads). Cut out the coarse stem from the wedges before cooking. Or, quarter heads and shred them. Leave long, loose heads whole and cut heads across the leaves to shred.

Cooking: *To braise,* quickly blanch chopped or shredded green, Savoy, or red cabbage. (There is no need to blanch Napa cabbage.) Cook green, Savoy, and Napa cabbage with ⅓ cup stock or water and 2 tablespoons butter per pound, tightly covered, for 3–4 minutes. For red cabbage, increase liquid by 1 cup and cook 30 minutes. *To boil,* drop into boiling salted water, then simmer until just crisp-tender: 6–8 minutes for wedges, 3–5 minutes for shredded green, Savoy, or Napa cabbage. *To steam,* cook, covered, in a steamer over boiling water until tender.

Serving Ideas (4 ounces per portion)
• Add chopped fresh dill when braising green or Savoy cabbage.
• Blanch larger outer leaves of green or Savoy cabbage, then roll them up around a ground meat stuffing and simmer in a rich tomato sauce.
• Add sliced apples, cooked diced bacon, and warm spices (cinnamon, nutmeg) when braising red cabbage.
• Use shredded Napa cabbage raw in tossed salads.

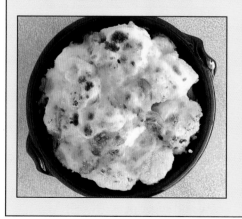

Cauliflower au Gratin

Cut a large cauliflower head into florets and steam until crisp-tender. Spread in a buttered gratin dish and scatter sautéed sliced mushrooms over the florets. Pour 2 cups hot cheese sauce (page 170) evenly over the top and sprinkle with a mixture of grated Cheddar cheese and fine dry bread crumbs. Brown under the broiler. *Serves 4.*

Brussels Sprouts

These miniature heads of cabbage are best cooked just until crisp-tender.

Preparation: Remove any discolored leaves. Trim the stems level with the heads. If cooking whole, cut an "x" in the base of the stem so that it will cook in the same time as the head.

Cooking: *To braise*, cook with ⅓ cup stock or water and 2 tablespoons butter per pound, covered, until just tender, 8–10 minutes. *To boil*, drop into boiling salted water, then simmer until just tender, 7–10 minutes. *To steam*, cook, covered, in a steamer over boiling water for 10–12 minutes.

Serving Ideas (4 ounces per portion)
- Toss with butter and orange rind.
- Toss with toasted nuts, braised or poached chestnuts, or sliced canned water chestnuts.
- Cut the heads lengthwise in half and blanch in boiling water 2–3 minutes; drain and refresh. Stir-fry in hot oil with minced fresh ginger and garlic until tender and lightly browned, 2–3 minutes.
- Shred and blanch 2–3 minutes; drain and refresh. Add minced onion and celery and toss with a lemony vinaigrette dressing (page 182).

Celery

Crisp green celery is a popular salad ingredient and favorite flavoring in soups, stews, and stuffings.

Preparation: Separate the stalks. Scrub with a vegetable brush under cold running water. Trim off the root end, leaves, and any blemishes (keep leaves for the stockpot). If the stalks have tough strings, remove these with a vegetable peeler. Cut as directed. For celery hearts, cut in half lengthwise. Trim off the leaves.

Cooking: *To steam-boil*, put in a pan with 1 inch of boiling salted water. Cover and cook until crisp-tender: 5–10 minutes for pieces, 10–20 minutes for hearts. *To braise*, cook slices with 2 tablespoons stock or water and 2 tablespoons butter per ½ pound, or hearts with 1 cup liquid, covered, until tender: 3 minutes for thin slices, 10–20 minutes for hearts.

Serving Ideas (4 ounces per portion)
- Stuff finger-length pieces of raw celery with blue cheese, flavored cream cheese, or peanut butter.
- Sprinkle braised celery with chopped walnuts and minced parsley.
- Braise celery hearts with chopped tomatoes and tarragon or thyme.

Mushrooms

Cultivated or common mushrooms are widely available; you may also find fresh wild mushrooms such as shiitake, oyster, chanterelle, and enoki.

Preparation: Rinse or wipe with a damp paper towel (don't leave in water as mushrooms absorb liquid readily). Trim gritty stems; cut off tough stems of wild mushrooms. Small mushrooms can be left whole; larger ones are normally halved, quartered, or sliced, or they may be diced or minced as required. Pull stems from large mushrooms to be stuffed.

Cooking: *To fry*, cook in hot butter and/or oil until tender, about 4 minutes, stirring frequently. The mushrooms will give up liquid; if the recipe directs, continue frying until the liquid has evaporated and the mushrooms have browned. *To broil*, brush with melted butter and/or oil. Broil about 4 inches from the heat, turning and basting occasionally, until tender and browned, 5–8 minutes.

Serving Ideas (4 ounces per portion)
- Fry sliced mushrooms with minced garlic and thyme.
- Top broiled mushroom caps with a pat of flavored butter (page 174).

PREPARING ASPARAGUS

When asparagus is young and tender, you need do nothing more than trim off the ends of the stalks. However, larger spears, with stalk ends that are tough and woody, require some further preparation.

A Standing Alternative

Asparagus spears can be cooked loose and flat in simmering water (as described below) or they can be tied into bundles and cooked standing upright in a tall pot. With the latter method, the tips are kept above the water so they cook gently in the steam.

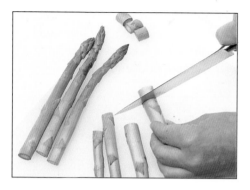

1 ▲ Cut off the tough, woody ends. Cut the spears so they are all about the same length.

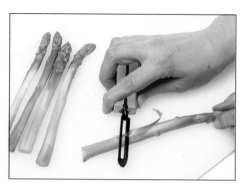

2 ▲ If you like, remove the skin: Lay a spear flat and hold it just below the tip. With a vegetable peeler, shave off the skin, working lengthwise down the spear to the end of the stalk. Roll the spear so you can remove the skin from all sides.

Asparagus with Ham

SERVES 4

1½–2 pounds medium asparagus spears, prepared for cooking

¾ cup clarified butter (page 176)

2 teaspoons lemon juice

2 tablespoons minced scallions

1 tablespoon minced parsley

salt and pepper

4 slices Westphalian ham or prosciutto

1 ▼ Half fill a large frying pan with salted water. Bring to a boil. Simmer asparagus spears until they are just tender, 4–5 minutes. (Pierce the stalk to test.) Remove and drain.

2 Combine the clarified butter, lemon juice, scallions, and herbs in a small saucepan. Season with salt and pepper to taste. Heat the herb butter until it is lukewarm.

3 Divide the asparagus among 4 warm plates. Drape a slice of ham over each portion. Spoon the herb butter over the top and serve.

PREPARING FRESH CORN

Sweet, tender corn is a favorite, eaten on the cob or off – as kernels in soups, salad, casseroles, etc. Buy the freshest corn you can find, still in its husk.

Cooking Corn on the Cob
Bring a large pot of water to a boil and add 1 teaspoon sugar. Drop freshly prepared ears of corn into the water. Bring back to a boil and simmer until just tender, 4–7 minutes (test by piercing a kernel with the tip of a sharp knife). Alternatively, steam the corn with a little boiling water in a covered saucepan. Drain well before serving.

1 ▲ Just before cooking, strip off the husks and pull off all the silk. (If grilling or oven-roasting in the husk, just pull back the husks and remove the silk, then reshape.) Trim the stalk so it is level with the base of the ear.

2 ▲ To remove the kernels: Use a sharp knife to cut them lengthwise, several rows at a time, from the cob. Alternatively, use a corn scraper or stripper. If the recipe directs, set each cob upright on a plate and run the blunt edge of the knife down the cob to scrape off the milky liquid.

Corn and Zucchini Succotash

SERVES 4

4 bacon slices
1 onion, chopped
1 small green bell pepper, seeded and diced
kernels scraped from 6 ears of fresh corn
1½ cups diced zucchini
½ cup whipping cream
salt and pepper

1 ▲ Fry the bacon until it is crisp. Remove and drain on paper towels. Pour off all but a thin film of bacon fat.

2 ◄ Add the onion and green pepper. Fry until soft, stirring occasionally. Add the corn kernels. Cover and cook 10 minutes over low heat. Stir in the zucchini and cream. Season with salt and pepper. Cook, covered, until all the vegetables are tender, about 10 minutes longer. Crumble the bacon and stir it in. Taste and adjust the seasoning, and serve.

PEELING AND SEEDING TOMATOES

Some tomatoes have tough skins. In cooking, these, and the seeds, are separated from the flesh and they can spoil the appearance and texture of a dish. In addition, some people find tomato skins indigestible. So, unless a soup, sauce, or other dish is puréed in a food mill or pressed through a strainer before serving, it is best to peel and seed the tomatoes before cooking.

If the tomatoes have tender skins and they will be eaten raw, or only briefly cooked, removing the skin is less essential, but many people prefer to peel raw tomatoes as well.

1 ▲ To peel tomatoes: Cut a small cross in the skin at the base of each tomato. Immerse, 3 or 4 at a time, in boiling water. After the cut skin begins to roll back, about 10 seconds, lift the tomatoes out and immerse in ice water. Drain and peel.

2 ▲ To seed tomatoes: Cut out the core, then cut each tomato in half crosswise (around the "equator"). Gently squeeze each half and shake the seeds and juice into a bowl. Scrape out any remaining seeds with the tip of a spoon. Discard the seeds.

Spicy Tomato Barbecue Sauce

SERVES 6

2 tablespoons vegetable oil

1 onion, minced

1 garlic clove, minced

1 cup tomato purée

1 cup peeled, seeded, and chopped tomatoes

½ cup cider vinegar

1 tablespoon Worcestershire sauce

⅓ cup firmly packed light brown sugar

2 tablespoons chili powder, or to taste

1 bay leaf

few drops of mesquite liquid smoke (optional)

salt and pepper

1 ▶ Heat the oil in a saucepan, add the onion, and cook until soft, stirring occasionally. Stir in the garlic and cook 30 seconds. Add the tomato purée, tomatoes, vinegar, Worcestershire sauce, brown sugar, chili powder, bay leaf, and liquid smoke, if using. Season with salt and pepper to taste.

2 Bring to a boil, reduce the heat, and simmer 15 minutes, stirring from time to time. Taste and adjust the seasoning, if needed.

3 Use as a basting sauce for grilled hamburgers, chicken, spareribs, and steak. Serve additional sauce to accompany the grilled food.

ROASTING AND PEELING BELL PEPPERS

There are several methods for peeling bell peppers, the most basic of which is shaving off the skin with a vegetable peeler. However, because peppers have awkward curves, other methods, such as roasting, are often easier. Roasting peppers also heightens the sweetness of the flesh.

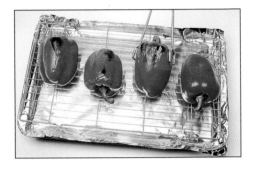

Handling Chili Peppers
Do not touch eyes and lips when handling chilies, and afterwards be sure to wash your hands well. Better yet, wear rubber gloves. Remove skin, core, and seeds from chilies as for bell peppers.

1 ▲ Set the peppers on a rack in a broiler pan and broil close to the heat. Turn the peppers to char and blister the skin all over. Alternatively, spear the pepper on a long-handled fork and hold it over a flame – over a gas burner or charcoal fire – turning the pepper slowly so that the skin is charred and blistered on all sides.

2 ▲ Once the skin is charred, put the peppers in a plastic bag and seal it. Let cool – the steam trapped inside the bag will help loosen the skin. When the peppers are cool enough to handle, peel with the help of a small knife. (Work over a bowl so you can save the juices.) Cut out the stem and core; scrape out any remaining seeds.

Marinated Pepper Salad with Cheese

SERVES 6

3 small bell peppers of different colors

6 tablespoons olive or salad oil

3 tablespoons fresh lime juice

2 tablespoons fresh lemon juice

1 teaspoon Worcestershire sauce

1 small garlic clove, finely minced (optional)

salt and pepper

½ pound mozzarella or firm goat cheese, sliced

½ cup coarsely chopped toasted walnuts or pecans, for garnishing

1 Roast the peppers, then peel them, reserving the juices. Cut the roasted pepper flesh lengthwise into strips.

2 Combine the oil, lime and lemon juices, Worcestershire sauce, and garlic, if using, in a bowl. Season to taste with salt and pepper.

3 ◀ Add the pepper strips and juices and toss to mix thoroughly with the marinade. Cover and marinate 1–2 hours at room temperature.

4 To serve, arrange the pepper salad and overlapping slices of cheese on individual plates. Garnish with chopped nuts.

PREPARING AND COOKING GLOBE ARTICHOKES

Artichokes can be served whole, with or without a stuffing, or just the meaty bottoms, or bases, may be used. Very small artichokes, 2½ inches or less in diameter, are often called hearts; this can be confusing, as artichoke bottoms are also sometimes called hearts. These baby artichokes are best braised whole, or halved or quartered, with a little stock, tightly covered, until tender. Be sure to rub all cut surfaces with lemon juice as you work and use a stainless-steel knife, to prevent darkening and discoloration.

1 ▲ For whole artichokes: Break off the stem close to the base. Cut off the pointed top about one-third of the way down. Snip off the pointed end of each large outside leaf using scissors. Open up the leaves and rinse thoroughly between them.

2 ▲ For artichoke bottoms: Break off all the coarse outer leaves down to the pale inner leaves. Scrape off the fuzzy center, or "choke," (or do this after cooking) and peel away all the leaves with a stainless-steel knife, leaving just the edible base or bottom.

Artichokes with Herb Butter
Serve boiled artichokes hot with clarified butter (page 176) mixed with freshly chopped dill and parsley or other herbs.

3 ▲ To cook whole artichokes:
Bring a large pot of salted water to a boil. Add the juice of 1 lemon or ¼ cup vinegar. Add the prepared artichokes and put a plate on top to keep them submerged. Cover and simmer until you can pierce the stem end easily with a fork: 15–20 minutes for small artichokes, 25–50 minutes for large artichokes.

4 ▲ Remove and drain well, upside down. Open up the leaves so you can insert a spoon into the center and scrape out the fuzzy choke.

Eating a Whole Artichoke
One by one, pull off the leaves and dip the base into the sauce. Scrape the flesh from the base of the leaf with your teeth, then discard the leaf. When you have removed all the large leaves, you will have exposed the fuzzy choke. Scrape this off and discard it. Cut the meaty bottom, or base, of the artichoke with a fork for eating.

5 ▲ To cook artichoke bottoms:
Boil gently in salted water to cover until tender, 15–20 minutes.

Ideas for Artichokes
● Serve boiled artichokes hot with Hollandaise sauce (page 178).
● Serve boiled artichokes cool (not chilled) with a vinaigrette dressing (page 182) or mayonnaise (page 180).
● Serve cool boiled artichoke bottoms filled with shrimp or crab mayonnaise salad.
● Boil artichoke bottoms with flavorings such as garlic, bay leaf, and black peppercorns. Drain and let cool, then slice and marinate in a vinaigrette dressing (page 182), with chopped onion and olives.

CHOPPING AND MINCING VEGETABLES

In countless recipes, vegetables and other ingredients need to be chopped to varying degrees of fineness. Very fine chopping is called mincing.

For most chopping, use a large, sharp chef's knife. You can also use a food processor, but take care not to over-process vegetables to a pulp.

Cheese and Herb Dip

Combine 1 cup cream cheese and 1 cup cottage cheese in a food processor or blender and blend until smooth. Turn the cheese mixture into a bowl and stir in 2 tablespoons minced fresh dill and ¾ cup minced chives. Season to taste with salt and pepper. If the dip is too thick, stir in a few spoonfuls of half-and-half or milk. Cover and chill for at least 1 hour before serving, with vegetables, crackers, or potato chips for dipping. *Makes 2½ cups.*

Peeling Whole Garlic

If you want to peel garlic and keep the clove whole, drop it into boiling water, count to 30, then drain and rinse with cold water. The skin will slip off easily.

1 ▲ To chop an onion: Peel it, leaving on the root end to hold the onion together. Cut it in half, straight through the root.

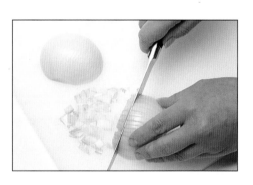

3 ▲ Make vertical lengthwise cuts in the onion half, again not cutting the root. Finally, cut across the onion to chop it, guiding the side of the knife with your knuckles. Discard the root.

5 ▲ Crush the peeled clove again with the knife to flatten it, then begin to chop it. When it is coarsely chopped, continue chopping and crushing it until it is finely minced. Hold the tip of the knife on the board and raise and lower the knife handle with your other hand, moving the blade back and forth over the garlic.

2 ▲ Put one half flat on the work surface and hold the onion steady at the root end. With a chef's knife, make horizontal cuts in the onion half to the root, but without cutting all the way through it.

4 ▲ To mince garlic: Set a chef's knife flat on top of the clove and bang it gently with the side of your fist to crush the garlic slightly and loosen the skin. Remove the skin.

6 ▲ To chop fresh herbs: Hold the leaves or sprigs together in a bunch and chop coarsely, then continue mincing as for garlic (without crushing). You can also use this method of mincing for vegetables and fresh ginger.

CUBING AND DICING VEGETABLES

When vegetables play a starring role in a dish, they should be cut into neat shapes such as cubes or dice. This also promotes even cooking. Cubes are generally ½-inch square, and dice are ⅛- to ¼-inch square.

Coarsely Chopping Vegetables
For coarsely chopped vegetables, follow the steps here, without shaving off curved sides. There is no need to cut uniform slices and strips. Alternatively, you can coarsely chop vegetables in a food processor by pulsing, but take care not to turn the vegetables into a purée (this can happen very quickly with juicy kinds like onions, leeks, celery, and bell peppers).

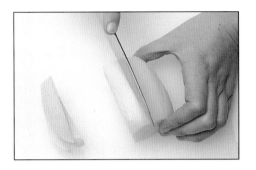

1 ▲ Peel the vegetable, if directed. If it is long, like a carrot or celery stalk, cut it across into pieces about 3-inches long. This will make cubing and dicing easier. For the neatest appearance, shave off curved sides so the pieces of vegetable have straight edges. Lay the vegetable flat and cut it lengthwise into uniform slices of the required thickness, guiding the side of the knife with your knuckles.

2 ▲ Stack the slices and cut lengthwise into uniform strips of the required thickness. Gather the strips together and cut across the strips into cubes or dice.

Home-Fried Potatoes

SERVES 4

1½ pounds boiling potatoes, peeled and cut into ½-inch cubes
3 tablespoons vegetable oil
½ cup chopped onion
1–2 tablespoons butter
salt and pepper

1 ▼ Put the potatoes in a saucepan and cover with cold salted water. Bring to a boil. Simmer 1 minute, then drain well in a colander. Turn onto a dish towel and pat dry.

2 Heat the oil in a frying pan over medium-high heat. Add the potato cubes and fry until they start to turn golden, about 10 minutes. Stir and turn the potatoes frequently so they brown evenly on all sides.

3 Add the onion and cook, stirring, until the potatoes are just tender. Add the butter. Season with salt and pepper. Cook 2 minutes longer, stirring constantly. Serve hot.

CUTTING VEGETABLE MATCHSTICKS

These decorative shapes, also called "julienne," are simple to cut yet look very special. Many other foods can also be cut into matchsticks, for example citrus rind, fresh ginger, cooked meats, hard cheese, and firm fruits such as apple.

For matchsticks, vegetables should be peeled and cut across into pieces about 2 inches long. If necessary, cut off curved sides so the vegetable has straight edges.

1 ▲ Lay each piece of vegetable flat and cut it lengthwise into slices ⅛-inch thick or less, guiding the side of the knife with your knuckles.

2 ▲ Stack the vegetable slices and cut them lengthwise into strips about ⅛-inch thick or less.

Stir-Fried Vegetables

SERVES 4

2½ tablespoons peanut or vegetable oil

1½ tablespoons sesame seeds

2 carrots, cut into matchsticks

¼ pound thin young green beans, blanched 2 minutes and refreshed

6 fresh shiitake mushrooms, stems removed and caps thinly sliced

2 thin yellow crookneck squash or zucchini, cut into matchsticks

1 tablespoon soy sauce

few drops of oriental sesame oil

1 ▲ Heat ½ tablespoon of the oil in a hot wok or frying pan. Add the sesame seeds and cook, stirring and shaking the pan, until the seeds are golden, about 1 minute. Turn the seeds onto paper towels to drain.

2 ◄ Heat the remaining oil. Add the carrots and stir-fry 2 minutes. Add the beans and mushrooms. Stir-fry 1 minute. Add the squash and stir-fry until all the vegetables are crisp-tender, 2–3 minutes longer. Add the soy sauce and sesame oil. Toss well and serve with the sesame seeds sprinkled on top.

SHREDDING VEGETABLE HEADS

Leaf vegetables that form compact heads, such as cabbage and lettuce, are often shredded for cooking or using in a salad. A large sharp knife is essential for good results.

Alternatively, you can use the appropriate blade in a food processor.

Keep Knives Sharp
Vegetable preparation is easy with sharp knives. Hone the edge regularly with a sharpening steel.

1 ▲ Cut the head in half through the core. Cut each half in half. Cut out the core from each quarter. Discard any damaged outside leaves.

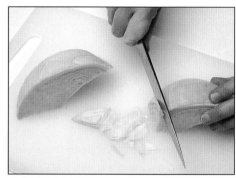

2 ▲ Set each quarter flat on a cut surface and slice across into shreds of the required thickness, guiding the side of the knife with your knuckles.

Hot Slaw

SERVES 4–6

2 tablespoons butter

4 cups firmly packed shredded white cabbage

1 teaspoon caraway seeds

salt and pepper

½ cup sour cream

1 teaspoon sugar

1 tablespoon cider vinegar

1 ▲ Melt the butter in a large frying pan. Add the cabbage and sprinkle with the caraway seeds. Season with salt and pepper.

2 Cook over low heat, stirring and turning the cabbage, until it is crisp-tender and just beginning to turn golden. Remove from the heat and turn into a large bowl.

3 ◀ Stir together the sour cream, sugar, and cider vinegar. Add to the cabbage, toss to combine well, and serve immediately.

SHREDDING VEGETABLE LEAVES

Cut individual leaves – cabbage, lettuce, spinach and other greens, and herbs such as basil – into neat shreds with this method.

<table>
<tr><td>

A Clean Cut
Leaves of very tender greens such as basil and Bibb lettuce can turn black at the cut edge if the cut is not clean. To avoid this, be sure the knife is very sharp, and cut straight down through the roll.

</td></tr>
</table>

1 ▲ Stack the leaves, 6–8 at a time, and roll up tightly parallel with the central rib. If the leaves are very large, roll them up individually.

2 ▲ With a sharp knife, slice across the roll into shreds of the required thickness, guiding the side of the knife with your knuckles.

Chinese-Style Vegetable and Noodle Soup

SERVES 4

5 cups vegetable or chicken stock

1 garlic clove, lightly crushed with the flat side of a knife

1-inch peeled cube of fresh ginger, cut into fine shreds

2 tablespoons soy sauce

1 tablespoon cider vinegar

3 ounces fresh shiitake or button mushrooms, stems removed and thinly sliced

2 large scallions, thinly sliced on the diagonal

1½ ounces vermicelli or other fine noodles

2 cups shredded Napa cabbage

1 tablespoon fresh coriander leaves (cilantro)

1 Pour the stock into a saucepan. Add the garlic, ginger, soy sauce, and vinegar. Bring to a boil, then cover the pan and reduce the heat to very low. Let simmer gently for about 10 minutes. Remove the garlic clove and discard it.

2 ◄ Add the sliced mushrooms and scallions and bring the soup back to a boil. Reduce the heat and simmer, uncovered, for 5 minutes, stirring occasionally. Add the noodles and shredded Napa cabbage. Simmer until the noodles and vegetables are just tender, 3–4 minutes longer. Stir in the coriander leaves. Simmer 1 minute longer. Serve the soup hot.

Blanching and Refreshing

Foods are blanched for several reasons: to loosen skins before peeling (tomatoes, peaches, and nuts), to set color and flavor (for vegetables before freezing), to reduce bitterness (in some vegetables), to firm flesh (sweetbreads), and to remove excess salt (country ham, bacon). Vegetables are often blanched as an initial cooking, when further cooking is to be done by stir-frying or a brief reheating in butter before serving, or if they are to be used in a salad. After blanching, most foods are "refreshed" to stop them cooking any further.

1 ▲ To blanch: Immerse the food in a large pan of boiling water (ideally use a wire basket or strainer so the food can be lifted out easily). Bring the water back to a boil and boil for the time directed, usually 1–2 minutes. Immediately lift the food out of the water (in its basket or with a slotted spoon or drain in a colander).

2 ▲ To refresh: Quickly immerse the food in ice water or hold under cold running water. If the recipe directs, leave until it has cooled completely. Drain well.

Broccoli, Cauliflower, and Carrot Salad

Serves 4

1 small head of cauliflower, cut into florets and stems trimmed
½ pound broccoli, cut into florets and stems trimmed
2 carrots, thickly sliced
⅓ cup vegetable oil
¼ cup coarsely chopped almonds
2 tablespoons red wine vinegar
½ teaspoon ground cumin
salt and pepper

1 Blanch the cauliflower, broccoli, and carrots separately in boiling salted water, allowing 10 minutes for the cauliflower and 5 minutes for the broccoli and carrots. Drain well and refresh in ice water.

2 ▶ Heat 1 tablespoon of the oil in a small frying pan. Add the almonds. Fry until golden brown, about 5 minutes, stirring frequently. Drain on paper towels and let cool.

3 Combine the remaining oil with the vinegar, cumin, salt, and pepper in a large bowl. Whisk well together. Add the vegetables and toss to coat with the dressing. Scatter the almonds on top. Serve at room temperature.

SWEATING

Sweating is a common preliminary step in vegetable cooking, particularly for onions and leeks. This process, which is essentially a form of steaming, draws out the juices and develops the vegetable's flavor.

1 ▲ Heat fat (usually butter) over low heat in a heavy saucepan or frying pan that has a tight fitting lid. Add the vegetable and stir to coat with the melted fat.

2 ▲ Cover the pan tightly and cook gently until the vegetable is softened but not brown; onions will be translucent. This can take 10–15 minutes or longer. Uncover to stir occasionally during the cooking.

Pasta with Zucchini and Walnut Sauce

SERVES 4

5 tablespoons butter
1 large yellow onion, halved and thinly sliced
1 pound zucchini, very thinly sliced
¾ pound short pasta shapes such as penne, ziti, rotini, or fusilli
½ cup coarsely chopped walnuts
3 tablespoons minced fresh parsley
2 tablespoons half-and-half
salt and pepper
freshly grated Parmesan cheese, for serving

1 ▲ Melt the butter in a frying pan and add the onion. Cover and sweat for 5 minutes, then add the zucchini.

2 Stir well, cover again, and sweat until the vegetables are very soft, stirring occasionally.

3 Meanwhile, bring a large pot of salted water to a boil. Add the pasta to the boiling water, stir, and cook until it is just tender to the bite ("al dente"), about 10 minutes. Check the package directions for timing.

4 While the pasta is cooking, add the walnuts, parsley, and half-and-half to the zucchini mixture and stir well. Season to taste with salt and pepper.

5 Drain the pasta and return it to the pot. Add the zucchini sauce and mix well together. Serve immediately, with plenty of Parmesan cheese sprinkled on top.

MASHING AND PURÉEING

The smooth texture of a mashed or puréed vegetable is very appealing, perhaps because it reminds us of childhood food. Vegetables to be finished this way may be first boiled, steamed, sweated, or baked.

Carrot Purée

Thinly slice 1½ pounds carrots. Put them in a saucepan, cover with water, and add a pinch of salt. Bring to a boil and simmer until tender, 10–15 minutes. Drain well, then purée the carrots in a food processor. Add 2 tablespoons butter, ¼ cup each milk and orange juice, and ½ teaspoon ground cardamom or ⅛ teaspoon grated nutmeg. Season with salt and pepper. Reheat, stirring frequently. *Serves 4.*

Whipped Sweet Potatoes

Mash 1½ pounds boiled or baked sweet potatoes with an electric mixer. Add butter, ¼ cup orange juice, and ¼ teaspoon ground cinnamon; beat well.

1 ▲ To mash potatoes and sweet potatoes or yams: Put the warm, freshly cooked potatoes through a potato ricer. With a wooden spoon, beat in butter and milk or cream, then season to taste.

3 ▲ To purée other root vegetables and most squashes: Put the freshly cooked vegetable in a food processor and process until smooth, scraping down the sides of the container as necessary. Season to taste.

2 ▲ Alternatively, beat them with an electric mixer. A third method, less successful, is to use a potato masher. Do not use a food processor for puréeing starchy vegetables such as potatoes; it will make them gluey.

4 ▲ To purée vegetables with fibers: Use a vegetable mill for fibrous vegetables, such as green beans, legumes, or stringy squashes, unless you are prepared to push the food-processor purée through a strainer.

5 ◄ To purée greens: Remove the stems of leaves such as spinach or chard before cooking. Purée in a food processor. Be sure to squeeze out as much water as possible, both before and after puréeing, especially if adding cream. Season to taste.

Mashed Potatoes with Celery Root

SERVES 4

2 pounds baking potatoes, peeled

¾ pound celery root

3 tablespoons butter

½ cup sour cream

⅛ teaspoon grated nutmeg

salt and pepper

1 Cut up the potatoes, if large. Bring to a boil in salted water, then simmer until very tender, about 20 minutes.

2 ▲ Meanwhile, peel the celery root, chop it coarsely, and drop immediately into a pan of salted water. (If exposed to the air too long, celery root will turn brown.) Bring to a boil, then simmer until very tender, 15–20 minutes.

3 ▲ Drain the potatoes and return them to the saucepan. Return to very low heat for 1–2 minutes to evaporate excess moisture, shaking the pan to turn the potatoes.

4 Press the potatoes through a potato ricer into a warmed bowl. Drain the celery root and purée in a food processor. Add to the bowl.

~ **VARIATION** ~

Substitute 1 medium-size head of rutabaga for the celery root. The rutabaga can be puréed with a potato ricer along with the potatoes or in a food processor.

5 ▼ Add the butter, sour cream, and nutmeg. Season to taste with salt and pepper. Beat well with a wooden spoon or, for a fluffier result, with an electric mixer. Serve hot.

MAKING VEGETABLE STOCK

Adapt the ingredients for this fresh-flavored stock to what you have on hand. Refrigerate, covered, for up to 5 days or freeze for up to 1 month.

MAKES ABOUT 2½ QUARTS

2 large onions, coarsely chopped
2 leeks, sliced
3 garlic cloves, crushed with the flat side of a knife
3 carrots, coarsely chopped
4 celery stalks, coarsely chopped
a large strip of lemon rind
a handful of parsley stems (about 12)
a few fresh thyme sprigs
2 bay leaves
2½ quarts water

1 ▲ Put the vegetables, strip of lemon rind, herbs, and water in a stockpot and bring to a boil. Skim off the foam that rises to the surface, doing so frequently at first, and then just from time to time.

2 ▲ Reduce the heat and simmer, uncovered, for 30 minutes. Strain the stock and let it cool.

Vegetable and Herb Chowder

SERVES 4

2 tablespoons butter
1 onion, minced
1 leek, thinly sliced
1 celery stalk, diced
1 bell pepper, yellow or green, seeded and diced
2 tablespoons minced fresh parsley
1 tablespoon flour
1 quart vegetable stock
¾ pound boiling potatoes, peeled and diced
a few fresh thyme sprigs, or ½ teaspoon dried thyme
1 bay leaf
¼ pound string beans, thinly sliced on the diagonal
½ cup milk
salt and pepper

1 ▲ Melt the butter in a heavy saucepan or Dutch oven and add the onion, leek, celery, bell pepper, and parsley. Cover and cook over low heat until the vegetables are soft.

2 Add the flour and stir until well blended. Add the stock slowly, stirring to combine. Bring to a boil, stirring frequently.

3 ▼ Add the potatoes, thyme, and bay leaf. Simmer, uncovered, about 10 minutes.

4 Add the beans and simmer until all the vegetables are tender, 10–15 minutes longer.

5 Stir in the milk. Season with salt and pepper. Heat through. Before serving, discard the thyme stems and bay leaf. Serve hot.

Preparing Salad Greens

Crisp, fresh green and variegated leaves are very appetizing. Use them as the background for a vegetable, fish, meat, or fruit salad, or make the leaves the focus.

Lettuce

There are four main types of lettuce: crisphead, with solid heads of tightly packed, crisp leaves (iceberg); butterhead, with looser heads of soft-textured leaves (Bibb or limestone, Boston); romaine, with its elongated head of crisp leaves; and looseleaf, with leaves that do not form a head (salad bowl, oak leaf).

Preparation: Discard wilted or damaged leaves. Twist or cut out the central core. Rinse the leaves thoroughly in cold water and soak briefly to draw out any grit trapped in the folds. Drain and blot or spin dry. If the leaves are large, tear in pieces.

Other Salad Ingredients

To provide contrast in texture and flavor, add brightly colored and crunchy, sharp-flavored leaves, such as radicchio or red cabbage, with plain leaves. Cucumber, scallions, and carrot are also appealing in a mixed salad, as are raw or lightly cooked green beans or snow peas. Nuts or dried fruit are tasty additions, as are shredded or cubed cheese, or croutons.

Endive and Escarole

These members of the chicory family bring an appealing bitterness to salads. The smooth, pale leaves of Belgian endive are more delicate and sweet than those of curly endive (sometimes labeled chicory), which has frilly green leaves with a coarse texture. Escarole has broader, fleshier leaves with jagged edges and a firm texture.

Preparation: Trim the base and cut out the core. Discard wilted or damaged leaves. Rinse and dry the leaves. If large, tear in smaller pieces.

Lamb's Lettuce

Also know as corn salad or "mâche," this salad green has a pleasantly firm, chewy texture and mild, slightly nutty flavor. The leaves are small and may be spoon-shaped or round.

Preparation: Remove any wilted or damaged leaves. Trim roots. Rinse well, as the leaves can be sandy.

Arugula

In a salad of mixed greens, the pungent peppery, nutty taste of arugula is unmistakable and welcome. This member of the mustard family, also called rocket, has deep green leaves with curved edges and a texture somewhat like spinach.

Preparation: Discard any wilted or damaged leaves. Pull off roots. Rinse thoroughly and dry on paper towels – it's best not to use a salad spinner, which could bruise the leaves.

Watercress

Another member of the mustard family, the round dark green leaves have a wonderful peppery flavor that enlivens any salad, and the fresh, attractive appearance of watercress makes it a popular garnish.

Preparation: Discard wilted or damaged leaves and snap off thick stems. Rinse well and spin dry.

Wilted Spinach Salad

SERVES 6

1 pound fresh young spinach leaves
½ pound sliced bacon
¼ cup red wine vinegar
¼ cup water
4 teaspoons sugar
1 teaspoon dry English mustard
salt and pepper
8 scallions, thinly sliced
6 radishes, thinly sliced
2 hard-boiled eggs, coarsely grated

3 ▲ Combine the vinegar, water, sugar, mustard, salt, and pepper in a bowl and stir until smoothly blended. Add to the bacon fat in the pan. Bring the dressing to a boil, stirring.

4 ▼ Pour the hot dressing over the spinach leaves. Sprinkle on the bacon, scallions, radishes, and eggs and toss well. Serve immediately.

1 ▲ Pull any coarse stems from the spinach leaves. Rinse them, dry them well, and put in a large salad bowl.

2 ▲ Fry the bacon slices until crisp and brown. Remove them and drain on paper towels. Crumble the bacon and set aside.

RINSING AND CRISPING SALAD GREENS

It is vital that all salad leaves be thoroughly rinsed to remove any grit or insects, as well as residues of sprays. Just as important is to dry the salad leaves thoroughly so that the dressing will not be diluted.

Lettuce with Blue Cheese Dressing

For each serving, use 1 small head of Bibb lettuce or heart of Boston lettuce, washed and spun or blotted dry. Top with 3–4 tablespoons blue cheese dressing (page 180). Garnish with cherry tomatoes and chives, if desired.

Salad Success

● Dress salad greens just before serving, otherwise the leaves will wilt and become unpleasantly soggy.

● Match the dressing to the greens: sharp leaves need hearty flavors, but the same dressing used on delicate greens would overpower them.

● Be imaginative with salad additions. A little crumbled goat cheese, for instance, can lift a plain salad, especially with a sprinkling of fresh herbs or nuts.

1 ▲ Discard any wilted, discolored, or damaged leaves. For spinach, watercress, and similar greens, pull off the stems. Trim off any roots.

2 ▲ For leaves in compact or loose heads, pull them individually from the core or stem.

3 ▲ Put the leaves in a sink or large bowl of cold water and swirl them around to wash off any dirt or insects. Let settle 1-2 minutes.

4 ▲ Lift the leaves out of the water onto a dish towel and pat dry gently with paper towels or another dish towel.

5 ▲ Alternatively, put the washed leaves in a salad spinner to spin off the water. (Do not use a salad spinner for leaves that bruise easily.)

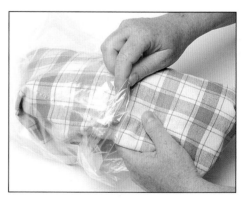

6 ▲ Wrap the leaves loosely in a clean dish towel or paper towels and put in a large plastic bag. Refrigerate about 1 hour. When assembling the salad, tear any large leaves into smaller, bite-sized pieces.

Tossed Salad with Oranges and Avocado

SERVES 4

1 head of Boston or Bibb lettuce

1 small bunch of watercress

a few leaves of curly endive

1 small bunch of arugula

1 red onion, thinly sliced into rings

2 seedless oranges, peeled and sectioned

1 ripe avocado, peeled, seeded, and cubed

½ cup walnut pieces, toasted

FOR THE DRESSING

6 tablespoons salad oil

1 tablespoon walnut oil

3 tablespoons lemon juice

2 tablespoons orange juice

1 teaspoon grated orange rind

1 teaspoon Dijon-style mustard

pinch of sugar

salt and pepper

1 ▲ Combine all the dressing ingredients in a bowl or screwtop jar. Whisk or shake well together.

~ **VARIATION** ~

For Green Salad with Tuna and Peppers, omit oranges and walnuts. Add 1 7-ounce can drained, flaked tuna and 1 roasted bell pepper (page 123), peeled and thinly sliced.

2 ▼ Put the salad greens in a bowl and add the onion, orange sections, and avocado cubes.

3 ▲ Add the dressing and toss the salad to combine well.

4 Scatter the walnuts on top and serve immediately.

PREPARING LEGUMES

Legumes – beans, peas, and lentils – are a high-protein food. They keep well, making them a useful pantry staple. Most dried legumes require the same initial preparation.

An Extra Safeguard

To remove potentially harmful toxins when cooking dried beans, boil, uncovered, for 10 minutes before reducing the heat to a simmer for the rest of the time.

1 ▲ First rinse the legumes and pick out any small stones.

2 ▲ To soak dried beans and peas: Put them in a bowl, cover with plenty of cold water, and let soak at least 4 hours. (Lentils do not need soaking.)

3 ▲ A quick alternative method is to put the dried beans or peas in a large pan of water, bring to a boil and boil 2 minutes, then let soak 1 hour.

4 ▲ In either case, drain the legumes and rinse them well. They are now ready for cooking as the recipe directs.

5 ▲ To cook: Put the soaked and drained beans or peas or the lentils in a pan of fresh cold water (3 parts water to 1 part legumes) and bring to a boil. Then cover the pan, reduce the heat, and simmer until tender.

A LOOK AT LEGUMES

Dried beans, peas, and lentils range widely in color, shape, and size. They are endlessly versatile.

Some of the most commonly available beans include: **Great Northern**, small to medium-sized, kidney-shaped, white; **kidney**, medium-sized, kidney-shaped, smooth, shiny, may be reddish-brown or white (called cannellini beans); **navy**, small, oval, smooth, off-white; **black** (also called turtle beans), which are small, oval, smooth, shiny, jet-black; **pinto**, small, oval, smooth, beige with brown specks.

Other legumes include: **black-eyed peas**, small, oval, smooth, creamy color, with small cream-centered black dot in center on one side; **chickpeas** (also called garbanzo beans), medium-sized, round, not smooth, beige-tan; **peas**, small, round, or split in half, may be gray-green or yellow; **lentils**, tiny, disk-shaped, smooth, may be brownish-green, reddish-orange, or yellow.

All legumes are easy to prepare, and they can be used in all sorts of ways – in casseroles, soups, stews, purées, and salads.

The minimum soaking time for dried legumes is 4 hours, but they can be soaked overnight if that is more convenient. Lentils do not need soaking, and it is not essential for split peas, although they may be soaked to speed cooking.

Most dried legumes require about 1½–2 hours' cooking time. This includes black beans, pinto beans, navy beans, Great Northern beans, kidney beans, and chickpeas. Black-eyed peas and split peas require less time, about 1–1¼ hours. Lentils cook in less than ½ hour.

Split Pea Soup

SERVES 4–6

2 tablespoons butter

1 large onion, chopped

1 large celery stalk with leaves, chopped

2 carrots, chopped

1 smoked ham hock, about 1 pound

2 quarts water

2 cups green split peas

2 tablespoons minced fresh parsley, plus more for garnishing

½ teaspoon dried thyme

1 bay leaf

about 2 tablespoons lemon juice

salt and pepper

1 ▲ Melt the butter in a large pot. Add the onion, celery, and carrots and cook, stirring occasionally, until they are soft.

2 ▲ Add the remaining ingredients. Bring to a boil, cover, and simmer over very low heat until the peas are very tender, about 2 hours.

3 ▼ Remove the ham hock. Let it cool slightly, then remove the skin and cut the meat from the bones. Discard skin and bones; cut the meat into chunks.

4 ▲ Return the chunks of ham to the soup. Discard the bay leaf. Taste and adjust the seasoning with more lemon juice, salt, and pepper.

5 Serve hot, sprinkled with parsley.

Tuna and Black-Eyed Pea Salad

1 cup dried black-eyed peas
½ cup garlic vinaigrette (page 182)
½ cup minced red onion
3 tablespoons chopped fresh parsley
1 7-ounce can tuna, drained
cherry tomatoes, for garnishing

2 ▲ Pour the vinaigrette dressing over the beans and mix well.

4 ▲ Add the tuna and stir gently into the salad.

5 Garnish with halved cherry tomatoes and serve at cool room temperature.

1 ▲ Soak the black-eyed peas for at least 4 hours. Drain, then cook in fresh water until tender. Drain well and let cool slightly.

3 ▲ Add the onion and parsley and stir to combine.

~ **VARIATION** ~

For Italian Bean Salad, use cannellini beans (canned, if desired, for quicker preparation) instead of black-eyed peas.

Garbanzo-Chili Dip

2 cups dried chickpeas (garbanzo beans), soaked overnight, cooked, and drained
¼ cup cream cheese
3 tablespoons lemon juice
2 tablespoons olive oil
1–2 garlic cloves, minced
1–2 tablespoons tequila (optional)
⅓ cup seeded and chopped mild green chili peppers (fresh or canned)
salt
¼ cup pine nuts, for garnishing
hot tortilla or corn chips, for serving

1 Combine the chickpeas, cream cheese, lemon juice, oil, garlic, and tequila in a blender or food processor. Blend until smooth.

2 ▲ Turn into a bowl and stir in the chili peppers. Season with salt. Cover and chill at least 1 hour.

3 ▲ Toast the pine nuts in a dry skillet over medium heat. Serve the dip at room temperature, with pine nuts sprinkled over the surface and hot tortilla or corn chips.

Garbanzo-Chili Dip (left), Tuna and Black-Eyed Pea Salad

Eggs

~

The endlessly versatile egg lends itself to easy and exciting suppers, snacks, brunches, and desserts. From fried eggs to soufflés, the techniques for cooking eggs are essentially simple. A little practice will give you confidence.

Boiling Eggs

The derisive expression, "can't boil an egg," indicates the importance of this basic cooking skill, although, to be accurate, eggs are simmered rather than boiled.

For many people, a soft-boiled egg with toast is a favorite breakfast. But the soft-boiled egg and its cousin the coddled egg have many delicious applications. If they are to be peeled for serving, cook them for the longest time suggested below. The salt in the cooking water aids in peeling.

Hard-boiled eggs make classic salads and sandwich fillings, as well as cold first course and buffet dishes and hot main dishes.

1 ▲ To hard-boil eggs: Bring a pan of well-salted water to a boil. Using a slotted spoon, lower each egg into the water. Reduce the heat so the water is just simmering gently. Cook 10 minutes. Immediately plunge the eggs into a bowl of ice water and let cool.

2 ▲ When the eggs are cool enough to handle, peel them. If they are not to be used immediately, keep the peeled eggs in a bowl of cold salted water. Or, store the eggs, still in the shell, in the refrigerator; they will keep up to 1 week.

Egg, Potato, and Bean Salad
Bring a pot of salted water to a boil. Add 1 pound small unpeeled new potatoes. Bring back to a boil and simmer 10 minutes. Add ½ pound thin green beans ("haricots verts") and simmer until the potatoes and beans are just tender, 4–5 minutes longer. Drain well in a colander and refresh under cold running water. Turn the vegetables into a large bowl. Sprinkle ¼ cup olive oil and 2 tablespoons balsamic vinegar over them. Season with salt and pepper and toss well. Scatter 2 grated hard-boiled eggs and 3 tablespoons coarsely shredded mixed fresh mint and basil over the top. Serve warm or at room temperature. *Serves 4–6.*

3 ▲ To coddle eggs: Lower them into a pan of boiling salted water. Cover the pan and remove it from the heat. Let stand until the eggs are done to your taste, 6–8 minutes. Lift out each egg and place it in an egg cup for serving; cut off the top of the shell so the egg can be scooped out. Or, plunge the eggs into a bowl of cold water and cool, then peel carefully. To reheat for serving, immerse in a bowl of hot water for 1–2 minutes.

Hard-Boiled Egg Tips
- Always cool hard-boiled eggs in ice water. The abrupt temperature change helps prevent a gray layer from forming around the egg yolk.
- To peel hard-boiled eggs, tap them gently on a hard surface to crack the shell. Carefully peel under cold running water.

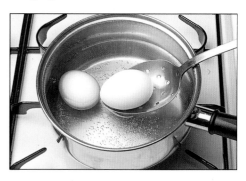

4 ▲ To soft-boil eggs: Bring a pan of well-salted water to a boil. Using a slotted spoon, lower each egg into the water. Reduce the heat so the water just simmers. Cook until the eggs are done to your taste, 3–5 minutes (depending on how firm you like the white to be; the yolk will be runny).

Ideas for Soft-Boiled and Coddled Eggs
- For *Caviar-Crowned Eggs:* Cut the top ¾ inch from each egg, in its shell. Put a spoonful of sour cream and caviar on the egg.
- For *Smoked-Salmon Eggs:* Prepare as above and top each with a spoonful each of sour cream and diced smoked salmon.
- Put a hot peeled egg in the center of a bowl of cream of spinach or watercress soup.

Caesar Salad

Serves 6

¾ cup salad oil, preferably olive oil

2 cups 1-inch cubes of French or Italian bread

1 large garlic clove, crushed with the flat side of a knife

2 small heads of romaine lettuce, separated into leaves, rinsed, and crisped

salt and pepper

2 eggs, soft-boiled 1 minute

⅓ cup lemon juice

⅔ cup freshly grated Parmesan cheese

6 anchovy fillets, drained and finely chopped (optional)

Ideas for Hard-Boiled Eggs

● For *Deviled Eggs*: Halve the eggs lengthwise and scoop out the yolks. Mash the yolks with a fork and mix with enough mayonnaise to make a creamy consistency. Season with Dijon-style mustard, salt, and pepper. Spoon or pipe the yolk mixture into the hollows in the egg-white halves and sprinkle the tops with a little paprika or cayenne.

● For *Herb-Stuffed Eggs*: Add minced fresh herbs such as parsley, tarragon, and chives to the egg yolk and mayonnaise mixture; omit the mustard.

● For *Egg Salad*: Grate or chop eggs. Mix with minced scallions or red onion to taste and a little minced parsley. Bind with mayonnaise. Season with mustard.

● For *Eggs in Aspic*: Put cooled peeled eggs in individual ramekins and surround with chopped herbs in aspic. Refrigerate to set.

● For *Eggs in Cream Sauce*: Add whole or quartered eggs to hot mushroom or mustard sauce (page 170). Add 1 cup slow-cooked onions (page 114). Simmer gently 1–2 minutes to heat through.

1 ▼ Heat ¼ cup of the oil in a large frying pan. Add the bread cubes and garlic. Fry, stirring and turning constantly, until the cubes are golden brown all over. Drain on paper towels. Discard the garlic.

2 Tear large lettuce leaves into smaller pieces. Put all the lettuce in a large salad bowl.

3 ▲ Add the remaining oil and season with salt and pepper. Toss the leaves to coat well.

4 Break the eggs on top. Sprinkle with the lemon juice. Toss well again.

5 Add the cheese and anchovies, if using. Toss gently to mix.

6 Scatter the toasted bread cubes on top and serve immediately.

SCRAMBLING EGGS

Tender, creamy scrambled eggs are perfect for breakfast or brunch, but you can also add flavorings for a more unusual snack or supper dish.

Ideas for Scrambled Eggs
● Add minced fresh herbs (chives, tarragon) to the beaten eggs.
● Cook diced vegetables (onions, mushrooms, bell peppers) or ham in the butter before adding the eggs.
● Stir in a little grated cheese or bits of cream cheese just before the eggs have finished cooking.
● Fold small cooked shelled shrimp into scrambled eggs.

1 ▲ Put the eggs in a bowl and add a little salt and pepper. Beat the eggs with a fork until they are well blended. Melt butter in a frying pan over medium-low heat (butter should cover the bottom of the pan generously). Pour in the beaten eggs.

2 ▲ Cook, scraping up and turning the eggs over, until they are softly set and still moist, 3–5 minutes. The eggs will continue to cook after being removed from the heat, so undercook them slightly even if you prefer a firmer end result.

Scrambled Eggs with Smoked Salmon

SERVES 4

6 eggs
salt and pepper
4 tablespoons butter
2 tablespoons whipping cream
¼ cup mayonnaise
4 slices of pumpernickel or whole-wheat bread, crusts trimmed
¼ pound thinly sliced smoked salmon
lumpfish or salmon caviar, for garnishing

1 ▲ Season the eggs with salt and pepper. Scramble them using half of the butter. Mix in the cream just before they have finished cooking.

2 Remove from the heat and mix in the mayonnaise. Let cool.

3 Spread the slices of bread with the remaining butter. Cover with smoked salmon, trimming it to fit. Cut in half.

4 Divide the scrambled eggs among the plates, spreading it neatly on the smoked salmon. Top each serving with a heaped tablespoon of caviar.

FRYING EGGS

Short-order cooks know that people have strong feelings about how their eggs should be fried. However they're cooked, fried eggs are natural partners for bacon and other breakfast fare.

1 Heat butter, bacon fat, or oil in a frying pan (to cover the bottom generously) over medium heat. When the fat is sizzling, break each egg and slip it into the pan.

2 ◀ Fry until the egg white is just set and opaque or more firm, according to your taste, 1–1½ minutes. The yolk will still be runny and the base of the egg will be golden brown and crisp. The egg is ready to serve now, for "sunny-side up." Or, for "over easy," gently turn the fried egg over with a slotted spatula, taking care not to break the yolk. Cook until the other side is just browned, 10–15 seconds.

Fried Eggs and Sausage on Tortillas

SERVES 4

½ pound ground pork

½ small onion, minced

1 tablespoon chili powder (or to taste)

½ teaspoon ground cumin

½ teaspoon dried oregano

1 tablespoon vinegar

1 garlic clove, minced

salt and pepper

oil, for frying

4 large corn tortillas

4 eggs

4 tablespoons butter or bacon fat

Mexican hot sauce or salsa, for serving

1 ▲ Put the pork in a bowl and add the onion, spices, oregano, vinegar, garlic, salt, and pepper. Mix well, cover, and refrigerate overnight.

2 ▼ Cook the pork mixture in a large frying pan until it is browned and crumbly, stirring occasionally.

3 Meanwhile, heat 1 inch of oil in a wide saucepan to 365°F. Fry the tortillas until they are crisp and golden brown, keeping them flat. Drain on paper towels and put on a baking sheet. Keep warm in the oven.

4 Fry the eggs in the butter or bacon fat (or use oil for frying if you prefer).

5 Put a tortilla on each plate. Using a slotted spoon, divide the pork mixture among the tortillas. Top each serving with a fried egg. Serve accompanied by hot sauce or salsa.

POACHING EGGS

The perfect poached egg has a neat oval shape, a tender white, and a soft yolk. It is unbeatable on a slice of hot buttered toast, or it can be partnered with vegetables (artichoke bottoms, asparagus), seafood (crab, smoked salmon), or meat (ham, bacon, steak) and dressed with a rich sauce. Use the freshest eggs possible because they will be the easiest to poach.

1 First, bring a large, deep pan of water to a boil.

2 ▲ Break each egg and slip it gently into the water. Reduce the heat to low so the water is just simmering. Poach until the eggs are done, 3–4 minutes.

3 ▲ With a slotted spoon, lift out each egg and press it gently; the white should feel just firm but the yolk should still be soft.

> **The Clotting Factor**
> If your eggs are more than a few days old, adding white wine vinegar to the poaching water will help the egg white to coagulate, although it will slightly flavor the egg. Use 2 tablespoons vinegar to each quart of water.

4 ◄ If there are any strings of cooked egg white, trim them off with a knife or kitchen scissors. Drain briefly on paper towels. Serve immediately, if wished. Or, warm up the eggs in a bowl of hot water for serving. If the eggs will be served cold, immerse them in a bowl of ice water until needed. Drain the eggs and blot dry gently with paper towels before serving.

Poached Eggs Florentine

SERVES 4

1½ pounds spinach leaves, shredded
2 tablespoons butter
3–4 tablespoons whipping cream
⅛ teaspoon grated nutmeg
salt and pepper
4 eggs
1 cup cheese sauce made with Swiss cheese and no mustard (page 170)
¼ cup shredded Swiss cheese

1 Preheat the broiler.

2 Put the spinach in a large pan with the butter. Cover and cook until the leaves are wilted. Uncover and boil to evaporate the excess liquid.

3 ▲ Mix in the cream, nutmeg, and seasonings. Poach the eggs.

4 Divide the spinach among 4 individual shallow gratin dishes or a large gratin dish. Spread it evenly and make hollows for the eggs. Set a poached egg in each hollow.

5 ▼ Coat the eggs lightly with the cheese sauce. Sprinkle with the shredded cheese. Broil until the cheese has melted and is lightly browned, 2–3 minutes. Serve immediately.

BAKING EGGS

Baking, or shirring, is one of the simplest ways to cook eggs, yet it produces elegant results. The eggs can be baked individually, in buttered pots (ramekins) or small shallow dishes, or several can be baked in a large dish, on a bed of vegetables, sauce, etc.

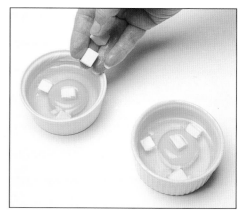

Ideas for Baked Eggs
- Coat buttered ramekins with freshly grated Parmesan cheese. Dot the eggs with butter and sprinkle each egg very lightly with Parmesan before baking.
- Put a little diced cooked ham, or a few sautéed sliced mushrooms, or crisp croutons, garlic flavored if preferred, in the bottom of each ramekin before breaking in the egg.
- Bake eggs on a bed of creamed spinach, mashed potato or other root vegetables, or puréed broccoli or peas.
- Bake eggs on a bed of tomato sauce and roasted vegetables (page 173).
- Bake eggs in hollows made in a cooked stuffing, such as sausage stuffing for chicken (page 13) or smoked ham and almond stuffing for turkey (page 27).
- Bake potatoes, then cut off a lengthwise slice from one side. Scoop out the flesh, leaving a shell ⅛- to ¼-inch thick. Mash the potato with butter, milk, salt, and pepper. Spoon it back into the potato shells and press down firmly. Make a hollow in the top of the mashed potato in each shell and break in an egg. Drizzle a little melted butter over the egg. Bake at 400°F to set the egg white, 5–7 minutes.

1 ▲ To bake in individual ramekins: Butter the dishes and sprinkle them with salt and pepper. Break an egg into each, taking care not to pierce the yolk.

3 ▲ Set the dishes in a baking pan. Add enough water to come halfway up the sides of the dishes. Bring to a simmer on top of the stove. Transfer to a preheated 400°F oven. Bake until the whites are just set and the yolks still soft, 5–7 minutes.

2 ▲ Dot the top of each egg with a few small pieces of butter, or add 1 tablespoon of whipping cream to each ramekin.

4 ▲ To bake on a bed: Spread a hot savory mixture in a buttered shallow baking dish or in individual ramekins or gratin dishes. Make hollows in the mixture with the back of a spoon. Break an egg into each hollow.

5 ◀ According to recipe directions, dot the eggs with butter, sprinkle with cheese, drizzle with cream, etc. (These toppings help to moisten and flavor the eggs during cooking.) Bake until the whites are just set and the yolks are still soft.

Eggs Baked in Hash

SERVES 6

4 tablespoons butter
1 large onion, chopped
3 cups chopped cooked ham
3 cups chopped cooked potatoes
1 cup shredded sharp Cheddar cheese
2 tablespoons ketchup
1–2 tablespoons Worcestershire sauce
salt and pepper
6 eggs
few drops of hot pepper sauce
chopped fresh parsley, for garnishing

1 Preheat the oven to 325°F.

2 Melt 2 tablespoons butter in a frying pan. Cook the onion until soft, stirring occasionally.

3 ▲ Turn the onion into a bowl. Add the ham, potatoes, cheese, ketchup, and Worcestershire sauce. Season with salt and pepper. Stir the mixture to combine well.

4 ▲ Spread the hash evenly in a buttered baking dish in a layer about 1-inch deep. Bake 10 minutes.

5 ▼ Make 6 hollows in the hash. Slip an egg into each.

6 Melt the remaining butter in a small pan. Season with hot pepper sauce to taste.

7 ▲ Drizzle the seasoned butter over the eggs and hash.

8 Bake until the eggs are set and cooked to your taste, 15–20 minutes longer. Serve hot, in the dish, garnished with parsley.

MAKING A ROLLED OR FOLDED OMELET

The versatile rolled or folded omelet can be served plain or filled. There are also flat omelets and soufflé omelets, which may be filled as well. At its simplest, an omelet is made with 2 or 3 eggs, 1–2 teaspoons water, salt, and pepper.

1 ▲ Break the eggs into a bowl and add the water and some salt and pepper. Beat with a fork until just blended but not frothy.

2 ▲ In an 8-inch omelet pan, melt 1–1½ tablespoons butter over medium-high heat. Tilt and rotate the pan so the bottom and sides are thoroughly coated with butter.

Omelet Fillings

• Add 1 tablespoon minced fresh herbs (a mixture of parsley, chives, and tarragon, for example) to the beaten eggs.

• Scatter 2–3 tablespoons shredded cheese (Swiss, Cheddar) over the omelet before rolling or folding.

• Sauté peeled, seeded, and chopped tomatoes in butter 1–2 minutes. Season with salt and pepper and stir in a little chopped fresh basil. Use to fill the omelet.

• Fill the omelet with strips of prosciutto or cooked ham, or with roasted vegetables (page 173), sautéed sliced mushrooms, slow-cooked onions (page 114), home-fried potatoes (page 126), or buttered asparagus tips.

• Warm leftover pasta (buttered or in sauce); if the shape is long, such as spaghetti, cut it into short pieces. If using buttered pasta, add strips of canned pimiento, sliced black olives, capers, etc. Use to fill the omelet, roll or fold, and sprinkle the top with grated Parmesan cheese.

3 ▲ When the butter is foaming and just beginning to turn golden, pour in the egg mixture. Tilt and rotate the pan to spread the eggs in an even layer over the bottom.

4 ▲ Cook until the omelet starts to set on the base, 5–10 seconds. With a thin spatula, lift the cooked base and tilt the pan so the uncooked egg mixture runs underneath onto the hot pan. Continue cooking in this way until most of the omelet is set but the top is still moist and creamy.

The Right Pan

Although you can make an omelet in a frying pan or skillet, a special omelet pan, with its curved edge, will make rolling or folding and turning out the omelet easier.

5 ▲ With the spatula, loosen the edge of the omelet on one side and tilt the pan so that a third of the omelet rolls over onto itself. (Or, just fold the omelet over in half.)

6 ▲ Continue loosening the omelet from its rolled edge, holding the pan over a warmed plate. As the omelet slides out of the pan onto the plate, tilt the pan so the omelet rolls over again on itself into thirds, using the edge of the pan to guide it.

Omelet Foo Yung

SERVES 4

1 tablespoon peanut or vegetable oil

½ cup chopped scallions

¼ cup diced celery

2 teaspoons minced fresh ginger

1 garlic clove, minced

½ cup shelled cooked small shrimp

½ cup crabmeat

¼ cup diced cooked ham

1½ tablespoons chopped fresh coriander
(cilantro)

1–2 tablespoons soy sauce, plus more for
serving

8 or 12 eggs

salt and pepper

4–6 tablespoons butter

1 Heat the oil in a frying pan over medium heat. Add the scallions, celery, ginger, and garlic and cook 1 minute, stirring frequently.

2 ▼ Add the shrimp, crabmeat, and ham. Sprinkle with the coriander and soy sauce. Reduce the heat to low and leave the mixture to heat through, stirring occasionally.

3 ▲ Meanwhile, make 4 omelets: use 2 or 3 eggs for each, season, and cook each in 1–1½ tablespoons of the butter. Before rolling or folding each omelet, spoon one-quarter of the shrimp and crab filling over the center. Serve hot, with more soy sauce for sprinkling.

MAKING A FLAT OMELET

Called a "frittata" in Italy and a "tortilla" in Spain, a flat omelet is thicker than a rolled or folded omelet. It is usually cut into wedges for serving hot, warm, or cold. Use a pan with a heatproof handle, or wrap the handle well with foil.

Fillings used for rolled or folded omelets can be used in flat ones, too. The quantities here will make a flat omelet to serve 4.

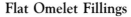

Flat Omelet Fillings

- Prepare ½ quantity home-fried potatoes (page 126). Spread out the cooked potatoes in the frying pan. Pour the egg mixture over the potatoes and continue cooking as described.
- Prepare roasted vegetables (page 173). Transfer to the frying pan and spread them out before pouring in the egg mixture. Continue cooking as described.
- Roast and peel 2 bell peppers and cut into thin strips. Cook 1 minced onion with garlic in oil and butter in a frying pan over medium heat until very soft. Stir in the pepper strips and some thawed, frozen peas. Spread out the vegetables in the pan. Pour in the egg mixture and continue cooking as described.

1 ▲ Break 8 eggs into a bowl and season with salt and pepper. Beat lightly with a fork. Meanwhile, preheat the broiler.

3 ▲ When the fat is sizzling and just beginning to turn golden, pour in the egg mixture. Tilt and rotate the pan to spread the eggs in an even layer over the bottom. Reduce the heat to low. (If the omelet has other ingredients, add them now, or spread in the pan before pouring in the egg mixture.)

Flat Omelet with Ham and Cheese
For each 8-egg omelet, scatter ¾ cup cooked ham strips and 3–4 tablespoons finely chopped scallions or red onion in the pan immediately after pouring in the egg mixture. Before transferring the omelet to the broiler, sprinkle 3–4 tablespoons of freshly grated Parmesan cheese or about ½ cup of shredded Cheddar or Swiss cheese evenly over the top. Serve the omelet hot or warm, cut into wedges. *Serves 4.*

2 ▲ In a 9- or 10-inch frying pan with a heatproof handle, melt 1 tablespoon butter with 1 tablespoon oil over medium heat. Tilt and rotate the pan to coat the bottom and sides.

4 ▲ Cook until the omelet starts to set on the base, 5–10 seconds. With a thin spatula, lift the cooked base and tilt the pan so the uncooked egg mixture runs underneath onto the hot pan. Continue cooking in this way until most of the omelet is set but the top is still moist and creamy.

5 ▲ Transfer the pan to the broiler, setting it 3–4 inches from the heat. Cook until the omelet is lightly browned and just set, 3–4 minutes.

MAKING A SOUFFLÉ OMELET

This cross between a flat omelet and a soufflé starts cooking on top of the stove and finishes in the oven. Fillings are normally sweet.

1 ▲ Separate 4 eggs. To the yolks, add 6 tablespoons sugar and beat with an electric mixer until thick and pale. Preheat the oven to 350°F.

2 ▲ Beat the egg whites until they hold stiff peaks. (Add a pinch of cream of tartar if not using a copper bowl.)

Soufflé Omelet Fillings

● Mix lightly crushed berries (raspberries, strawberries, blackberries, etc.) with a dash of Cognac, orange liqueur, or kirsch. Use to fill the omelet. Drizzle a little warmed honey over the top and serve with sweetened whipped cream (page 160) or sour cream.

● Add 2 tablespoons orange-flavored liqueur to the egg yolks with the sugar. Fill the omelet with sweet orange sections. Sprinkle the folded omelet with confectioners' sugar and pour on 3 tablespoons warmed orange-flavored liqueur. Set alight, and serve flaming.

3 ▲ With a rubber spatula, fold the egg whites into the yolk mixture as lightly as possible, cutting down to the bottom of the bowl and turning the mixture over, while rotating the bowl at the same time.

4 ▲ Heat a 9- or 10-inch frying pan with an ovenproof handle over medium-high heat. Melt enough butter in the pan to cover the bottom generously. Tilt the pan to coat the bottom and sides. Pour in the egg mixture. Reduce the heat to low.

Soufflé Omelet with Peaches
For each 4-egg omelet, spread 2 tablespoons warmed apricot, raspberry or strawberry jam over the cooked omelet and top with a peeled and thinly sliced peach. After folding, sprinkle with confectioners' sugar. Decorate with berries, if desired. *Serves 2.*

5 ▲ Cook, without stirring, until the omelet is puffy and set around the edges but still soft in the center, about 5 minutes. Transfer the pan to the oven. Bake until the top is set and lightly browned, 3–5 minutes.

6 ▲ Spread a filling over the center. Fold the omelet in half. Turn it onto a warmed plate and finish as the recipe directs. Serve immediately.

MAKING A SOUFFLÉ

Despite their reputation as tricky, soufflés are not difficult to make. The base for a soufflé is simply a thick sauce (sweet or savory) or a purée. Into this, stiffly beaten egg whites are folded, and the whole is baked until it has risen and is lightly set.

Proper preparation of the dish, enabling the soufflé to "climb" up the sides, encourages rising. Generously butter or oil the dish, including the top edge. If the recipe directs, coat the bottom and sides with a thin layer of crumbs, grated cheese, sugar, etc.

1 ▲ Separate the eggs, taking care that there is no trace of egg yolk in the whites. (It is best to separate 1 egg at a time and check each white before adding to the rest.)

2 ▲ For a savory soufflé, make a thick white sauce. Beat in the yolks and the soufflé flavoring. For a sweet soufflé, make a thick custard sauce using the yolks; mix in the flavoring.

3 ▲ In a large, scrupulously clean bowl, beat the egg whites until they hold stiff peaks when the beaters are lifted. (Any grease on the bowl or beaters will minimize volume.) If not using a copper bowl, add a pinch of cream of tartar once the whites are frothy. For a sweet soufflé, add sugar once the whites hold soft peaks (the tips flop over), then continue beating.

4 ▲ Add one-quarter of the egg whites to the sauce base. Using a large metal spoon or a rubber spatula, stir the whites in to lighten the base. Add the remaining whites and fold them in as lightly as possible by cutting down with the spatula to the bottom of the bowl and then turning the mixture over, while rotating the bowl.

5 ▲ Spoon the mixture into the prepared dish. Bake in a preheated oven until the soufflé has risen about 2 inches above the rim of the dish and is lightly browned. Serve the soufflé immediately because it will only hold its puff out of the oven for a few minutes before it begins to deflate.

Separating Eggs
It is easier to separate the yolks and whites if eggs are cold, so take the eggs straight from the refrigerator. Tap the egg once or twice against the rim of a small bowl to crack the shell. Break open the shell and hold half in each hand. Carefully transfer the unbroken yolk from one half shell to the other several times, letting the egg white dribble into the bowl. Put the yolk in a second bowl.

Cheese Soufflé
Butter a 1½-quart soufflé dish and coat it with fine bread crumbs. Make 1 cup thick blond or béchamel sauce (page 170). Add 4 egg yolks and 1 cup grated sharp cheese (Swiss, Cheddar, blue, or a mixture of Parmesan and Swiss cheeses). If desired, season with 2 teaspoons Dijon-style mustard. Beat 6 egg whites until they hold stiff peaks; fold into the sauce base. Bake in a preheated 400°F oven 20–25 minutes. *Serves 4.*

Amaretto Soufflé

SERVES 6

6 amaretti cookies, coarsely crushed
6 tablespoons Amaretto liqueur
4 eggs, separated, plus 1 egg white
7 tablespoons sugar
2 tablespoons flour
1 cup milk
pinch of cream of tartar (if needed)
confectioners' sugar, for decorating

1 Preheat the oven to 400°F. Butter a 1½-quart soufflé dish and sprinkle the inside with superfine sugar.

2 Put the cookies in a bowl. Sprinkle them with 2 tablespoons of the Amaretto liqueur and set aside.

3 ▲ Mix together the 4 egg yolks, 2 tablespoons of the sugar, and the flour.

4 ▲ Heat the milk just to a boil in a heavy saucepan. Gradually add the hot milk to the egg mixture, stirring.

5 Pour the mixture back into the saucepan. Set over medium-low heat and simmer gently until thickened, 3–4 minutes, stirring constantly.

6 ▲ Add the remaining Amaretto liqueur. Remove from the heat.

7 In a scrupulously clean, greasefree bowl, beat the 5 egg whites until they will hold soft peaks. (If not using a copper bowl, add the cream of tartar as soon as the whites are frothy.) Add the remaining sugar and continue beating until stiff.

8 Add about one-quarter of the whites to the liqueur mixture and stir in with a rubber spatula. Add the remaining whites and fold in gently.

9 Spoon half of the mixture into the prepared soufflé dish. Cover with a layer of the moistened amaretti cookies, then spoon the remaining soufflé mixture on top.

10 Bake until the soufflé is risen and lightly browned, about 20 minutes. Sprinkle with sifted confectioners' sugar and serve immediately.

~ **COOK'S TIP** ~

Some people like soufflés to be completely cooked. Others prefer a soft, creamy center. The choice is up to you. To check the degree of doneness, quickly insert a skewer into the center: it will come out almost clean or with moist particles clinging to it.

MAKING SIMPLE MERINGUE

There are two types of this egg-white-and-sugar foam: a soft meringue used as an insulating topping for pies and baked Alaska and a firm meringue that can be shaped into containers or cake layers for luscious fillings.

Take care when separating the egg whites and yolks because even the smallest trace of yolk will prevent the whites from being beaten to their maximum volume. All equipment used must be scrupulously clean and free of grease.

Meringue Nests
Make a firm meringue using 2 egg whites and ½ cup superfine sugar. Spoon large mounds of meringue onto a baking sheet lined with parchment paper. Slightly hollow out the center of each with the back of the spoon, to make a nest shape. Alternatively, put the meringue into a pastry bag fitted with a ½-inch plain tip and pipe the nest shapes. Sprinkle lightly with a little extra sugar. Dry in a preheated 200°F oven until crisp and firm to the touch but not brown, 3–4 hours. Let cool. To serve, fill with sweetened whipped cream and fresh berries or other fruit. *Makes 4–6.*

1 ▲ Put the egg whites in a large, scrupulously clean and greasefree bowl. With a whisk or electric mixer, beat the whites until they are foamy. If not using a copper bowl, add a pinch of cream of tartar.

3 ▲ For a soft meringue: Sprinkle the sugar over the whites, beating constantly. Continue beating until the meringue is glossy and holds stiff peaks when the whisk or beaters are lifted, about 1 minute. The meringue is now ready to be spread over a pie filling or used for baked Alaska.

Sweetened Whipped Cream
This is used as a topping and filling for many hot and cold desserts. Whip 1 cup chilled whipping cream until it starts to thicken. Add 2 tablespoons sifted confectioners' sugar and continue whipping until the cream holds a soft peak on the beaters. If desired, the cream may be flavored with ½ teaspoon vanilla extract, ¼ teaspoon almond extract, or 2 teaspoons Cognac or liqueur, added with the sugar.

2 ▲ Continue beating until the whites hold soft peaks when the whisk or beaters are lifted (the tips of the peaks will flop over).

4 ▲ For a firm meringue: Add a little of the sugar (about ½ tablespoon for each egg white). Continue beating until the meringue is glossy and holds stiff peaks.

5 ▲ Add the remaining sugar to the bowl, with a flavoring if the recipe directs. With a rubber spatula, fold the sugar into the meringue as lightly as possible by cutting down with the spatula to the bottom of the bowl and then turning the mixture over. The meringue is now ready to be shaped into containers or cake layers.

Lemon Meringue Pie

SERVES 6–8

1⅓ cups sugar

¼ cup cornstarch

pinch of salt

2 teaspoons finely grated lemon rind

½ cup fresh lemon juice

1 cup water

3 eggs, separated

3 tablespoons butter

9-inch pie shell, made from basic pie pastry (page 222) or tart pastry (page 230), baked "blind" (page 232)

pinch of cream of tartar (if needed)

1 ▼ Combine 1 cup sugar, the cornstarch, salt, and lemon rind in a saucepan. Stir in the lemon juice and water until smoothly blended.

2 Bring to a boil over medium-high heat, stirring constantly. Simmer until thickened, about 1 minute.

3 Blend in the egg yolks. Cook over medium-low heat about 2 minutes longer, stirring constantly.

4 Remove from the heat. Add the butter and mix well.

5 ▲ Pour the lemon filling into the pie shell. Spread it evenly and smooth the surface. Let cool completely.

6 Preheat the oven to 350°F.

7 In a scrupulously clean, greasefree bowl, beat the egg whites until they will hold soft peaks. (If not using a copper bowl, add the cream of tartar as soon as the whites are frothy.) Add the remaining sugar and continue beating until stiff and glossy.

8 ▲ Spread the meringue evenly over the filling. Take care to seal it to the edges of the pie shell all around.

9 Bake until the meringue is just set and lightly golden brown on the surface, 10–15 minutes. Let cool before serving.

~ COOK'S TIP ~

Egg whites can be beaten to their greatest volume if they are at room temperature rather than cold. A copper bowl and wire balloon whisk are the best tools to use, although a stainless steel bowl and electric mixer produce very good results. Take care not to overbeat whites (they will start to look grainy and then will separate into lumps and liquid). Using a copper bowl helps produce a stable foam that is hard to overbeat; adding a pinch of cream of tartar has the same effect.

MAKING A BATTER

Batters consist mainly of flour, eggs, and liquid. They may be thick – for making fritters or coating food to be fried – or thin and pourable, for pancakes, waffles, and crêpes. For a very light result, the eggs can be separated and the whites beaten and folded in.

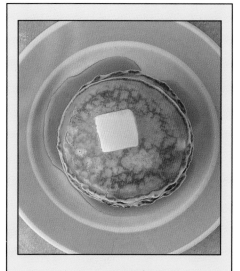

Perfect Pancakes
Make the batter with 1¾ cups flour, 3 tablespoons sugar, 2 teaspoons baking powder, ½ teaspoon salt, 2 eggs, 1¼ cups milk, and 3 tablespoons melted butter. Put the batter in a pitcher for easy pouring, or ladle it from the bowl. Heat a lightly oiled frying pan or griddle over medium heat. It is ready for cooking when a few drops of water sprinkled on the surface jump and sizzle immediately. Pour the batter onto the hot surface, using 3–4 tablespoons for each pancake and keeping them spaced well apart. Cook until about half of the bubbles on the surface have popped and the edges of the pancakes are slightly dry. Turn the pancakes over and cook until the other side is golden brown, about 1 minute. Serve the pancakes hot, with butter and maple syrup, or a syrup of your choice. *Serves 4–6.*

1 ▲ Sift the flour into a bowl along with other dry ingredients such as sugar, baking powder or soda, salt, spices, etc.

2 ▲ Make a well in the center of the dry ingredients and put in the eggs or egg yolks and some of the liquid.

3 ▲ With a wooden spoon, beat together the eggs and liquid in the well just to mix them.

4 ▲ Gradually draw in some of the flour from the sides, stirring vigorously.

5 ▲ When the mixture is smooth, stir in the remaining liquid. The trick is not to overmix – stir just until the ingredients are combined.

6 ▲ If the recipe directs, beat egg whites to a soft peak and fold them into the batter. Do this just before using the batter.

MAKING CRÊPES

These thin, lacy French pancakes are wonderfully versatile. They can be served very simply with just lemon juice and sugar, or turned into more elaborate dishes: folded and warmed in a sauce, rolled around a savory or sweet filling, or stacked in layers like a cake with filling between.

MAKES ABOUT 12

1 cup flour

2 teaspoons sugar (for sweet crêpes)

2 extra large eggs

about 1½ cups milk

2 tablespoons melted butter, plus more for frying (or oil, for frying)

Crêpes with Ricotta and Peaches
Combine 2 cups ricotta cheese, ¼ cup confectioners' sugar, 1 teaspoon vanilla extract, and 2 tablespoons brandy in a bowl. Mix well. Add 4 large, ripe peaches, peeled and diced, and fold in gently. Divide the ricotta and peach mixture among 12 crêpes and spread it evenly over them. Fold each crêpe in half and then in half again, into quarters. Arrange the crêpes in a buttered large oval baking dish, slightly overlapping them. Brush with 2 tablespoons melted butter and sprinkle generously with confectioners' sugar. Bake in a preheated 375°F oven for 10 minutes. Serve the crêpes hot, with raspberry sauce (page 194). *Serves 4.*

1 ▲ Make the crêpe batter and let stand at least 20 minutes. Heat an 8-inch crêpe pan over medium heat. The pan is ready for cooking when a few drops of water sprinkled on the surface sizzle immediately. Grease the pan lightly with melted butter or oil. Ladle or pour 3–4 tablespoons batter into the pan. Quickly tilt and rotate the pan so that the batter spreads out to cover the bottom thinly and evenly; pour out any excess batter.

3 ▲ **To fill crêpes:** For folded crêpes, spread 3–4 tablespoons of filling evenly over each crêpe. Fold in half, then in half again, into quarters. For rolled crêpes, put 3–4 tablespoons of filling near one edge of each crêpe and roll up tightly from that side. To make packages, spoon 3–4 tablespoons of filling in the center of each crêpe. Fold in 2 opposite sides, over the filling, then fold in the other 2 sides. Turn the package over before serving or putting in a baking dish. Filled crêpes are usually baked before serving to heat them through and to brown any topping that may be added.

2 ▲ Cook until the crêpe is set and small holes have appeared, 30–45 seconds. If the cooking seems to be taking too long, increase the heat slightly. Lift the edge of the crêpe with a metal spatula; the base of the crêpe should be lightly brown. Shake the pan vigorously back and forth to loosen the crêpe completely, then turn or flip it over. Cook the other side about 30 seconds. Stack cooked crêpes until ready to fill.

Crêpe-Making Tips
• Crêpe batter should be made at least 20 minutes before using. Refrigerate if holding it longer.
• The batter can be made in a blender or food processor. It must have time to stand before using, as this method incorporates more air.
• Crêpe batter should be the consistency of heavy cream. If it doesn't flow smoothly to make a thin crêpe, add a little more liquid.
• If the batter is lumpy, strain it.
• For best results use a crêpe pan, with a flat bottom and sides that angle straight out without curving.
• Your first crêpe may well be unsuccessful because it will test the consistency of the batter and the temperature of the pan, both of which may need adjusting.
• If more convenient, make crêpes ahead of time. Stack them up as you make them, layered with waxed paper. Let cool completely, then wrap in foil. Refrigerate up to 3 days or freeze for 1 month.

MAKING STIRRED CUSTARD

A homemade stirred custard is a luscious sauce for many hot and cold desserts. It is also the basis for a very rich ice cream, which is essentially a frozen stirred custard enriched with cream.

The secret for success is patience. Don't try to hurry the cooking of the custard by raising the heat.

MAKES ABOUT 2 CUPS

2 cups milk
1 vanilla bean, split in half
4 egg yolks
3–4 tablespoons sugar

Custard Variations
- Use 1 teaspoon vanilla extract instead of the vanilla bean. Omit steps 1 and 2, and add the extract after straining the custard.
- For *Chocolate Custard*: Add 2 ounces semisweet chocolate, grated, to the hot milk and sugar mixture. Stir until smooth before adding to the egg yolks.
- For *Mocha Custard*: Add 2 ounces semisweet chocolate, grated, and 2 teaspoons instant coffee powder or granules.
- For *Orange Custard*: Omit the vanilla bean and instead infuse the milk with the finely pared rind of 1 orange.
- For *Liqueur Custard*: Add 2–3 tablespoons Cognac, kirsch, or other liqueur to the custard.

Damage Repair
If the custard gets too hot and starts to curdle, remove it from the heat immediately and pour it into a bowl. Whisk vigorously until smooth, 2–3 seconds. Then pour it back into the pan and continue cooking.

1 ▲ Put the milk in a heavy-based saucepan. Hold the vanilla bean over the pan and scrape out the tiny black seeds into the milk. Add the split bean to the milk.

3 ▲ In a bowl, lightly beat the egg yolks with the sugar until smoothly blended and creamy. Gradually add the hot milk to the egg yolks, stirring constantly.

5 ▲ Cook, stirring constantly, until the custard thickens to a creamy consistency that coats the spoon, 10–12 minutes. Immediately remove the pan of custard from over the pan of hot water.

2 ▲ Heat the milk until bubbles appear around the edge. Remove from the heat, cover, and set aside to infuse 10 minutes. Remove the split vanilla bean.

4 ▲ Pour the mixture into the top of a double boiler. Set over the bottom pan containing hot water. Put on a medium-low heat, so the water stays below a boil.

6 ▲ Strain the custard into a bowl. If using cold, sprinkle a little superfine sugar over the surface of the custard to help prevent a skin from forming. Set the bowl in a container of ice water and let cool.

English Trifle

SERVES 6 OR MORE

6 cups 1-inch cubes of spongecake (page 244), pound cake (page 238), or coarsely crumbled ladyfingers
¼ cup cream sherry wine
⅓ cup raspberry preserves
1 pint raspberries
2 cups stirred custard, flavored with 2 tablespoons cream sherry
¾ cup sweetened whipped cream (page 160)
toasted sliced almonds and mint leaves, for garnishing

1 Spread half of the cake cubes or ladyfingers over the bottom of a large serving bowl. (A glass bowl is best for presentation.)

2 ▲ Sprinkle half of the sherry over the cake to moisten it. Spoon over half of the preserves, dotting them evenly over the cake cubes.

3 ▲ Reserve a few raspberries for garnish. Make a layer of half of the remaining raspberries on top.

4 ▼ Pour over half of the custard, covering the fruit and cake. Repeat the layers. Cover and chill for at least 2 hours.

5 ▲ Before serving, spoon the sweetened whipped cream evenly over the top. To decorate, sprinkle with toasted almonds and arrange the reserved raspberries and the mint leaves on the top.

~ VARIATIONS ~

If preferred, use other fruit in the trifle, with preserves and liqueur to suit: apricots, strawberries, etc.

COOKING IN A WATER BATH

Setting a dish in a pan of water for cooking insures that delicate mixtures, such as custards and baked eggs, do not overheat and curdle. The pan of water, called a water bath or "bain marie," can be used on top of the stove or in the oven.

A double boiler is a type of water bath, where the pan containing the delicate mixture – stirred custard for example – is set over hot water rather than in it.

1 ◄ Set the dish or dishes in a roasting pan or a wide shallow saucepan. Pour enough water into the pan to come halfway up the sides of the dishes. Set the pan over medium-high heat and bring the water almost to a boil. Reduce the heat so the water is just simmering, or not moving at all, according to recipe directions. Or, if directed, transfer the dishes, in the water bath, to the oven to finish cooking.

Baked Custard with Praline Topping

SERVES 6

2 cups whipping cream
4 egg yolks
¼ cup granulated sugar
1 teaspoon vanilla extract
¼ cup superfine sugar
¼ cup minced pecans

1 Preheat the oven to 300°F.

2 Heat the cream in a saucepan until bubbles form around the edge.

3 Meanwhile, beat the egg yolks with the granulated sugar until the mixture is pale and creamy. Gradually stir the hot cream into the egg yolk mixture. Stir in the vanilla.

4 Strain the mixture into a pitcher. Pour it into 6 ramekins. Set the ramekins in a water bath and bring the water to a boil on top of the stove.

5 Transfer to the oven and bake until the custards are just set, 20–25 minutes. Remove from the water bath and let cool. Cover and chill.

6 Preheat the broiler.

7 Mix together the superfine sugar and the pecans. Sprinkle over the tops of the custards in an even layer.

8 ▲ Set the ramekins in a baking pan containing ice water. Broil, about 5 inches from the heat, until the sugar has melted and caramelized. Turn the ramekins so the sugar browns evenly. Let cool and set before serving.

SAUCES

~

A sauce can make plain food memorable, and most sauces are quick and easy. A simple flavored butter gives fish a lift. Or vary a basic white sauce with cheese, mushrooms, or herbs to enliven a casserole or baked pasta.

MAKING BASIC WHITE SAUCE

Some modern chefs consider flour-thickened sauces old-fashioned and replace them with butter sauces, reduction sauces, or sauces using vegetable purées or cream. But a basic white sauce is essential in many dishes, and lends itself to endless variation. This recipe makes a medium-thick sauce that coats food.

MAKES ABOUT 2 CUPS

3 tablespoons butter
3 tablespoons flour
2 cups milk
⅛ teaspoon grated nutmeg
salt and pepper

1 ▲ Melt the butter in a heavy saucepan over low heat. Remove the pan from the heat and stir in the flour to make a smooth, soft paste (called a "roux" in French).

2 ▲ Add about one-quarter of the milk and mix it in well with a whisk. When it is smooth, mix in the remaining milk.

3 ▲ Set the pan over medium-high heat and bring to a boil, whisking constantly.

Saucemaking Tips

● A whisk will blend the mixture more thoroughly than a spoon and will help avoid lumps. In the event of a lumpy sauce, pour it into a fine-mesh strainer and push it through, then reheat it, whisking constantly.

● White sauces can be made ahead of time. Pour the sauce into a bowl or other container, dab the surface with butter, and let cool. Cover and refrigerate up to 2 days. Before serving, whisk over medium heat until boiling.

4 ▲ When the sauce bubbles and starts to thicken, reduce the heat to very low and simmer gently, whisking well from time to time, for 5–10 minutes. The sauce will continue to thicken slightly. Add the nutmeg and season to taste with salt and pepper.

White Sauce Variations

● For *Thin White Sauce* (to use as a base for cream soups or with creamed vegetables or meat): Use 2 tablespoons butter and 2 tablespoons flour to 2 cups milk.

● For *Thick White Sauce* (to use as a soufflé base or to bind croquettes): Use 6 tablespoons butter and ⅓ cup flour to 2 cups milk.

● For *Blond Sauce*: Add the flour to the melted butter and cook, stirring constantly, until the roux is a pale beige color, 1–2 minutes. Heat the liquid before adding it, off the heat. Bring to a boil, whisking, and simmer 3–5 minutes.

● For *Velouté Sauce*: Cook the roux as for a blond sauce until it is lightly browned and smells nutty, about 3 minutes. Use hot chicken or fish stock, or a mixture of stock and wine, instead of milk.

● For *Béchamel Sauce*: Heat the milk with a slice of onion, 1 bay leaf, and a few black peppercorns until scalded. Remove from the heat, cover, and let infuse 20 minutes. Strain before adding to the roux, made as for blond sauce.

● For *Cream Sauce*: Substitute cream for ½–1 cup of the milk.

● For *Cheese Sauce*: Stir 1–2 cups shredded cheese and 1–2 teaspoons spicy brown mustard into white, blond, or béchamel sauce; add a pinch of cayenne instead of the nutmeg. Choose a well-flavored cheese that melts easily.

● For *Mustard Sauce*: Stir 1 tablespoon Dijon-style mustard and ½ teaspoon sugar into white, blond, or béchamel sauce.

● For *Mushroom Sauce*: Cook 2 cups sliced mushrooms in 1–2 tablespoons butter until soft; continue cooking until excess liquid has evaporated. Add to white, blond, béchamel, velouté, or cheese sauce.

MAKING ICE CREAM

At its most basic, homemade ice cream is just frozen cream, sweetened and flavored. More often it has a stirred custard base enriched with cream. Flavorings range from ever-popular vanilla and chocolate to fresh fruit and liqueur, and many others.

An electric ice cream machine makes light work of the task of churning and freezing ice cream. Models and capacities vary, so follow the manufacturer's instructions.

1 Make a stirred custard, using cream or a mixture of milk and cream. For ice cream, the custard should be quite sweet. Strain and leave to cool.

2 ▶ Pour into an ice cream machine and freeze following manufacturer's instructions. Serve as soon as possible after making. If the ice cream is left in the freezer and becomes very hard, let it soften for 20 minutes at room temperature before serving.

Old-Fashioned Chocolate Ice Cream

MAKES ABOUT 1 QUART

| 3 cups whipping cream |
| 1 cup milk |
| 1 vanilla bean, split in half |
| ¾ cup granulated sugar |
| 4 ounces semisweet chocolate, grated |
| 4 egg yolks |
| ½ teaspoon superfine sugar |

1 Put 1 cup of the whipping cream and all of the milk in a heavy-based saucepan with the vanilla bean. Heat until bubbles appear around the edge.

2 ▲ Off the heat, add the granulated sugar and the chocolate, then heat the mixture almost to boiling point, stirring until smooth.

3 In a bowl, lightly beat the egg yolks until smooth. Add the hot mixture to the egg yolks, stirring constantly.

4 Pour into the top of a double boiler set over hot water. Cook, stirring constantly, until the custard thickens enough to coat the spoon. Strain into a bowl and stir in the remaining cream. Sprinkle the surface with superfine sugar. Let cool to room temperature.

5 Pour into an ice cream machine and freeze.

Ice Cream Variations
- For *Rich Vanilla Ice Cream*: Omit the chocolate.
- For *Strawberry Ice Cream*: Omit chocolate. Mash 1½ pints hulled strawberries with a little lemon juice and 2–3 tablespoons sugar. Add before freezing.
- For *Peach Ice Cream*: Omit the chocolate. Mash 6 large ripe peaches, peeled and pitted. Add to custard before freezing.

Moussaka

SERVES 4–6

2 eggplants, weighing about 1½ pounds, trimmed and sliced crosswise
about ½ cup olive oil
1 large onion, chopped
1–2 garlic cloves, minced
1½ pounds ground lean lamb
1 cup peeled, seeded, and chopped tomatoes or canned crushed tomatoes
2 tablespoons chopped fresh parsley
1 tablespoon chopped fresh marjoram, or 1 teaspoon dried oregano
½ teaspoon ground cinnamon
2 tablespoons tomato paste
salt and pepper
2 cups hot white or blond sauce
1 egg yolk

1 Preheat the broiler.

2 ▲ Spread out the eggplant slices on a large baking sheet and brush them with a little oil. Broil until lightly browned and beginning to soften. Turn the eggplant slices over and brush the other side with oil. Broil until lightly browned and soft.

~ **VARIATION** ~

Use leftover roast lamb or beef, minced, instead of fresh ground lamb.

3 Meanwhile, heat 2 tablespoons oil in a frying pan and cook the onion, stirring occasionally, until soft.

4 ▲ Add the garlic and lamb and cook until the meat is browned and crumbly, stirring frequently. Stir in the tomatoes. Bring the mixture to a boil and simmer until the excess liquid has evaporated.

5 Add the herbs, cinnamon, and tomato paste. Season to taste with salt and pepper.

6 Preheat the oven to 375°F.

7 Layer the lamb mixture and the eggplant slices in a baking dish, starting with meat and ending with eggplant slices.

8 ▼ Mix together the sauce and egg yolk. Pour this over the top layer of eggplant slices in an even layer.

9 Bake until the sauce is golden and the moussaka is bubbling, about 30 minutes. Serve hot, in the baking dish.

MAKING BASIC TOMATO SAUCE

Tomato sauce is a useful standby to have on hand in the refrigerator or freezer. When tomatoes are in season make a large batch. At other times of the year, use canned whole Italian plum tomatoes (drain, cut in half, scrape out seeds, and chop).

MAKES ABOUT 2½ CUPS

2 tablespoons butter
4 cups peeled, seeded, and finely chopped tomatoes
¼–½ teaspoon sugar
salt and pepper

1 ▲ Melt the butter in a heavy-based saucepan over low heat. Add the tomatoes and stir to mix with the butter. Cover and cook 5 minutes.

2 ▲ Uncover and stir in the sugar. Partly cover the pan and let simmer gently, stirring occasionally, until the tomatoes have softened and the sauce is thick, about 30 minutes.

3 ▲ Season the sauce to taste with salt and pepper. Use immediately, or cool and then refrigerate or freeze.

Eggs Baked in Tomato Sauce
For each serving, put 1½ tablespoons of tomato sauce in a lightly buttered ramekin. Break an egg into the ramekin and sprinkle with pepper to taste and 1 tablespoon of freshly grated Parmesan or Cheddar cheese. Put the ramekins in a baking dish and add cold water to come halfway up the sides of the ramekins. Bring to a boil on top of the stove, then transfer to a pre-heated 400°F oven and bake until the eggs are set, about 5–7 minutes. Serve immediately.

Tomato Sauce Variations
- For *Rich Tomato Sauce*: Stir another 1–2 tablespoons butter into the sauce before serving.
- For *Smooth Tomato Sauce*: Purée in a blender or food processor.
- For *Tomato-Garlic Sauce*: Use 1 tablespoon olive oil instead of butter. In a separate small pan, cook 1–2 minced garlic cloves in 1 tablespoon olive oil until soft, about 1 minute. Add this garlic oil to the tomato sauce for the last 5 minutes of cooking.
- For *Tomato-Herb Sauce*: Stir ¼–½ cup minced fresh herbs (parsley, basil, chives, thyme, oregano, marjoram – singly or a mixture) into tomato sauce or tomato-garlic sauce before serving.
- For *Italian Tomato Sauce*: Mince 1 onion, 1 small carrot, and 1 celery stalk. Cook in 2 table-spoons olive oil until soft. Add 1–2 minced garlic cloves and cook 1 minute longer. Add the tomatoes with 1 bay leaf and 1 large sprig of fresh rosemary or ½ teaspoon crumbled dried rose-mary. Continue cooking as for tomato sauce. Discard the bay leaf and rosemary stem before serving.
- For *Tomato-Wine Sauce*: Mince 3 shallots or ½ onion and cook in 2 tablespoons butter or olive oil until soft. Add 1 minced garlic clove and cook 1 minute longer. Stir in ½ cup dry white wine, bring to a boil, and boil until almost completely evaporated. Add the tomatoes and continue cooking as for tomato sauce. If a smooth sauce is wanted, purée in a blender or food processor.
- For *Tomato-Mushroom Sauce*: Slice ½–¾ pound mushrooms and fry in the butter, adding more if needed, until lightly browned. Add the tomatoes and continue cooking as for tomato sauce.

Pasta with Tomato Sauce and Roasted Vegetables

SERVES 4

1 eggplant

2 zucchini

1 large onion

2 red or yellow bell peppers, seeded

1 pound tomatoes, preferably plum-type

2–3 garlic cloves, coarsely chopped

¼ cup olive oil

salt and pepper

1 cup smooth tomato sauce

⅓ cup halved black olives

¾–1 pound dried pasta shapes, such as
   rigatoni or penne

¼ cup shredded fresh basil

Parmesan or Romano cheese, for serving

1 Preheat the oven to 500°F.

2 ▲ Cut the eggplant, zucchini, onion, bell peppers, and tomatoes into 1½-inch chunks. Discard the tomato seeds.

3 ▲ Spread out the vegetables in a large roasting pan. Sprinkle the garlic and oil over the vegetables and stir and turn to mix evenly. Season with salt and pepper.

4 Roast the vegetables until they are soft and browned (don't worry if the edges are charred black), about 30 minutes. Stir halfway through.

5 ▼ Scrape the vegetable mixture into a saucepan. Add the tomato sauce and olives.

6 Bring a large pot of water to a boil. Add the pasta and cook until it is just tender to the bite ("al dente").

7 Meanwhile, heat the tomato and roasted vegetable sauce. Taste and adjust the seasoning.

8 Drain the pasta and return it to the pot. Add the tomato and roasted vegetable sauce and mix to combine well. Serve hot, sprinkled with the basil. If desired, serve with freshly grated Parmesan or Romano cheese.

Making Flavored Butters

A pat of flavored butter melting over hot, freshly cooked vegetables, meat, or seafood is an impressive finishing touch. Yet flavored butters are so easy to make. They can be used as a spread for sandwiches or canapés, too. In addition to savory flavored butters, you can make sweet butters to serve with pancakes, waffles, and warm breads and rolls.

Makes about ½ cup

1 stick (8 tablespoons) butter, preferably unsalted, at room temperature
flavoring of choice (see butter flavorings)
salt and pepper (for savory butters)

Butter Flavorings
- For *Herb Butter*: Use 2–4 tablespoons minced fresh herbs (parsley, chives, tarragon, thyme, marjoram, mint, etc.), singly or in combinations of 2 or 3, and a squeeze of lemon juice.
- For *Mustard Butter*: Use 1 tablespoon Dijon-style mustard or spicy brown mustard.
- For *Citrus Butter*: Use 2 teaspoons orange or lime juice, or 1 teaspoon lemon juice, and the grated rind of 1 orange, lime, or lemon (or 2 limes, if small).
- For *Cilantro-Lime Butter*: Mince 1 cup loosely packed fresh coriander leaves (cilantro). Mix into the soft butter with the grated rind and juice of 1 lime.
- For *Parsley and Lemon Butter* ("beurre maître d'hôtel"): Use 2 tablespoons minced parsley and 1 tablespoon lemon juice.
- For *Tomato Butter*: Use 1 tablespoon tomato paste.
- For *Garlic Butter*: Use 1–2 minced garlic cloves.
- For *Sweet Orange Butter*: Use 1–2 tablespoons confectioners' sugar, 2 teaspoons orange juice, and the grated rind of 1 orange.
- For *Honey Butter*: Use ¼ cup honey; beat in gradually.
- For *Maple Butter*: Use ¼ cup maple syrup; beat in gradually.
- For *Cinnamon Butter*: Use 1–2 tablespoons confectioners' sugar and ½ teaspoon ground cinnamon.
- For *Almond Butter*: Use ¼ cup finely ground almonds.

1 ▲ For a savory butter: Put the butter in a mixing bowl and beat with a wooden spoon or electric mixer until soft. Add the flavoring. Season savory butters to taste with salt and pepper. Blend well.

2 ▲ Transfer the butter to a piece of wax paper and shape it into a neat roll, handling it as little as possible because the heat of your hands can melt it. Wrap and refrigerate until firm. Cut the roll into neat disks.

3 ▲ Alternatively, flatten with the back of a spoon or knife until it is about ¼-inch thick. Refrigerate until firm, and stamp out small rounds or other shapes using a cookie cutter.

4 ▲ For a sweet butter: Put the butter in a mixing bowl and beat with an electric mixer or wooden spoon until fluffy. Add the flavoring and blend well. Spoon into a serving bowl, cover, and refrigerate until firm.

Freezing Flavored Butters
Flavored butters can be frozen and then used straight from the freezer. Wrap the paper-wrapped roll in foil for storage.

Fish Steaks with Cilantro-Lime Butter

SERVES 4

1½ pounds swordfish or mahimahi steak, 1-inch thick, cut into 4 pieces

¼ cup vegetable oil

2 tablespoons lemon juice

1 tablespoon lime juice

salt and pepper

4 tablespoons cilantro-lime butter

1 ▲ Lay the fish steaks side by side in a shallow dish. Combine the oil, juices, salt, and pepper and pour over the fish. Cover and refrigerate 1–2 hours, turning the fish once or twice.

2 Preheat the broiler or prepare a charcoal fire.

3 ▼ Drain the fish and arrange on the rack in the broiler pan, or set on the grill over the hot coals. Broil or grill about 5 inches from the heat until just firm to the touch but still moist in the center, 3–4 minutes. Turn the steaks over once.

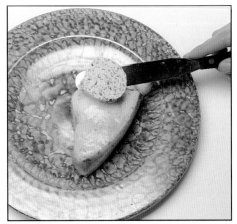

~ **VARIATIONS** ~

For Salmon Steaks with Citrus Butter, brush 4 1-inch-thick salmon steaks lightly with oil on both sides and season. Broil or grill 4–5 minutes on each side. Top with citrus butter to serve. For Mackerel Fillets with Mustard Butter, brush 4 unskinned mackerel fillets (about 8 ounces each) with oil and season. Broil or grill 3–4 minutes on each side. Top with mustard butter to serve.

4 ▲ When done, transfer to warmed plates and top each fish steak with a pat of the cilantro-lime butter. Serve immediately.

MAKING CLARIFIED BUTTER

Also known as drawn butter, this is butter from which the milk solids have been removed. The result is a clear yellow fat that can be heated to a higher temperature than ordinary butter without burning.

This makes clarified butter excellent for pan-frying. It is also used as a dip for seafood, such as lobster and crab, and globe artichokes.

MAKES ABOUT ¾ CUP

2 sticks (1 cup) butter

Keeping Butter Longer
Since clarification removes impurities, clarified butter keeps well – several weeks in the refrigerator, longer in the freezer.

1 ▲ Put the butter in a heavy saucepan over low heat. Melt gently. Skim off all the froth from the surface. You will then see a clear yellow layer on top of a milky layer.

2 Carefully pour the clear fat into a bowl or measure. Stop pouring when you reach the milky layer, leaving it in the pan. Discard the milky residue, or add it to soups.

Lobster Tail with Drawn Butter
Drop 4 ½-pound raw lobster tails (thawed if frozen) into a large pot of boiling salted water. Bring back to a boil and simmer until the shells are bright red and the meat is opaque, 8–12 minutes. Drain and serve hot, with clarified butter. *Serves 4.*

Chicken Liver Pâté

SERVES 6 OR MORE

4 tablespoons butter

1 onion, minced

¾ pound chicken livers, trimmed of all dark or greenish parts

¼ cup medium or cream sherry wine

2 tablespoons cream cheese

1–2 tablespoons lemon juice

2 hard-boiled eggs, chopped

salt and pepper

4–6 tablespoons clarified butter

1 Melt the butter in a frying pan. Add the onion and livers and cook until the onion is soft and the livers are lightly browned and no longer pink in the center.

2 Add the sherry and boil until reduced by half. Let cool slightly.

3 ▲ Turn the mixture into a blender or food processor and add the cream cheese and 1 tablespoon lemon juice. Blend until smooth.

4 Add the hard-boiled eggs to the mixture and blend briefly. Season to taste with salt and pepper, and add more lemon juice if desired.

5 ▼ Pack the liver pâté into a mold or individual ramekins. Smooth the top with a knife or metal spatula.

6 Spoon a layer of clarified butter over the surface of the pâté. Refrigerate until firm. Serve at room temperature, with hot toast, crackers, or French bread.

MAKING SIMPLIFIED HOLLANDAISE SAUCE

This classic of French cuisine has a reputation for being difficult to make. It does require care: if the sauce becomes too hot, it will separate. However, a method proposed by Harold McGee, of putting all the ingredients in the pan at once – rather than the traditional method of cooking the egg yolks to thicken them and then slowly beating in melted butter – lowers the chance of failure. Just take it slow, and beat constantly.

MAKES ABOUT 1¼ CUPS

3 egg yolks

1 tablespoon lemon juice, plus more if needed

pinch of cayenne

salt and pepper

2 sticks (1 cup) butter, preferably unsalted, cut into 1-tablespoon chunks

Saucemaking Tips
● If your sauce does separate into soft curds and clear butterfat, don't despair. As long as the egg yolks haven't scrambled, you can rescue the sauce. Remove the pan from the heat, add 1–2 teaspoons of water, and whisk vigorously. If the sauce doesn't re-form and become creamy, put 1–2 teaspoons of water in a bowl and whisk in the separated sauce, drop by drop at first and then in a thin stream.
● Hollandaise and Béarnaise sauces can be kept warm for up to 30 minutes before serving. Set the saucepan in a water bath (a roasting pan half-filled with hot water) over very low heat, or on a warming tray, and whisk occasionally. Alternatively, they can be made 2–3 hours ahead and kept in a wide-mouth thermos container until serving.

1 ▲ Combine the egg yolks, lemon juice, cayenne, salt, and pepper in a heavy saucepan. Whisk together until thoroughly blended.

3 ▲ When all the butter has melted and has been blended into the egg-yolk base, continue whisking until the sauce just thickens to a creamy consistency. Taste the sauce and add more lemon juice, salt, and pepper if needed.

2 ▲ Add the butter and set the pan over medium heat. Whisk constantly so that as the butter melts, it is blended into the egg-yolk base. Regulate the heat so it melts gradually.

The Hollandaise Family
● For *Mousseline Sauce*: Let the sauce cool slightly, then whisk in ½ cup whipped cream.
● For *Béarnaise Sauce*: Combine ⅓ cup white wine vinegar, 2 chopped shallots, 1 tablespoon chopped fresh tarragon or 1 teaspoon dried tarragon, and a little pepper in a small saucepan. Boil to reduce to about 1 tablespoon. Let cool. Continue as for Hollandaise sauce, using the strained vinegar reduction in place of the lemon juice. Before serving, stir in another ½–1 tablespoon chopped fresh tarragon, if desired.

Asparagus with Hollandaise Sauce
Trim the stalks of 1½ pounds asparagus, cutting off any woody ends, and peel, if desired. Arrange the asparagus spears on a rack in a steamer over simmering water, cover tightly, and steam until just tender when pierced with the tip of a knife, about 8–12 minutes. Transfer the asparagus to warmed plates and spoon over the Hollandaise sauce. *Serves 4.*

Eggs Benedict

SERVES 6

6 slices of ham, preferably country-style

6 eggs

3 English muffins, split in half

1¼ cups warm Hollandaise sauce

1 Preheat the broiler.

2 ▲ Cut rounds from the ham that are about the same diameter as the muffin halves.

3 ▲ Arrange the ham slices on the rack in the broiler pan. Broil until they are hot and golden brown.

4 Meanwhile, poach the eggs in barely simmering water, until done (the white just firm, but the yolk still soft), 3–4 minutes. Remove, drain, trim them if necessary, and keep warm.

5 ▼ Toast the muffin halves. Put one half, cut-side up, on each warmed plate. Arrange a slice of ham on the muffin and top with a poached egg.

6 Spoon the Hollandaise sauce over the egg and serve immediately.

~ **VARIATIONS** ~

If preferred, fry the ham in butter rather than broiling it. Use slices of Canadian bacon (2 per serving) instead of ham. Replace the ham with hot asparagus spears or sliced mushrooms sautéed in butter. If desired, use toasted rounds of brioche or whole-wheat bread instead of muffins.

MAKING MAYONNAISE

This cold emulsified sauce of oil and egg yolks has thousands of uses – as an integral part of a dish or as an accompaniment, in sandwiches and in salad dressings. It can be varied enormously by using different oils, vinegars, and flavorings.

MAKES ABOUT 1½ CUPS

2 egg yolks

salt and pepper

1½ cups oil (vegetable, corn, or olive)

1–2 tablespoons lemon juice or white wine vinegar

1–2 teaspoons Dijon-style mustard

1 ▲ Put the egg yolks in a bowl and add a pinch of salt. Beat together well.

2 ▲ Add the oil, 1–2 teaspoons at a time, beating constantly with a whisk or electric mixer.

3 ▲ After about one-quarter of the oil has been added very slowly and absorbed, beat in 1–2 teaspoons of the lemon juice or vinegar.

4 ▲ Continue beating in the oil, in a thin, steady stream now. As the mayonnaise thickens, add another teaspoon of lemon juice or vinegar.

5 ◄ When all the oil has been beaten in, add the mustard. Taste the mayonnaise and add more lemon juice or vinegar. Season with salt and pepper to taste. If the mayonnaise is too thick, beat in a spoonful or two of water. Homemade mayonnaise will keep, covered, in the refrigerator, for up to 1 week.

Mayonnaise Variations
● For *Garlic Mayonnaise*: Mince 3–6 garlic cloves. Beat with the egg yolks and salt. Beat in oil (vegetable and olive) as above.
● For *Spicy Mayonnaise*: Increase mustard to 1 tablespoon and add 1 teaspoon Worcestershire sauce and a dash of hot pepper sauce.
● For *Green Mayonnaise*: Combine 1 cup each parsley sprigs and watercress sprigs in a blender or food processor. Add 3–4 chopped scallions and 1 chopped garlic clove. Blend until coarse-fine. Add ½ cup mayonnaise and blend until smooth. Season to taste.
● For *Blue Cheese Dressing*: Mix ½ pound crumbled blue cheese into the mayonnaise; thin with milk.

Raw Egg Alert
Eggs can harbor salmonella bacteria, so there is some risk of food poisoning if you eat raw eggs (as in homemade mayonnaise) or undercooked eggs (as in Hollandaise sauce). The elderly, infants, pregnant women, and those who are ill are the most susceptible.

Seafood Salad with Garlic Mayonnaise
Make a bed of salad greens (green and red leaf lettuces, arugula, etc.) on 4 individual plates or in stemmed goblets. Arrange 6–8 ounces fresh white crabmeat and ½ pound cooked, peeled medium shrimp on top. Spoon garlic mayonnaise over the seafood and sprinkle with a little paprika. *Serves 4.*

Salmon Cakes with Spicy Mayonnaise

SERVES 4

2 boiling potatoes, about ¾ pound, unpeeled

¾ pound salmon fillet, skinned and minced

2–3 tablespoons chopped fresh dill

1 tablespoon lemon juice

salt and pepper

flour for coating

3 tablespoons vegetable oil

¾–1 cup spicy mayonnaise

1 Put the potatoes in a saucepan of boiling salted water and parboil them for 15 minutes.

2 ▲ Meanwhile, combine the salmon, dill, lemon juice, salt, and pepper in a large bowl.

3 Drain the potatoes and let them cool. When they are cool enough to handle, peel them.

4 Shred the potatoes into strips on the coarse side of a box grater.

~ **COOK'S TIP** ~

The potatoes will be sticky – it is their starch that helps hold the cakes together. If necessary, you can dampen your hands a little when shaping the cakes, but do not get the cakes too wet.

5 Add to the salmon mixture. Mix gently together with your fingers, breaking up the strips of potato as little as possible.

6 ▼ Divide the salmon and potato mixture into 8 portions. Shape each into a compact patty, pressing well together. Flatten the patties to about ⅜-inch thickness.

7 ▲ Coat the patties lightly with flour, shaking off excess.

8 Heat the oil in a large frying pan. Add the salmon cakes and fry until crisp and golden brown on both sides, about 5 minutes.

9 Drain the salmon cakes on paper towels, and serve with the spicy mayonnaise.

Making Vinaigrette Dressing

A good vinaigrette can do more than dress a salad. It can also be used to baste meat, poultry, seafood, or vegetables during cooking; and it can be used as a flavoring and tenderizing marinade. The basic mixture of oil, vinegar, and seasoning lends itself to many variations.

The basic vinaigrette dressing will keep in the refrigerator, in a tightly closed container, for several weeks. Add flavorings, particularly fresh herbs, just before serving.

A Handy Holder
If more convenient, you can make vinaigrette dressing in a screwtop jar. Combine all the ingredients in the jar, cover, and shake well to mix and emulsify.

Makes just over ¾ cup

3 tablespoons wine vinegar

salt and pepper

½ cup plus 2 tablespoons vegetable oil

1 ▲ Put the vinegar, salt, and pepper in a bowl and whisk together to dissolve the salt. Gradually add the oil, stirring with the whisk. Taste and add more salt and pepper if needed.

Varying the Ingredients
● Use red or white wine vinegar. Or, use herb- or fruit-flavored wine vinegar.
● Use lemon juice instead of vinegar.
● Replace 1 tablespoon of the vinegar with wine.
● Use olive oil, or a mixture of vegetable and olive oils.
● Use ½ cup olive oil and 2 tablespoons walnut or hazelnut oil.
● Add 1–2 tablespoons Dijon-style mustard to the vinegar before adding the oil.
● Add 1 minced garlic clove before whisking in the oil.
● Add 1–2 tablespoons minced fresh herbs (parsley, basil, chives, thyme, etc.) to the vinaigrette.

Orange Chicken Salad

Serves 4

3 large seedless oranges

1 cup rice

2 cups water

salt and pepper

¾ cup vinaigrette dressing, made with red wine vinegar and a mixture of olive and vegetable oils

½ teaspoon sugar

2 teaspoons Dijon-style mustard

4 cups diced cooked chicken

3 tablespoons scissor-snipped chives

½ cup toasted cashew nuts

cucumber slices, for garnishing

1 Thinly peel 1 orange, taking only the colored part of the rind and leaving the white pith; reserve the rind. Then peel off the white pith. Peel the remaining oranges.

2 Combine the orange rind, rice, and water in a saucepan. Add a pinch of salt. Bring to a boil, then cover and steam over very low heat until the rice is tender, 15–18 minutes.

3 ▼ Section the oranges: slide a knife down one side of a section along the dividing membrane, then down the other, cutting out each section. Reserve the sections and add the juice to the vinaigrette, then whisk in the sugar and mustard. Taste for seasoning.

4 When the rice is cooked, remove it from the heat and let it cool slightly, uncovered. Discard the orange rind.

5 Turn the rice into a bowl and add half of the dressing. Toss well and let cool completely.

6 ▲ Add the chicken, chives, cashews, and orange sections to the rice with the remaining dressing. Toss gently. Serve at room temperature, garnished with cucumber slices.

Fruit, Chocolate & Nuts

~

*Fruit, the focus of many desserts, and some main courses as
well, lends itself equally to homey or dramatic presentations.
And chocolate, everyone's favorite indulgence, is easy to use –
just follow a few simple rules. Nuts enhance them both.*

PREPARING FRESH FRUIT

PEELING AND TRIMMING FRUIT

Citrus fruit

To peel completely, cut a slice from the top and base. Set the fruit base down on a work surface. Using a small sharp knife, cut off the peel lengthwise in thick strips, taking the colored rind and all the white pith (which has a bitter taste). Cut following the curve of the fruit.

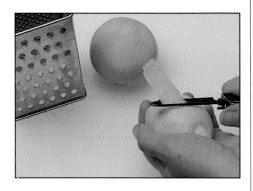

To remove colored rind (or "zest"), use a vegetable peeler to shave off the rind in thick strips, taking none of the white pith. Use these strips whole or cut them into fine shreds with a sharp knife, according to recipe directions. Or, rub the fruit against the fine holes of a metal grater, turning the fruit so you take just the colored rind and not the white pith. Or, use a special tool, called a citrus zester, to take fine threads of rind. (Mince the threads as an alternative to grating.)

Kiwi fruit

Follow citrus fruit technique, taking off the peel thinly in lengthwise strips.

Apples, pears, quinces, mangoes, papayas

Use a small sharp knife or a vegetable peeler. Take off the peel in long strips, as thinly as possible.

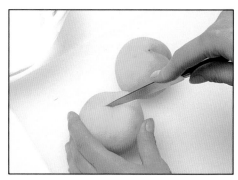

Peaches, apricots

Cut a cross in the base. Immerse the fruit in boiling water. Leave 10–30 seconds (according to ripeness), then drain and immerse in ice water. The skin should slip off easily.

Pineapple

Cut off the leafy crown. Cut a slice from the base and set the pineapple upright. With a sharp knife, cut off the peel lengthwise, cutting thickly to remove the brown "eyes" with it.

Bananas, litchis, avocado

Make a small cut and remove the peel with your fingers.

Passion fruit, pomegranates

Cut in half, or cut a slice off the top. With a spoon, scoop the flesh and seeds into a bowl.

Star fruit (carambola)

Trim off the tough, darkened edges of the five segments.

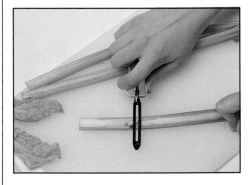

Rhubarb

Cut off the leaves and discard them (they are poisonous). Peel off any tough skin.

Fresh currants (red, black, white)
Pull through the tines of a fork to remove the currants from the stem.

Fresh dates
Squeeze gently at the stem end to remove the rather tough skin.

CORING AND PITTING OR SEEDING FRUIT

Apples, pears, quinces
For whole fruit, use an apple corer to stamp out the whole core from stem end to base. Alternatively, working up from the base, use a melon baller to cut out the core. Leave the stem end intact.

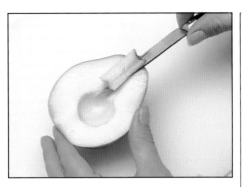

For halves, use a melon baller to scoop out the core. Cut out the stem and base with a small sharp knife.
For quarters, cut out the stem and core with a serrated knife.

Citrus fruit
With the tip of a pointed knife, nick out seeds from slices or sections.

Cherries
Use a cherry pitter for the neatest results.

Peaches, apricots, nectarines, plums
Cut the fruit in half, cutting around the indentation. Twist the halves apart. Lift out the pit, or lever it out with the tip of a sharp knife.

Fresh dates
Cut the fruit lengthwise in half and lift out the pit. Or, if the fruit is to be used whole, cut in from the stem end with a thin-bladed knife to loosen the pit, then remove it.

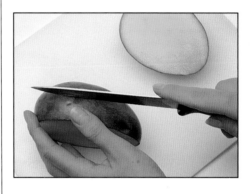

Mangoes
Cut lengthwise on either side of the large flat seed in the center. Curve the cut slightly to follow the shape of the seed. Also, cut the flesh from the two thin ends of the seed.

Papayas, melons
Cut the fruit in half. Scoop out the seeds from the central hollow, then scrape away any fibers.

Pineapple

For spears and wedges, cut out the core neatly with a sharp knife.

For rings, cut out the core with a small cookie cutter.

Grapes

Cut the fruit lengthwise in half. Use a small knife to nick out the seeds. Alternatively, use the curved end of a sterilized bobby pin.

Gooseberries

Use scissors to trim off the stem and flower ends.

Star fruit (carambola), watermelon

With the tip of a pointed knife, nick out seeds from slices.

Strawberries

Use a special huller to remove leafy green top and central core. Or, cut these out with a small sharp knife.

Avocado

Cut the fruit in half lengthwise. Stick the tip of a sharp knife into the seed and lever it out without damaging the surrounding flesh.

CUTTING FRUIT

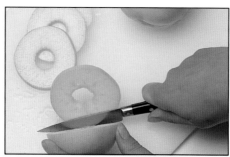

Apples, quinces

For rings, remove the core and seeds with an apple corer. Set the fruit on its side and cut across into thick or thin rings, as required.

For slices, cut the fruit in half and remove core and seeds with a melon baller. Set one half cut-side down and

cut it across into neat slices, thick or thin according to recipe directions. Or, cut the fruit into quarters and remove core and seeds with a knife. Cut lengthwise into neat slices.

Pears

For "fans," cut the fruit in half and remove core and seeds with a melon baller. Set one half cut-side down and cut lengthwise into thin slices, not cutting all the way through at the stem end. Gently fan out the slices so they are overlapping each other evenly. Transfer the pear fan to plate or pastry shell using a metal spatula.

For slices, follow apple technique.

Keeping Fresh Color

If exposed to the air for long, the cut flesh of some fruits and vegetables starts to turn brown. Those that tend to brown include apples, bananas, peaches, and avocado. So if prepared fruit has to wait before being served or cooked, sprinkle the cut surfaces with lemon juice. Or, you can immerse hard fruits in water and lemon juice, but do not soak or the fruit may become soggy.

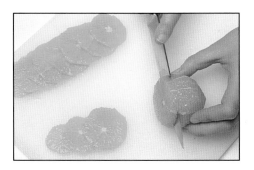

Citrus fruit

For slices, using a serrated knife, cut the fruit across into neat slices.

For sections, hold the peeled fruit in your cupped palm, over a bowl to catch the juice. Working from the side of the fruit to the center, slide the knife down one side of a separating membrane to free the flesh from it. Then slide the knife down the other side of that section to free it from the membrane there. Drop the section into the bowl. Continue cutting out the sections, folding back the membrane like the pages of a book as you work. When all the sections have been cut out, squeeze all the juice from the membrane.

Peaches, nectarines, apricots, plums

For slices, follow apple technique.

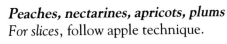

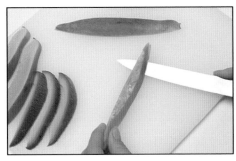

Papayas, avocado

For slices, follow apple technique. Or, cut the unpeeled fruit into wedges, removing the central seeds or seed. Set each wedge peel side down and slide the knife down the length to cut the flesh away from the peel.
For fans, follow pear technique.

Melon

For slices, follow papaya technique.
For balls, use a melon baller.

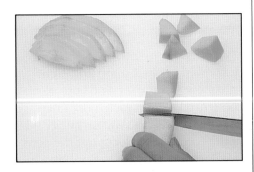

Mangoes

Cut the peeled flesh into slices or cubes, according to recipe directions.

Bananas Baked with Rum

Quarter 4 bananas and put in a small baking dish. Sprinkle with a mixture of ¼ cup melted butter, 3 tablespoons light brown sugar, 1–2 tablespoons lemon juice, and 6 tablespoons light rum or orange juice. Turn to coat the pieces. Bake at 400°F for 20 minutes, basting occasionally. Serve hot. *Serves 4.*

Pineapple

For spears, cut the peeled fruit lengthwise in half and then into quarters. Cut each quarter into spears and cut out the core.
For chunks, cut the peeled fruit into spears. Remove the core. Cut across each spear into chunks.
For rings, cut the peeled fruit across into slices. Stamp out the central core from each slice using a cookie cutter.

Kiwi fruit, Star fruit (carambola)

Cut the fruit across into neat slices; discard the ends.

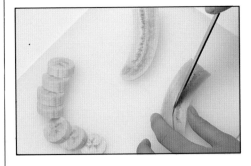

Banana

Cut the fruit across into neat slices. Or, cut in half and then lengthwise into quarters.

PREPARING FRESH PINEAPPLE

Pineapple can be prepared in many
decorative ways, apart from rings,
spears, and cubes.

Spiked Pineapple Boat
Cut 2 small to medium-sized
pineapples in half and scoop out
the flesh. Cut the pineapple flesh
into neat, small pieces. Put them
back in the pineapple halves.
Sprinkle each half with 1–2 tablespoons rum, kirsch, apricot brandy,
or Grand Marnier. If desired,
sprinkle with a little sugar to
taste. Toss the fruit to mix the
liquor and sugar evenly. Cover
tightly and chill 20–30 minutes
before serving. *Serves 4.*

1 ▲ **For a pineapple boat**: Trim off
any browned ends from the green
leaves of the crown. Trim the stem
end if necessary. With a long sharp
knife, cut the pineapple lengthwise in
half, through the crown.

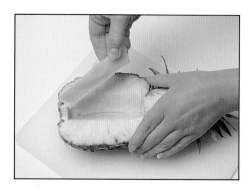

3 ▲ With a small sharp knife, cut
straight across the top and bottom of
the central core in each half. Then
cut lengthwise at a slant on either side
of the core. This will cut out the core
in a V-shape.

5 ▲ **For pineapple wedges**: Trim the
crown and base as above. Cut the fruit
lengthwise in half, through the crown,
and then into quarters.

2 ▲ Cut a thin slice from the base of
each half so it has a flat surface and
will not rock.

4 ▲ With a curved serrated
grapefruit knife, cut out the flesh from
each half. The boats are now ready for
filling with a salad, a dessert, or with
ice cream, fruit ice, or sorbet.

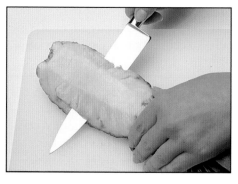

6 ▲ Cut the central core from each
quarter. Slide the knife under the
flesh to loosen it from the peel, but
leave it in place.

7 ▲ Cut across the flesh on each
wedge. Pull out the slices slightly in
alternate directions. If desired,
sprinkle the fruit lightly with sugar
before serving.

Peanut-Chicken Salad in Pineapple Boats

SERVES 4

2 small ripe pineapples

2 cups cooked chicken breast, cut into bite-size pieces

2 celery stalks, diced

½ cup chopped scallions, white and green parts

1½ cups seedless green grapes

⅓ cup coarsely chopped salted peanuts

FOR THE DRESSING

⅓ cup smooth peanut butter

½ cup mayonnaise

2 tablespoons half-and-half or milk

1 garlic clove, minced

1 teaspoon mild curry powder

1 tablespoon apricot jam

salt and pepper

1 Make 4 pineapple boats from the pineapples. Cut the flesh removed from the boats into bite-size pieces.

2 ▲ Combine the pineapple flesh, chicken, celery, scallions, and grapes in a bowl.

~ **VARIATION** ~

For Mango Turkey Salad in Pineapple Boats, use cooked turkey breast meat instead of chicken and cubed mango flesh in place of grapes. Omit the peanuts.

3 ▼ Put all the dressing ingredients in another bowl and mix with a wooden spoon or whisk until thoroughly blended. Season with salt and pepper. (The dressing will be thick, but will be thinned by the juices from the pineapple.)

4 ▲ Add the dressing to the pineapple and chicken mixture. Fold together gently but thoroughly.

5 Divide the chicken salad among the pineapple boats. Sprinkle the peanuts over the top before serving.

PREPARING MELON

Melons make attractive containers for salads, both sweet and savory. Small melons can be used for individual servings, while large watermelons will hold salads to serve a crowd, providing a festive centerpiece at the same time!

Special tools, such as melon cutters with V- and U-shaped blades, and melon ballers, make decorative preparation easier.

1 ◄ For a plain edge: Cut the melon in half and scoop out the central seeds. Remove most of the flesh with a melon baller. Or, cut it out with a grapefruit knife or scoop it out with a large spoon. Reserve the flesh for the salad. Continue scraping out the flesh, to leave an even, usually thin, layer.

2 ▲ For a zigzag edge: First cut a line around the circumference of the melon to ensure that your finished edge will be straight. Using a sharp knife, insert it on the cut line at an angle. Continue making an angled cut about ½- to 2-inches long, according to the size of the melon. Cut all the way to the center of the melon. Remove the knife.

3 ▲ Insert the knife at the top of the angled cut and cut back down to the line at a right angle to the first cut, forming a V. Continue cutting V-shapes in this way all around the melon. If available, a special melon cutter with a V-shaped blade will make the job easier.

4 ▲ Lift the melon halves apart. Remove the seeds and scoop out the flesh as above.

Watermelon Basket
Cut a watermelon basket as directed above. Scoop out the flesh with a melon baller and nick out as many of the black seeds as you can. Mix the watermelon balls with balls of cantaloupe and honeydew melon, blueberries, and strawberries. Pile the fruit back in the watermelon basket for serving.

Citrus Garnishes
The technique for preparing melons can also be used for lemons and oranges. These make attractive containers for cold and iced desserts. Another idea: Cut a lemon in half with a zigzag edge, but don't hollow out the halves. Instead, trim the base of each so it will sit flat, then dip the points of the V's in minced parsley. Serve these lemon halves instead of wedges with fish.

5 ▲ For a scalloped edge: You can do this freehand following the technique for cutting a zigzag edge, but instead cutting curves. However, it is much easier, and the results are better, if you use a special melon cutter with a U-shaped blade.

6 ▲ For a melon basket: Cut a plain, zigzag, or scalloped edge, starting just off center. Cut around the melon to a point opposite where you started.

7 ▲ Cut up over the top of the melon and down to the point you began. Lift off the freed wedge of melon. Repeat on the other end.

8 ▲ Cut out the flesh from under the "handle." Cut or scoop the flesh from the melon as before.

Melon Salad with Herbs

SERVES 4 AS A FIRST COURSE

| 2 small cantaloupe melons |
| ½ honeydew melon |
| ½ hothouse cucumber |
| 1 cup small cherry tomatoes |
| 1½ tablespoons minced fresh parsley |
| 1 tablespoon snipped fresh chives |
| 1 tablespoon chopped fresh mint |

FOR THE DRESSING

| 6 tablespoons salad oil |
| 2 tablespoons red wine vinegar |
| 1 teaspoon sugar |
| salt and pepper |

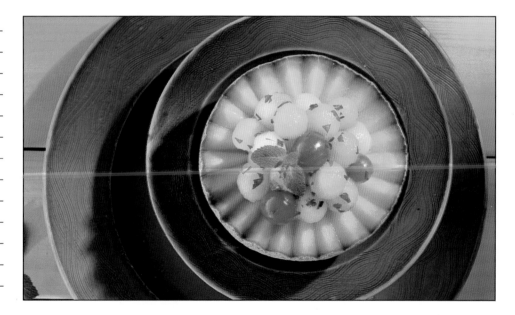

1 Cut the cantaloupes in half, with a plain, zigzag, or scalloped edge. Scoop out the seeds and central fibers. Using a melon baller, take small balls of flesh and put them in a bowl. Scrape some of the remaining flesh from the melon halves. Set the melon shells aside.

2 Remove seeds and fibers from the honeydew melon. Scoop out the flesh in small balls and add to the cantaloupe balls.

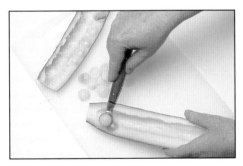

3 ▲ Use the melon baller to make balls of cucumber, or cut into cubes.

4 Add the cucumber to the melon balls with the cherry tomatoes.

5 For the dressing, combine the ingredients in a screwtop jar and shake well. Add the dressing to the bowl and toss together. Cover and refrigerate the salad 2–3 hours.

6 Just before serving, stir in the herbs. Divide the salad among the melon shells, with all the juice.

Making a Berry Sauce

A smooth, uncooked berry sauce, called a "coulis" in French, has a refreshing flavor and beautiful color. According to how much sugar you add, a berry sauce can be a sweet complement or tart contrast to cake, pastry, ice cream, or a fruit dessert.

You can use fresh or frozen berries for the sauce. If using frozen berries, partially thaw them and drain on paper towels before puréeing.

Makes about 1 cup

1 pint berries (raspberries, strawberries, blackberries, boysenberries, etc.)	
¼–½ cup confectioners' sugar	
squeeze of lemon juice (optional)	
1–2 tablespoons kirsch or fruit liqueur (optional)	

1 ▲ Hull the berries if necessary. Put them in a bowl of cold water and swirl them around briefly. Scoop out and spread on paper towels. Pat dry. Purée the berries in a blender or food processor. Turn the machine on and off a few times and scrape down the bowl to be sure all the berries are evenly puréed.

2 ▲ For raspberries, blackberries, and other berries with small seeds, press the purée through a fine-mesh nylon strainer. Add confectioners' sugar to taste, plus a little lemon juice and/or liqueur – framboise – if desired (for example, raspberry liqueur for a raspberry sauce). Stir well to dissolve the sugar completely.

Iced Macaroon Cream with Raspberry Sauce

Serves 6–8

3 cups whipping cream	
¼ cup brandy	
2 tablespoons sugar	
12 crisp almond macaroons (about 4 ounces), coarsely crushed	
raspberries, for decorating	
1 cup raspberry sauce, for serving	

2 Add the brandy and sugar. Continue whipping until the cream will hold stiff peaks.

3 ▼ Add the macaroons and fold evenly into the cream.

~ VARIATIONS ~

Use coarsely broken meringue nests (page 160) instead of macaroons. Use orange juice instead of brandy.

4 Spoon into 6 1-cup or 8 ¾-cup ramekins, or a 1½-quart smooth-sided mold. Press in evenly to be sure there are no air pockets. Smooth the surface. Cover and freeze until firm. (Do not freeze more than 1 day.)

5 ▼ To serve, dip the molds in hot water for 5–10 seconds, then invert onto a serving plate. Lift off the molds. Refrigerate the desserts 15–20 minutes, to soften slightly.

1 ▲ Put the cream in a large bowl, preferably chilled, and whip until it starts to thicken.

6 Decorate with raspberries and serve with the raspberry sauce.

MAKING SORBETS AND FRUIT ICES

Sorbets and fruit ices are most refreshing desserts. A fruit ice is made by freezing a sweetened fruit purée, whereas a sorbet is made from fruit juice or purée mixed with a sugar syrup. In addition, there are sorbets based on wine or liqueur. The Italian "granita" uses the same mixture as a sorbet, but it is stirred during freezing to give it its characteristic coarse texture. A sherbet normally contains milk or cream.

Strawberry Ice

Purée 1½ pints strawberries with ½ cup sugar and ½ cup orange juice in a blender or food processor. Be sure the sugar has dissolved completely. Add 1 tablespoon lemon juice. Taste the mixture and add more sugar or orange or lemon juice, if required. (The mixture should be well flavored.) Chill, then transfer to an ice cream machine and freeze until firm. *Makes about 2½ cups.*

Variations
• Use raspberries or blackberries instead of strawberries.
• Use 4 cups peeled, sliced, and pitted peaches or nectarines instead of strawberries.
• Add 1–2 tablespoons of fruit liqueur (to match the fruit used).

1 ▲ For a fruit ice: Prepare the fruit, removing peel, pits, hulls, stems, etc. Purée the fruit with sugar and liquid in a blender or food processor until very smooth. Be sure that the sugar has dissolved completely.

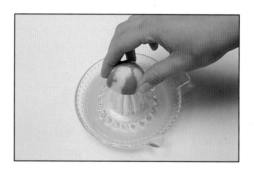

3 ▲ For a sorbet: If using citrus fruit, peel off strips of rind. Squeeze the juice from the fruit. Alternatively, purée fruit in a blender or food processor (first cooking if necessary).

5 ▲ Stir in the fruit juice or purée. Strain the mixture into a bowl, if necessary, and chill well. Then transfer the mixture to an ice cream machine and freeze following the manufacturer's instructions.

2 ▲ Add additional flavorings as directed in the recipe (alcohol, herbs, for example). If using berries with seeds (raspberries, blackberries, etc.), press the purée through a fine-mesh nylon strainer. Chill the purée well. Then transfer to an ice cream machine and freeze following manufacturer's instructions.

4 ▲ Put the strips of rind (or other flavorings such as vanilla bean, spices) in a saucepan with sugar and water and bring to a boil, stirring to dissolve the sugar. Let cool.

Still-Freezing Fruit Ice
If you don't have an ice cream machine, you can "still-freeze" the fruit ice or sorbet in the freezer. Pour it into a metal pan or tray, cover, and freeze until set around the edge. Turn it into a bowl and break it into small pieces. Beat with an electric mixer or in a food processor until slushy. Return to the metal pan and freeze again until set around the edge. Repeat the beating once or twice more, then let freeze until firm.

Mango Sorbet

SERVES 6

¾ cup sugar

¾ cup water

a large strip of orange rind

1 large mango, peeled, pitted, and cubed

¼ cup orange juice

1 Combine the sugar, water, and orange rind in a saucepan. Bring to a boil, stirring to dissolve the sugar. Let the sugar syrup cool.

2 ▼ Purée the mango with the orange juice in a blender or food processor. There should be about 2 cups of purée.

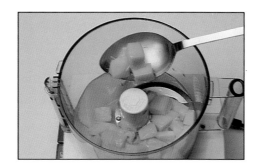

3 ▲ Add the purée to the cooled sugar syrup and mix well. Strain. Taste the mixture (it should be well flavored). Chill. Transfer to an ice cream machine and freeze until firm.

Sorbet Variations

● For *Banana Sorbet*: Peel and cube 4–5 large bananas. Purée with 2 tablespoons lemon juice to make about 2 cups. If desired, replace the orange rind in the sugar syrup with 2–3 whole cloves, or omit the rind.

● For *Papaya Sorbet*: Peel, seed, and cube 1½ pounds papaya. Purée with 3 tablespoons lime juice to make about 2 cups. Replace the orange rind with lime rind.

● For *Passion Fruit Sorbet*: Halve 16 or more passion fruit and scoop out the seeds and pulp (there should be about 2 cups). Work in a blender or food processor until the seeds are like coarse pepper. Omit the orange juice and rind. Add the passion fruit to the sugar syrup, then press through a wire strainer before freezing.

● For *Lemon Sorbet*: Make the sugar syrup with 2 cups sugar, 2 cups water, and 2 tablespoons finely grated lemon rind. Add ¾ cup fresh lemon juice. Do not strain before freezing.

Making Fruit Crisp

This well-loved dessert is simple and satisfying. It consists of fruit baked with a sweet, crumbly topping. Almost any fruit can be used, and the topping can be varied in many ways, according to your preferences and what you have on hand.

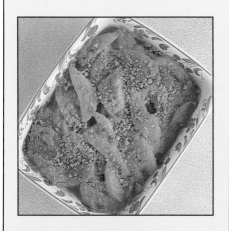

Pear Crisp
Make the crumb mixture with ¾ cup flour, ¾ cup packed light brown sugar, 1 teaspoon ground ginger, and 1 stick (8 tablespoons) butter. Add ½ cup chopped walnuts and mix lightly. Toss 5 cups sliced firm pears with ½–1 cup sugar and 1–2 tablespoons flour. Assemble the crisp and bake in a preheated 375°F oven 30–35 minutes. Serve warm, with cream or ice cream. *Serves 4–6.*

Variation
● Use apples instead of pears, and cinnamon instead of ginger.

Fruit Betty
A betty is another popular baked dessert, similar to a fruit crisp. It consists of alternate layers of sweetened and spiced fruit and buttered bread crumbs or cubes. Betties have been made in the United States since colonial times.

1 ▲ First, prepare the topping: Combine the dry ingredients (flour and sugar plus oats or other cereal, coconut, nuts, spices, etc.) in a bowl. Add the fat (butter or margarine).

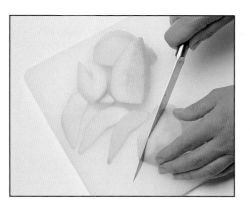

3 ▲ Prepare the fruit as directed in the recipe, by peeling, pitting or coring, slicing or cubing.

5 ▲ Scatter the crumb mixture on top to cover the fruit in an even layer.

2 ▲ Cut or rub the fat into the dry ingredients as if making pastry dough. Do not overmix the topping. The finished texture should be like coarse crumbs.

4 ▲ If the recipe directs, toss the fruit with sugar or a sweet syrup and spices. Add flour or cornstarch for thickening the fruit juices, if directed. Spread the fruit in a baking dish.

6 ▲ Bake until the fruit is tender and the topping is golden brown and crisp. Serve warm, with whipped cream, sour cream, or ice cream.

Spiced Peach Crisp

SERVES 6

3 pounds ripe but firm peaches, peeled, cored, and sliced

¼ cup sugar

½ teaspoon ground cinnamon

1 teaspoon lemon juice

whipped cream or vanilla ice cream, for serving (optional)

FOR THE TOPPING

½ cup flour

¼ teaspoon ground cinnamon

¼ teaspoon ground allspice

1 cup rolled oats

1 cup packed light brown sugar

1 stick (8 tablespoons) butter

1 Preheat the oven to 375°F.

2 ▼ For the topping, sift the flour and spices into a bowl. Add the oats and sugar and stir to combine. Cut in the butter until the mixture resembles coarse crumbs.

3 Toss the peaches with the sugar, cinnamon, and lemon juice. Put the fruit in an 8- or 9-inch diameter baking dish.

4 ▲ Scatter the topping over the fruit in an even layer. Bake 30–35 minutes. Serve warm, with whipped cream or ice cream, if desired.

~ VARIATION ~

Use apricots or nectarines instead of peaches. Substitute nutmeg for the cinnamon, if desired.

MAKING A STEAMED PUDDING

Steamed puddings, many with fruit, range from light sponges to rich suet puddings, and the variety of flavorings is infinite, both sweet and savory. Puddings may be steamed on top of the stove or in the oven. A pressure cooker can also be used. Some puddings are wrapped in greased foil rather than being cooked in a basin or mold.

First prepare the steamer. For cooking on top of the stove, you can use either a large saucepan with tight-fitting lid or a proper steamer. For oven steaming, use a deep casserole or roasting pan.

1 If using a saucepan, it is necessary to have something to help you put the pudding in the pan and then lift it out after cooking. Unless you are wrapping the pudding in a cloth (the knot at the top makes a convenient handle), use a wire steaming basket with handles or make a sling of foil. Put enough water into the saucepan or steamer to one-quarter fill it, and bring to the boil. Boil water in the kettle too.

2 ▲ Generously butter the pudding basin or mold(s). Put a disc of buttered waxed paper in the bottom. Make the pudding mixture. Turn it into the basin or mold(s), which should be about two-thirds full.

3 ▲ Cover the basin or mold(s). This must be done carefully so that the steam from the boiling water does not fall on the pudding, making it soggy. First lay a disc of buttered greaseproof paper on top.

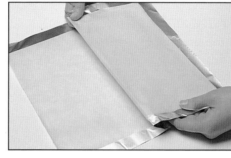

4 ▲ To cover with foil, lay a piece of foil on another piece of paper. Holding the paper and foil together, fold a 1-inch pleat across the center (the pleat will allow for the pudding rising above the basin rim).

5 ▲ Smooth the paper and fold down over the edge. Wrap a piece of string twice around the basin, just below the rim, and tie firmly. Trim off the corners with scissors.

6 ▲ To cover with a cloth, use a square of cotton that is about three times larger than the top of the basin or mold(s). Lay it over the buttered paper, pleat and tie with string as above. Bring the corners of the cloth up over the top and tie opposite ones together in knots.

7 ▲ Lower the basin or mold(s) into the boiling water in the saucepan or steamer, or arrange in the roasting pan. Pour enough boiling water into the pan to come halfway up the sides of the basin or mold(s).

8 Cover tightly with a lid or foil. Set over a moderately low heat on top of the stove or put into a preheated 350°F oven. The water in the steamer should simmer but not boil up over the top of the pudding. Steam for the required time, topping up with more boiling water if needed. (With oven steaming you will need to replenish the water less often as there is much less evaporation.) When cooked, remove the basin or mold(s) from the water and cool for a few minutes. Remove the covering, set a serving plate, inverted, on top of the basin or mold(s) and, holding them firmly together, turn them over. Lift off the mold and serve.

Apple and Kumquat Sponge Puddings

SERVES 8

¾ cup butter, at room temperature

2 cups cooking apples, peeled and thinly sliced

1 cup kumquats, thinly sliced

¾ cup golden sugar

2 eggs

1 cup self-rising flour

FOR THE SAUCE

1 cup kumquats, thinly sliced

⅓ cup sugar

1 cup water

1 cup crème fraîche

1 teaspoon cornstarch mixed with 2 teaspoons water

lemon juice to taste

1 Prepare the steamer. Butter eight ⅔ cup dariole molds or ramekins and put a disc of buttered waxed paper on the bottom of each one.

2 ▲ Melt 2 tablespoons butter in a frying pan. Add the apples, kumquats and 1 tablespoon sugar and cook over a moderate heat for 5–8 minutes or until the apples start to soften and the sugar begins to caramelize. Remove from the heat and leave to cool.

3 Meanwhile, cream the remaining butter with the remaining sugar until the mixture is pale and fluffy. Add the eggs, one at a time, beating well after each addition. Fold in the flour.

4 ▼ Divide the apple and kumquat mixture among the prepared molds. Top with the sponge mixture.

5 Cover the molds and put into the steamer. Steam on top of the stove for 45 minutes. If oven-steaming, cook for 30 minutes.

6 For the sauce, put the kumquats, sugar and water in a frying pan and bring to a boil, stirring to dissolve the sugar. Simmer for 5 minutes.

7 ▲ Stir in the crème fraîche and bring back to a boil, stirring.

8 Remove from the heat and whisk in the cornstarch mixture. Return the pan to the heat and simmer gently for 2 minutes, stirring. Add lemon juice to taste.

9 Turn out the puddings and serve hot, with the sauce.

MELTING CHOCOLATE

If chocolate is overheated, it can burn and develop a grainy texture. So care must be taken when melting it. If the chocolate is being melted with butter or a large quantity of liquid, this can be done in a heavy-based pan over medium-low heat. When melting chocolate alone, use the water-bath principle described here.

For the richest, most intense chocolate flavor in cakes, cookies, and candies, use a chocolate that contains a lot of chocolate liquor (the pure chocolate essence), and cocoa butter (a natural vegetable fat) rather than vegetable oil. Unsweetened chocolate, also called baking or cooking chocolate, is unadulterated chocolate liquor, with at least 50 percent cocoa butter to give it its smooth texture. Of the sweetened chocolates available, bittersweet contains the most chocolate liquor (at least 35 percent).

1 ▲ First, cut the chocolate into small pieces with a sharp knife. This will enable the chocolate to be melted quickly and evenly.

3 ▲ According to recipe directions, a liquid may be added, such as milk, or water, or a fat such as butter or margarine.

2 ▲ Put the chocolate in a double boiler or bowl set over a saucepan of almost simmering water. The base of the bowl should not touch the water.

4 ▲ Heat gently until the chocolate is melted and smooth, stirring occasionally. Remove from the heat.

Spiced Mocha Drink
Chop 6 ounces milk chocolate. Melt it with ½ cup light cream. Add 3 cups hot black coffee and ¼ teaspoon ground cinnamon. Beat with a whisk until foamy. Serve hot, topped with a dollop of whipped cream, or let cool and chill, then serve over ice. *Serves 4.*

5 ▲ Alternatively, arrange the chocolate in a glass container and melt it in a microwave oven (consult manufacturer's handbook for timings).

Moisture Problems
If any steam from boiling water gets into the chocolate while melting, it can turn into a solid mass. If this happens, stir in a little shortening (1 teaspoon to each ounce of chocolate).

Bittersweet Chocolate Sauce

MAKES ABOUT 2 CUPS

¼ cup sugar

⅓ cup water

8 ounces bittersweet chocolate, chopped into small pieces

1 cup whipping cream

1 teaspoon vanilla extract

~ VARIATION ~

If preferred, use 5 ounces semi-sweet chocolate and 3 ounces unsweetened chocolate.

---

1 Combine the sugar and water in a heavy-based saucepan. Bring to a boil, stirring to dissolve the sugar.

2 ▲ Add the chocolate and remove the pan from the heat.

3 ▲ Stir until the mixture is smooth, then stir in the cream and vanilla. Serve the sauce warm or cooled, over ice cream, cream puffs, etc.

Chocolate Truffles

MAKES ABOUT 24

8 ounces bittersweet or semisweet chocolate, chopped into small pieces

¼ cup whipping cream

unsweetened cocoa powder

1 ▲ Put the chocolate in a bowl set over a pan of hot water or in the top of a double boiler. Heat until melted and smooth, stirring occasionally.

2 ▼ Remove from the pan of hot water. Add the cream and stir well. Let cool.

3 Cover and refrigerate until the mixture is just firm enough to hold its shape, about 35 minutes.

4 Sift a layer of cocoa powder onto a plate or shallow dish.

5 ▲ Take a heaping teaspoonful of the chocolate mixture and shape it into a ball.

6 ▲ Roll in the cocoa to coat all over in an even layer. Shake off excess cocoa. Set the truffle on a tray.

7 Continue shaping and coating the remaining truffles, setting them on the tray in a single layer, not touching each other.

8 Cover and refrigerate. Remove from the refrigerator 15 minutes before serving.

~ **VARIATIONS** ~

For Liqueur-Flavored Truffles, add 2 tablespoons cherry or apricot brandy or orange liqueur.
For Coated Truffles, roll the truffles in minced toasted hazelnuts or other nuts, or in finely grated sweet chocolate instead of cocoa.

Chocolate Nut Cake

SERVES 6–8

6 ounces semisweet chocolate, chopped into small pieces

1 stick (8 tablespoons) butter, preferabiy unsalted

1 cup sugar

4 eggs, separated

1 cup freshly ground unsalted macadamia nuts or almonds

¼ cup flour

pinch of cream of tartar (if needed)

sweetened whipped cream (page 160), for serving

1 Preheat the oven to 325°F. Grease a 9-inch round cake pan and line the bottom with greased paper. Dust the pan with unsweetened cocoa powder.

2 Combine the chocolate and butter in a heavy-based saucepan. Set over medium-low heat and stir until melted and smooth. Let cool.

3 ▲ Beat together the sugar and egg yolks until pale and thick.

4 ▲ Add the chocolate mixture, nuts, and flour and beat in gently.

5 In another large bowl, scrupulously clean and greasefree, and using clean beaters, beat the egg whites until they will hold stiff peaks. (If not using a copper bowl, add the cream of tartar when the whites are frothy.)

6 ▲ Add about one-quarter of the whites to the chocolate mixture and mix in gently. It is not necessary to blend thoroughly.

7 ▲ Add the remaining whites and fold them in gently but thoroughly using a rubber spatula.

8 Pour the batter into the prepared pan. Bake until a skewer inserted into the center of the cake comes out clean, 1–1¼ hours.

9 Cool in the pan 10 minutes, then turn out onto a wire rack to cool completely. Serve with sweetened whipped cream.

PREPARING NUTS

Nuts are enjoyed as a snack or with cocktails, as well as being an important ingredient or garnish in many dishes, from breakfast cereals and breads to salads, main dishes, vegetables and grains, and desserts.

Some nuts may be bought complete with their brown, papery skins. The skin often has a bitter taste and so should be removed before the nuts are used. The flavor of all nuts is improved by toasting; this makes them appealing crisp, too.

1 ▲ To skin almonds and pistachios: Put the nuts in a bowl and cover with boiling water. Let stand 2 minutes. (This is called blanching.) Drain the nuts and let them cool slightly. Squeeze or rub each nut with your fingers to remove the skins.

2 ▲ To skin hazelnuts and Brazils: Spread the nuts on a baking sheet. Toast in a preheated 350°F oven to dry the skins, 10–15 minutes. Wrap the nuts in a rough dish towel and rub to remove the skin. Pick off any bits of skin still adhering to the nuts.

Hot Cocktail Nuts
Combine 3 tablespoons corn oil, 2 halved garlic cloves, and 1 teaspoon dried hot red pepper flakes in a saucepan. Heat 1 minute, stirring. Discard the garlic. Add 1½ cups mixed nuts, such as skinned almonds, walnuts, skinned peanuts, skinned hazelnuts, and stir well. Add salt to taste. Pour the mixture onto a baking sheet and bake in a preheated 300°F oven about 20 minutes, stirring occasionally. Drain the nuts on paper towels and let cool before serving.

3 ▲ To oven-toast or broil-toast nuts: Spread the nuts on a baking sheet. Toast in a preheated 350°F oven or under the broiler, 5–6 inches from the heat, until golden brown and smelling nutty. Stir occasionally.

5 ▲ To grind nuts: Using a nut mill or a clean coffee grinder, grind a small batch of nuts at a time so that you can be sure of getting an even texture. As soon as the nuts have a fine texture, stop grinding: If overworked, they will turn to a paste.

4 ▲ To fry-toast nuts: Put the nuts in a frying pan, with no fat. Toast over medium heat until golden brown. Stir constantly and watch carefully because nuts scorch easily.

6 ▲ You can also grind nuts in a food processor, but it is not as easy to get an even texture, and thus there is more risk of overworking the nuts to a paste. To prevent this, grind the nuts with some of the sugar or flour called for in the recipe.

Bread Pudding with Pecans

1¾ cups milk

1¾ cups whipping cream or half-and-half

¾ cup sugar

3 eggs, beaten to mix

2 teaspoons grated orange rind

1 teaspoon vanilla extract

24 slices of day-old French bread, ½-inch thick

¾ cup chopped toasted pecans

confectioners' sugar, for sprinkling

whipped cream or sour cream and maple syrup, for serving

1 ▲ Put 1½ cups each of the milk and cream in a saucepan. Add the sugar. Warm over low heat, stirring to dissolve the sugar. Remove from the heat and let cool. Add the eggs, orange rind, and vanilla and mix well.

2 ▲ Arrange half of the bread slices in a buttered 9- or 10-inch baking dish. Scatter ½ cup of the pecans over the bread. Arrange the remaining bread slices on top and scatter on the rest of the pecans.

3 ▼ Pour the egg mixture evenly over the bread slices. Let soak 30 minutes. Press the top layer of bread down into the liquid once or twice.

4 Preheat the oven to 350°F.

5 If the top layer of bread slices looks dry and all the liquid has been absorbed, moisten with the remaining milk and cream.

6 ▲ Set the baking dish in a roasting pan. Add enough water to the pan to come halfway up the sides of the dish. Bring the water to a boil.

7 Transfer to the oven. Bake until the pudding is set and golden brown on top, about 40 minutes. Sprinkle the top of the pudding with sifted confectioners' sugar and serve warm, with whipped cream or sour cream and maple syrup, if desired.

BREADS

~

The enticing aroma of fresh bread baking is enough to lure
anyone to the kitchen, and the enjoyment of homemade
muffins, bread, and rolls is even better than the anticipation.
You can make your own pizza dough, too.

MAKING QUICK BREADS AND MUFFINS

As their name denotes, these breads are fast and easy to make. The leavening agent reacts quickly with moisture and heat to make the breads and muffins rise, without the need for a rising period before baking.

The leavening agent is usually baking soda or baking powder, which is a mixture of baking soda and an acid salt such as cream of tartar. It will start to work as soon as it comes into contact with liquid, so don't mix the dry and liquid ingredients until just before you are ready to fill the muffin cups and bake.

In addition to the thick-batter quick breads discussed here, there are also thin-batter quick breads such as pancakes and waffles, and quick breads that are made from soft doughs such as biscuits.

1 ▲ For muffins: Combine the dry ingredients in a bowl. It is a good idea to sift the flour with the leavening agent, salt, and any spices to mix them. Add the liquid ingredients and stir just until the dry ingredients are moistened; the batter will not be smooth. Do not overmix in an attempt to remove all the lumps. If you do, the muffins will not be tender and will have tunnels in them.

2 ▲ Divide the batter evenly among the greased muffin cups (or line the cups with paper cupcake liners), filling them about two-thirds full. Bake until golden brown and a wooden skewer inserted in the center comes out clean. To prevent soggy bottoms, remove the muffins immediately from the cups to a wire rack. Let cool, and serve warm or at room temperature.

Granola Muffins
Make the batter from 1 cup flour, 2½ teaspoons baking powder, 2 tablespoons sugar, 1 cup milk, ¼ cup melted butter or corn oil, and 1 egg, adding 1¾ cups granola-type cereal with raisins to the dry ingredients. Pour into muffins cups (2½- to 2¾-inch diameter, 1½-inches deep). Bake in a preheated 400°F oven until golden brown, about 20 minutes. *Makes 10.*

3 ▲ For fruit and/or nut breads: Method 1: Stir together all the liquid ingredients. Add the dry ingredients and beat just until smoothly blended. Method 2: Beat the butter with the sugar until the mixture is light and fluffy. Beat in the eggs followed by the other liquid ingredients. Stir in the dry ingredients. Pour the batter into a prepared pan (typically a loaf pan). Bake until a wooden skewer inserted in the center comes out clean. If the bread is browning too quickly, cover the top with foil.

4 ▲ Cool in the pan 5 minutes, then unmold onto a wire rack to cool completely. A lengthwise crack on the surface is characteristic of quick breads. For easier slicing, wrap the bread in wax paper and overwrap in foil, then store overnight at room temperature.

Banana Bread

MAKES 1 LOAF

1½ cups flour
2¼ teaspoons baking powder
½ teaspoon salt
¾ teaspoon ground cinnamon (optional)
¼ cup wheat germ
5 tablespoons butter, at room temperature, or ⅓ cup shortening
⅔ cup sugar
¾ teaspoon grated lemon rind
1¼ cups mashed ripe bananas (2–3 bananas)
2 eggs, beaten to mix

1 Preheat the oven to 350°F. Grease and flour an 8½- × 4½-inch loaf pan.

2 ▲ Sift the flour, baking powder, salt, and cinnamon, if using, into a bowl. Stir in the wheat germ.

3 ▲ In another bowl, beat the butter or shortening with the sugar and lemon rind until the mixture is light and fluffy.

4 ▲ Add the mashed bananas and eggs and mix well.

5 Add the dry ingredients and blend quickly and evenly.

~ **VARIATION** ~

For Banana Walnut Bread, add ½–¾ cup finely chopped walnuts with the dry ingredients.

6 ▼ Spoon into the prepared loaf pan. Bake until a wooden skewer inserted in the center comes out clean, about 1 hour.

7 Let the bread cool in the pan about 5 minutes, then unmould onto a wire rack to cool completely.

MAKING BISCUITS

Biscuits are quick breads made with a soft dough. The dough may be rolled out and cut into shapes, or it may be dropped from a spoon onto a baking sheet, or molded.

This dough has many uses. Fruit cobblers have a biscuit dough crust. Dumplings are also a type of biscuit.

1 Sift the dry ingredients into a bowl (flour, baking powder with or without soda, salt, sugar, spices, etc).

2 ▲ Add the fat (butter, margarine, shortening, etc.). With a pastry blender or two knives used scissor-fashion, cut the fat into the dry ingredients until the mixture resembles fine crumbs, or rub in the fat with your fingertips.

3 ▲ **For rolled-out biscuits**: Add the liquid ingredients (milk, cream, buttermilk, eggs). Stir with a fork until the dry ingredients are thoroughly moistened and will come together in a ball of fairly soft dough in the center of the bowl.

Baking Powder Biscuits
Make the biscuit dough using 2 cups flour, 1 tablespoon baking powder, ½ teaspoon salt, 1 stick (8 tablespoons) chilled butter or ½ cup shortening, and ⅔–¾ cup milk. Roll or pat out the dough and cut out 2½-inch rounds. Bake the biscuits in a preheated 450°F oven for 10–12 minutes. *Makes about 10.*

4 ▲ Turn the dough onto a lightly floured surface. Knead it very lightly, folding and pressing, to mix evenly, about 30 seconds. Roll or pat out the dough to ½- to ¾-inch thickness.

6 ▲ **For drop biscuits**: Add the liquid ingredients, using more than for a rolled-out dough. Stir with a fork until evenly mixed. Using a floured spoon, drop scoops of batter onto an ungreased baking sheet, leaving space around each biscuit. Bake until puffed and golden brown.

5 ▲ With a floured, sharp-edged cutter, cut out rounds or other shapes. Or, cut with a floured knife. Arrange on an ungreased baking sheet (not touching if you want crusts all around, touching if you want soft sides). Brush the tops with beaten egg or cream if the recipe directs. Bake until golden brown. Serve immediately.

Cutting Tips
● Be sure the cutter or knife is sharp so that the edges of the biscuit shapes are not compressed; this would prevent rising.
● Cut the shapes close together so that you won't have to reroll the dough more than once.
● If necessary, a short, sturdy drinking glass can be pressed into service as a cutter. Flour the rim well and do not press too hard.

Berry Shortcake

SERVES 8

1¼ cups whipping cream

¼ cup confectioners' sugar

2 pints berries (strawberries or mixed berries), halved or sliced if large

⅓ cup granulated sugar, or to taste

FOR THE SHORTCAKE BISCUIT

2 cups flour

2 teaspoons baking powder

⅓ cup granulated sugar

1 stick (8 tablespoons) butter

⅓ cup milk

1 extra-large egg

1 Preheat the oven to 450°F. Grease an 8-inch round cake pan.

2 For the shortcake biscuit, sift the flour, baking powder, and sugar into a bowl. Add the butter and cut or rub in until the mixture resembles fine crumbs. Combine the milk and egg. Add to the crumb mixture and stir just until evenly mixed to a soft dough.

3 Put the dough in the prepared pan and pat out to an even layer. Bake until a wooden skewer inserted in the center comes out clean, 15–20 minutes. Let cool slightly.

4 ▲ Whip the cream until it starts to thicken. Add the confectioners' sugar and continue whipping until the cream will hold soft peaks.

5 Put the berries in a bowl. Sprinkle with the granulated sugar and toss together lightly. Cover and set aside for the berries to render some juice.

6 ▼ Remove the shortcake biscuit from the pan. With a long, serrated knife, split it horizontally into two equal layers.

7 ▲ Put the bottom layer on a serving plate. Top with half of the berries and most of the cream. Set the second layer on top and press down gently. Spoon the remaining berries over the top layer (or serve them separately) and add the remaining cream in small, decorative dollops.

MAKING YEAST DOUGH

Making bread is a very enjoyable and satisfying culinary experience – with no other preparation do you have such "hands-on" contact. From the kneading through to the shaping of the risen dough, you are working with a living organism, yeast, not a chemical leavening agent. Yeast is available either dry or fresh. Active dry yeast keeps longer. Compressed fresh yeast should be refrigerated.

Everyday White Bread
Mix 2 packages active dry yeast with ⅓ cup warm water; add 1 teaspoon sugar. Sift 5½ cups flour into a large bowl with ½ table-spoon salt and 1 tablespoon sugar. Make a well in the center and add the yeast mixture, 1 cup warm milk, ¾ cup warm water, and 2 tablespoons melted and cooled butter. Mix to a soft dough, adding more flour if necessary, then knead until smooth and elastic. Let rise until doubled in bulk. Punch the dough to deflate it. Divide it in half and shape each piece into a loaf, tucking the ends under. Put in 2 greased 8½- × 4½-inch loaf pans. Leave in a warm place to rise, 30–45 minutes. If desired, lightly beat 1 egg with 1 tablespoon milk and glaze the tops of the loaves. Bake in a preheated 450°F oven 35–40 minutes. *Makes 2 loaves.*

1 ▲ Put the yeast in a small bowl and add some of the warm liquid (105–110°F) called for in the recipe. Let dry yeast soak for 1 minute, then whisk to dissolve; mash fresh yeast to blend. Add a little sugar if the recipe directs.

3 ▲ Using your fingers or a spoon, gradually draw the flour into the liquids. Continue until all the flour is incorporated and the dough pulls away from the sides of the bowl. If the dough feels too soft and wet, work in a little more flour. If it will not come together, add a little more liquid.

5 ▲ Shape the dough into a ball. Put it in a lightly greased bowl and rotate the dough so that the surface is lightly greased all over. Cover the bowl with a towel or plastic wrap. Set it aside in a warm, draft-free place (about 80°F).

2 ▲ Sift the flour into a large warm bowl (with other dry ingredients such as salt). Make a well in the center and add the yeast mixture plus any other liquid ingredients.

4 ▲ Turn the dough onto a lightly floured surface. Fold the dough over onto itself toward you, and then press it down away from you with the heels of your hands. Rotate the dough slightly and fold and press it again. Knead until the dough looks satiny and feels elastic, about 10 minutes.

6 ▲ Let the dough rise until it is doubled in bulk, 1–1½ hours. To test if it is sufficiently risen, press a finger about 1 inch into the dough and withdraw it quickly: the indentation should remain.

7 ▲ Gently punch the center of the dough with your fist to deflate it and fold the edges to the center. Turn the dough onto a lightly floured surface and knead it again for 2–3 minutes. If the recipe directs, shape it into a ball again and let rise a second time.

8 ▲ Shape the dough into loaves, rolls, or other shapes as directed. Put into prepared pans or onto baking sheets. Cover and let rise in a warm place again, ¾–1 hour. If the recipe directs, glaze the loaves or rolls before baking.

9 ▲ Bake in the center of a preheated oven until well risen and golden brown. To test for doneness, turn out of the pan and tap the base with your knuckle. If it sounds hollow, it is fully cooked. Immediately transfer to a wire rack for cooling.

SHAPING ROLLS

A basket of freshly baked rolls, in decorative shapes, is a delightful accompaniment for soups or salads. After shaping, arrange the rolls on a baking sheet, leaving space around each roll for spreading, and let rise for 30 minutes before baking.

Working with Yeast
- A ¼-ounce package of active dry yeast contains 1 tablespoon. One cake of compressed fresh yeast is equivalent to a package of dry yeast. For quick-rising dry yeast, combine it with the flour and other dry ingredients, then add the liquids (which should be warmer than for ordinary active dry yeast). Or, follow recipe directions.
- If you are in any doubt about the freshness of the yeast, it is a good idea to "proof" it: set the yeast mixture in a warm place. After 5–10 minutes, the mixture should be foamy. If it isn't, discard it and start again.

1 ▲ For Parker House rolls: Roll out the risen dough to ¼-inch thickness and cut out 2½- to 3-inch rounds, using a floured cutter. Brush the rounds with melted butter. Fold them in half, slightly off-center so the top overlaps the bottom. Press the folded edge firmly. Arrange on a greased baking sheet.

2 ▲ For butterhorn rolls: Roll out the risen dough to a large round about ¼-inch thick. Brush with melted butter. With a sharp knife, cut into wedges that are 2½–3 inches at their wide end. Roll up each wedge, from the wide end. Set the rolls on a greased baking sheet, placing the points underneath.

3 ◄ For bowknot rolls: Divide the risen dough into pieces. Roll each with your palms on a lightly floured surface to make ropes that are about ½-inch thick. Divide the ropes into 9-inch lengths. Tie each length of dough loosely into a knot, tucking the ends under. Arrange the rolls on a greased baking sheet.

Two-Tone Bread

MAKES 2 LOAVES

2 packages active dry yeast
½ cup warm water (105–110°F)
⅓ cup sugar
5¼–5½ cups all-purpose flour
½ tablespoon salt
2½ cups warm milk (105–110°F)
⅓ cup shortening or butter, melted and cooled
3 tablespoons dark molasses
2¼ cups whole-wheat flour

1 Dissolve the yeast in the water. Whisk in 1 teaspoon of the sugar.

2 Sift 3 cups of the all-purpose flour, the remaining sugar, and salt into a large warm bowl. Make a well in the center and put in the yeast mixture, milk, and shortening or butter. Gradually draw in the flour and mix to a smooth, soft batter.

3 ▲ Divide the batter in half and put one portion in another bowl. To the first half add 2¼ cups all-purpose flour and mix together to a moderately stiff dough. If necessary, add 1–2 tablespoons more warm water.

4 Turn onto a lightly floured surface and knead until smooth and elastic. Shape into a ball. Put in a greased bowl and rotate to grease the dough all over. Cover the bowl with a towel or plastic wrap.

5 ▲ To the second portion of batter add the molasses and whole-wheat flour. Mix together. If necessary, add the remaining all-purpose flour to make a moderately stiff dough. Turn onto a lightly floured surface and knead until smooth and elastic. Shape into a ball and put in a greased bowl.

6 Cover the bowls and let the dough rise in a warm place until doubled in bulk, 1–1¼ hours. Grease two 8½- × 4½-inch loaf pans.

7 Punch the balls of dough to deflate them. Divide each ball of dough in half. On a lightly floured surface, roll out half of the light dough to a rectangle about 12 × 8 inches. Roll out half of the dark dough to a rectangle of the same size.

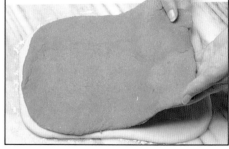

8 ▲ Set the dark dough rectangle on top of the light one. Roll up tightly from a short side. Set in a greased pan. Repeat with the remaining dark and light dough. Cover the pans and let the dough rise until doubled in bulk, ¾–1 hour.

9 Preheat the oven to 425°F. Bake the loaves 30–35 minutes.

Cinnamon-Walnut Rolls

MAKES ABOUT 24

2 packages active dry yeast
½ cup warm water (105–110°F)
6–6½ cups flour
¼ cup granulated sugar
2 teaspoons salt
1½ cups warm milk (105–110°F)
11 tablespoons butter, melted and cooled
2 eggs
1½ teaspoons grated orange rind
1½ cups confectioners' sugar
3–4 tablespoons orange juice

FOR THE FILLING

½ cup granulated sugar
½ cup finely chopped walnuts
1½ teaspoons ground cinnamon

1 Dissolve the yeast in the water.

2 Sift 6 cups of the flour, the granulated sugar, and salt into a large warm bowl. Make a well in the center and put in the yeast mixture, milk, half of the butter, the eggs, and grated orange rind.

3 Gradually draw the flour into the liquids and mix until the dough pulls away from the sides of the bowl. If the dough feels too soft, work in a little of the remaining flour.

4 Turn onto a lightly floured surface and knead until satiny smooth and elastic. Shape into a ball. Put in a greased bowl and rotate to grease the dough all over. Cover the bowl and let the dough rise in a warm place until doubled in bulk. Grease two 9- or 10-inch round cake pans.

5 With your fist gently punch down the dough to deflate it. Divide it in half. On a lightly floured surface, roll out one piece of dough to a 12- × 8-inch rectangle.

6 ▲ For the filling, put the sugar, chopped nuts, and cinnamon into a bowl. Mix the ingredients together until well combined.

7 ▲ Brush the dough with half of the remaining melted butter. Sprinkle half of the topping evenly over the surface. Roll up tightly from a long side and pinch the seam to seal it.

8 ▲ With a sharp knife, cut the roll across into 1-inch pieces. Arrange the pieces, on their cut sides, in one of the prepared pans. Repeat with the second portion of dough and the remaining melted butter and filling.

9 Cover the pans with a cloth and let the rolls rise in a warm place until very puffy, about 30 minutes. Preheat the oven to 375°F.

10 Bake the rolls until golden, 30–40 minutes. Transfer to a wire rack.

11 Stir the confectioners' sugar with enough orange juice to make a smooth icing of pourable consistency. Drizzle the icing over the rolls and let stand to cool and set.

MAKING PIZZA DOUGH

The range of toppings for a pizza is virtually limitless. Although you can buy pizza bases, it's very easy to make your own at home, and takes much less time than you would expect.

MAKES A 14-INCH PIZZA BASE

2 teaspoons active dry yeast
¾ cup warm water (105–110°F)
2¼ cups flour
1 teaspoon salt
1½ tablespoons olive oil

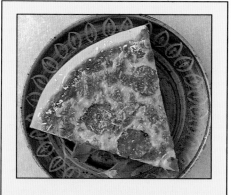

Tomato and Mozzarella Pizza
Spread 1 cup tomato-garlic sauce (page 172) over the pizza base, not quite to the edges. Scatter 1 cup shredded mozzarella cheese evenly over the sauce (plus thinly sliced pepperoni or salami if desired). Finish with a sprinkling of 2 table-spoons freshly grated Parmesan cheese and a drizzle of olive oil. Bake in a preheated 475°F oven 15–20 minutes.

Food Processor Pizza Dough
Combine the flour, salt, yeast mixture, and olive oil in the processor container. Process briefly, then add the rest of the warm water. Work until the dough begins to form a ball. Process 3–4 minutes to knead the dough, then knead it by hand for 2–3 minutes.

1 ▲ Put the yeast in a small bowl, add ¼ cup of the water, and let it soak 1 minute. Whisk lightly with a fork until dissolved.

3 ▲ Using your fingers, gradually draw the flour into the liquids. Continue mixing until all the flour is incorporated and the dough will just hold together.

5 ▲ Cover the bowl with plastic wrap. Set aside in a warm place to let the dough rise until doubled in bulk, about 1 hour. Turn the dough onto the lightly floured surface again. Gently punch down the dough to deflate it. Knead lightly until smooth.

2 ▲ Sift the flour and salt into a large warm bowl. Make a well in the center and add the yeast mixture, olive oil, and remaining warm water.

4 ▲ Turn the dough onto a lightly floured surface. Knead it until it is smooth and silky, about 10 minutes. Shape the dough into a ball. Put it in an oiled bowl and rotate to coat the surface with oil.

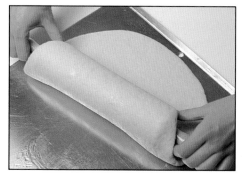

6 ▲ Roll out the dough into a round or square about ¼-inch thick. Transfer it to a lightly oiled metal pizza tray or baking sheet. Add the topping as directed in the recipe. Bake until the pizza crust is puffy and well browned. Serve hot.

Goat Cheese, Basil, and Olive Pizza

SERVES 2–4

1 cup tomato-garlic sauce (page 172)

14-inch pizza dough base

3 tomatoes, preferably plum-type, sliced

6 ounces firm goat cheese, cut into small cubes or crumbled

½ cup fresh basil leaves, torn if large

18 large black olives, preferably Greek Kalamata olives

2 tablespoons freshly grated Parmesan cheese

2 tablespoons olive oil

1 Preheat the oven to 475°F.

2 ▲ Spread the tomato sauce over the pizza base, not quite to the edges. Arrange the tomato slices on top.

3 Scatter the goat cheese evenly over the tomato slices, followed by the basil leaves and olives.

~ COOK'S TIP ~

A stoneware pizza baking brick or stone will give a pizza a very crisp crust, similar to restaurant pizza. A flat terracotta tile will give the same result. The pizza is assembled on a cornmeal-dusted wooden paddle, and then slid onto the stone for baking.

4 ▼ Sprinkle with the Parmesan and then the olive oil.

5 Bake until the pizza crust is puffy and well browned and the topping is golden brown, 15–20 minutes.

~ VARIATIONS ~

For Tuna Pizza, spread with tomato-herb sauce (page 172). Top with ½ cup thinly sliced scallions and 7 ounces drained, flaked canned tuna. Make a lattice of anchovy fillets on top and put a black olive in each space. Sprinkle generously with grated Parmesan and Swiss cheeses and drizzle with olive oil. For Mushroom Pizza, spread with tomato-garlic sauce (page 172). Scatter 2 cups sliced mushrooms on top, 1 cup shredded mozzarella cheese, and 2 tablespoons each grated Parmesan and olive oil.

PASTRY & CAKES

~

*A reputation for good cooking is often built on pastries and
cakes. A solid grounding in the basic skills takes the mystery
out of pie pastry and cream puffs, spongecakes and jelly rolls,
and helps you enjoy the creativity of beautiful baking.*

MAKING BASIC PIE PASTRY

A tender, flaky piecrust sets off any pie filling to perfection. The pastry dough here uses shortening, which makes a dough that is easy to roll out and line into pie plates. It is an excellent all-purpose pastry dough.

FOR A 9-INCH SINGLE-CRUST PIE

1¼ cups flour
¼ teaspoon salt
½ cup shortening
3–4 tablespoons ice water

1 ▲ Sift the flour and salt into a bowl. Add the shortening. Cut or rub it into the flour until it is in pieces the size of small peas.

2 ▲ Sprinkle 3 tablespoons water over the mixture. With a fork, toss gently to mix and moisten it.

Pastrymaking Tips

● A pastry blender works very well, but you can also use two knives, scissor-fashion, to cut the fat into the flour, or rub in the fat with your fingertips.

● It helps if the fat is cold and firm, particularly if making the dough in a food processor or if using butter for tart pastry. If the fat softens too much when being blended into the flour, the pastry may be oily.

● Liquids used in pastrymaking should be ice cold so that they will not melt the fat.

● When cutting or rubbing the fat into the flour, if it should begin to soften and feel oily, put the bowl in the refrigerator to chill 20–30 minutes, then continue.

● When adding the liquid, start with the smaller amount (added all at once, not in a dribble), and only add more if the mixture will not come together. Too much water will result in tough pastry.

● When gathering the mixture together into a ball of dough, handle it as little as possible; overworked pastry will not be tender.

● To avoid shrinkage, refrigerate the pastry dough before rolling out and baking.

3 ▲ Press the dough into a ball. If it is too dry to form a dough, add the remaining water.

5 ▲ To make pastry in a food processor: Combine the flour, salt, and shortening in the work bowl. Process, turning the machine on and off, just until the mixture is crumbly. Add the ice water and process again briefly – just until the dough starts to pull away from the sides of the bowl. It should still look crumbly. Remove the dough from the processor bowl and gather it into a ball. Wrap and refrigerate.

4 ▲ Wrap the ball of dough with plastic wrap or wax paper and refrigerate at least 45 minutes.

Pastry Variations

● For *Whole-Wheat Pie Pastry*: Use 1 cup all-purpose flour and ⅓ cup whole-wheat flour. Increase the ice water to 4–5 tablespoons.

● For *Nut Pie Pastry*: Add ¼ cup finely chopped walnuts or pecans to the flour mixture.

● For *Spice Pie Pastry*: Sift 1 teaspoon cinnamon with the flour.

● For a *Double-Crust Pie*: Use 2¼ cups flour, ½ teaspoon salt, ¾ cup shortening, and 6–7 tablespoons ice water for basic pie pastry. (For nut or spice pastry, double the additions, using ½ cup finely chopped nuts added to the flour or 2 teaspoons cinnamon sifted with the flour.) Divide dough in half, shape into balls, and wrap separately.

Sweet Potato Pie

SERVES 6–8

1½ pounds sweet potatoes, unpeeled

¾ cup firmly packed light brown sugar

2 eggs, separated

pinch of salt

1 teaspoon ground cinnamon

½ teaspoon ground ginger

¼ teaspoon grated nutmeg

¾ cup whipping cream

pinch of cream of tartar (if needed)

9-inch pie shell made from plain or spice pie pastry

1 Put the sweet potatoes in a saucepan of boiling water. Simmer until tender, 20–25 minutes. Drain and let cool. When the sweet potatoes are cool enough to handle, peel them.

2 ▲ Purée the sweet potatoes in a blender or food processor; there should be 1½ cups of purée.

3 Preheat the oven to 375°F.

4 ▲ Combine the purée, sugar, egg yolks, salt, and spices in a bowl. Stir well to dissolve the sugar. Add the cream and stir to mix.

5 In another bowl, scrupulously clean and greasefree, beat the egg whites until they will hold a soft peak (the tips will just flop over). If not using a copper bowl, add the cream of tartar when the whites are frothy.

6 ▼ Stir one-quarter of the whites into the sweet potato mixture to lighten it. Fold in the remaining whites with a metal spoon or rubber spatula.

7 Pour the filling into the pie shell and spread it out evenly. Bake until the filling is set and lightly golden brown and the pastry is golden, 40–45 minutes. The filling will rise during baking but will fall again when the pie cools. Serve warm or at room temperature. If desired, the pie can be accompanied by ice cream or sweetened whipped cream.

~ **VARIATION** ~

For Pumpkin Pie, use fresh or canned pumpkin instead of sweet potatoes.

Rolling Out and Lining a Pie Plate

A neat crust that doesn't distort or shrink in baking is the desired result. The key to success is handling the dough gently.

First remove the chilled dough from the refrigerator and let it soften slightly at room temperature. Unwrap and put it on a lightly floured surface. Flatten the dough into a neat, round disk. Sprinkle the top with a little flour. Lightly flour the rolling pin.

Rolling Out and Lining Tips

● A pastry cloth and a stockinette cover for your rolling pin will ensure that your pastry dough does not stick when rolling out.
● Reflour the surface and rolling pin if the dough starts to stick.
● Should the dough tear, patch the hole with a small piece of moistened dough.
● When rolling out and lining the pie plate, do not stretch the dough. It will only shrink back during baking, spoiling the shape of the pie shell.
● Once or twice during rolling out, gently push in the edges of the dough with your cupped palms, to keep the circular shape.
● A pastry scraper will help lift the dough from the work surface, to wrap it around the rolling pin.
● Pie plates made from heat-resistant glass or dull-finish metal such as heavyweight aluminum will give a crisp crust.
● When finishing the edge, be sure to hook the dough over the rim all the way around or to press the dough firmly to the rim. This will prevent the dough pulling away should it start to shrink slightly during baking.
● To prevent the edge of the pie-crust from overbrowning, cover it with foil. Remove the foil half-way through baking.

1 ▲ Using even pressure, start rolling out the dough, working from the center to the edge each time and easing the pressure slightly as you reach the edge.

3 ▲ Continue rolling out until the dough circle is about 2 inches larger all around than the pie plate. The dough will be about ⅛-inch thick.

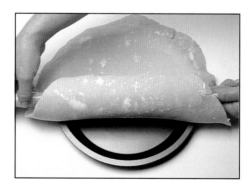

5 ▲ Hold the pin over the pie plate and gently unroll the dough so it drapes into the plate, centering it as much as possible.

2 ▲ Lift up the dough and give it a quarter turn from time to time during the rolling. This will prevent the dough sticking to the surface, and will help keep the thickness even.

4 ▲ Set the rolling pin on the dough, near one side of the circle. Fold the outside edge of dough over the pin, then roll the pin over the dough to wrap the dough around it. Do this gently and loosely.

6 ▲ With your fingertips, ease the dough into the plate, gently pressing it smoothly over the bottom and up the side. With kitchen scissors or a knife, trim the dough according to the edge to be made.

FINISHING THE EDGE OF A PIE

1 ▲ For a fork-finished edge: Trim the dough even with the rim and press it flat. Firmly and evenly press the tines of a fork all around the edge. If the fork sticks, dip it in flour.

2 ▲ For a fluted or pinched edge: Trim the dough to leave a ½-inch overhang all around. Fold the extra dough under to build up the edge. Put the knuckle or tip of the index finger of one hand inside the edge, pointing directly out. With the thumb and index finger of your other hand, pinch the dough edge around your index finger into a "V" shape. Continue all the way around the edge.

3 ▲ For a ruffled or scalloped edge: Trim the dough to leave a ½-inch overhang all around. Fold the extra dough under to build up the edge. Hold the thumb and index finger of one hand 1 inch apart, inside the edge, pointing directly out. With the index finger of your other hand, gently pull the dough between them, to the end of the rim. Continue all the way around the edge.

Apple and Cherry Streusel Pie
Mix together 3 cups peeled, cored, and sliced apples, 2 cups pitted tart red cherries, and ½ cup firmly packed light brown sugar. Put the fruit mixture into a 9-inch pie shell and spread out evenly. For the topping, combine ⅔ cup flour, ½ cup firmly packed brown sugar, and 1 teaspoon ground cinnamon. Cut in 6 tablespoons butter until the mixture resembles coarse crumbs. Sprinkle evenly over the fruit. Bake in a preheated 375°F oven until golden brown, about 45 minutes. *Serves 6.*

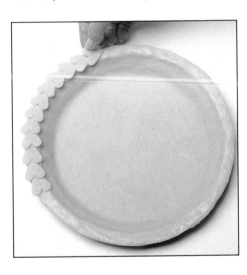

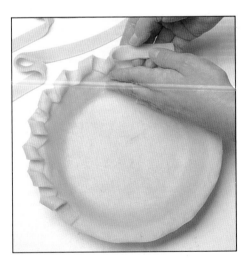

4 ▲ For a cutout edge: Trim the dough even with the rim of the pie plate and press it flat on the rim. With a small cookie cutter, cut out shapes from the dough trimmings. Moisten the edge of the pastry shell and press the cutouts in place, overlapping them slightly if desired.

5 ▲ For a ribbon edge: Trim the dough even with the rim of the pie plate and press it flat on the rim. Cut long strips, about ¾-inch wide, from the dough trimmings. Moisten the edge and press one end of a strip onto it. Twist the strip gently and press it onto the edge again. Continue all the way around the edge.

MAKING A DOUBLE-CRUST PIE

Two tender pastry layers enveloping a sweet filling – what could be nicer? It is easy to see why the double-crust pie is an American institution.

Apple Pie
Combine 6 cups peeled, cored, and thinly sliced apples, 1 tablespoon flour, ½ cup sugar, and ¾ teaspoon apple pie spice. Toss together until the fruit is evenly coated with the sugar and flour. Use to fill the pie (use spice pie pastry if desired). Bake in a preheated 375°F oven until the pastry is golden brown and the fruit is tender (test with a skewer through a slit in the crust), about 45 minutes. Cool on a rack.

1 ▲ Roll out half of the pastry dough on a floured surface and line a pie plate. Trim the dough even with the rim of the pie plate.

2 ▲ Put in the filling. Brush the edge of the pie shell evenly with water to moisten it.

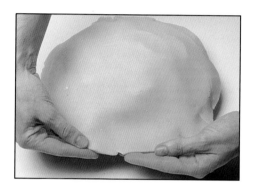

3 ▲ Roll out a second piece of dough to a circle that is about 1 inch larger all around than the pie plate. Roll it up around the rolling pin and unroll it over the pie. Press the edges together.

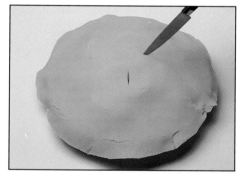

4 ▲ Trim the edge of the top crust to leave a ½-inch overhang. Cut slits or a design in the center. These will act as steam vents during baking.

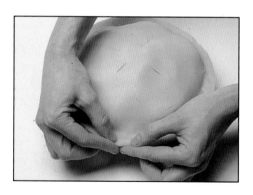

5 ▲ Fold the overhang under the edge of the bottom crust. Press the two crusts together gently and evenly to seal. Finish the edge, as desired.

6 ▲ Brush the top crust with milk or cream for a shiny finish. Or, brush with 1 egg yolk mixed with 1 teaspoon water for a glazed golden-brown finish. Or, brush with water and then sprinkle with sugar or cinnamon-sugar for a sugary crust.

7 ▲ If desired, cut out decorative shapes from the dough trimmings, rolled out as thinly as possible. Moisten the cutouts with a little water and press them onto the top crust. Glaze the decorations before baking.

Blueberry Pie

SERVES 6–8

pastry for a 9-inch double-crust pie
(page 222, pastry variations)

4 cups blueberries

¾ cup plus 1 tablespoon sugar

3 tablespoons flour

1 teaspoon grated orange rind

¼ teaspoon grated nutmeg

2 tablespoons orange juice

1 teaspoon lemon juice

1 Preheat the oven to 375°F.

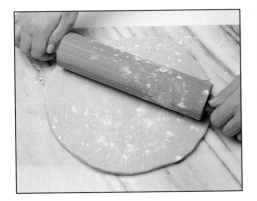

2 ▲ On a lightly floured surface, roll out half of the pastry and use to line a 9-inch pie plate.

3 ▲ Combine the blueberries, ¾ cup of the sugar, the flour, orange rind, and nutmeg in a bowl. Toss the mixture gently to coat the fruit evenly with the dry ingredients.

4 ▼ Pour the blueberry mixture into the pie shell and spread it evenly. Sprinkle over the citrus juices.

5 Roll out the remaining pastry and cover the pie. Cut out small decorative shapes or cut 2–3 slits for steam vents. Finish the edge as desired.

6 ▲ Brush the top crust lightly with water and sprinkle evenly with the remaining sugar.

7 Bake until the pastry is golden brown, about 45 minutes. Serve warm or at room temperature.

Making a Lattice Top

A woven pastry lattice is a very attractive finish for a pie. Prepare pastry dough for a double-crust pie.

Roll out half of the pastry dough and line the pie plate. Trim the dough to leave a ½-inch overhang all around. Put in the filling. Roll out the second piece of dough into a circle that is about 2 inches larger all around than the pie plate.

1 ▲ With the help of a ruler, cut neat, straight strips of dough that are about ½-inch wide, using a knife or fluted pastry wheel.

2 ▲ **For a square woven lattice**: Lay half of the strips across the pie filling, keeping them neatly parallel and spacing them evenly.

Apricot Lattice Pie
Combine 6 cups peeled, pitted, thinly sliced apricots, 2 tablespoons flour, and ½ cup sugar. Toss to coat the fruit evenly. Fill the pie shell and make a lattice top. Glaze with milk and bake in a preheated 375°F oven until the pastry is golden brown and the filling is bubbling, about 45 minutes. Cool on a wire rack.

3 ▲ Fold back every other strip from the center. Lay another strip across the center, on the flat strips, at right angles to them. Lay the folded strips flat again.

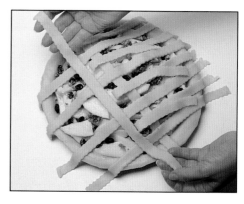

4 ▲ Now fold back those strips that were not folded the first time. Lay another strip across those that are flat now, spacing this new strip evenly from the center strip.

5 ▲ Continue folding the strips in this way until half of the lattice is completed. Repeat on the other half of the pie.

6 ▲ Trim the ends of the strips even with the rim of the pie plate. Moisten the edge of the bottom crust and press the strips gently to it to seal. Finish the edge.

7 ▲ **For a diamond lattice**: Weave as above, laying the intersecting strips diagonally instead of at right angles. Or, lay half the strips over the filling and the remaining strips on top.

Walnut and Pear Lattice Pie

nut pie pastry for a 9-inch double-crust
   pie (page 222, pastry variations)

6 cups peeled, cored, and thinly sliced
   pears

⅓ cup granulated sugar

¼ cup flour

½ teaspoon grated lemon rind

¼ cup raisins

¼ cup chopped walnuts

½ teaspoon ground cinnamon

½ cup confectioners' sugar

1 tablespoon lemon juice

about 2 teaspoons cold water

1 Preheat the oven to 375°F.

2 Roll out half of the pastry dough
and use to line a 9-inch pie plate that
is about 2 inches deep.

3 ▲ Combine the pears, granulated
sugar, flour, and lemon rind in a bowl.
Toss gently to combine the fruit with
the dry ingredients. Mix in the
raisins, nuts, and cinnamon.

~ COOK'S TIP ~

For a simple cutout lattice top, roll
out the dough for the top into a
circle. Using a small cookie cutter,
cut out shapes in a pattern,
spacing them evenly and not too
close together.

4 ▲ Put the pear filling into the pie
shell and spread it evenly.

5 Roll out the remaining pastry
dough and use to make a lattice top.

6 Bake until the pastry is golden
brown, about 55 minutes.

7 Combine the confectioners' sugar,
lemon juice, and water in a bowl and
stir until smoothly blended.

8 ▼ Remove the pie from the oven.
With a spoon, drizzle the confectioners'
sugar glaze evenly over the top of the
pie, on pastry and filling. Let the pie
cool on a wire rack before serving.

MAKING TART PASTRY

The pastry for tarts and quiches is made mainly with butter, giving a rich and crumbly result. The more butter used, the richer the pastry will be – almost like a cookie dough – and the harder to roll out. If you have difficulty rolling it, you can press it into the pan instead, or roll it out between sheets of plastic wrap for easier handling.

Tart pastry, like pie pastry, can be made by hand or in a food processor. The tips for making, handling, and using pie pastry found on pages 222–224 apply equally to tart pastry.

FOR A 9-INCH TART SHELL

1½ cups flour
½ teaspoon salt
6 tablespoons butter, chilled
3 tablespoons shortening
1 egg yolk
¼ teaspoon lemon juice
2–3 tablespoons ice water

1 ▲ Sift the flour and salt into a bowl. Add the butter and shortening. Cut or rub into the flour until the mixture resembles coarse meal.

2 ▲ In a small bowl, mix the egg yolk, lemon juice, and 2 tablespoons water. Add to the flour mixture. With a fork, toss gently to mix and moisten.

3 ▲ Press the dough into a rough ball. If it is too dry to come together, add the remaining water. Turn onto the work surface or a pastry board.

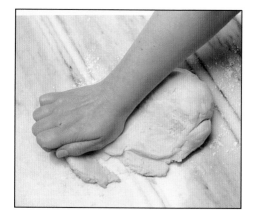

4 ▲ With the heel of your hand, push small portions of dough away from you, smearing them on the work surface.

Tart Pastry Variations

● For *Sweet Tart Pastry*: Reduce the amount of salt to ¼ teaspoon and add 1 tablespoon sugar, sifting it with the flour.
● For *Rich Tart Pastry*: Use 1½ cups flour, ½ teaspoon salt, 9 tablespoons butter, 2 egg yolks, and 1–2 tablespoons ice water.
● For *Rich Sweet Tart Pastry*: Make rich tart pastry, adding 3 tablespoons sugar with the flour and ½ teaspoon vanilla extract with the egg yolks.

5 ▲ Continue mixing the dough in this way until it feels pliable and can be peeled easily off the surface.

6 ▲ Press the dough into a smooth ball. Wrap with plastic wrap and refrigerate at least 2 hours.

LINING A TART PAN OR FLAN RING

A tart pan is shallow, with no rim. Its straight sides (smooth or fluted) give a tart or quiche the traditional shape. The most useful pans have removable bottoms, making it easy to unmold a tart. Flan rings, also called tart bands, are straight-sided metal rings that are set on a baking sheet. In addition to these, there are porcelain quiche dishes and small, individual tartlet tins or molds, both plain and fluted.

Pecan Tartlets

Line six 4-inch tartlet shells with tart pastry. Divide 1½ cups pecan halves among them. In a bowl, beat 3 eggs to mix. Add 2 tablespoons melted butter, 1 cup light corn syrup, and ½ teaspoon vanilla extract. In another bowl, sift together 1 cup sugar and 1 tablespoon flour. Add to the egg mixture and stir until evenly blended. Divide among the tartlet shells and let stand until the nuts rise to the surface. Bake in a preheated 350°F oven until a knife inserted in the filling near the center comes out clean, 35–40 minutes. Let cool on a wire rack before serving. *Makes 6.*

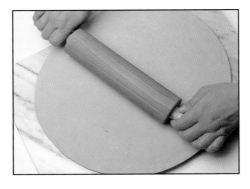

1 ▲ Remove the chilled dough from the refrigerator and let it soften slightly at room temperature. Roll out to a circle that is about 2 inches larger all around than the tart pan. It will be about ⅛-inch thick.

3 ▲ With your fingertips, ease the dough into the pan, gently pressing it smoothly over the bottom, without stretching it.

5 ▲ Roll the rolling pin over the top of the pan to cut off excess pastry dough. Smooth the cut edge and press it against the side of the pan, if necessary, to keep it in place.

2 ▲ Roll up the dough around the rolling pin, then unroll it over the pan, draping it gently.

4 ▲ Fold the overhanging dough down inside the pan, to thicken the side of the pastry shell. Smooth and press the side of the shell against the side of the pan.

6 ▲ For tartlet molds: Arrange them close together and unroll the dough over the molds, draping it loosely. Roll the rolling pin over the top to cut off excess pastry. Press into the bottom and sides of the molds.

BAKING A PASTRY SHELL WITHOUT A FILLING

Baked custard and cream fillings can make pastry soggy, so the shells for these pies and tarts are often prebaked before the filling is added and the final baking is done. Such prebaking is referred to as baking "blind." The technique is also used for pastry shells that are to be filled with an uncooked or precooked mixture.

The purpose of using weights is to prevent the bottom of the pastry shell from rising too much and becoming distorted, thus keeping its neat shape.

1 ▲ Set the pie plate, tart pan, or flan ring on a sheet of parchment paper or foil. Draw or mark around its base. Cut out a circle about 3 inches larger all around than the drawn or marked one.

2 ▲ Roll out the pastry dough and use to line the pie plate, tart pan, or flan ring set on a baking sheet. Prick the bottom of the pastry shell all over with a fork.

Fresh Strawberry Tart

Make the shell using sweet tart pastry or rich sweet tart pastry. Bake it "blind" and then let it cool. Combine 14 ounces cream cheese, ¼ cup sugar, 1 egg yolk, and ¼ cup whipping cream. Beat until smooth. Fold in 1 stiffly beaten egg white. Pour the mixture into the tart shell and spread it evenly. Bake at 350°F until the filling is softly set, 15–20 minutes; it will set further as it cools. Let cool. Arrange halved strawberries neatly over the surface in concentric circles. Heat ½ cup red currant jelly until it melts; brush it all over the berries to glaze them. Let cool and set before serving. *Serves 6.*

3 ▲ Lay the circle of parchment paper or foil in the pastry shell and press it smoothly over the bottom and up the side.

4 ▲ Put enough dried beans or pie weights in the shell to cover the bottom thickly.

5 ▲ For partially baked pastry: Bake the shell in a preheated 400°F oven until it is slightly dry and set, 15–20 minutes. Remove the paper or foil and beans. It is now ready to be filled and baked further.

6 ▲ For fully baked pastry: After baking 15 minutes, remove the paper or foil and beans. Prick the bottom again with a fork. Return to the oven and continue baking until golden brown, 5–10 minutes longer. Let cool completely before adding the filling.

Quiche Lorraine

SERVES 6

½ pound sliced bacon, cut across into ½-inch pieces

9-inch tart shell, made with tart pastry (page 230) and partially baked "blind"

3 eggs

2 egg yolks

1½ cups whipping cream

½ cup milk

salt and pepper

1 Preheat the oven to 400°F.

2 ▲ Fry the bacon over medium heat until it is crisp and has rendered most of its fat. Drain on paper towels.

3 ▲ Scatter the bacon in the partially baked tart shell.

4 Beat together the eggs, egg yolks, cream, and milk. Season with salt and pepper.

5 ▼ Pour the egg mixture into the pastry shell.

6 Bake until the filling is set and golden brown and the pastry is golden, 35–40 minutes. Serve warm or at room temperature.

~ VARIATIONS ~

Add ¾ cup shredded Gruyère or Swiss cheese with the bacon. Replace the bacon with diced cooked ham, if desired. For a vegetarian quiche, omit the bacon. Slice 1 pound zucchini and fry in a little oil until lightly browned on both sides. Drain on paper towels, then arrange in the tart shell. Scatter ½ cup shredded cheese on top. Make the egg mixture with 4 eggs, 1 cup cream, ¼ cup milk, ⅛ teaspoon grated nutmeg, salt, and pepper.

MAKING A CRUMB CRUST

A crumb crust is one of the simplest piecrusts to make, and the variations in flavoring are almost endless. Crumbs from any dry cookie can be used as well as cracker crumbs. You can also use bread crumbs and cake crumbs. Most crumb crusts are sweet, to hold sweet fillings, but there are also unsweetened crumb crusts for savory cheesecakes.

MAKES AN 8- OR 9-INCH CRUST

1¾ cups fine crumbs (see below)
½ cup butter, melted
3–4 tablespoons sugar (optional)

1 ▲ Combine the crumbs, melted butter, and sugar, plus other flavorings, if using. Stir well to mix.

2 ▲ Turn the crumb mixture into a buttered 8-inch springform cake pan or 9-inch pie plate. Spread it evenly over the bottom and up the side.

Crumb Crust Flavorings

● Use graham crackers, plain or cinnamon-flavored. Sweeten with sugar to taste. For plain crackers, add 1 teaspoon ground cinnamon or ginger or ½ teaspoon freshly grated nutmeg.
● Use plain graham crackers and sweeten with sugar to taste. Add 1 teaspoon grated lemon rind or 2 teaspoons grated orange rind.
● Use 1 cup graham cracker crumbs and ½ cup ground or very finely chopped nuts (almonds, hazelnuts, pecans, or walnuts).
● Use vanilla or chocolate wafers, gingersnaps, shortbread, amaretti cookies, or crisp macaroons. No sugar is needed.
● Use saltines or crackers for cheese, without adding sugar, for a savory filling.

3 ▲ With the back of a large spoon or your fingers, press the crumb mixture firmly against the pie plate, to pack the crumbs into a solid crust.

4 ▲ According to recipe directions, refrigerate the crust to set it, usually at least 1 hour. Or, bake the crust in a preheated 350°F oven 8–10 minutes; let cool before filling.

Crushing the Crumbs

To make fine crumbs, break the cookies or crackers into small pieces. Put them, a small batch at a time, in a heavy-duty plastic bag and roll over them with a rolling pin. Or, grind finely in a blender or food processor.

Easy Chocolate Cream Pie

Prepare the crumb crust using chocolate wafers and pressing it into a 9-inch pie plate. Bake and let cool. Melt 6 ounces semisweet chocolate with 3 tablespoons milk; let cool. Whip 2 cups heavy whipping cream until thick. Fold the cream into the cooled chocolate. Spread evenly in the crust. Cover and refrigerate until firm. Just before serving, garnish with chocolate curls or grated chocolate. *Serves 6.*

Rich Orange Cheesecake

SERVES 8

1½ pounds cream cheese, at room
    temperature

1 cup sugar

2 tablespoons flour

3 eggs

1 stick (8 tablespoons) butter, melted

1 teaspoon vanilla extract

1 tablespoon grated orange rind

8-inch crumb crust, made in a
    springform cake pan with graham
    crackers and orange rind, chilled

4 sweet oranges, peeled and sectioned

squeeze of lemon juice

1–2 tablespoons orange liqueur
    (optional)

1 Preheat the oven to 300°F.

2 ▲ Combine the cream cheese,
sugar, and flour in a bowl. Beat until
light and fluffy.

3 ▲ Add the eggs, butter, vanilla,
and orange rind and beat until
smoothly blended.

4 ▲ Pour the filling into the crumb
crust. Set the springform pan on a
baking sheet.

5 Bake until the filling is gently set,
1–1¼ hours (it will continue to firm
up as it cools). If the top browns too
quickly, cover with foil. Turn off the
oven and open the door.

6 Let the cheesecake cool in the
oven. When it is cold, cover and
refrigerate overnight.

7 Mix together the orange sections,
lemon juice, and liqueur, if using.
Serve with the cheesecake.

~ VARIATIONS ~

For Lemon Cheesecake, use
1½ teaspoons lemon rind instead
of orange in the filling. For a
lighter cheesecake, use a mixture
of ricotta cheese and cream
cheese, worked in a food processor
until smooth.

CREAM-PUFF PASTRY

Unlike other pastries, where the fat is cut into the flour, with cream-puff pastry (also called choux pastry) the butter is melted with water and then the flour is added, followed by eggs. The result is more of a paste than a pastry. It is easy to make, but take care in measuring the ingredients.

FOR 18 SMALL PUFFS OR 12 ECLAIRS

1 stick (8 tablespoons) butter, cut into pieces

1 cup water

2 teaspoons sugar (optional)

¼ teaspoon salt

1 cup flour

4 eggs, beaten to mix

Shaping Cream-Puff Pastry
- For *large puffs*: Use two large spoons dipped in water (and your wet fingers, if necessary). Drop the paste in 2- or 2½-inch-wide blobs on the paper-lined baking sheet, leaving 1½–2 inches between each. Alternatively, for well-shaped puffs, pipe the paste using a pastry bag fitted with a ¾-inch plain tube.
- For *small puffs or profiteroles*: Use two small spoons or a pastry bag fitted with a ½-inch tube, and shape 1-inch-wide blobs.
- For *éclairs*: Use a pastry bag fitted with a ¾-inch plain tube. Pipe strips 4- to 5-inches long.
- For a *ring*: Draw a 12-inch circle on the parchment paper. Spoon the paste in large blobs on it. Or, pipe 2 rings on either side of the circle and a third ring on top.

Baking Cream-Puff Pastry
Large puffs and éclairs need 30–35 minutes, small puffs 20–25 minutes, rings 40–45 minutes.

1 ▲ Combine the butter, water, sugar, if using, and salt in a large heavy-based saucepan. Bring to a boil over medium-high heat, stirring occasionally to help melt the butter.

3 ▲ Return the pan to medium heat and cook, stirring, until the mixture will form a ball, pulling away from the side of the pan. This will take about 1 minute. Remove from the heat again and let cool 3–5 minutes.

5 ▲ While still warm, shape large cream puffs, éclairs, small puffs or profiteroles, or large rings on a baking sheet lined with parchment paper.

2 ▲ As soon as the mixture is boiling, remove the pan from the heat. Add the flour all at once and beat vigorously with a wooden spoon to mix the flour into the liquid.

4 ▲ Add a little of the beaten egg and beat well with the spoon or an electric mixer to incorporate. Add a little more egg and beat in well. Continue beating in the eggs until the mixture becomes a smooth, shiny paste thick enough to hold its shape.

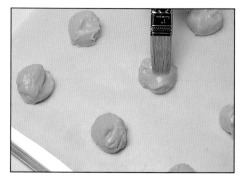

6 ▲ Brush with an egg glaze made by beating 1 egg with 1 teaspoon cold water. Put into a preheated 425°F oven, then reduce the heat to 400°F. Bake until puffed and golden brown.

7 ▶ When baked (see baking times, left) make a slit in the side of each puff or éclair, or several around a ring, with the tip of a knife to let the steam inside escape. Return to the turned-off oven and dry out 5–10 minutes. Cool on a wire rack. Shortly before serving, split the pastries open horizontally and fill as desired.

Fillings for Cream-Puff Pastry
● Fill sweet puffs, éclairs, or pro-fiteroles with sweetened whipped cream (page 160), or ice cream (page 167). Serve with bittersweet chocolate sauce (page 203).
● Fill savory puffs with egg salad or hot creamed chicken.

Hot Cheddar Puffs

MAKES ABOUT 28 APPETIZER PUFFS

4 tablespoons butter, cut into pieces

1 cup water

½ teaspoon salt

1 cup flour

¼ teaspoon mustard powder

⅛ teaspoon hot paprika

½ cup grated sharp Cheddar cheese

4 eggs, beaten

1 egg, beaten with 1 teaspoon cold water, for glazing

FOR THE FILLING

½ pound cream cheese, at room temperature

2 tablespoons smooth, spicy fruit sauce

¼ cup diced canned pimiento

2 tablespoons chopped black or green olives

1 Preheat the oven to 425°F.

2 Make the cream-puff pastry, adding the mustard and paprika with the flour and beating in the cheese before the eggs. Shape into small puffs on a baking sheet lined with parchment paper. Brush with the egg glaze.

3 Put them in the oven and immediately reduce the temperature to 400°F. Bake until risen, golden brown, and crisp, 20–25 minutes.

4 ▲ Meanwhile, for the filling, beat the cream cheese with the spicy fruit sauce until well blended. Mix in the pimiento and olives.

5 Cut a slit in the side of each puff and return to the turned-off oven to dry out about 10 minutes.

6 ▼ While the puffs are still warm, fill them with the cheese filling, piping or spooning it carefully into the slit cut in the side of each puff. Serve warm.

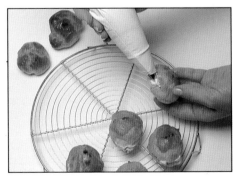

MAKING A BUTTER CAKE

The butter cake, with its tender crumb and rich, moist flavor, is always popular. It is delicious enough to be served plain, with just a dusting of sugar (as with pound cake), or it can be layered and frosted.

To make a butter cake, the fat and sugar are "creamed" together before the eggs and dry ingredients are added. The fat (butter, margarine, or shortening) should be soft enough to be beaten, so if necessary remove it from the refrigerator and let it stand at room temperature at least 30 minutes. For best results, the eggs should be at room temperature, too.

Pound Cake
Make the batter using 2 sticks (½ pound) butter, 2 cups sugar, 4 eggs, 3 cups cake flour, ¼ teaspoon salt, ½ teaspoon baking soda, 1¼ cups milk, ½ teaspoon vanilla extract, and 1 teaspoon almond extract. Pour into a greased and floured 9- × 5-inch loaf pan. Bake in a preheated 350°F oven for about 1½ hours. Cool in the pan 15 minutes, then unmold onto a wire rack to cool completely. Dust with confectioners' sugar before serving.

1 ▲ Sift the flour with the salt, leavening agent(s), and any other dry ingredients, such as spices or cocoa powder. Set aside.

3 ▲ Add the sugar to the creamed fat gradually. With the mixer at medium-high speed, beat it into the fat until the mixture is pale and very fluffy, 4–5 minutes. The sugar should be completely incorporated. During this process, air will be beaten into the mixture, which will help the cake to rise.

5 ▲ Add the dry ingredients to the beaten mixture, beating at low speed just until smoothly combined.

2 ▲ Put the fat in a large, deep bowl and beat with an electric mixer at medium speed until the texture is soft and pliable.

4 ▲ Add the eggs or egg yolks, one at a time, beating well after each addition (about 45 seconds). Scrape the bowl often so all the ingredients are evenly combined. When adding the eggs, the mixture may begin to curdle, especially if the eggs are cold. If this happens, add 1 tablespoon of the measured flour.

6 ▲ If the recipe calls for any liquid, add it in small portions alternately with portions of the dry ingredients.

7 ▲ If the recipe directs, beat egg whites separately until frothy, add sugar, and continue beating until stiff peaks form. Fold into the batter.

8 ▲ Pour the batter into a cake pan or pans, prepared according to recipe directions, and bake as directed.

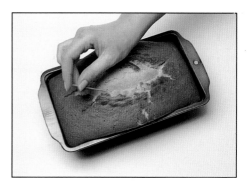

9 ▲ To test butter cakes for doneness, insert a cake tester, skewer, or wooden toothpick into the center; it should come out clean.

MAKING SEVEN-MINUTE FROSTING

This fluffy white frosting has an attractive gloss and a texture like divinity candy. It is ideal for filling and frosting layer cakes.

MAKES ENOUGH TO FROST THE TOP AND SIDES OF TWO 9-INCH CAKE LAYERS

1½ cups sugar
¼ teaspoon cream of tartar
2 egg whites
¼ cup cold water
1 tablespoon light corn syrup
2 teaspoons vanilla extract

1 ▲ Combine the sugar, cream of tartar, egg whites, water, and corn syrup in a large heatproof bowl or large double boiler. Stir just to mix.

2 ▲ Set the bowl over a saucepan of boiling water. The base of the bowl should not touch the water.

Seven-Minute Frosting Variations
- For *Orange Frosting*: Use orange juice instead of water and add 1 teaspoon grated orange rind. Reduce the vanilla to ½ teaspoon.
- For *Lemon Frosting*: Use 2 tablespoons each lemon juice and water and add ½ teaspoon grated lemon rind. Reduce the vanilla to ½ teaspoon.

3 ▲ Beat with a handheld electric mixer at high speed until the frosting is thick and white, and will form stiff peaks, about 7 minutes.

4 ▲ Remove from the heat. Add the vanilla and continue beating until the frosting has cooled slightly, about 3 minutes. Use immediately.

Coconut Lime Layer Cake

SERVES 8 OR MORE

2½ cups cake flour
2½ teaspoons baking powder
¼ teaspoon salt
10 tablespoons butter, at room temperature
1½ cups sugar
2 teaspoons grated lime rind
3 eggs
½ cup fresh lime juice (from about 4–5 limes)
½ cup water
¾ cup sweetened flaked coconut
1 recipe quantity seven-minute frosting (page 239)

1 Preheat the oven to 350°F. Grease two 9-inch layer cake pans and line the bottoms with greased wax or parchment paper.

2 Sift together the flour, baking powder, and salt.

3 In a large bowl, beat the butter until it is soft and pliable. Add the sugar and lime rind and beat until the mixture is pale and fluffy. Beat in the eggs, one at a time.

4 ▲ Beat in the sifted dry ingredients in small portions, alternating with the lime juice and water. When the mixture is smooth, gently stir in ½ cup of the coconut.

5 ▲ Divide the batter between the prepared pans and spread it evenly to the sides. Bake the cake layers until done, 30–35 minutes.

6 ▲ Remove the cake layers from the oven and set them, in their pans, on a wire rack. Let cool 10 minutes. Then unmold and peel off the lining paper. Cool completely on the rack.

7 ▲ Spread the remaining coconut in another cake pan. Bake until golden brown, stirring occasionally. Watch carefully so that the coconut does not get too dark. Let cool.

8 ▲ Put one of the cake layers, base up, on a serving plate. Spread a layer of frosting evenly over the cake.

9 ▲ Set the second layer on top, base down. Spread the remaining frosting all over the top and around sides of the cake.

10 ▲ Scatter the toasted coconut over the top of the cake and let set before serving.

MAKING A ONE-BOWL CAKE

Many cakes are made by an easy "one-bowl" method where all the ingredients are combined in a bowl and beaten thoroughly. The mixture can also be made in a food processor, but take care not to overprocess.

Chiffon cakes are a variation on this theme. The eggs are separated and the batter is made by the one-bowl method using the yolks. The whites are beaten separately and then folded into the batter.

1 ▲ Sift the dry ingredients (flour, salt, leavening agents, spices, and so on) into a bowl.

2 ▲ Add the liquid ingredients (eggs, melted fat, milk, fruit juices, and so on) and beat until smooth, with an electric mixer for speed. Pour the batter into the prepared pans and bake as directed.

MAKING BUTTER FROSTING

Simple to make and easy to spread, butter frosting is ideal for butter cakes, layer cakes, and spongecakes. The basic vanilla frosting can be varied with many other flavors, and it can be tinted with food coloring, too.

MAKES ENOUGH TO FROST THE TOP AND SIDES OF TWO 9-INCH CAKE LAYERS

9 tablespoons butter, preferably unsalted, at room temperature

3 cups confectioners' sugar, sifted

1½ teaspoons vanilla extract

about 2 tablespoons milk

1 ▲ Put the butter in a deep mixing bowl and beat it with an electric mixer at medium speed, or a wooden spoon, until it is soft and pliable.

2 ▲ Gradually add the confectioners' sugar, and beat at medium-high speed. Continue beating until the mixture is pale and fluffy.

3 ▲ Add the vanilla extract and 1 tablespoon milk. Beat until smooth and of a spreading consistency. If it is too thick, beat in more milk. If too thin, beat in more sugar.

Butter Frosting Variations
• For *Orange or Lemon Butter Frosting*: Grate the rind from 1 small orange or ½ lemon; squeeze the juice. Beat in the rind with the sugar; use juice instead of the vanilla and milk.
• For *Chocolate Butter Frosting*: Add 6 tablespoons unsweetened cocoa powder, beating it in with the sugar. Increase milk to 3–4 tablespoons.

• For *Mocha Butter Frosting*: Warm the milk and dissolve 1 tablespoon instant coffee powder in it; cool and use to make chocolate butter frosting, adding more milk if needed.
• For *Coffee Butter Frosting*: Warm the milk and dissolve 1½ tablespoons of instant coffee powder in it; cool before adding to the butter frosting.

German Chocolate Cupcakes

MAKES 24

4 ounces sweet cooking chocolate, cut into small pieces
¼ cup water
2 cups cake flour
1 teaspoon baking powder
½ teaspoon baking soda
pinch of salt
1½ cups sugar
¾ cup butter or shortening, at room temperature
⅔ cup buttermilk or milk
1 teaspoon vanilla extract
3 eggs
1 recipe quantity butter frosting, flavored to taste

1 Preheat the oven to 350°F. Grease and flour 24 muffin pans, 2½ to 2¾ inches in diameter, or line them with paper cupcake liners.

2 ▲ Put the chocolate and water in a bowl set over a pan of almost simmering water. Heat until melted and smooth, stirring. Remove from the heat and let cool.

3 Sift the flour, baking powder, soda, salt, and sugar into a large bowl. Add the chocolate mixture, butter, buttermilk, and vanilla.

4 ▲ With an electric mixer on medium-low speed, beat until smoothly blended. Increase the speed to high and beat 2 minutes. Add the eggs and beat 2 minutes.

5 Divide the batter evenly among the muffin pans.

6 Bake until a toothpick inserted into the center of a cupcake comes out clean, 20–25 minutes. Cool in the pans 10 minutes, then unmold and let cool completely on a wire rack.

7 ▼ Frost the top of each cupcake with butter frosting, swirling it into a peak in the center.

MAKING A CLASSIC SPONGECAKE

The classic spongecake contains no fat and no leavening agents – just eggs, sugar, and flour. The light, airy texture of the finished cake depends on the air beaten into the batter.

Sometimes the eggs are separated for a spongecake and sometimes the cake is enriched with butter (called a "genoise", or butter spongecake).

Spongecake can be simply dusted with confectioners' sugar, layered with sweetened whipped cream, filled with preserves or fruit if desired, or used to make a jelly roll.

If you use a countertop electric mixer to beat the eggs and sugar, or if using separated eggs, there is no need to set the bowl over a pan of simmering water.

Basic Spongecake
Make the cake batter using 4 whole eggs, ¾ cup sugar, and ¾ cup cake flour. Pour the batter into a greased, bottom-lined, and floured 9-inch round cake pan. Bake in a preheated 350°F oven 30–35 minutes. Let the cake cool in the pan 10 minutes, then un-mold onto a wire rack and cool completely. Before serving, peel off the lining paper. Dust lightly with confectioners' sugar.

1 ▲ In a bowl, combine the eggs (at room temperature) and sugar. Set the bowl over a saucepan of simmering water; the base of the bowl should not touch the water.

3 ▲ Lift out the beaters; the mixture on the beaters should trail back onto the surface of the remaining mixture in the bowl to make a ribbon that holds it shape.

5 ▲ Sift the flour and fold it into the mixture, cutting in to the bottom of the bowl with a rubber spatula or large metal spoon, and turning the batter over, working gently yet thoroughly, to retain the volume of the egg and sugar mixture.

2 ▲ Beat with a handheld electric mixer at medium-high speed until the mixture is very thick and pale, about 10 minutes.

4 ▲ Remove the bowl from over the pan of water and continue beating until the mixture is cool, 2–3 minutes.

6 ▲ Pour the batter into the prepared pan or pans and bake as directed. To test if a spongecake is done, press the center lightly with your fingertip: the cake should spring back.

Lemon Spongecake with Cream Cheese Frosting

SERVES 8 OR MORE

4 eggs
¾ cup granulated sugar
¾ cup cake flour
1 teaspoon grated lemon rind
FOR THE FROSTING
¾ cup (6 ounces) cream cheese, at room temperature
4 tablespoons butter, at room temperature
4 cups confectioners' sugar
3–4 tablespoons fresh lemon juice

1 Preheat the oven to 350°F. Grease, line the bottom, and flour a 9-inch cake pan.

2 Put the eggs and sugar in a large bowl (over a pan of just simmering water if not using a countertop electric mixer). Beat until the mixture is thick and pale. Remove the bowl from the pan of water and continue beating until the mixture is cool. Beat in the lemon rind.

3 Sift the flour and fold it into the mixture with a rubber spatula. Pour the batter into the prepared pan. Bake 35–40 minutes. Let cool.

4 ▲ For the frosting, beat the cream cheese with the butter until smooth. Gradually beat in the sugar. Beat in enough lemon juice to make a fluffy frosting that has a smooth spreadable consistency.

5 ▼ When the cake is cold, cut it into two layers with a long serrated knife, holding it steady with one hand on top. (First, wrap a piece of string around the cake, at the point where you want to cut. Make sure it is level, then pull taut to make an indentation in the cake side to follow while slicing. Remove string before slicing.)

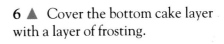

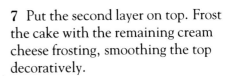

6 ▲ Cover the bottom cake layer with a layer of frosting.

7 Put the second layer on top. Frost the cake with the remaining cream cheese frosting, smoothing the top decoratively.

PREPARING CAKE PANS

Instructions vary from recipe to recipe for preparing cake pans. Some are simply greased, some are greased and floured, some are lined with paper. There are some (such as for angel food cakes) that are not greased at all. The preparation required is based on the type of cake batter and the length of the baking time.

Flavorful Coatings
Some cake recipes direct that the greased pan be coated with sugar, cocoa powder, or fine crumbs. Follow the method for flouring.

1 ▲   To grease a pan: Use butter, shortening, oil, or vegetable cooking spray. If using butter or shortening, hold a small piece in a paper towel (or use your fingers), and rub it all over the bottom and up the side of the pan to make a thin, even coating. If using oil, brush it on with a pastry brush.

2 ▲   To flour a pan: Put a small scoopful of flour in the center of the greased pan. Tip and rotate the pan so that the flour spreads and coats all over the bottom and up the side. Turn the pan over and shake out excess flour, tapping the base of the pan to dislodge any pockets of flour.

3 ▲   To line the bottom of a pan: Use wax or parchment paper. Set the pan on the paper and draw around the base. Cut out this circle, square, or rectangle, cutting just inside the drawn line. Press the paper circle smoothly onto the bottom of the pan.

4 ▲   To line the sides of a pan: Cut a strip of wax or parchment paper long enough to wrap around the outside of the pan and overlap by 1½ inches. The strip should be wide enough to extend 1 inch above the rim of the cake pan.

5 ▲   Fold the strip lengthwise at the 1-inch point and crease it firmly. With scissors, snip at regular intervals along the 1-inch fold, from the edge to the crease. Line the side of the pan, putting the snipped part of the strip on the bottom of the pan.

6 ▲   For square and rectangular cake pans, fold the paper and crease it with your fingernail to fit snugly into the corners of the pan. Then press the bottom paper lining into place.

7 ▲   If the recipe directs, grease the paper before you put it in the pan. If the pan is to be floured, do this after the paper is in place.

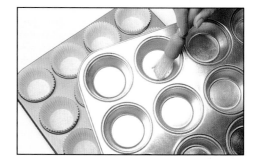

8 ▲   To line muffin cups: Use paper cupcake liners of the required size. Or grease and flour the cups.

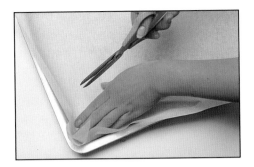

9 ▲ To line a jelly-roll pan: Cut a rectangle of wax or parchment paper 2 inches larger all around than the pan. Grease the bottom of the pan lightly to prevent the paper slipping.

10 ▲ Lay the paper evenly in the pan. With the a table knife, press the paper into the angle all around the bottom of the pan, creasing the paper firmly but not cutting it.

11 ▲ With scissors, snip the paper in the corners, from top to bottom, so it will fit neatly into them. Grease the paper according to recipe directions, unless using nonstick silicone paper.

MAKING A SPONGECAKE WITH SEPARATED EGGS

This version of spongecake is easier to make than the classic spongecake that uses whole eggs, but the results are no less tender and delicious. There is no need to set the bowl over a pan of simmering water for beating, although if you are using a hand whisk, rather than an electric mixer or rotary beater, you may want to do so to speed up the thickening of the egg yolk and sugar mixture and to increase its volume. Bowls and beaters used with egg whites must be scrupulously clean and greasefree.

1 ▲ Separate the eggs, taking care that there is no trace of yolk with the whites. Put the yolks and whites in separate large bowls.

2 ▲ Add most of the sugar to the yolks. With a handheld or countertop electric mixer, beat at medium-high speed until the mixture is very thick and pale. Lift out the beaters. The mixture on the beaters should trail back onto the surface of the remaining mixture in the bowl to make a ribbon that holds its shape.

3 ▲ Beat the egg whites until they form soft peaks (if not using a copper bowl, add a pinch of cream of tartar once the whites become frothy). Add the remaining sugar and beat until the whites will form stiff peaks.

4 ▲ With a rubber spatula, fold the sifted flour into the egg-yolk mixture, then fold in the beaten egg whites. Fold gently but thoroughly. Pour the batter into the prepared pan or pans and bake as directed.

A Butter Spongecake
This whisked sponge, made with whole or separated eggs, is more rich and trickier to make, as melted butter is folded in just before pouring into the pan.

MAKING A JELLY ROLL

A rolled spongecake reveals an attractive swirl of filling when it is sliced. Some filling ideas are sweetened whipped cream (page 160), ice cream (page 167), fruit preserves, or butter frosting (page 242).

The spongecake batter can be made using whole or separated eggs.

Line the pan with wax paper or baking parchment. Grease and dust with flour.

1 ▲ Pour the batter into the prepared pan and spread it evenly into the corners with a metal spatula. Bake as directed in the recipe.

2 ▲ Spread a dish towel flat and lay a sheet of parchment paper on top. Sprinkle the paper evenly as directed with granulated or confectioners' sugar, cocoa powder, or a spice mixture. Invert the cake onto the paper.

Chocolate Ice Cream Roll

Make the spongecake batter using 4 eggs, separated, ⅔ cup sugar, and ⅔ cup cake flour sifted with 3 tablespoons unsweetened cocoa powder. Pour into a prepared 15- × 10-inch jelly roll pan. Bake in a preheated 375°F oven about 15 minutes. Turn out, roll up, and let cool. When cold, unroll the cake and spread with 2½ cups softened vanilla or chocolate ice cream. Roll up the cake again, wrap in foil, and freeze until firm. About 30 minutes before serving, transfer the cake to the refrigerator. Sprinkle with granulated or confectioners' sugar before serving. If desired, serve with warm bittersweet chocolate sauce (page 203). *Serves 6–8.*

3 ▲ Carefully peel off the lining paper from the cake. If necessary, trim off any crisp crust from the side of the cake.

4 ▲ Carefully roll up the cake, with the paper inside, starting from a short side. Wrap the towel around the cake roll and let cool on a wire rack.

5 ▲ Remove the towel and unroll the cake. Lift off the paper. Spread the chosen filling over the cake.

6 ▲ Roll the cake up again, using the paper to help move it forward. Sprinkle with sugar or frost, as the recipe directs.

Yule Log Cake

SERVES 8 OR MORE

4 eggs, separated
¾ cup sugar
1 teaspoon vanilla extract
pinch of cream of tartar (if needed)
¾ cup cake flour, sifted
1 cup whipping cream
10 ounces bittersweet chocolate, chopped
2 tablespoons rum or Cognac

1 Preheat the oven to 375°F. Grease, line the bottom, and flour a 15- × 10-inch jelly roll pan.

2 Put the egg yolks in a large bowl. Reserve 2 tablespoons sugar; add the remainder to the egg yolks. Beat until pale and thick. Beat in the vanilla.

3 In another bowl, scrupulously clean and greasefree, beat the egg whites (with the cream of tartar if not using a copper bowl) until they will hold soft peaks. Add the reserved sugar and continue beating until the whites are glossy and will hold stiff peaks.

4 Add the flour to the egg yolk mixture in 2 batches and gently fold it in. Add one-quarter of the egg whites and fold in to lighten the mixture. Fold in the remaining whites.

5 ▲ Spread the batter in the prepared pan. Bake about 15 minutes.

6 Turn onto paper sprinkled with superfine sugar. Roll up and let cool.

7 Bring the cream to a boil in a small saucepan. Put the chocolate in a bowl, add the cream, and stir until the chocolate has melted.

8 ▲ Beat the chocolate mixture until it is fluffy and has thickened to a spreading consistency. Spoon one-third of the chocolate mixture into another bowl. Mix in rum or Cognac.

9 Unroll the cake. Spread the rum and chocolate mixture evenly over the surface. Roll up the cake again.

10 Cut off about one-quarter of the cake, at an angle. Place it against the side of the larger piece of cake, to resemble a branch from a tree trunk.

11 ▼ Spread the remaining chocolate mixture all over the cake. Mark with the tines of a fork to resemble bark. Before serving, add Christmas decorations, such as sprigs of holly, and dust with a little confectioners' sugar "snow", if desired.

MAKING CAKES BY THE MELTING METHOD

Cakes made by the melting method are wonderfully moist and keep quite well. Ingredients such as sugar, syrup (treacle, honey, corn syrup) and fat are warmed together until melted and smoothly combined before being added to the dry ingredients.

Fruit Cake
Sift 2 cups self-rising flour, a pinch of salt and 1 teaspoon mixed spice. Melt together 8 tablespoons butter or shortening, ½ cup brown sugar, ⅔ cup water and the grated zest and juice of 1 orange. When smooth, add ½ cup each golden raisins, currants and raisins and simmer gently for about 10 minutes, stirring occasionally. Cool. Add the fruit mixture to the dry ingredients. Add ¼ cup each chopped candied cherries and chopped candied peel, 1 tablespoon orange marmalade and 2 beaten eggs. Mix thoroughly. Pour into a greased and lined 8-inch round cake pan. Bake at 325°F for 1½ hours or until firm and golden; a skewer inserted in the center should come out clean. Cool in the pan for 30 minutes before turning out onto a wire rack.

1 ▲ Sift the dry ingredients (such as flour, rising agent, salt, ground spices) into a large bowl.

2 ▲ Put the sugar and/or syrup and fat in a saucepan with any other ingredients specified in the recipe. Warm over a low heat, stirring occasionally, until the fat has melted and sugar dissolved. The mixture should not boil.

3 ▲ If the recipe instructs, warm fruit in the syrup mixture. Remove from the heat and leave to cool slightly (if too hot, it will not combine well with dry ingredients).

4 ▲ Make a well in the center of the dry ingredients and pour in the cooled melted mixture. Add beaten eggs and any other liquid ingredients (milk, water, etc) and beat to a smooth, thick batter.

5 ▲ If called for in the recipe, stir in fruit and/or nuts (if these have not been warmed in the syrup). Turn the cake mixture into a lined tin and bake according to the recipe.

Maturing for flavor
Melting-method cakes taste best if they are allowed to "mature" before serving. After the cake has cooled completely, wrap it in wax paper and then overwrap in foil. Keep it in a cool place for 1–2 days before cutting into slices.

Rich Sticky Gingerbread

MAKES AN 8-INCH SQUARE CAKE

2 cups flour
pinch of salt
1 teaspoon baking soda
2 teaspoons ground ginger
1 teaspoon apple spice
8 tablespoons butter or margarine
4 ounces corn syrup
4 ounces molasses
¼ cup brown sugar
2 eggs, beaten
½ cup milk
½ cup golden raisins or chopped stem ginger (optional)
FOR THE ICING (OPTIONAL)
1 cup confectioners' sugar
about 4 teaspoons water

1 ▲ Preheat a 350°F oven. Grease and line an 8-inch cake pan, using waxed paper.

2 ▲ Sift the flour, salt, baking soda and spices into a bowl.

3 Put the butter or margarine, corn syrup, molasses and brown sugar in a saucepan and warm over a gentle heat, stirring occasionally, until the fat has melted and the mixture is smooth. Remove from the heat and leave to cool slightly.

4 ▼ Make a well in the center of the dry ingredients and add the melted mixture, the beaten eggs and milk. Beat with a wooden spoon until the mixture is smooth. Add the golden raisins or ginger, if using.

5 Turn the cake mixture into the prepared pan. Bake for 1 hour. To test if the gingerbread is done, press it lightly in the center; it should spring back. Allow to cool in the pan for 5 minutes before turning out onto a wire rack to cool completely.

6 ▲ If frosting the gingerbread, sift the confectioners' sugar into a bowl and add 3 teaspoons of the water. Stir to mix. Add more water, 1 teaspoon at a time until the frosting is smooth and has a pouring consistency. Pour over the gingerbread. Leave to set before serving.

INTRODUCTION

~

American home cooking means putting together weekday meals and having friends and relatives over for dinner. It means rummaging through notebooks and file-card boxes to find a special aunt's recipe for roast turkey or a neighbor's elegant chocolate cake.

In preparing this book, we brought together old-time favorites and added new ideas, which reflect the appearance of exotic and specialty ingredients in local markets, and the evolution of the way we eat. But here each recipe is brought to life, every step of the way, in pictures.

It's easy to learn basic cooking know-how with the help of this book. With pictures to guide you at every stage, even a beginner can cook meals with confidence. For the experienced cook, the step-by-step photographs serve as memory-joggers. You will practically be able to cook at a glance from a treasury of over 200 recipes.

To start off a meal or sit down to a simple one, there are chunky soups and cold ones, plus sandwiches to eat with both hands, and appetizers plain and fancy. The seafood recipes take full advantage of our fish- and shellfish-stocked lakes and coastal waters. For many people, meat and poultry are the heart of a meal, and the choice here includes long-simmered as well as speedy dishes. If you have shifted the balance of your diet to grains and fresh produce, you will find recipes for pasta and pizza, beans and vegetables. Baking may be a luxury these days, but with the particulars spelled out, it requires less effort to fill the kitchen with fragrant smells.

Here is American family cooking in all its variety. From the category of foods that mean home and comfort, we chose such standbys as macaroni and cheese, chicken potpie and peach cobbler. Sometimes we put a twist on the basics, offering cornish game hens with cranberry sauce, guacamole cheese-burgers and chocolate brownie sundaes. Regional and immigrant specialties are represented with tacos, jambalaya, calzone, pork with sauerkraut, and more.

The only thing that's missing in *American Home Cooking* are the aromas. Still, there's no substitute for experience. Only you know the quirks of your oven and how to get the best from your equipment. Setting out all the ingredients before beginning and measuring accurately is just sound culinary practice. Even perfect technique won't remedy lack of flavor. Good ingredients are essential to good cooking. Stay in tune with the seasons, choosing fruits and vegetables at their peak. And remember to taste and adjust the seasoning, if necessary, before serving.

Our hectic schedules leave us less time in the kitchen these days, but we hope this book rekindles the pleasures of family cooking. Homemade can make a comeback in your house with the help of *American Home Cooking*.

SOUPS, SANDWICHES
& APPETIZERS

~

Here are soups smooth and creamy, icy and refreshing, or hearty, to start a meal or be a meal in themselves; tempting sandwiches, both hot and cold; and sumptuous party fare.

Winter Vegetable Soup

SERVES 8

1 medium-size head of Savoy cabbage,
   quartered and cored

2 tablespoons corn oil

4 carrots, thinly sliced

2 celery stalks, thinly sliced

2 parsnips, diced

6 cups chicken stock

3 medium-size potatoes, diced

2 zucchini, sliced

1 small red bell pepper, seeded and
   diced

2 cups cauliflower florets

2 tomatoes, seeded and diced

½ teaspoon fresh thyme leaves or ¼
   teaspoon dried thyme

2 tablespoons chopped fresh parsley

salt and pepper

1 Slice the cabbage quarters into thin strips across the leaves.

2 ▲ Heat the oil in a large saucepan. Add the cabbage, carrots, celery, and parsnips and cook 10–15 minutes over medium heat, stirring frequently.

3 Stir the stock into the vegetables and bring to a boil. Skim off any foam that rises to the top.

4 ▲ Add the potatoes, zucchini, bell pepper, cauliflower and tomatoes with the herbs, and salt and pepper to taste. Bring back to a boil. Reduce the heat to low, cover the pan, and simmer until the vegetables are tender, 15–20 minutes.

Fresh Tomato Soup

SERVES 4

2 tablespoons butter or margarine

1 onion, chopped

2 pounds tomatoes, quartered

2 carrots, chopped

2 cups chicken stock

2 tablespoons chopped fresh parsley

½ teaspoon fresh thyme leaves or ¼
   teaspoon dried thyme

⅓ cup whipping cream (optional)

salt and pepper

1 Melt the butter or margarine in a large saucepan. Add the onion and cook until softened, about 5 minutes.

2 ▲ Stir in the tomatoes, carrots, chicken stock, parsley and thyme. Bring to a boil. Reduce the heat to low, cover the pan, and simmer until tender, 15–20 minutes.

3 ▼ Purée the soup in a vegetable mill. Return the puréed soup to the saucepan.

4 Stir in the cream, if using, and reheat gently. Season with salt and pepper. Ladle into warmed soup bowls and serve hot, sprinkled with a little more thyme, if you wish.

~ **COOK'S TIP** ~

Meaty and flavorful Italian plum tomatoes are ideal for this soup.

Winter Vegetable Soup (top), Fresh Tomato soup

Carrot Soup with Ginger

SERVES 6

2 tablespoons butter or margarine

1 onion, chopped

1 celery stalk, chopped

1 medium-size potato, chopped

1½ pounds carrots, chopped

2 teaspoons minced fresh gingerroot

5 cups chicken stock

⅓ cup whipping cream

¼ teaspoon grated nutmeg

salt and pepper

1 ▼ Combine the butter or margarine, onion, and celery and cook until softened, about 5 minutes.

2 Stir in the potato, carrots, gingerroot, and stock. Bring to a boil. Reduce the heat to low, cover the pan, and simmer 20 minutes.

3 ▲ Pour the soup into a food processor or blender and process until smooth. Alternatively, use a vegetable mill to purée the soup. Return the soup to the pan. Stir in the cream and nutmeg, and add salt and pepper to taste. Reheat gently for serving.

Minted Pea Soup

SERVES 6

2 tablespoons butter or margarine

1 onion, chopped

1 small head of Boston lettuce, shredded

2 pounds shelled fresh green peas or frozen peas, thawed

6 cups chicken stock

3 tablespoons chopped fresh mint

salt and pepper

¾ cup whipping cream

fresh mint sprigs, for garnishing

1 ▲ Melt the butter or margarine in a large saucepan. Add the onion and cook until softened, about 5 minutes.

2 ▲ Stir in the lettuce, peas, stock, and mint. Bring to a boil. Reduce the heat to low, cover the pan, and simmer 15 minutes.

~ VARIATION ~

To serve cold, refrigerate the puréed soup until thoroughly chilled, 3–4 hours. Stir all the cream into the soup just before serving, or keep some to swirl onto the surface of each serving.

3 Pour the soup into a blender or food processor and process until smooth. Alternatively, purée the soup in a vegetable mill. Return the puréed soup to the pan. Season to taste.

4 ▲ Stir in ½ cup of the cream and reheat gently. Ladle into bowls and serve with the remaining cream. For a decorative effect, pour a scant tablespoon of cream in a spiral design into the center of each serving, or stir it in and garnish with sprigs of mint.

Carrot Soup with Ginger (top), Minted Pea Soup

Chilled Avocado and Zucchini Soup

SERVES 6

4 cups chicken stock

1 pound zucchini, sliced

2 large, very ripe avocados

3 tablespoons fresh lemon juice

¾ cup plain yogurt

2 teaspoons Worcestershire sauce

½ teaspoon chili powder

⅛ teaspoon sugar

dash of hot pepper sauce

salt

1 In a large saucepan, bring the chicken stock to a boil.

2 ▲ Add the zucchini and simmer until soft, 10–15 minutes. Let cool.

3 ▲ Peel the avocados. Remove and discard the pits. Cut the flesh into chunks and put in a food processor or blender. Add the lemon juice and process until smooth.

4 ▲ Using a slotted spoon, transfer the zucchini to the food processor or blender; reserve the stock. Process the zucchini with the avocado purée.

5 ▲ Pour the avocado-zucchini purée into a bowl. Stir in the reserved stock. Add ½ cup of the yogurt, the Worcestershire sauce, chili powder, sugar, hot pepper sauce, and salt to taste. Mix well. Cover tightly and chill 3–4 hours.

6 To serve, ladle the soup into bowls. Swirl the remaining yogurt on the surface.

Chicken Noodle Soup

Serves 8

1 3-pound chicken, cut in pieces
2 onions, quartered
1 parsnip, quartered
2 carrots, quartered
½ teaspoon salt
1 bay leaf
2 allspice berries
4 black peppercorns
3 quarts water
1 cup very thin egg noodles
sprigs of fresh dill, for garnishing

1 ▲ In a large stockpot, combine the chicken pieces, onions, parsnip, carrots, salt, bay leaf, allspice berries and peppercorns.

2 ▲ Add the water to the pot and bring to a boil, skimming frequently.

3 Reduce the heat to low and simmer 1½ hours, skimming occasionally.

4 Strain the broth through a fine-mesh strainer into a bowl. Refrigerate overnight.

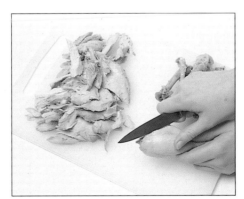

5 ▲ When the chicken pieces are cool enough to handle, remove the meat from the bones. Discard the bones, skin, vegetables, and flavorings. Chop the chicken meat and refrigerate overnight.

6 Remove the solidified fat from the surface of the chilled broth. Pour the broth into a saucepan and bring to a boil. Taste the broth; if a more concentrated flavor is wanted, boil 10 minutes to reduce slightly.

7 ▲ Add the chicken meat and noodles to the broth and cook until the noodles are tender, about 8 minutes (check package directions for timing). Serve hot, garnished with dill sprigs.

Green Bean and Parmesan Soup

SERVES 4

2 tablespoons butter or margarine

½ pound green beans, trimmed

1 garlic clove, minced

2 cups vegetable stock

salt and pepper

½ cup freshly grated Parmesan cheese

¼ cup light cream

2 tablespoons chopped fresh parsley

1 Melt the butter or margarine in a medium saucepan. Add the green beans and garlic and cook 2–3 minutes over medium heat, stirring frequently.

2 ▲ Stir in the stock and season with salt and pepper. Bring to a boil. Reduce the heat and simmer, uncovered, until the beans are tender, 10–15 minutes.

3 ▼ Pour the soup into a blender or food processor and process until smooth. Alternatively, purée the soup in a food mill. Return to the pan. Stir in the cheese and cream. Sprinkle with the parsley and serve.

Hearty Lentil Soup

SERVES 6

1 cup brown lentils

4 cups chicken stock

1 cup water

¼ cup dry red wine

1½ pounds ripe tomatoes, peeled, seeded, and chopped, or 2 cups canned crushed tomatoes

1 carrot, sliced

1 onion, chopped

1 celery stalk, sliced

1 garlic clove, minced

¼ teaspoon ground coriander

2 teaspoons chopped fresh basil, or ½ teaspoon dried basil

1 bay leaf

6 tablespoons freshly grated Parmesan cheese

1 ▲ Rinse the lentils and discard any discolored ones and any stones.

2 ▲ Combine the lentils, stock, water, wine, tomatoes, carrot, onion, celery, and garlic in a large saucepan. Add the coriander, basil, and bay leaf.

3 ▼ Bring to a boil, reduce the heat to low, cover, and simmer until the lentils are just tender, 20–25 minutes, stirring occasionally.

4 Discard the bay leaf. Ladle the soup into 6 soup bowls and sprinkle each with 1 tablespoon of the cheese.

> **~ VARIATION ~**
>
> For a more substantial soup, add about 1 cup finely chopped cooked ham for the last 10 minutes of cooking.

Green Bean and Parmesan Soup (top), Hearty Lentil Soup

Black and White Bean Soup

SERVES 8

2 cups dry black (turtle) beans, soaked overnight

2 quarts water

6 garlic cloves, minced

2 cups dry navy or Great Northern beans, soaked overnight

6 tablespoons balsamic vinegar

4 jalapeño peppers, seeded and chopped

6 scallions, finely chopped

juice of 1 lime

¼ cup olive oil

¼ cup chopped fresh coriander (cilantro), plus more for garnishing

salt and pepper

1 Drain and rinse the black beans. Place them in a large saucepan with half the water and garlic. Bring to a boil. Reduce the heat to low, cover the pan, and simmer until the beans are soft, about 1½ hours.

2 Drain and rinse the white beans. Put them in another saucepan with the remaining water and garlic. Bring to a boil, cover, and simmer until soft, about 1 hour.

3 ▲ Purée the cooked white beans in a food processor or blender. Stir in the vinegar, jalapeños, and half the scallions. Return to the saucepan and reheat gently.

4 Purée the cooked black beans in the food processor or blender. Return to the saucepan and stir in the lime juice, olive oil, coriander, and the remaining scallions. Reheat gently.

5 ▲ Season both soups with salt and pepper. To serve, place a ladleful of each puréed soup in each soup bowl, side by side. Swirl the two soups together with a toothpick. If liked, garnish with extra chopped fresh coriander.

Butternut Squash Bisque

SERVES 4

2 tablespoons butter or margarine

2 small onions, finely chopped

1 pound butternut squash, peeled, seeded, and cubed

5 cups chicken stock

½ pound potatoes, cubed

1 teaspoon paprika

½ cup whipping cream (optional)

salt and pepper

1½ tablespoons chopped fresh chives, plus whole chives, for garnishing

1 Melt the butter or margarine in a large saucepan. Add the onions and cook until soft, about 5 minutes.

2 ▲ Add the squash, stock, potatoes, and paprika. Bring to a boil. Reduce the heat to low, cover the pan, and simmer until the vegetables are soft, about 35 minutes.

3 Pour the soup into a food processor or blender and process until smooth. Return the soup to the pan and stir in the cream, if using. Season with salt and pepper. Reheat gently.

4 ▲ Stir in the chopped chives just before serving. If liked, garnish each serving with a few whole chives.

Black and White Bean Soup (top), Butternut Squash Bisque

Mozzarella, Tomato, and Pesto Sandwiches

SERVES 4

4 small round Italian or French bread rolls

½ cup freshly made or bottled pesto sauce

½ pound mozzarella cheese, thinly sliced

4 medium tomatoes, thinly sliced

3 tablespoons olive oil

fresh basil leaves, for garnishing

1 With a serrated knife, cut each roll open in half. Spread 1 tablespoon of pesto sauce over the cut side of each half.

3 ▲ Drizzle the olive oil over the cheese and tomatoes.

4 Replace the top half of each roll; garnish with basil leaves, if you wish.

2 ▲ Arrange alternating slices of mozzarella cheese and tomato on the bottom half of each roll.

Salad-Stuffed Pita Pockets

SERVES 6

½ small head of iceberg lettuce, cut in fine strips across the leaves

½ hothouse cucumber, diced

9 cherry tomatoes, halved

2 scallions, finely chopped

½ cup crumbled feta cheese

8 black olives, pitted and chopped

6 oblong pita breads, cut in half crosswise

FOR THE DRESSING

1 small garlic clove, minced

⅛ teaspoon salt

1 teaspoon fresh lemon juice

2 tablespoons olive oil

1 teaspoon chopped fresh mint

pepper

1 ▲ In a bowl, combine the lettuce, cucumber, tomatoes, scallions, feta cheese, and olives.

2 ▲ For the dressing, combine all the ingredients in a small screwtop jar and shake well to mix.

3 ▲ Pour the dressing over the salad and toss together.

4 ▲ Gently open the pita bread halves. Fill the pockets with the salad. Serve immediately.

Mozzarella, Tomato and Pesto Sandwiches (top), Salad-Stuffed Pita Pockets

Club Sandwiches

SERVES 4

8 bacon slices

12 slices of white bread or rectangular brioche, toasted

½ cup mayonnaise

¼–½ pound cooked chicken breast meat, sliced

8 large lettuce leaves

salt and pepper

1 beefsteak tomato, cut across in 4 slices

1 ▼ In a heavy skillet, fry the bacon until crisp and the fat is rendered. Drain on paper towels.

2 Lay 4 slices of toast on a flat surface. Spread them with some of the mayonnaise.

3 ▲ Top each slice with one-quarter of the chicken and a lettuce leaf. Season with salt and pepper.

4 ▲ Spread 4 of the remaining toast slices with mayonnaise. Lay them on top of the lettuce.

5 ▲ Top each sandwich with a slice of tomato, 2 bacon slices, and another lettuce leaf.

6 Spread the remaining slices of toast with the rest of the mayonnaise. Place them on top of the sandwiches, mayonnaise-side down.

7 Cut each sandwich into four triangles and secure each triangle with a toothpick.

Chili Dogs

SERVES 6

6 frankfurters

6 hot dog buns, split open

2 tablespoons butter or margarine, at
    room temperature

⅓ cup shredded cheddar cheese

⅓ cup chopped red onion

FOR THE CHILI

2 tablespoons corn oil

1 small onion, chopped

1 small green bell pepper, seeded and
    chopped

½ pound ground beef

1 cup tomato sauce

½ cup drained canned red kidney beans

2 teaspoons chili powder, or to taste

salt and pepper

3 ▼ Stir in the tomato sauce, beans, chili powder, and salt and pepper to taste. Cover the pan and simmer 10 minutes.

4 Meanwhile, put the frankfurters in a saucepan and cover with cold water. Bring to a boil. Remove from the heat, cover, and let stand 5 minutes.

5 ▲ Spread both sides of each hot dog bun with the butter or margarine. Fry in a hot skillet until golden brown on both sides.

6 To serve, put a frankfurter in each bun. Top with chili and sprinkle with cheese and onion. Serve immediately.

1 ▲ For the chili, heat the oil in a skillet. Add the onion and green bell pepper and cook until softened, about 5 minutes.

2 ▲ Add the beef and cook until well browned, stirring frequently and breaking up lumps with the side of a wooden spatula.

Grilled Cheddar and Chutney Sandwiches

SERVES 4

3 tablespoons butter or margarine

3 large garlic cloves, minced

⅓ cup homemade or bottled mango chutney

8 slices of white bread

½ pound cheddar cheese, shredded

1 ▲ Melt the butter or margarine in a small saucepan. Add the garlic and cook until softened but not brown, about 2 minutes, stirring. Remove from the heat.

2 ▲ Spread the chutney on 4 slices of bread.

3 ▲ Divide the cheese among the bread slices, spreading it evenly. Top with the remaining bread slices.

4 ▲ Brush both sides of each sandwich with the garlic butter.

5 Fry the sandwiches in a hot skillet over medium heat until golden brown, about 2 minutes on each side. Serve immediately.

~ **COOK'S TIP** ~

Well aged sharp cheddar cheese works best in combination with the strong flavors of the chutney and garlic.

Tuna and Sun-Dried Tomato Sandwiches

SERVES 4

2 7-ounce cans tuna fish, drained

2 tablespoons finely chopped black olives, preferably Kalamata

¼ cup finely chopped drained sun-dried tomatoes packed in oil

3 scallions, finely chopped

4 round Italian or French bread rolls, split open

1 cup arugula or small lettuce leaves

FOR THE DRESSING

1½ tablespoons red wine vinegar

5 tablespoons olive oil

¼ cup chopped fresh basil

salt and pepper

1 ▼ For the dressing, combine the vinegar and oil in a mixing bowl. Whisk until an emulsion is formed. Stir in the basil. Season with salt and pepper.

2 Add the tuna, olives, sun-dried tomatoes, and scallions and stir.

3 ▲ Divide the tuna mixture among the rolls. Top with the arugula or lettuce leaves and replace the tops of the rolls, pressing them on firmly.

Grilled Cheddar and Chutney Sandwiches (top), Tuna and Sun-Dried Tomato Sandwiches

Roast Beef Sandwiches with Horseradish Sauce

SERVES 4

4 slices of pumpernickel bread

¾ pound roast beef, thinly sliced

salt and pepper

⅓ cup mayonnaise

1½ tablespoons prepared horseradish

2 small tomatoes, seeded and chopped

2 kosher dill pickle spears, chopped

fresh dill sprigs, for garnishing

1 ▲ Lay the slices of pumpernickel on a flat surface. Divide the slices of roast beef among the pumpernickel, folding the slices in half, if large. Season with salt and pepper.

2 In a small bowl, combine the mayonnaise and horseradish. Stir in the tomatoes and dill pickle.

3 ▲ Spoon the horseradish mayonnaise onto the beef. Garnish with dill sprigs and serve.

Roast Pork and Coleslaw Sandwiches

SERVES 6

¾ cup mayonnaise

2 tablespoons ketchup

¼–½ teaspoon cayenne

1 tablespoon light brown sugar

1 pound roast pork, thinly sliced

1 pound green or white cabbage, cut in wedges

2 carrots, finely shredded

1 small green bell pepper, seeded and diced

½ small red onion, finely chopped

12 small round Italian or French bread rolls, split open

1 ▲ In a bowl, combine the mayonnaise, ketchup, cayenne, and brown sugar. Stir well.

2 Stack the slices of roast pork. With a sharp knife, cut them into matchstick strips.

3 Remove the cores from the cabbage wedges. Lay them on a chopping board and cut into fine strips across the leaves.

4 ▲ Add the pork, cabbage, carrots, green bell pepper, and red onion to the mayonnaise mixture. Toss to mix.

5 ▲ Fill the split bread rolls with the pork coleslaw.

~ VARIATIONS ~

Instead of roast pork, substitute cooked ham or turkey, and prepare as above. For a change of pace, try tuna in place of meat.

Roast Beef Sandwiches with Horseradish Sauce (top), Roast Pork and Coleslaw Sandwiches

Baby Baked Potatoes with Blue Cheese Topping

MAKES 20

20 small new potatoes

¼ cup vegetable oil

coarse salt

½ cup sour cream

¼ cup crumbled blue cheese

2 tablespoons chopped fresh chives

1 Preheat the oven to 350°F.

2 Wash and dry the potatoes. Pour the oil into a bowl. Add the potatoes and toss to coat well with oil.

3 ▼ Dip the potatoes in the coarse salt to coat lightly. Spread out the potatoes on a baking sheet. Bake until tender, 45–50 minutes.

4 ▲ In a small bowl, combine the sour cream and blue cheese.

5 ▲ Cut a cross in the top of each potato. Press with your fingers to open the potatoes.

6 ▲ Top each potato with a dollop of the cheese mixture. Sprinkle with chives and serve immediately.

Guacamole with Cumin Tortilla Chips

SERVES 10

2 very ripe avocados

2 shallots or scallions, chopped

2 tablespoons fresh lime juice

1 teaspoon salt

2 teaspoons chili powder

1 medium-size tomato, seeded and
chopped

FOR THE CUMIN TORTILLA CHIPS

3 tablespoons corn oil

1½ teaspoons ground cumin

1 teaspoon salt

9 6-inch corn tortillas, each cut in 6
triangles

1 Preheat the oven to 300°F.

2 ▲ For the tortilla chips, combine the oil, cumin, and salt in a bowl.

3 ▲ Spread the tortilla triangles on 2 baking sheets. Brush the seasoned oil on both sides. Bake until they are crisp and golden, about 20 minutes, turning once or twice and brushing with the seasoned oil. Let cool.

4 ▼ Peel the avocados, discard the pits, and chop the flesh. In a food processor or blender, combine the avocados, shallots or scallions, lime juice, salt, and chili powder. Process until smooth.

5 ▲ Transfer the mixture to a bowl. Gently stir in the chopped tomato.

6 Serve the guacamole in a bowl in the center of a platter, surrounded with the cumin tortilla chips.

Cornmeal and Smoked Salmon Muffins

MAKES 25

½ cup cornmeal

¼ cup flour

½ teaspoon baking powder

⅛ teaspoon salt

1 tablespoon sugar

1 egg

½ cup buttermilk

¼ cup light cream

½ cup smoked salmon, cut in fine strips

1 Preheat the oven to 400°F. Grease a mini-muffin tray.

2 In a mixing bowl, combine the cornmeal, flour, baking powder, salt, and sugar. Set aside.

3 ▼ In another bowl, mix together the egg, buttermilk, and cream. Gradually add the egg mixture to the cornmeal mixture, stirring quickly until just combined.

4 ▲ Stir the smoked salmon strips into the batter.

5 Fill the mini-muffin pans three-quarters full with the batter. Bake until slightly risen and golden brown, 18–20 minutes. Let cool 5 minutes in the pans on a wire rack before unmolding.

Black Bean and Tomato Salsa in Corncups

MAKES 30

1 15-ounce can black (turtle) beans, rinsed and drained

2 tomatoes, seeded and diced

1 garlic clove, minced

1 shallot, minced

1 jalapeño pepper, seeded and chopped

1 teaspoon finely grated lime rind

1 tablespoon olive oil

2 tablespoons fresh lime juice

2 teaspoons maple syrup

salt and pepper

3 tablespoons chopped fresh coriander (cilantro)

FOR THE CORNCUPS

10 6-inch corn tortillas

3–4 tablespoons corn oil, for brushing

1 Preheat the oven to 400°F.

2 ▼ For the corncups, using a 2-inch round cookie cutter, cut 3 rounds from each tortilla, pressing firmly to cut through. Discard the tortilla trimmings. Brush both sides of each tortilla round with oil.

3 Press the tortilla rounds into the cups of 2–3 mini-muffin trays. Bake until the corncups are crisp, about 6 minutes. Let cool on a wire rack.

4 ▲ In a mixing bowl, combine the beans, tomatoes, garlic, shallot, jalapeño, lime rind, oil, lime juice, and maple syrup. Stir in salt and pepper to taste.

5 Place a spoonful of the bean and tomato salsa in each corncup. Sprinkle with the chopped coriander just before serving.

Cornmeal and Smoked Salmon Muffins (top), Black Bean and Tomato Salsa in Corncups

Cornmeal and Smoked Salmon Muffins

MAKES 25

½ cup cornmeal

¼ cup flour

½ teaspoon baking powder

⅛ teaspoon salt

1 tablespoon sugar

1 egg

½ cup buttermilk

¼ cup light cream

½ cup smoked salmon, cut in fine strips

1 Preheat the oven to 400°F. Grease a mini-muffin tray.

2 In a mixing bowl, combine the cornmeal, flour, baking powder, salt, and sugar. Set aside.

3 ▼ In another bowl, mix together the egg, buttermilk, and cream. Gradually add the egg mixture to the cornmeal mixture, stirring quickly until just combined.

4 ▲ Stir the smoked salmon strips into the batter.

5 Fill the mini-muffin pans three-quarters full with the batter. Bake until slightly risen and golden brown, 18–20 minutes. Let cool 5 minutes in the pans on a wire rack before unmolding.

Black Bean and Tomato Salsa in Corncups

MAKES 30

1 15-ounce can black (turtle) beans, rinsed and drained

2 tomatoes, seeded and diced

1 garlic clove, minced

1 shallot, minced

1 jalapeño pepper, seeded and chopped

1 teaspoon finely grated lime rind

1 tablespoon olive oil

2 tablespoons fresh lime juice

2 teaspoons maple syrup

salt and pepper

3 tablespoons chopped fresh coriander (cilantro)

FOR THE CORNCUPS

10 6-inch corn tortillas

3–4 tablespoons corn oil, for brushing

1 Preheat the oven to 400°F.

2 ▼ For the corncups, using a 2-inch round cookie cutter, cut 3 rounds from each tortilla, pressing firmly to cut through. Discard the tortilla trimmings. Brush both sides of each tortilla round with oil.

4 ▲ In a mixing bowl, combine the beans, tomatoes, garlic, shallot, jalapeño, lime rind, oil, lime juice, and maple syrup. Stir in salt and pepper to taste.

3 Press the tortilla rounds into the cups of 2–3 mini-muffin trays. Bake until the corncups are crisp, about 6 minutes. Let cool on a wire rack.

5 Place a spoonful of the bean and tomato salsa in each corncup. Sprinkle with the chopped coriander just before serving.

Cornmeal and Smoked Salmon Muffins (top), Black Bean and Tomato Salsa in Corncups

Guacamole with Cumin Tortilla Chips

SERVES 10

2 very ripe avocados

2 shallots or scallions, chopped

2 tablespoons fresh lime juice

1 teaspoon salt

2 teaspoons chili powder

1 medium-size tomato, seeded and chopped

FOR THE CUMIN TORTILLA CHIPS

3 tablespoons corn oil

1½ teaspoons ground cumin

1 teaspoon salt

9 6-inch corn tortillas, each cut in 6 triangles

1 Preheat the oven to 300°F.

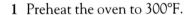

2 ▲ For the tortilla chips, combine the oil, cumin, and salt in a bowl.

3 ▲ Spread the tortilla triangles on 2 baking sheets. Brush the seasoned oil on both sides. Bake until they are crisp and golden, about 20 minutes, turning once or twice and brushing with the seasoned oil. Let cool.

4 ▼ Peel the avocados, discard the pits, and chop the flesh. In a food processor or blender, combine the avocados, shallots or scallions, lime juice, salt, and chili powder. Process until smooth.

5 ▲ Transfer the mixture to a bowl. Gently stir in the chopped tomato.

6 Serve the guacamole in a bowl in the center of a platter, surrounded with the cumin tortilla chips.

Buckwheat Blinis with Marinated Salmon

MAKES 25

½ pound salmon fillet, skinned

juice of 1 lime

¼ cup extra-virgin olive oil

pinch salt

3 tablespoons chopped fresh dill

⅔ cup sour cream

¼ avocado, peeled and diced

3 tablespoons chopped fresh chives

fresh dill sprigs, for garnishing

FOR THE BLINIS

¾ cup buckwheat flour

2 teaspoons sugar

1 egg

½ cup milk

2 tablespoons butter or margarine, melted

½ teaspoon cream of tartar

¼ teaspoon baking soda

1 tablespoon water

1 ▲ With a long, sharp knife, slice the salmon as thinly as possible. Place the slices, in one layer, in a large non-metallic dish.

~ **COOK'S TIP** ~

For easy entertaining, make the blinis early in the day and store, covered. To serve, arrange the blinis on a baking sheet, and reheat in a preheated 400°F oven until hot, about 3–4 minutes.

2 ▲ In a small bowl, combine the lime juice, olive oil, salt, and chopped dill. Pour the mixture over the salmon. Cover tightly and refrigerate several hours or overnight.

3 ▲ For the blinis, combine the buckwheat flour and sugar in a mixing bowl. Set aside.

4 ▲ In a small bowl, beat together the egg, milk, and butter or margarine. Gradually stir the egg mixture into the flour mixture. Stir in the cream of tartar, baking soda, and water.

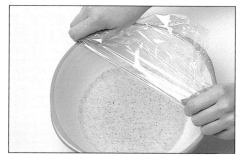

5 ▲ Cover the bowl and let the batter stand 1 hour.

6 With a sharp knife, cut the marinated salmon in thin strips.

7 ▲ To cook the blinis, heat a heavy nonstick skillet. Using a small ladle or large spoon, drop the batter into the skillet to make small pancakes about 2 inches in diameter. When bubbles appear on the surface, turn over. Cook until the other side is golden brown, 1–2 minutes longer. Transfer the blinis to a plate and continue until all the batter is used.

8 ▲ To serve, place a teaspoon of sour cream on each blini and top with marinated salmon. Sprinkle with diced avocado and chopped chives and garnish with dill sprigs.

Cheese Twists with Cranberry Sauce

MAKES 12

6 large sheets of phyllo pastry

½ cup (1 stick) butter or margarine, melted

½ pound Brie cheese, finely diced (rind removed, if wished)

FOR THE SAUCE

1 cup cranberries

2 tablespoons light brown sugar

1 For the sauce, combine the cranberries and sugar in a small saucepan with just enough water to cover. Bring to a boil and simmer until the cranberries "pop", about 3 minutes, stirring.

2 ▼ Pour the cranberry mixture into a blender or food processor and process until finely chopped. Press it through a fine-mesh nylon strainer into a bowl. Taste and add more sugar if needed. Set aside.

3 Preheat the oven to 450°F.

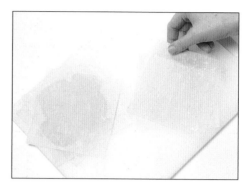

4 ▲ To make the cheese parcels, cut the phyllo pastry into 36 pieces 5-inches square. Lay one pastry square on a flat surface and brush with some of the butter or margarine. Lay a second pastry square on top, placing it so the corners are not on top of each other. Brush with butter. Lay a third pastry square on top, again placing it so the corners are not on top of the others, thus forming a 12-pointed star.

5 Put a heaping tablespoon of the diced cheese in the center of each pastry star.

6 ▲ Bring the points of each pastry star up over the cheese and twist to close securely. Fold back the tips of the points.

7 Arrange the packages on a baking sheet. Bake until the pastry is crisp and golden brown, 10–15 minutes.

8 Meanwhile, gently reheat the cranberry sauce. Serve the cheese twists hot with the sauce.

Bean Nachos

SERVES 8

2 tablespoons corn oil

2 onions, chopped

2 garlic cloves, chopped

3 jalapeño peppers, seeded and chopped

1½ tablespoons mild chili powder

1 16-ounce can red kidney beans,
   drained and liquid reserved

3 tablespoons chopped fresh coriander
   (cilantro)

nacho chips (fried tortilla rounds) or
   tortilla chips, for serving

2 cups shredded cheddar cheese

½ cup pitted black olives, thinly sliced

fresh coriander (cilantro) sprigs, for
   garnishing

1 Preheat the oven to 425°F.

2 ▼ Heat the oil in a skillet. Add the onions, garlic, and jalapeños and cook until soft, about 5 minutes. Add the chili powder and cook 1 minute more.

~ VARIATION ~

To serve as a bean dip, stir in the cheese and olives. Transfer the bean mixture to a round earthenware dish. Bake until the cheese melts and browns slightly, 10–15 minutes. Garnish with coriander, and serve with tortilla chips for dipping.

3 ▲ Stir the beans into the onion mixture with ½ cup of the reserved can liquid. Cook until thickened, about 10 minutes, mashing the beans with a fork from time to time. Remove the pan from the heat and stir in the chopped coriander.

4 ▼ Put a little of the bean mixture on each nacho chip. Top each nacho with a little cheese and a slice of olive. Arrange on a baking sheet.

5 Bake until the cheese has melted and is beginning to brown, 5–10 minutes. Serve immediately. Garnish with coriander, if liked.

Spinach and Feta Phyllo Triangles

SERVES 20

2 tablespoons olive oil
2 shallots, finely chopped
1 pound frozen spinach, thawed
¼ pound feta cheese, crumbled
⅓ cup walnut pieces, chopped
¼ teaspoon grated nutmeg
salt and pepper
4 large or 8 small sheets phyllo pastry
½ cup (1 stick) butter or margarine, melted

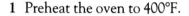

1 Preheat the oven to 400°F.

2 ▲ Heat the olive oil in a skillet. Add the shallots and cook until softened, about 5 minutes.

3 ▲ A handful at a time, squeeze all the liquid out of the spinach. Add the spinach to the shallots. Increase the heat to high and cook, stirring, until all excess moisture has evaporated, about 5 minutes.

4 ▲ Transfer the spinach mixture to a bowl. Let cool. Stir in the feta and walnuts. Season with nutmeg, salt and pepper.

5 ▲ Lay a phyllo sheet on a flat surface. (Keep the remaining phyllo covered with a damp cloth to prevent it drying out.) Brush with some of the butter or margarine. Lay a second phyllo sheet on top of the first. With scissors, cut the layered phyllo pastry lengthwise into 3-inch-wide strips.

~ **VARIATION** ~

For an alternative filling, omit the spinach and shallots. Use ¾ pound goat cheese, crumbled, instead of the feta cheese, and ½ cup toasted pine nuts instead of the walnuts. Mix the cheese with the olive oil and 1 tablespoon chopped fresh basil. Assemble as above.

6 ▲ Place a tablespoonful of the spinach mixture at the end of one strip of phyllo pastry.

7 ▲ Fold a bottom corner of the pastry over the filling to form a triangle, then continue folding over the pastry strip to the other end. Fill and shape the triangles until all the ingredients are used.

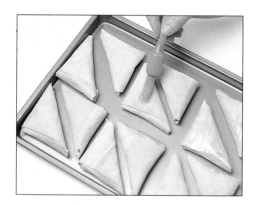

8 ▲ Set the triangles on baking sheets and brush with butter. Bake the phyllo triangles until they are crispy and golden brown, about 10 minutes. Serve hot.

Potato Pancakes with Lemon-Chive Cream

MAKES 40

2 tablespoons butter or margarine

1 shallot, finely chopped

1 egg

½ pound potatoes

oil for frying

FOR THE LEMON-CHIVE CREAM

½ cup cream cheese, at room temperature

2 tablespoons sour cream

1 teaspoon finely grated lemon rind

1 tablespoon fresh lemon juice

1 tablespoon chopped fresh chives

1 Melt the butter or margarine in a small skillet. Add the shallot and cook until softened, about 3 minutes. Set aside and let cool.

2 Beat the egg in a large mixing bowl until light and frothy.

3 Coarsely grate the potatoes. Add them to the bowl and mix with the egg until completely coated. Season generously with salt and pepper. Add the shallot and mix well.

4 ▼ For the lemon-chive cream, combine the cream cheese and sour cream in a bowl. Beat until smooth. Add the lemon rind and juice and chives. Set aside.

5 ▲ Heat ¼ inch of oil in a skillet. Drop teaspoonfuls of the potato mixture into the hot oil and press them with the back of a spoon to make flat rounds. Fry until well browned, 2–3 minutes on each side. Drain on paper towels and keep warm while frying the remaining pancakes.

6 Serve the pancakes hot, with the lemon-chive cream for spooning on top, or for dipping.

Crab-Stuffed Cherry Tomatoes

MAKES 40

¼ pound lump crab meat

1 teaspoon chili sauce

¼ teaspoon Dijon-style mustard

2 tablespoons mayonnaise

½ teaspoon Worcestershire sauce

2 scallions, finely chopped

1 tablespoon chopped fresh basil

1 tablespoon chopped fresh chives

40 cherry tomatoes

salt

1 In a mixing bowl, combine the crab meat, chili sauce, mustard, mayonnaise, Worcestershire sauce, scallions, and herbs. Mix well. Cover and refrigerate until needed.

2 ▲ Using a serrated knife, cut a very thin slice from the stem end of each tomato. Carefully scoop out the pulp and seeds with the tip of a teaspoon.

3 Sprinkle the insides of the tomato shells lightly with salt. Invert them on paper towels and let them drain 15 minutes.

4 ▲ Using a small spoon, stuff the tomatoes with the crab, mounding the filling slightly on top. Serve cold.

Potato Pancakes with Lemon-Chive Cream (top), Crab-Stuffed Cherry Tomatoes

FISH & SEAFOOD

~

Whether fresh from the sea, or frozen or canned, fish and seafood make nutritious and easy-to-prepare dishes. The recipes here offer exciting ideas, from rich casseroles and chowders to tasty kabobs and broiled steaks.

Swordfish with Orange-Caper Sauce

SERVES 4

¼ cup fresh orange juice

1 teaspoon soy sauce

2 tablespoons olive oil

4 swordfish steaks (about ½ pound each)

salt and pepper

3 tablespoons cold butter or margarine, cut in pieces

2 tablespoons capers in vinegar

1 tablespoon chopped fresh parsley

1 In a small bowl, combine the orange juice, soy sauce, and 1 tablespoon of the olive oil. Whisk to mix.

2 Lay the swordfish steaks in a shallow baking dish. Pour the orange-soy mixture over them and sprinkle with salt and pepper.

3 Heat the remaining tablespoon of olive oil in a heavy skillet over medium-high heat.

4 ▲ Drain the swordfish steaks, reserving the marinade. Add the steaks to the skillet and cook until the fish flakes easily when tested with a fork, 3–4 minutes on each side, basting occasionally with the reserved marinade. Transfer the swordfish steaks to a warmed serving platter.

5 ▲ Pour the reserved marinade into the skillet and cook 1 minute, stirring to mix in the cooking juices. Add the butter or margarine, capers with their vinegar, and parsley. Cook until the butter has melted and the sauce is slightly syrupy.

6 Pour the sauce over the swordfish steaks and serve immediately.

Tuna Steaks with Ginger-Soy Vinaigrette

SERVES 6

6 tuna steaks (about 2 pounds)

FOR THE VINAIGRETTE

1-inch piece of fresh gingerroot, peeled and finely grated

2 scallions, thinly sliced

2 tablespoons chopped fresh chives

grated rind and juice of 1 lime

2 tablespoons dry sherry wine

1 tablespoon soy sauce

½ cup olive oil

salt and pepper

1 ▲ For the vinaigrette, combine the gingerroot, scallions, chives, lime rind and juice, sherry, and soy sauce. Add the olive oil and whisk to mix. Season with salt and pepper. Set aside.

2 Preheat the broiler. Sprinkle the tuna steaks with salt and pepper.

3 ▼ Arrange the tuna steaks on the rack in the broiler pan. Broil about 3 inches from the heat for about 5 minutes on each side, until the fish flakes easily when tested with a fork.

4 Arrange the cooked fish on a warmed serving platter or individual plates. Spoon the ginger vinaigrette over the fish, and serve.

Swordfish with Orange-Caper Sauce (top), Tuna Steaks with Ginger-Soy Vinaigrette

Cornmeal-Coated Cod with Tomato Sauce

SERVES 4

3 tablespoons cornmeal

½ teaspoon salt

¼ teaspoon hot chili powder or cayenne

4 cod steaks, each 1-inch thick (about 1½ pounds)

2 tablespoons corn oil

fresh basil sprigs, for garnishing

FOR THE TOMATO SAUCE

2 tablespoons olive oil

1 shallot or ½ small onion, finely chopped

1 garlic clove, minced

1 pound ripe tomatoes, chopped, or 1 16-ounce can crushed tomatoes

⅛ teaspoon sugar

¼ cup dry white wine

2 tablespoons chopped fresh basil or ½ teaspoon dried basil

salt and pepper

1 For the sauce, heat the oil in a saucepan. Add the shallot or onion and the garlic and cook until soft, about 5 minutes. Stir in the tomatoes, sugar, wine, and basil. Bring to a boil. Simmer until thickened, 10–15 minutes.

2 ▲ Work the sauce through a vegetable mill or strainer until smooth. Return it to the pan. Season with salt and pepper. Set aside.

3 ▲ Combine the cornmeal, salt, and chili powder or cayenne on a sheet of wax paper.

4 ▲ Rinse the cod steaks, then dip them on both sides into the cornmeal mixture, patting gently to make an even coating.

5 ▲ Heat the corn oil in a large frying pan. Add the cod steaks and cook until golden brown and the flesh will flake easily when tested with a fork, about 5 minutes on each side. Cook in batches if necessary. Meanwhile, reheat the tomato sauce.

6 Garnish the cod steaks with basil sprigs and serve with the tomato sauce.

Cajun Blackened Swordfish

SERVES 4

1 teaspoon onion powder
1 teaspoon garlic salt
2 teaspoons paprika
1 teaspoon ground cumin
1 teaspoon mustard powder
1 teaspoon cayenne
2 teaspoons dried thyme
2 teaspoons dried oregano
½ teaspoon salt
1 teaspoon pepper
4 swordfish steaks (about 1½ pounds)
4 tablespoons butter or margarine, melted
dill sprigs, for garnishing

1 In a small bowl, combine all the spices, herbs, and seasonings.

2 ▲ Brush both sides of the fish steaks with some of the melted butter or margarine.

3 ▲ Coat both sides of the fish steaks with the seasoning mixture, rubbing it in well.

4 Heat a large heavy skillet until a drop of water sprinkled on the surface sizzles, about 5 minutes.

5 ▲ Drizzle 2 teaspoons of the remaining butter or margarine over the fish steaks. Add the steaks to the skillet, butter-side down, and cook until the underside is blackened, 2–3 minutes.

6 ▲ Drizzle another 2 teaspoons melted butter or margarine over the fish, then turn the steaks over. Cook until the second side is blackened and the fish flakes easily when tested with a fork, 2–3 minutes more.

7 Transfer the fish to warmed plates, garnish with dill, and drizzle with the remaining butter or margarine.

Salmon Steaks with Lime Butter

SERVES 4

4 salmon steaks (about 1½ pounds)

salt and pepper

FOR THE LIME BUTTER

4 tablespoons butter or margarine, at room temperature

1 tablespoon chopped fresh coriander (cilantro), or 1 teaspoon dried coriander

1 teaspoon finely grated lime rind

1 tablespoon fresh lime juice

1 For the lime butter, combine the butter or margarine, coriander, and lime rind and juice in a bowl. Mix well with a fork.

2 ▲ Transfer the lime butter to a piece of wax paper and shape into a log. Roll in the paper until smooth and round. Refrigerate until firm, about 1 hour.

3 Preheat the broiler.

4 ▼ Sprinkle the salmon steaks with salt and pepper. Arrange them on the rack in the broiler pan. Broil about 3 inches from the heat, 5 minutes on each side.

5 Unwrap the lime butter and cut into 4 pieces. Top each salmon steak with a pat of lime butter and serve.

Citrus Fish Fillets

SERVES 6

1–2 tablespoons butter or margarine, melted

2 pounds sole fillets

salt and pepper

1 teaspoon grated lemon rind

1 teaspoon grated orange rind

2 tablespoons fresh orange juice

⅓ cup whipping cream

1 tablespoon chopped fresh basil

fresh basil sprigs, for garnishing

1 Preheat the oven to 350°F. Generously grease a large baking dish with the melted butter or margarine.

~ **VARIATION** ~

Use an equal amount of grapefruit rind and juice to replace the lemon and orange.

2 ▲ Lay the fish fillets skin-side down in the baking dish, in one layer. Sprinkle with salt and pepper.

3 ▲ In a small bowl, combine the lemon and orange rinds and orange juice. Pour the mixture over the fish.

4 Bake until the fish flakes easily when tested with a fork, 15–20 minutes. Transfer the fish to a warmed serving platter.

5 ▲ Strain the juices from the baking dish into a small saucepan. Stir in the cream and chopped basil. Boil until thickened, about 5 minutes.

6 Spoon the citrus cream over the fish fillets. Garnish with basil sprigs and serve.

Salmon Steaks with Lime Butter (top), Citrus Fish Fillets

Sweet and Spicy Salmon Fillets

SERVES 6

2 pounds salmon fillet, cut in 6 pieces

½ cup honey

¼ cup soy sauce

juice of 1 lime

1 tablespoon sesame oil

¼ teaspoon hot red pepper flakes

¼ teaspoon crushed black peppercorns

~ COOK'S TIP ~

The acid in the citrus juice begins to "cook" the fish, so broiling on one side only is sufficient.

---

1 Place the salmon pieces skin-side down in a large baking dish, in one layer.

2 ▲ In a bowl, combine the honey, soy sauce, lime juice, sesame oil, pepper flakes, and peppercorns.

3 ▲ Pour the mixture over the fish. Cover and let marinate 30 minutes.

4 Preheat the broiler. Remove the fish from the marinade and arrange on the rack in the broiler pan, skin-side down. Broil about 3 inches from the heat until the fish flakes easily when tested with a fork, 6–8 minutes.

Peppercorn-Crusted Cod Steaks

SERVES 4

1 teaspoon each pink, white, and green peppercorns

3 tablespoons butter or margarine

4 cod steaks, each 1-inch thick (about 1 pound)

salt

½ cup fish stock or bottled clam juice

½ cup whipping cream

¼ cup chopped fresh chives

1 ▼ Wrap the peppercorns in a dish towel or heavy plastic bag and crush with a rolling pin.

2 Melt the butter or margarine in a large frying pan. Remove from the heat. Brush the cod steaks with some of the butter or margarine.

3 ▲ Press the crushed peppercorns onto both sides of the cod steaks. Season with salt.

4 Heat the frying pan. Add the cod steaks and cook over medium-low heat until the fish flakes easily when tested with a fork, about 4 minutes on each side. Transfer the steaks to a warmed serving platter.

5 ▲ Add the stock or clam juice and cream to the frying pan and bring to a boil, stirring well. Boil until reduced by half, about 5 minutes. Remove from the heat and stir in the chives.

6 Pour the sauce over the fish and serve immediately.

~ VARIATION ~

In place of cod, use monkfish, cut into steaks or thick fillets. The flavor is similar to lobster.

Sweet and Spicy Salmon Fillets (top), Peppercorn-Crusted Cod Steaks

Breaded Fish with Tartare Sauce

SERVES 4

½ cup dry bread crumbs

1 teaspoon dried oregano

½ teaspoon cayenne

1 cup milk

2 teaspoons salt

4 pieces of cod fillet (about 1½ pounds)

3 tablespoons butter or margarine, melted

FOR THE TARTARE SAUCE

½ cup mayonnaise

½ teaspoon Dijon-style mustard

1 kosher dill pickle spear, finely chopped

1 tablespoon drained capers, chopped

1 teaspoon chopped fresh parsley

1 teaspoon chopped fresh chives

1 teaspoon chopped fresh tarragon

salt and pepper

1 Preheat the oven to 450°F. Grease a shallow glass or porcelain baking dish.

2 ▲ Combine the bread crumbs, oregano, and cayenne on a plate and blend together. Mix the milk with the salt in a bowl, stirring well to dissolve the salt.

3 ▲ Dip the pieces of cod fillet in the milk, then transfer to the plate and coat with the bread crumb mixture.

4 ▲ Arrange the coated fish in the prepared baking dish, in one layer. Drizzle the melted butter or margarine over the fish.

5 Bake until the fish flakes easily when tested with a fork, 10–15 minutes.

6 ▲ Meanwhile, for the tartare sauce, combine all the ingredients in a small bowl. Stir gently to mix well.

7 Serve the fish hot, accompanied by the tartare sauce.

Stuffed Sole Rolls

SERVES 4

8 skinless sole fillets (about 1 pound)

1 tablespoon butter or margarine, cut in 8 pieces

¼ cup dry white wine

paprika, for garnishing

FOR THE STUFFING

2 tablespoons butter or margarine

1 small onion, finely chopped

1 handful of fresh spinach leaves, shredded (1 cup firmly packed)

2 tablespoons pine nuts, toasted

2 tablespoons raisins

2 tablespoons fresh bread crumbs

⅛ teaspoon ground cinnamon

salt and pepper

1 Preheat the oven to 400°F. Butter a shallow baking dish.

2 ▲ For the stuffing, melt the butter or margarine in a small saucepan. Add the onion and cook over medium heat until softened, about 5 minutes. Stir in the spinach and cook, stirring constantly, until the spinach wilts and renders its liquid.

~ **VARIATION** ~

Instead of sole, other lean fish fillets may be used, such as flounder, whitefish, perch, or orange roughy.

3 Add the pine nuts, raisins, bread crumbs, cinnamon, and a little salt and pepper. Raise the heat and cook until most of the liquid has evaporated, stirring constantly. Remove from the heat.

4 ▲ Sprinkle the sole fillets with salt and pepper. Place a spoonful of the spinach stuffing at one end of each fillet. Roll up and secure with a wooden toothpick, if necessary.

5 ▲ Place the sole rolls in the prepared baking dish. Put a small piece of butter or margarine on each roll. Pour the wine over the fish. Cover the baking dish with foil and bake until the fish flakes easily when tested with a fork, about 15 minutes.

6 Serve on warmed plates with a little of the cooking juices spooned over the fish.

Red Snapper Veracruz

SERVES 4

3 tablespoons flour

salt and pepper

1½ pounds red snapper fillets or other firm white-fish fillets

1 tablespoon butter or margarine

2 tablespoons olive oil

1 onion, sliced

2 garlic cloves, chopped

¼ teaspoon ground cumin

1½ cups peeled, seeded, and chopped fresh tomatoes or canned crushed tomatoes

½ cup fresh orange juice

orange wedges, for garnishing

1 ▼ Put the flour on a plate and season with salt and pepper. Coat the fish fillets lightly with the seasoned flour, shaking off any excess.

2 Heat the butter or margarine and half the oil in a large skillet. Add the fish fillets to the skillet and cook until golden brown and the flesh flakes easily when tested with a fork, about 3 minutes on each side.

3 ▲ When the fish is cooked, transfer to a heated serving platter. Cover with foil and keep warm while making the sauce.

4 ▲ Heat the remaining oil in the skillet. Add the onion and garlic and cook until softened, about 5 minutes.

5 ▲ Stir in the cumin, tomatoes, and orange juice. Bring to a boil and cook until thickened, about 10 minutes, stirring frequently.

6 Garnish the fish with orange wedges. Pass the sauce separately.

Baked Stuffed Trout

SERVES 4

2 tablespoons butter or margarine

1 onion, chopped

1 celery stalk, diced

1 cup fresh bread cubes

1 tablespoon fresh thyme leaves or 1
    teaspoon dried thyme

salt and pepper

4 trout, dressed (about ½ pound each)

8 bacon slices

celery leaves or parsley, for garnishing

1 Preheat the oven to 450°F.

2 ▲ Melt the butter or margarine in a frying pan. Add the onion and celery and cook until softened, about 5 minutes. Remove the pan from the heat. Add the bread cubes, thyme, and season with salt and pepper to taste. Stir to mix well.

3 ▲ Season the cavity of each trout with salt and pepper.

4 ▲ Stuff each trout with the bread mixture, dividing it evenly among the fish. If necessary, secure the openings with wooden toothpicks.

5 ▼ Wrap 2 bacon slices around each stuffed trout. Arrange in a baking dish, in one layer.

6 Bake until the fish flakes easily when tested with a fork and the bacon is crisp, 35–40 minutes. Serve garnished with celery leaves or sprigs of parsley.

Halibut with Lemon-Pineapple Relish

SERVES 4

4 halibut steaks (about 1½ pounds)

2 tablespoons butter or margarine, melted

salt and pepper

fresh mint sprigs, for garnishing

FOR THE RELISH

½ cup finely diced fresh pineapple

2 tablespoons diced red bell pepper

1 tablespoon minced red onion

finely grated rind of 1 lemon

1 tablespoon lemon juice

1 teaspoon honey

2 tablespoons chopped fresh mint

1 For the relish, combine the pineapple, bell pepper, red onion, lemon rind and juice, and honey in a small bowl. Stir to mix. Cover with plastic wrap and refrigerate 30 minutes.

2 Preheat the broiler.

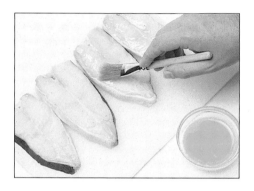

3 ▲ Brush the halibut with butter or margarine and sprinkle with salt and pepper. Arrange on the rack in the broiler pan, buttered-side up.

4 Broil the steaks about 3 inches from the heat, turning once and brushing with the remaining butter or margarine, about 5 minutes on each side. Transfer to warmed serving plates.

5 ▲ Stir the chopped mint into the pineapple relish. Garnish the halibut with mint sprigs and serve with the relish.

Fish Chowder

SERVES 4

3 thick-cut bacon slices, cut in small pieces

1 large onion, chopped

2 large potatoes, cut in ¾-inch cubes (about 1½ pounds)

salt and pepper

4 cups fish stock or bottled clam juice

1 pound skinless haddock or cod fillet, cut in 1-inch cubes

2 tablespoons chopped fresh parsley

1 tablespoon chopped fresh chives

1 cup whipping cream or whole milk

1 Fry the bacon in a deep saucepan until the fat is rendered. Add the onion and potatoes and cook over low heat, without browning, about 10 minutes. Season to taste with salt and pepper.

2 ▲ Pour off excess bacon fat from the pan. Add the fish stock to the pan and bring to a boil. Simmer until the vegetables are tender, 15–20 minutes.

3 ▲ Stir in the cubes of fish, the parsley, and chives. Simmer until the fish is just cooked, 3–4 minutes.

4 Stir the cream or milk into the chowder and reheat gently. Season to taste and serve immediately.

Halibut with Lemon-Pineapple Relish (top), Fish Chowder

Crab Cakes

SERVES 3 OR 6

1 pound fresh lump crab meat

1 egg, well beaten

1 teaspoon Dijon-style mustard

2 teaspoons prepared horseradish

2 teaspoons Worcestershire sauce

8 scallions, finely chopped

¼ cup chopped fresh parsley

1½ cups fresh bread crumbs

salt and pepper

1 tablespoon whipping cream (optional)

½ cup dry bread crumbs

3 tablespoons butter or margarine

lemon wedges, for serving

1 In a mixing bowl, combine the crab meat, egg, mustard, horseradish, Worcestershire sauce, scallions, parsley, fresh bread crumbs, and seasoning. Mix gently, leaving the pieces of crab meat as large as possible. If the mixture is too dry to hold together, add the cream.

2 ▲ Divide the crab mixture into 6 portions and shape each into a patty.

3 ▲ Put the dry bread crumbs on a plate. Coat the crab cakes on both sides with crumbs.

4 Melt the butter or margarine in a skillet. Fry the crab cakes until golden, about 3 minutes on each side. Add more fat if necessary.

5 Serve 1 or 2 per person, with lemon wedges.

Baked Stuffed Crab

SERVES 4

4 freshly cooked crabs

1 celery stalk, diced

1 scallion, finely chopped

1 small fresh green chili pepper, seeded and finely chopped

⅓ cup mayonnaise

2 tablespoons fresh lemon juice

1 tablespoon chopped fresh chives

salt and pepper

½ cup fresh bread crumbs

½ cup grated Monterey Jack cheese

2 tablespoons butter or margarine, melted

parsley sprigs, for garnishing

1 Preheat the oven to 375°F.

2 ▼ Pull the claws and legs from each crab. Separate the body from the shell. Scoop out the meat from the shell. Discard the feathery gills and the intestines; remove the meat and coral from the body. Crack the claws, and remove the meat.

3 Scrub the shells. Cut into the seam on the underside with scissors. The inner part of the shell should break off cleanly along the seam, enlarging the opening. Rinse the shells and dry them well.

4 In a bowl, combine the crab meat, celery, scallion, chili pepper, mayonnaise, lemon juice, and chives. Season with salt and pepper to taste and mix well.

5 In another bowl, toss together the bread crumbs, cheese, and melted butter or margarine.

6 ▲ Pile the crab mixture into the shells. Sprinkle with the bread-cheese mixture. Bake until golden brown, about 20 minutes. Serve hot, garnished with parsley sprigs.

Crab Cakes (top), Baked Stuffed Crab

Paella

SERVES 6

4 tablespoons olive oil

1½ cups short-grain rice

1 large onion, chopped

1 red bell pepper, seeded and chopped

¾ pound squid, cleaned and cut in rings (optional)

2¼ cups fish or chicken stock

½ cup dry white wine

½ teaspoon saffron threads

1 large garlic clove, minced

1 cup canned crushed tomatoes

1 bay leaf

¼ teaspoon finely grated lemon rind

¼ pound chorizo or other spicy cooked sausage, cut across into ¼-inch slices

salt and pepper

1½ cups fresh or frozen green peas

¾ pound monkfish, skinned and cut in 1-inch pieces

24 mussels, well scrubbed

12 raw or cooked jumbo shrimp, peeled and deveined

1 ▼ Heat the olive oil in a large, wide skillet or paella pan. Add the rice and cook over medium-high heat until it begins to color, stirring frequently.

2 ▲ Stir in the onion and bell pepper and cook 2–3 minutes longer.

3 ▲ Add the squid, if using, and cook, stirring occasionally, until it is lightly browned.

4 Stir in the stock, wine, saffron, and garlic. Bring to a boil.

5 ▲ Add the tomatoes, bay leaf, lemon rind, and sausage. Season with salt and pepper. Return to a boil, then reduce the heat to low. Cover and simmer until the rice has absorbed most of the liquid, about 15 minutes.

6 ▲ Add the peas, monkfish, and mussels to the rice. Push the mussels down into the rice.

7 ▲ Gently stir in the shrimp. Cover and continue cooking until the mussels have opened and the rice is tender, about 5 minutes. Raw shrimp should have turned bright pink.

8 Taste and adjust the seasoning. Serve immediately in a heated serving dish or from the paella pan, if using.

~ COOK'S TIP ~

This recipe can be doubled to feed a crowd. Be sure to use a larger pan, such as a wide shallow flameproof casserole. The final simmering, after the pan has been covered (step 5), can be done in a preheated 375°F oven. If using a paella pan, cover with foil.

Seafood and Vegetable Stir-Fry

SERVES 4

1 pound rice vermicelli

2 tablespoons oil drained from sun-dried
tomatoes

½ cup sun-dried tomatoes packed in oil,
drained and sliced

½ cup scallions, cut diagonally in
½-inch pieces

2 large carrots, cut in thin sticks

1 zucchini, cut in thin sticks

½ pound raw shrimp, peeled and
deveined

½ pound sea scallops

1-inch piece of fresh gingerroot, peeled
and finely grated

3 tablespoons fresh lemon juice

3 tablespoons chopped fresh basil or 1
teaspoon dried basil

salt and pepper

1 ▲ Bring a large saucepan of water
to a boil. Add the rice vermicelli and
cook until tender (check package
directions for timing). Drain, rinse
with boiling water, and drain again
thoroughly. Keep warm.

2 ▲ Heat the oil in a wok over high
heat. Add the tomatoes, scallions,
and carrots and stir-fry 5 minutes.

3 ▲ Add the zucchini, shrimp,
scallops, and gingerroot. Stir-fry 3
minutes.

4 ▲ Add the lemon juice, basil, and
salt and pepper to taste and stir well.
Stir-fry until the shrimp are all pink,
about 2 more minutes.

5 Serve on the rice vermicelli.

Seafood Stew

SERVES 6

3 tablespoons olive oil

2 large onions, chopped

1 small green bell pepper, seeded and sliced

3 carrots, chopped

3 garlic cloves, minced

2 tablespoons tomato paste

2 16-ounce cans crushed tomatoes

¼ cup chopped fresh parsley

1 teaspoon fresh thyme leaves or ¼ teaspoon dried thyme

1 tablespoon chopped fresh basil or 1 teaspoon dried basil

½ cup dry white wine

1 pound raw shrimp, peeled and deveined

3 pounds mussels or clams (in shells), or a mixture of both, thoroughly cleaned

2 pounds halibut fillet, cut in 2- to 3-inch pieces

1½ cups fish stock or water

salt and pepper

extra chopped fresh herbs, for garnishing

1 ▲ Heat the oil in a flameproof casserole. Add the onions, green bell pepper, carrots, and garlic and cook until tender, about 5 minutes.

2 Add the tomato paste, canned tomatoes, herbs, and wine and stir well to combine. Bring to a boil and simmer 20 minutes.

3 ▲ Add the shrimp, mussels, clams, halibut pieces and stock. Season with salt and pepper.

4 ▲ Bring back to a boil, then reduce the heat and simmer until the shrimp turn pink, the pieces of fish will flake easily, and the mussels and clams open, about 5 minutes.

5 Serve in large soup plates, garnished with chopped herbs.

Shrimp Creole

SERVES 4

4 tablespoons butter or margarine

3 garlic cloves, minced

1 large onion, finely chopped

1 green bell pepper, seeded and finely chopped

1 cup chopped celery

2 cups canned crushed tomatoes

1 teaspoon sugar

2 teaspoons salt

1 bay leaf

1½ teaspoons fresh thyme leaves or ½ teaspoon dried thyme

¼ teaspoon cayenne

2 pounds raw shrimp, peeled and deveined

½ teaspoon grated lemon rind

2 tablespoons fresh lemon juice

pepper

1 Heat the butter or margarine in a flameproof casserole. Add the garlic, onion, bell pepper, and celery and cook until softened, about 5 minutes.

2 ▲ Add the tomatoes, sugar, salt, bay leaf, thyme, and cayenne. Bring to a boil. Reduce the heat and simmer 10 minutes.

3 ▲ Stir in the shrimp, lemon rind and juice, and pepper to taste. Cover and simmer until the shrimp turn pink, about 5 minutes.

4 Serve immediately on a bed of freshly cooked rice.

Shrimp in Creamy Mustard Sauce

SERVES 4

4 tablespoons butter or margarine

2 pounds raw shrimp, peeled and deveined

2 shallots, finely chopped

4 scallions, cut diagonally in ⅛-inch slices

2 tablespoons fresh lemon juice

½ cup dry white wine

½ cup whipping cream

2 tablespoons whole-grain mustard

salt and pepper

2 Melt the remaining butter or margarine in the skillet. Add the shallots and scallions and cook until softened, 3–4 minutes, stirring frequently.

3 ▲ Stir in the lemon juice and wine. Bring to a boil, scraping the bottom of the pan with a wooden spoon to mix in the cooking juices.

4 ▲ Add the cream. Simmer until the mixture thickens, 3–4 minutes, stirring frequently. Stir in the mustard.

5 Return the shrimp to the skillet and reheat briefly. Season with salt and pepper and serve.

1 Melt half the butter or margarine in a skillet over high heat. Add the shrimp and cook until they turn pink and opaque, about 2 minutes, stirring constantly. Remove with a slotted spoon and set aside.

Shrimp Creole (top), Shrimp in Creamy Mustard Sauce

New England Clambake with Lobster

SERVES 6

fresh seaweed

salt

6 1-pound lobsters

2 pounds pickling onions, peeled

2 pounds small red potatoes

3 dozen littleneck or cherrystone clams

6 ears of corn, husks and silk removed

1 cup (2 sticks) butter or margarine

3 tablespoons chopped fresh chives

1 Put a layer of seaweed in the bottom of a deep kettle containing 1 inch of salted water. Put the lobsters on top and cover with more seaweed.

2 Add the onions and potatoes. Cover the kettle and bring the water to a boil.

3 ▲ After 10 minutes, add the clams and the ears of corn. Cover again and cook until the clams have opened, the lobster shells are red, and the potatoes are tender, 15–20 minutes longer.

4 ▲ Meanwhile, in a small saucepan melt the butter or margarine and stir in the chives.

5 Discard the seaweed. Serve the lobsters and clams with the vegetables, accompanied by the chive butter.

Scallop Kabobs

SERVES 4

16 sea scallops

½ teaspoon ground ginger

1 8-ounce can pineapple chunks in juice, drained and juice reserved

1 small fresh red chili pepper, seeded and chopped

grated rind and juice of 1 lime

16 snow peas

16 cherry tomatoes

8 baby zucchini, halved

1 Put the scallops in a bowl. Add the ginger, the juice from the pineapple, the chili pepper, and lime rind and juice and stir well. Cover and let marinate at room temperature about 20 minutes, or 2 hours in the refrigerator.

2 Preheat the broiler.

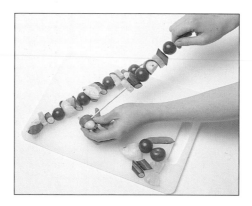

3 ▲ Drain the scallops, reserving their marinade. Wrap a snow pea around a scallop and thread onto 1 of 4 skewers. Thread on a cherry tomato, a piece of zucchini, and a piece of pineapple, followed by another snow pea-wrapped scallop. Repeat until all the ingredients have been used.

4 ▲ Lay the kabobs in the broiler pan and brush with the reserved marinade.

5 Broil about 3 inches from the heat, brushing frequently with the marinade and turning occasionally, until the scallops are opaque, 4–5 minutes.

6 Serve immediately, on a bed of cooked rice, if wished.

New England Clambake with Lobster (top), Scallop Kabobs

MEAT & POULTRY

~

For most people, meat and poultry are the heart of a good meal, so new and interesting recipes for beef, lamb, pork, chicken, and turkey are always welcome. Here are lots of good ideas, from snacks to barbecue fare, and stews to roasts.

Layered Meat Loaf with Fruit

SERVES 6

1½ pounds ground chuck

½ pound ground pork

2 eggs, lightly beaten

1 cup fresh bread crumbs

¼ teaspoon ground cinnamon

salt and pepper

FOR THE STUFFING

1 tablespoon butter or margarine

1 small onion, chopped

¼ cup chopped dried figs

¼ cup chopped dried apricots

¼ cup golden raisins

¼ cup pine nuts

½ cup dry white wine

2 tablespoons chopped fresh parsley

1 Preheat the oven to 350°F.

2 ▼ For the stuffing, melt the butter or margarine in a small frying pan. Add the onion and cook until softened, about 5 minutes. Stir in the figs, apricots, raisins, pine nuts and wine. Bring to a boil and boil to evaporate the liquid, about 5 minutes. Remove from the heat and stir in the parsley. Set aside.

3 In a bowl, mix together the beef, pork, eggs, bread crumbs, cinnamon, and a little salt and pepper.

4 ▲ Press half of the meat mixture over the bottom of a 9- × 5-inch loaf pan. Spoon the stuffing mixture over the meat. Spread the remaining meat mixture on top and press down gently.

5 Cover the pan with foil. Bake 1¼ hours. Pour off any excess fat from the pan. Let the meat loaf cool slightly before serving.

Steak with Spicy Mushroom Sauce

SERVES 4

5 tablespoons butter or margarine

1 pound mushrooms, quartered

1 shallot, finely chopped

¼ cup chopped fresh parsley

salt and pepper

4 beef top loin or rib eye steaks, each about 1-inch thick

1 onion, thinly sliced

⅛ teaspoon hot red pepper flakes

⅛ teaspoon cayenne

dash of hot pepper sauce

2 teaspoons Worcestershire sauce

2 teaspoons sugar

⅔ cup brandy

1 cup beef stock

1 ▼ Melt 2 tablespoons of the butter or margarine in a frying pan. Add the mushrooms and shallot, and cook until softened, about 5 minutes. Drain off the excess liquid. Sprinkle the mushrooms with the parsley and a little salt and pepper. Set aside.

2 Preheat the broiler. Sprinkle the steaks with salt and pepper and arrange them on the rack in the broiler pan. Set aside.

3 Melt the remaining butter or margarine in a saucepan. Add the onion and cook until softened, about 5 minutes. Stir in the red pepper flakes, cayenne, hot pepper sauce, Worcestershire sauce, sugar, and brandy. Bring to a boil and boil until the sauce is reduced by half.

4 Meanwhile, broil the steaks about 3 inches from the heat, 5 minutes on each side for medium-rare, 8 minutes on each side for medium.

5 While the steaks are cooking, add the stock to the sauce and boil again to reduce by half. Season to taste with salt and pepper. Stir in the cooked mushrooms.

6 Transfer the steaks to heated plates and spoon the sauce on top.

Layered Meat Loaf with Fruit (top), Steak with Spicy Mushroom Sauce

Guacamole Cheeseburgers

SERVES 6

2 pounds ground chuck

salt and pepper

6 slices of Swiss cheese

6 hamburger buns with sesame seeds, split and toasted

2 large tomatoes, sliced

FOR THE GUACAMOLE

1 large ripe avocado

1 scallion, chopped

2 teaspoons fresh lemon juice

1 teaspoon chili powder

2 tablespoons chopped fresh tomato

1 To make the guacamole, peel the avocado, discard the pit, and mash the flesh with a fork. Stir in the scallion, lemon juice, chili powder, and chopped tomato. Set aside.

2 Preheat the broiler.

3 ▼ Handling the beef as little as possible, divide it into 6 equal portions. Shape each portion into a ¾-inch-thick patty and season.

4 Arrange the patties on the rack in the broiler pan. Broil about 3 inches from the heat, 5 minutes on each side for medium-rare, 8 minutes on each side for well-done.

5 ▲ Top each hamburger with a slice of cheese and broil until melted, about 30 seconds.

6 Set a hamburger in each toasted bun. Top with a slice of tomato and a spoonful of guacamole and serve.

Chili con Carne

SERVES 8

3 tablespoons corn oil

1 large onion, chopped

2 pounds ground chuck

4 garlic cloves, minced

1 tablespoon light brown sugar

2-3 tablespoons chili powder

1 teaspoon ground cumin

1 teaspoon salt

1 teaspoon pepper

½ cup tomato paste

1 cup beer

2 cups tomato sauce

2 cups cooked or canned red kidney beans, rinsed and drained

FOR SERVING

1 pound spaghetti, broken in half

1 cup sour cream

2 cups shredded Monterey jack or cheddar cheese

1 Heat the oil in a deep saucepan and cook the onion until softened, about 5 minutes. Add the beef and cook until browned, breaking up the meat with the side of a spoon.

2 ▼ Stir in the garlic, brown sugar, chili powder, cumin, salt, and pepper. Add the tomato paste, beer, and tomato sauce and stir to mix. Bring to a boil. Reduce the heat, cover, and simmer 50 minutes.

3 ▲ Stir in the kidney beans and simmer 5 minutes longer, uncovered.

4 Meanwhile, cook the spaghetti in a large pot of boiling salted water until just tender (check package directions for cooking time). Drain.

5 To serve, put the spaghetti into a warmed bowl. Ladle the chili over the spaghetti and top with some of the sour cream and shredded cheese. Serve the remaining sour cream and cheese separately.

Guacamole Cheeseburgers (top), Chili con Carne

Old-Fashioned Beef Stew

SERVES 6

3 tablespoons corn oil

1 large onion, sliced

2 carrots, chopped

1 celery stalk, chopped

2 tablespoons flour

3 tablespoons paprika

2 pounds beef chuck steak, cubed

2 tablespoons tomato paste

1 cup red wine

2 cups beef stock

1 sprig of fresh thyme or 1 teaspoon dried thyme

1 bay leaf

salt and pepper

3 medium potatoes, cut into 1½-inch pieces

1 cup button mushrooms, quartered

1 Preheat the oven to 375°F.

2 ▼ Heat half the oil in a large flameproof casserole. Add the onion, carrots, and celery and cook until softened, about 5 minutes. Remove the vegetables with a slotted spoon and set aside.

3 ▲ Combine the flour and paprika in a plastic bag. Add the beef cubes and shake to coat them with the seasoned flour.

4 Heat the remaining oil in the casserole. Add the beef cubes and brown well on all sides, about 10 minutes.

5 Return the vegetables to the casserole. Stir in the tomato paste, red wine, stock, thyme, bay leaf, and a little salt and pepper. Bring to a boil.

6 ▲ Stir in the potatoes. Cover the casserole and transfer it to the oven. Cook 1 hour.

7 Stir in the mushrooms and continue cooking until the beef is very tender, about 30 minutes longer. Discard the bay leaf before serving.

Steak, Bell Pepper, and Corn Stir-Fry

SERVES 4

2–3 teaspoons chili powder

1 teaspoon ground cumin

½ teaspoon dried oregano

salt and pepper

1 pound beef top round steak, cut into thin strips

2 tablespoons corn oil

5 scallions, cut on the diagonal into 1-inch lengths

1 small green bell pepper, cored and thinly sliced

1 small red bell pepper, cored and thinly sliced

1 small yellow bell pepper, cored and thinly sliced

¼ pound baby corn, halved lengthwise, or 1 cup corn kernels

4 garlic cloves, minced

2 tablespoons fresh lime juice

2 tablespoons chopped fresh coriander leaves (cilantro)

1 ▼ In a medium bowl, combine the spices, oregano, and a little salt and pepper. Rub the mixture into the steak strips.

2 Heat half the oil in a wok or large frying pan over high heat. Add the steak strips and stir-fry until well browned on all sides, 3–4 minutes. Remove the steak from the wok with a slotted spoon and keep hot.

3 ▲ Heat the remaining oil in the wok and add the scallions, bell peppers, corn, and garlic. Stir-fry until the vegetables are crisp-tender, about 3 minutes.

4 ▼ Return the steak to the wok and toss briefly to mix with the vegetables and heat it through. Stir in the lime juice and coriander and serve.

Corned Beef Boiled Dinner

SERVES 6

2–2½ pounds corned beef brisket

1 teaspoon black peppercorns

2 bay leaves

1 small rutabaga, about 1 pound, cut into pieces

8 small white onions, peeled

8 small red potatoes

3 carrots, cut into sticks

1 small head of green cabbage, cut into 6 wedges

FOR THE SAUCE

⅓ cup red wine vinegar

5 tablespoons sugar

1 tablespoon mustard powder

4–5 tablespoons butter or margarine

salt and pepper

1 Put the brisket in a large pot. Add the peppercorns and bay leaves and cover with water. Bring to a boil. Reduce the heat and simmer until the beef is almost tender, about 2 hours.

2 ▼ Add the rutabaga, onions, potatoes, and carrots. Bring the liquid back to a boil, then reduce the heat and cover the pot. Simmer 10 minutes.

3 Add the cabbage wedges. Cover and cook 15 minutes longer.

4 With a slotted spoon, remove the meat and vegetables from the pot and keep them hot. Reserve 1½ cups of the cooking liquid.

5 ▲ For the sauce, combine the reserved cooking liquid, vinegar, sugar, and mustard in a small saucepan. Bring to a boil, then reduce the heat and simmer until thickened, about 5 minutes. Remove the pan from the heat and swirl in the butter or margarine. Season to taste with salt and pepper.

6 Slice the beef and arrange with the vegetables on a warmed platter. Serve with the sauce in a sauceboat.

Steak Sandwiches with Onions

SERVES 3

1 pound minute or sandwich steaks

salt and pepper

2 tablespoons butter or margarine

2 tablespoons corn oil

1 large onion, thinly sliced into rings

1 long flat loaf of Italian or French bread, split in half lengthwise, and cut into 3 sections

Dijon-style mustard, for serving

1 Sprinkle the steaks generously with salt and pepper.

2 ▲ Heat the butter or margarine and half of the oil in a frying pan. Add the onion and cook until browned and crispy, about 8 minutes. Remove the onion with a slotted spoon and drain on paper towels. Add the remaining oil to the pan.

3 ▼ Add the steaks to the frying pan and cook until well browned, about 3 minutes, turning once.

4 Divide the steak and onions among the bottom halves of the bread sections, and put on the tops. Serve on warmed plates with mustard.

Corned Beef Boiled Dinner (top), Steak Sandwiches with Onions

Pork with Mustard-Peppercorn Sauce

SERVES 4

SERVES 4

2 pork tenderloins, about ¾ pound each

2 tablespoons butter or margarine

1 tablespoon olive oil

1 tablespoon red wine vinegar

1 tablespoon whole-grain mustard

3 tablespoons whipping cream

1 tablespoon green peppercorns in brine, drained

pinch salt

1 Cut the pork tenderloins across into 1-inch-thick slices.

2 ▼ Heat the butter or margarine and oil in a frying pan. Add the slices of pork and fry until browned and cooked through, 5–8 minutes on each side. Transfer the pork to a warmed serving plate and keep hot.

3 ▼ Add the vinegar and mustard to the pan and cook 1 minute, stirring with a wooden spoon to loosen any particles attached to the bottom.

4 Stir in the cream, peppercorns, and salt. Boil 1 minute. Pour the sauce over the pork and serve immediately.

Pork Chop, Potato, and Apple Scallop

SERVES 6

2 cups apple juice

½ pound baking potatoes, peeled and cut into ½-inch slices

½ pound sweet potatoes, peeled and cut into ½-inch slices

1 pound apples, peeled, cored, and cut into ½-inch slices

salt and pepper

6 tablespoons flour

6 pork chops, cut 1-inch thick, trimmed of excess fat

4 tablespoons butter or margarine

3 tablespoons corn oil

6 fresh sage leaves

1 Preheat the oven to 350°F. Grease a 13- × 9-inch baking dish.

2 In a small saucepan, bring the apple juice to a boil.

3 ▼ Arrange a row of baking-potato slices at a short end of the prepared dish. Arrange a row of sweet-potato slices next to the first row, slightly overlapping it, and then a row of apple slices. Repeat the alternating overlapping rows to fill the dish. Sprinkle with salt and pepper.

4 Pour the apple juice over the potato and apple slices. Cover the dish with foil and bake 40 minutes.

5 ▲ Meanwhile, season the flour with salt and pepper. Coat the chops with the seasoned flour, shaking off any excess. Melt the butter or margarine with the oil in a frying pan. Fry the chops until well browned, about 5 minutes on each side.

6 Uncover the baking dish. Arrange the chops on top of the potatoes and apples. Put a sage leaf on each chop.

7 Return to the oven, uncovered, and cook until the potatoes and pork chops are tender and most of the liquid is absorbed, about 1 hour.

Pork with Mustard-Peppercorn Sauce (top), Pork Chop, Potato, and Apple Scallop

Pork Chops with Sauerkraut

SERVES 6

6 bacon slices, coarsely chopped

3 tablespoons flour

salt and pepper

6 boned top-loin pork chops or sirloin cutlets

2 teaspoons light brown sugar

1 garlic clove, minced

1½ pounds sauerkraut, rinsed

1 teaspoon juniper berries

1 teaspoon black peppercorns

1 cup beer

1 cup chicken stock

1 Preheat the oven to 350°F.

2 ▼ In a frying pan, fry the bacon until just beginning to brown. With a slotted spoon, transfer the bacon to a casserole dish.

3 ▲ Season the flour with salt and pepper. Coat the pork chops with the seasoned flour, shaking off any excess. Brown the chops in the bacon fat, about 5 minutes on each side. Remove and drain on paper towels.

4 ▲ Add the brown sugar and garlic to the fat in the frying pan and cook, stirring, for 3 minutes. Add the sauerkraut, juniper berries, and peppercorns.

5 ▲ Transfer the sauerkraut mixture to the casserole and mix with the bacon. Lay the pork chops on top. Pour the beer and chicken stock over the chops.

6 Place the casserole in the oven and cook until the chops are very tender, 45–55 minutes.

Barbecue Spareribs

SERVES 4

3 pounds meaty pork spareribs, in 2 pieces

½ cup corn oil

½ teaspoon paprika

FOR THE SAUCE

½ cup light brown sugar, firmly packed

2 teaspoons mustard powder

1 teaspoon salt

⅛ teaspoon pepper

½ teaspoon ground ginger

½ cup tomato sauce

½ cup fresh orange juice

1 small onion, finely chopped

1 garlic clove, minced

2 tablespoons chopped fresh parsley

1 tablespoon Worcestershire sauce

1 ▲ Preheat the oven to 375°F. Arrange the ribs in one layer in a roasting pan.

2 ▲ In a small bowl, combine the oil and paprika. Brush the mixture on the spareribs. Bake until the ribs are slightly crisp, 55–60 minutes.

3 ▼ Combine the sauce ingredients in a saucepan and bring to a boil. Simmer 5 minutes, stirring occasionally.

4 ▲ Pour off the fat from the roasting pan. Brush the ribs with half of the sauce and bake 20 minutes. Turn the ribs over and brush with the remaining sauce. Bake 20 minutes longer. Cut into sections for serving.

Pork Tostadas

1 garlic clove, minced
2 tablespoons corn oil
⅓ cup fresh lime juice
3 tablespoons Worcestershire sauce
⅛ teaspoon pepper
1¼ pounds pork cutlets, cut lengthwise into ⅜-inch-wide strips
1 large ripe avocado
½ cup loosely packed fresh coriander (cilantro) leaves, finely chopped
8 corn tortillas
1 onion, sliced
1 green bell pepper, seeded and sliced
black olives, for garnishing
FOR THE SALSA
1 cup cooked fresh or thawed frozen corn kernels
1 small red bell pepper, seeded and finely chopped
1 small red onion, thinly sliced
1 teaspoon honey
juice of 1 lime

1 ▼ In a medium bowl, combine the garlic, 1 tablespoon of the oil, the lime juice, Worcestershire sauce, and pepper. Add the pork strips and toss to coat. Let marinate 10–20 minutes, stirring the strips at least once.

2 ▲ Meanwhile, combine all the ingredients for the salsa in a bowl and mix well. Set aside.

3 ▲ Cut the avocado in half and remove the pit. Scrape the flesh into a bowl and mash it with a fork. Stir in the chopped coriander.

4 ▲ Preheat the oven to 350°F. Wrap the corn tortillas in foil and heat them in the oven for 10 minutes.

5 ▲ Meanwhile, heat the remaining oil in a frying pan. Add the onion and green bell pepper slices and cook until softened, about 5 minutes.

6 ▲ Add the pork strips to the frying pan and fry briskly, turning occasionally, until cooked and browned, about 5 minutes.

7 ▲ To serve, place a spoonful of the avocado on each of the heated tortillas. Top with some of the pork mixture and a spoonful of the salsa. Garnish with an olive, and serve with more salsa if you like.

Baked Sausages and Beans with Crispy Topping

SERVES 6

2 cups dry navy beans or Great Northern beans, soaked overnight and drained

1 onion, stuck with 4 cloves

3 tablespoons butter or margarine

1 pound pork link sausages

1 pound kielbasa sausage, cut into ½-inch slices

¼ pound bacon, chopped

1 large onion, finely chopped

2 garlic cloves, minced

1 16-ounce can crushed tomatoes

½ cup tomato paste

¼ cup maple syrup

2 tablespoons dark brown sugar

½ teaspoon mustard powder

¼ teaspoon salt

pepper

½ cup fresh bread crumbs

1 ▲ Put the beans in a saucepan and cover with fresh cold water. Add the clove-studded onion. Bring to a boil and boil until the beans are just tender, about 1 hour. Drain the beans. Discard the onion.

2 Preheat the oven to 350°F.

3 ▲ Melt half of the butter or margarine in a large flameproof casserole. Add the sausages, bacon, onion, and garlic and fry until the bacon and sausages are well browned.

4 ▲ Stir in the beans, tomatoes, tomato paste, maple syrup, brown sugar, mustard, salt, and pepper to taste. Bring to a boil.

5 ▲ Sprinkle the bread crumbs over the surface and dot with the remaining butter or margarine.

6 Transfer the casserole to the oven and bake until most of liquid has been absorbed by the beans and the top is crisp, about 1 hour.

Jambalaya

SERVES 6

2 tablespoons corn oil

4 skinless boneless chicken breast
halves, cut into chunks

1 pound spicy cooked sausage, sliced

6 ounces smoked ham, cubed

1 large onion, chopped

2 celery stalks, chopped

2 green bell peppers, seeded and
chopped

3 garlic cloves, minced

1 cup canned crushed tomatoes

2 cups chicken stock

1 teaspoon cayenne

1 sprig of fresh thyme or ¼ teaspoon
dried thyme

2 sprigs of flat-leaf (Italian) parsley

1 bay leaf

1½ cups rice

salt and pepper

4 scallions, finely chopped

1 ▼ Heat the oil in a large frying
pan. Add the chicken chunks and
sausage slices and cook until well
browned, about 5 minutes. Stir in the
ham cubes and cook 5 minutes longer.

2 Add the onion, celery, bell
peppers, garlic, tomatoes, stock,
cayenne, thyme, parsley, and bay leaf
to the frying pan. Bring to a boil,
stirring well.

3 ▲ Stir in the rice, and add salt and
and pepper to taste. When the liquid
returns to a boil, reduce the heat and
cover the pan tightly. Simmer 10
minutes.

4 Remove the pan from the heat and,
without removing the lid, set aside for
20 minutes, to let the rice finish
cooking.

5 ▲ Discard the bay leaf. Scatter the
chopped scallions on top of the
jambalaya just before serving.

Ham and Asparagus with Cheese Sauce

SERVES 4

24 asparagus spears

3 tablespoons butter or margarine

3 tablespoons flour

1½ cups milk

1 cup shredded Swiss cheese

⅛ teaspoon grated nutmeg

salt and pepper

12 thin slices of cooked ham or
    prosciutto

1 Trim tough stalk ends from the asparagus. Bring a wide shallow pan of salted water to a boil. Add the asparagus and simmer until barely tender, 5–7 minutes. Drain the asparagus in a colander, rinse with cold water, and spread out on paper towels to dry.

2 Preheat the broiler. Grease a 13- × 9-inch baking dish.

3 Melt the butter or margarine in a saucepan. Add the flour and cook 2 minutes, stirring. Stir in the milk. Bring to a boil, stirring constantly, and simmer until thickened, about 5 minutes.

4 ▲ Add ¾ cup of the cheese to the sauce. Season to taste with nutmeg, salt, and pepper. Keep warm.

5 ▲ Wrap a pair of asparagus spears in each slice of ham. Arrange in the prepared baking dish, in one layer.

6 Pour the sauce over the ham and asparagus rolls and sprinkle the remaining cheese on top. Broil about 3 inches from the heat until bubbling and golden brown, about 5 minutes. Serve hot.

Ham Steaks with Raisin Sauce

SERVES 4

⅓ cup raisins

1 cup warm water

½ teaspoon instant coffee

1 teaspoon cornstarch

3 tablespoons butter or margarine

4 ham steaks, about ¼ pound each,
    trimmed of excess fat

2 teaspoons dark brown sugar

2 teaspoons cider vinegar

2 teaspoons soy sauce

~ **VARIATION** ~

For a richer sauce, substitute an equal quantity of chopped prunes for the raisins.

1 ▼ In a small bowl, soak the raisins in half of the water to plump them, about 10 minutes.

2 Stir the coffee and cornstarch into the remaining water until smooth.

3 Melt the butter or margarine in a large frying pan. Add the ham steaks and cook over medium-low heat until lightly browned, about 5 minutes on each side.

4 ▲ Transfer the cooked steaks to a heated serving dish.

5 Drain the raisins and add them to the frying pan. Stir the coffee mixture to recombine it, then add to the pan with the sugar, vinegar, and soy sauce. Bring to a boil and simmer until slightly thickened, about 3 minutes, stirring constantly.

6 Spoon the raisin sauce over the ham steaks and serve.

Ham and Asparagus with Cheese Sauce (top), Ham Steaks with Raisin Sauce

Pesto Lamb Chops

SERVES 4

small bunch of fresh basil leaves

¼ cup pine nuts

2 garlic cloves, peeled

¼ cup freshly grated Parmesan cheese

½ cup extra-virgin olive oil

salt and pepper

4 lamb sirloin or blade chops, about ½ pound each

fresh basil sprigs, for garnishing

1 In a food processor or blender, combine the basil, pine nuts, garlic, and Parmesan cheese. Process until the ingredients are finely chopped. Gradually pour in the olive oil in a thin stream. Season to taste with salt and pepper. The sauce should be thin and creamy. Alternatively, use a mortar and pestle to make the sauce.

2 ▼ Put the lamb chops in a shallow dish that will hold them comfortably side by side. Pour the pesto sauce over the chops. Turn to coat on both sides. Let marinate 1 hour.

3 Preheat the broiler. Brush the rack in the broiler pan with olive oil.

4 ▲ Transfer the chops to the broiler rack. Broil about 3 inches from the heat until well browned and cooked to taste, about 15 minutes, turning once. Serve garnished with fresh basil sprigs.

Lamb and Bean Stew

SERVES 6

1½ cups dried red kidney beans, soaked overnight and drained

2 tablespoons vegetable oil

2 pounds lean boned lamb, cut into 1½-inch cubes

1 large onion, chopped

1 bay leaf

3 cups chicken stock

1 garlic clove, minced

salt and pepper

1 Put the beans in a large pot. Cover with fresh water, bring to a boil, and boil 10 minutes. Reduce the heat and simmer 30 minutes, then drain.

2 Meanwhile, heat the oil in another large pot. Add the lamb cubes and fry until browned all over. Remove the lamb with a slotted spoon and reserve until needed.

3 ▼ Add the onion to the hot oil and cook until softened, about 5 minutes.

4 ▲ Return the lamb cubes to the pot and add the drained beans, bay leaf, stock, garlic, and salt and pepper to taste. Bring to a boil. Reduce the heat, cover, and simmer 1¼ hours, or until the lamb and beans are tender.

5 Discard the bay leaf, and adjust the seasoning before serving.

Pesto Lamb Chops (top), Lamb and Bean Stew

Sesame Lamb Chops

SERVES 4

8 lamb rib chops
salt and pepper
1 egg
1 teaspoon Dijon-style mustard
3 tablespoons fine dry bread crumbs
3 tablespoons sesame seeds
2 tablespoons flour
2 tablespoons butter or margarine
1 tablespoon oil

1 ▼ If necessary, trim any excess fat from the chops. With a small knife, scrape all the meat and fat off the top 2 inches of the bone in each chop. Sprinkle the chops generously with salt and pepper.

2 ▲ In a bowl, beat the egg and mustard together. Pour into a shallow dish. In another dish, mix the bread crumbs and sesame seeds. Place the flour in a third dish.

3 ▲ Dredge each chop in flour, shaking off any excess. Dip in the egg and mustard mixture and then coat with the bread crumb mixture, pressing it on the meat to get an even coating. Refrigerate 15 minutes.

4 ▲ Heat the butter or margarine and oil in a frying pan. Add the chops and fry over medium heat until crisp and golden and cooked to taste, 4–5 minutes on each side, turning gently with tongs.

Roast Rack of Lamb

SERVES 4

2 racks of lamb, each with 8 chops, ends of bones scraped clean

¼ cup Dijon-style mustard

1½ tablespoons fresh rosemary or 1 tablespoon dried rosemary

salt and pepper

½ cup fine dry bread crumbs

¼ cup chopped fresh parsley

4 garlic cloves, minced

¼ cup olive oil

½ cup butter or margarine

1 cup chicken stock

4 In a small saucepan, melt half the butter or margarine. Stir in the remaining olive oil. Drizzle this mixture over the crumb coating.

5 Roast the racks of lamb, allowing 40 minutes for medium-rare meat and 50 minutes for medium.

6 Transfer the racks to a warmed serving platter, arranging them so the scraped ends of the bones are interlocked. Cover loosely with foil and set aside.

7 Pour the stock into the roasting pan and bring to a boil, scraping the bottom of the pan with a wooden spoon to mix in all the cooking juices. Remove from the heat and swirl in the remaining butter or margarine. Pour the gravy into a warmed sauceboat.

8 To serve, carve each rack by cutting down between the chop bones, or cut down after every 2 bones for double chops.

1 Preheat the oven to 425°F.

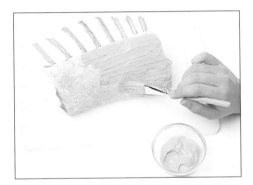

2 ▲ Brush the meaty side of the racks with the mustard. Sprinkle with the rosemary, salt, and pepper.

3 ▲ In a bowl, mix the bread crumbs with the parsley, garlic, and half of the olive oil. Press this mixture evenly over the mustard on the racks of lamb. Wrap the scraped bone ends with foil. Put the racks in a roasting pan.

Glazed Lamb Kabobs

SERVES 4

1 pound boned leg of lamb, cut into
  1-inch cubes

3 medium zucchini, cut into ½-inch
  slices

¼ cup mint jelly

2 tablespoons fresh lemon juice

2 tablespoons olive oil

1 tablespoon chopped fresh mint

~ **VARIATION** ~

Substitute an equal quantity of
orange marmalade for the mint
jelly. Instead of fresh mint, use
2 teaspoons of grated orange rind.

1 Preheat the broiler.

2 Thread the cubes of lamb and slices
of zucchini alternately onto metal or
wooden skewers.

3 ▲ Combine the mint jelly, lemon
juice, olive oil, and chopped mint in a
small saucepan. Stir over low heat
until the jelly melts.

4 ▼ Brush the lamb and zucchini
with the mint glaze. Lay them on the
rack in the broiler pan.

5 Cook under the broiler, about 3
inches from the heat, until browned
and cooked to taste, 10–12 minutes,
turning the skewers frequently. Serve
on a bed of rice, if wished.

Lamb Burgers with Cucumber-Mint Relish

SERVES 4

1½ pounds ground lamb

1 medium onion, finely chopped

1 tablespoon paprika

2 tablespoons chopped fresh parsley

2 tablespoons chopped fresh mint or 1
  tablespoon dried mint

salt and pepper

4 hamburger buns with sesame seeds,
  split open

FOR THE RELISH

2 medium hothouse cucumbers, thinly
  sliced

1 small red onion, thinly sliced

3 tablespoons fresh lime juice

2 teaspoons vegetable oil

½ cup chopped fresh mint or 2
  tablespoons dried mint

2 scallions, finely chopped

1 To make the relish, combine the
cucumbers, red onion, lime juice, oil,
mint, and scallions in a non-metallic
bowl. Cover the mixture and
refrigerate at least 2 hours.

2 ▲ In a bowl, combine the lamb,
onion, paprika, parsley, mint, and a
little salt and pepper. Mix thoroughly.

3 Preheat the broiler.

4 ▲ Divide the lamb mixture into 4
equal portions and shape each into a
1-inch-thick patty.

5 Broil the burgers, about 3 inches
from the heat, allowing 5 minutes on
each side for medium and 8 minutes
on each side for well-done. At the
same time, toast the cut surfaces of the
buns briefly under the broiler.

6 Serve the lamb burgers in the buns,
with the cucumber-mint relish.

Glazed Lamb Kabobs (top), Lamb Burgers with Cucumber-Mint Relish

Chicken Breasts with Prunes and Almonds

SERVES 4

2 tablespoons butter or margarine

1 tablespoon corn oil

2½ pounds chicken breast halves

3 cups chicken stock

⅔ cup raisins

1 tablespoon fresh thyme leaves or 1 teaspoon dried thyme

3 fresh sage leaves, chopped

¼ cup chopped fresh parsley

1 tablespoon chopped fresh marjoram or 1 teaspoon dried marjoram

1 cup fresh bread crumbs

½ cup ground almonds

12 prunes, pitted

4–6 whole cloves

½ teaspoon ground mace

pinch of saffron threads, crumbled

salt and pepper

⅓ cup sliced almonds, toasted

1 ▼ Melt the butter or margarine with the oil in a frying pan. Add the chicken and brown 10 minutes, turning once. Transfer the chicken pieces to a large pot.

~ COOK'S TIP ~

For ground almonds, chop whole or slivered almonds in a food processor until powdery.

2 ▲ Pour the stock into the pot and bring to a boil. Add all the remaining ingredients, except the toasted almonds, and stir well to mix. Simmer 45 minutes.

3 ▲ With tongs, remove the chicken from the pot and let cool. Bring the cooking liquid back to a boil and boil until well reduced, about 10 minutes, stirring frequently.

4 ▲ Remove the bones from the chicken and return the meat to the sauce. Heat through. Serve sprinkled with the toasted almonds.

Southern Fried Chicken

SERVES 4

½ cup buttermilk

1 3-pound chicken, cut into pieces

corn oil for frying

½ cup flour

1 tablespoon paprika

¼ teaspoon pepper

1 tablespoon water

1 ▼ Pour the buttermilk into a large bowl and add the chicken pieces. Stir to coat, then set aside for 5 minutes.

2 Heat a ¼-inch layer of oil in a large frying pan over medium-high heat. Do not let oil overheat.

3 ▲ In a bowl or plastic bag, combine the flour, paprika, and pepper. One by one, lift the chicken pieces out of the buttermilk and dip into the flour to coat all over, shaking off any excess.

4 ▼ Add the chicken pieces to the hot oil and fry until lightly browned, about 10 minutes, turning over halfway through cooking time.

5 ▲ Reduce the heat to low and add the water to the frying pan. Cover and cook 30 minutes, turning the pieces over at 10-minute intervals. Uncover the pan and continue cooking until the chicken is very tender and the coating is crisp, about 15 minutes, turning every 5 minutes. Serve hot.

Honey Roast Chicken

SERVES 4

1 3½-pound chicken
2 tablespoons clear honey
1 tablespoon brandy
1½ tablespoons flour
⅔ cup chicken stock
FOR THE STUFFING
2 shallots, chopped
4 bacon slices, chopped
½ cup button mushrooms, quartered
1 tablespoon butter or margarine
2 thick slices of white bread, diced
1 tablespoon chopped fresh parsley
salt and pepper

1 ▼ For the stuffing, gently fry the shallots, bacon, and mushrooms in a frying pan for 5 minutes. With a slotted spoon, transfer them to a bowl.

2 Pour off all but 2 tablespoons of bacon fat from the pan. Add the butter or margarine to the pan and fry the bread until golden brown. Add the bread to the bacon mixture. Stir in the parsley and salt and pepper to taste. Let cool.

3 Preheat the oven to 350°F.

4 ▲ Pack the stuffing into the body cavity of the chicken. Truss it with string, or secure with poultry pins, to keep it in a neat shape.

5 ▲ Transfer the chicken to a roasting pan which just holds it comfortably.

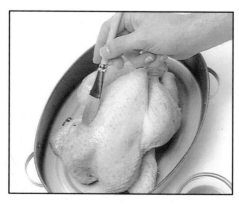

6 ▲ Mix the honey with the brandy. Brush half of the mixture over the chicken. Roast until the chicken is thoroughly cooked, about 1 hour 20 minutes. Baste the chicken frequently with the remaining honey mixture during roasting.

7 ▲ Transfer the chicken to a warmed serving platter. Cover with foil and set aside.

8 ▲ Strain the cooking juices into a degreasing pitcher. Set aside to let the fat rise to the surface.

9 ▲ Stir the flour into the sediments in the roasting pan. Add the lean part of the juices and the stock. Boil rapidly until the gravy has thickened, stirring constantly.

10 Pour the gravy into a warmed sauceboat and serve with the chicken.

Chicken Thighs Wrapped in Bacon

SERVES 4

16 bacon slices

8 chicken thighs, skin removed

FOR THE MARINADE

finely grated rind and juice of 1 orange

finely grated rind and juice of 1 lime

5 garlic cloves, minced

1 tablespoon chili powder

1 tablespoon paprika

1 teaspoon ground cumin

½ teaspoon dried oregano

1 tablespoon olive oil

1 For the marinade, combine the citrus rind and juice, garlic, chili powder, paprika, cumin, oregano, and olive oil in a bowl.

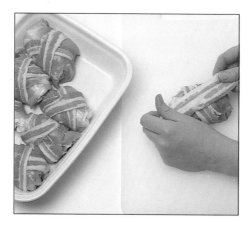

2 ▲ Wrap 2 slices of bacon around each chicken thigh in a cross shape. Secure with wooden toothpicks. Arrange the wrapped chicken thighs in a baking dish.

3 Pour the marinade over the chicken, cover, and let marinate 1 hour at room temperature or several hours in the refrigerator.

4 Preheat the oven to 375°F.

5 ▼ Put the baking dish in the oven and bake until the chicken is cooked through and the bacon is crisp, about 40 minutes for small thighs and 1 hour for large thighs. Skim excess fat from the sauce before serving. Rice is a good accompaniment because there is plenty of sauce.

Deviled Chicken Drumsticks

SERVES 4

2 tablespoons corn oil

8 chicken drumsticks, about 3 pounds

1 medium onion, chopped

½ cup water

¼ cup Dijon-style mustard

1 tablespoon prepared horseradish

1 tablespoon Worcestershire sauce

1 teaspoon light brown sugar

¼ teaspoon salt

parsley sprigs, for garnishing

1 Heat the oil in a frying pan. Add the chicken drumsticks and brown them on all sides. With a spatula or tongs, remove the drumsticks from the pan and drain on paper towels.

2 ▲ Add the onion to the hot oil and cook until softened, about 5 minutes. Return the chicken to the pan. Stir in the water, mustard, horseradish, Worcestershire sauce, brown sugar, and salt. Bring to a boil.

3 Reduce the heat to low. Cover the pan and simmer until the chicken is very tender, about 45 minutes, stirring occasionally.

4 ▼ Transfer the drumsticks to a warmed serving dish. Skim any fat off the cooking juices. Pour the juices over the chicken. Garnish with parsley and serve.

Chicken Thighs Wrapped in Bacon (top), Deviled Chicken Drumsticks

Cornish Game Hens with Cranberry Sauce

SERVES 4

4 Cornish game hens, with giblets, each about 1 pound
3 tablespoons butter or margarine
salt and pepper
1 onion, quartered
¼ cup port wine
⅔ cup chicken stock
2 tablespoons honey
1½ cups fresh cranberries

> ### ~ VARIATION ~
>
> For extra zest, add 2 tablespoons of finely grated orange rind to the sauce with the cranberries.

1 Preheat the oven to 450°F.

2 ▼ Smear the hens on all sides with 2 tablespoons of the butter or margarine. Arrange them, on their sides, in a roasting pan in which they will fit comfortably. Sprinkle them with salt and pepper. Add the onion quarters to the pan. Chop the gizzards and livers and arrange them around the hens.

3 ▲ Roast 20 minutes, basting often with the melted fat in the pan. Turn the hens onto their other sides and roast 20 minutes longer, basting often. Turn the hens breast up and continue roasting until they are cooked through, about 15 minutes. Transfer the hens to a warmed serving dish. Cover with foil and set aside.

4 Skim any fat off the juices in the roasting pan. Put the pan on top of the stove and bring the juices to a boil. Add the port wine and bring back to a boil, stirring well to dislodge any particles attached to the bottom of the pan.

5 ▲ Strain the sauce into a small saucepan. Add the stock, bring to a boil, and boil until reduced by half. Stir in the honey and cranberries. Simmer until the cranberries pop, about 3 minutes.

6 Remove the pan from the heat and swirl in the remaining butter or margarine. Season to taste with salt and pepper. Pour the sauce into a sauceboat and serve with the hens.

Barbecue Chicken

SERVES 4

3 tablespoons corn oil	
1 large onion, chopped	
¾ cup catsup	
¾ cup water	
2½ tablespoons fresh lemon juice	
1½ tablespoons prepared horseradish	
1 tablespoon light brown sugar	
1 tablespoon spicy brown mustard	
3 pounds chicken pieces	

1 Preheat the oven to 350°F.

2 ▲ Heat 1 tablespoon of the oil in a saucepan. Add the onion and cook until softened, about 5 minutes. Stir in the catsup, water, lemon juice, horseradish, brown sugar, and mustard and bring to a boil. Reduce the heat and simmer the sauce 10 minutes, stirring occasionally.

3 ▲ Heat the remaining oil in a heavy frying pan. Add the chicken pieces and brown on all sides. Drain the chicken pieces on paper towels.

4 ▼ Transfer the chicken pieces to a 11- × 1-inch baking dish and pour the sauce over the top.

5 ▲ Bake until the chicken is cooked and tender, about 1¼ hours, basting occasionally. Alternatively, grill over medium coals for 40–50 minutes, turning once and brushing frequently with the sauce.

Chicken Potpie

SERVES 6

4 tablespoons butter or margarine

1 medium onion, chopped

3 carrots, cut into ½-inch dice

1 parsnip, cut into ½-inch dice

3 tablespoons flour

1½ cups chicken stock

⅓ cup medium sherry wine

⅓ cup dry white wine

¾ cup whipping cream

⅔ cup frozen peas, thawed and well drained

3 cups cooked chicken meat, in chunks

1 teaspoon dried thyme

1 tablespoon minced fresh parsley

salt and pepper

FOR THE CRUST

1⅓ cups flour

½ teaspoon salt

½ cup shortening

2–3 tablespoons ice water

1 egg

2 tablespoons milk

1 ▲ For the crust, sift the flour and salt into a mixing bowl. Using a pastry blender, cut in the shortening until the mixture resembles coarse crumbs. Sprinkle in the water, 1 tablespoon at a time, tossing lightly with a fork until the dough will form a ball. Remove the dough, dust with flour, wrap, and refrigerate until required.

2 Preheat the oven to 400°F.

3 ▲ Heat half of the butter or margarine in a medium saucepan. Add the onion, carrots, and parsnip and cook until softened, about 10 minutes. Remove the vegetables from the pan with a slotted spoon.

4 ▲ Melt the remaining butter or margarine in the saucepan. Add the flour and cook 5 minutes, stirring constantly. Stir in the stock, sherry, and white wine. Bring the sauce to a boil, and continue boiling for 1 minute, stirring constantly.

5 ▲ Add the cream, peas, chicken, thyme, and parsley to the sauce. Season to taste with salt and pepper. Simmer 1 minute, stirring.

6 ▼ Transfer the chicken mixture to a 2-quart shallow baking dish.

7 On a lightly floured surface, roll out the dough to ½-inch thickness. Lay the dough over the baking dish and trim off the excess. Dampen the rim of the dish. With a fork, press the crust to the rim to seal.

8 Cut decorative shapes from the dough trimmings.

9 ▲ Lightly whisk the egg with the milk. Brush the pie crust all over with the egg wash. Arrange the dough shapes in an attractive design on top. Brush again with the egg wash. Make 1 or 2 holes in the crust so steam can escape during baking.

10 Bake the pie until the pastry is golden brown, about 35 minutes. Serve hot.

Chicken with Sweet Potatoes

SERVES 6

grated rind and juice of 1 large navel
  orange

⅓ cup soy sauce

1-inch piece of fresh gingerroot, peeled
  and finely grated

¼ teaspoon pepper

2½ pounds chicken pieces

½ cup flour

3 tablespoons corn oil

2 tablespoons butter or margarine

2 pounds sweet potatoes, peeled and cut
  into 1-inch pieces

3 tablespoons light brown sugar

1 ▲ In a plastic bag, combine the
orange rind and juice, soy sauce,
gingerroot, and pepper. Add the
chicken pieces. Put the bag in a
mixing bowl (this will keep the
chicken immersed in the marinade),
and seal. Let marinate in the
refrigerator overnight.

2 Preheat the oven to 425°F.

3 ▼ Drain the chicken, reserving the
marinade. Coat the pieces with flour,
shaking off any excess.

4 Heat 2 tablespoons of the oil in a
frying pan. Add the chicken pieces
and brown on all sides. Drain.

5 Put the remaining oil and the
butter or margarine in a 12- × 9-inch
baking dish. Heat in the oven a few
minutes.

6 ▲ Put the potato pieces in the
bottom of the dish, tossing well to
coat with the butter and oil. Arrange
the chicken pieces in a single layer on
top of the potatoes. Cover with foil
and bake 40 minutes.

7 Mix the reserved marinade with the
brown sugar. Remove the foil from the
baking dish and pour the marinade
mixture over the chicken and
potatoes. Bake uncovered until the
chicken and potatoes are cooked
through and tender, about 20
minutes.

Chicken Tacos

SERVES 4

1 3-pound chicken
1 teaspoon salt
12 taco shells
1½ cups shredded lettuce
1 cup chopped tomatoes
1 cup sour cream
1 cup shredded sharp cheddar cheese

FOR THE TACO SAUCE

1 cup tomato sauce
1–2 garlic cloves, minced
½ teaspoon cider vinegar
½ teaspoon dried oregano
½ teaspoon ground cumin
1–2 tablespoons chili powder

1 Put the chicken in a large pot and add the salt and enough water to cover. Bring to a boil. Reduce the heat and simmer until the chicken is thoroughly cooked, about 45 minutes. Remove the chicken from the pot and let cool. Reserve ½ cup of the chicken stock for the sauce.

2 ▲ Remove the chicken meat from the bones, discarding all skin. Chop the meat coarsely.

3 For the sauce, combine all the ingredients with the stock in a saucepan and bring to a boil. Stir in the chicken meat. Simmer until the sauce thickens considerably, about 20 minutes, stirring occasionally.

4 Preheat the oven to 350°F.

5 ▲ Spread out the taco shells on 2 baking sheets. Heat in the oven for 7 minutes.

6 Meanwhile, put the shredded lettuce, chopped tomatoes, sour cream, and shredded cheese in individual serving dishes.

7 ▲ To serve, spoon a little of the chicken mixture into each taco shell. Garnish with the lettuce, tomatoes, sour cream, and cheese.

Roast Turkey with Middle-Eastern Stuffing

1 12-pound turkey, with giblets
¾ cup softened butter or margarine
salt and pepper
1 lemon, quartered
2 onions, quartered
2 cups cold water
6 eggplants, 3–4 inches long (optional)
1 tablespoon cornstarch
parsley sprigs, for garnishing
FOR THE STUFFING
¼ cup pine nuts
1 cup couscous
1¼ cups boiling water
2 tablespoons butter or margarine
6 scallions, chopped
1 red bell pepper, seeded and chopped
⅓ cup raisins
½ teaspoon ground cumin
3 tablespoons chopped fresh parsley
1 tablespoon fresh lemon juice

1 Preheat the oven to 325°F. Put the pine nuts on a baking sheet and in the oven until golden brown, about 5–10 minutes, stirring occasionally.

2 For the stuffing, put the couscous into a large bowl and pour the boiling water over it. Let stand 10 minutes.

3 ▲ Add the pine nuts to the couscous with the rest of the stuffing ingredients. Mix with a fork to keep the grains of couscous separate.

4 Rinse the turkey inside and out with cold water. Pat dry. Gently slide your hand under the breast skin and loosen it from the meat.

5 ▲ Spread ½ cup of the softened butter or margarine under the skin all over the breast meat.

6 Fill the neck end of the turkey with stuffing without packing it down. Reserve any remaining stuffing to serve apart. Sew the neck flap with a trussing needle and thread or secure with poultry pins.

7 ▲ Sprinkle the body cavity with salt and pepper. Put the quartered lemon and one of the onions inside. Tie the legs together with string.

8 Smear the remaining butter or margarine all over the turkey. Wrap it loosely in foil and set in a roasting pan. Roast, allowing 25 minutes per pound. Remove the foil for the last 30 minutes of roasting. To test for doneness, pierce the thigh with the tip of a sharp knife; the juices that run out should be clear.

9 ▲ Meanwhile, put the giblets in a saucepan with the remaining onion and the water. Bring to a boil, simmer 1 hour, and strain.

10 If using, halve the eggplants and steam until tender, about 10 minutes. Scoop out the inside, leaving a thick shell, and fill with the remaining stuffing. Alternatively, serve the remaining stuffing apart.

11 When the turkey is done, transfer it to a warmed serving platter. Cover with foil and let rest 30 minutes.

12 ▲ Skim the fat off the drippings in the roasting pan. Stir the cornstarch into a little of the giblet stock until smooth. Add the remaining giblet stock to the roasting pan, then stir in the cornstarch mixture. Bring to a boil, scraping the bottom of the pan well with a wooden spoon. Simmer 15 minutes. Strain the gravy, and adjust the seasoning.

13 Garnish the turkey with the stuffed eggplants, if using, and parsley sprigs, and serve the gravy in a warmed sauceboat.

Sliced Turkey Sandwich

SERVES 4

4 tablespoons butter or margarine

1 shallot, finely chopped

½ pound button mushrooms, quartered

1¼ pounds roasted turkey breast

4 thick slices of whole-wheat bread

2 cups thick turkey gravy

parsley sprigs, for garnishing

1 Melt half the butter or margarine in a frying pan. Add the shallot and cook until softened, about 5 minutes.

~ **VARIATION** ~

If preferred, the sandwich bread may be toasted and buttered.

2 Add the mushrooms and cook until the moisture they render has evaporated, about 5 minutes, stirring occasionally.

3 ▲ Meanwhile, skin the turkey breast, and carve into 4 thick slices.

4 In a saucepan, reheat the turkey gravy. Stir in the shallot and mushrooms.

5 ▲ Spread the slices of bread with the remaining butter or margarine. Set a slice on each of 4 plates and top with the turkey slices. Pour the mushroom gravy over the turkey and serve hot, garnished with parsley.

Leftover Turkey Casserole

SERVES 6

½ cup corn oil

4 eggs

2 cups milk

1 cup flour

salt and pepper

1½ pounds cooked turkey meat, cubed

½ cup thick plain yogurt

3 cups cornflakes, crushed

1 Preheat the oven to 425°F.

2 Pour the oil into a 13- × 9-inch baking dish. Heat in the oven about 10 minutes.

3 Meanwhile, beat the eggs in a mixing bowl. Add the milk. Sift in the flour, and add a little salt and pepper. Mix until the batter is smooth. Set aside.

4 ▲ Coat the turkey cubes in the yogurt, then roll in the crushed cornflakes to coat all over.

5 ▲ Remove the baking dish from the oven and pour in the prepared batter. Arrange the turkey pieces on top. Return to the oven and bake until the batter is set and golden, 35–40 minutes. Serve hot.

Sliced Turkey Sandwich (top), Leftover Turkey Casserole

Turkey Kiev

4 turkey cutlets (boneless slices of breast), about 6 ounces each

salt and pepper

½ cup butter or margarine, chilled

1 teaspoon grated orange rind

2 tablespoons chopped fresh chives

flour, for dredging

3 eggs, beaten

1 cup fine dry bread crumbs

corn oil, for frying

orange wedges and parsley, for garnishing

1 ▼ Place each cutlet between 2 sheets of wax paper. With the flat side of a meat pounder, pound until about ¼-inch thick, being careful not to split the meat. Remove the wax paper. Sprinkle the cutlets with salt and pepper.

2 ▲ Cut the butter or margarine into 4 finger-shaped pieces. Place a piece crosswise in the middle of a cutlet. Sprinkle with a little orange rind and chives.

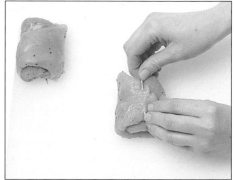

3 ▲ Fold in the 2 long sides of the cutlet, then roll up from a short end. Secure with wooden toothpicks. Repeat with the remaining cutlets.

4 Dredge each roll lightly with flour, shaking off any excess. Dip in the beaten eggs, then roll in the bread crumbs to coat evenly on all sides. Refrigerate 1 hour to set the breaded coating.

5 Pour enough oil into a frying pan to make a ½-inch layer and heat. Add the breaded turkey rolls to the hot oil and fry until crisp and golden on all sides, 15–20 minutes, turning gently with tongs.

6 Remove the toothpicks before serving. Garnish with orange wedges and parsley.

Turkey Scaloppine with Lemon and Sage

SERVES 4

4 turkey cutlets (boneless slices of breast), about 6 ounces each

salt and pepper

1 tablespoon freshly grated lemon rind

1 tablespoon chopped fresh sage or 1 teaspoon dried sage

¼ cup fresh lemon juice

6 tablespoons vegetable oil

1 cup fine dry bread crumbs

fresh sage leaves, for garnishing

lemon slices, for garnishing

1 Place each cutlet between 2 sheets of wax paper. With the flat side of a meat pounder, pound until about ¼-inch thick, being careful not to split the meat. Remove the wax paper. Sprinkle the cutlets with salt and pepper.

2 ▲ In a small bowl, combine the lemon rind, sage, lemon juice, and 2 tablespoons of the oil. Stir well to mix.

~ **VARIATION** ~

For a delicious alternative, substitute fresh tarragon leaves for the sage.

3 ▼ Arrange the turkey cutlets, in one layer, in 1 or 2 shallow baking dishes. Divide the lemon mixture evenly between the dishes and rub well into the turkey. Let marinate 20 minutes.

4 ▲ Heat the remaining oil in a frying pan. Dredge the turkey scaloppine in the bread crumbs, shaking off the excess. Fry in the hot oil until golden brown, about 2 minutes on each side. Serve garnished with sage leaves and lemon slices.

Turkey Chili

SERVES 8

2 tablespoons corn oil

1 medium onion, halved and thinly sliced

1 green bell pepper, seeded and diced

3 garlic cloves, minced

2 pounds ground turkey

2–3 tablespoons chili powder

1½ teaspoons ground cumin

1 teaspoon dried oregano

1 16-ounce can crushed tomatoes

2 tablespoons tomato paste

1 cup chicken stock

1 16-ounce can red kidney beans, drained and rinsed

¼ teaspoon salt

1 Heat the oil in a large saucepan over medium heat. Add the onion, green bell pepper, and garlic and cook until softened, about 5 minutes, stirring frequently.

2 ▼ Add the turkey and cook until it is lightly browned, about 5 minutes longer, stirring to break up the meat.

3 ▼ Stir in the chili powder, cumin, and oregano. Add the tomatoes, tomato paste, chicken stock, kidney beans, and salt, and stir well.

4 Bring to a boil, then reduce the heat and simmer 30 minutes, stirring occasionally. Serve the chili with boiled rice.

Turkey Tetrazzini

SERVES 4

5 tablespoons butter or margarine

4 cups thinly sliced mushrooms

¼ cup flour

1¾ cups milk

2 cups chicken stock

¼ cup dry white wine

10 ounces spaghetti

3 cups chopped cooked turkey meat

1 cup frozen peas, thawed and drained

⅔ cup freshly grated Parmesan cheese

salt and pepper

⅓ cup fine fresh bread crumbs

1 Preheat the oven to 375°F. Grease a shallow 3-quart baking dish.

2 ▲ Melt 4 tablespoons of the butter or margarine in a medium saucepan. Add the mushrooms and cook 5 minutes, stirring frequently. Stir in the flour and cook 3 minutes, stirring constantly. Pour in the milk, stock, and white wine and bring to a boil, stirring. Reduce the heat and simmer 5 minutes.

3 Meanwhile, cook the spaghetti in a large pot of boiling salted water until just tender (see package directions for suggested cooking time). Drain.

4 ▼ Transfer the spaghetti to a mixing bowl. Pour in the mushroom sauce and mix well. Stir in the turkey, peas, ⅓ cup of the Parmesan, and salt and pepper to taste. Transfer the mixture to the baking dish.

5 In a small bowl, combine the remaining Parmesan with the bread crumbs. Sprinkle evenly over the turkey mixture. Dot with the remaining butter or margarine, cut into pieces. Bake until bubbling and golden, 30–40 minutes. Serve hot, in the baking dish.

Turkey Chili (top), Turkey Tetrazzini

PASTA, PIZZA & GRAINS

~

*Versatile pasta and grains – rice, couscous, and bulgur wheat
– star in the recipes here, with a myriad of tasty sauces and
flavorings, for first courses or main dishes. And there are
pizzas with mouthwatering toppings.*

Spicy Cheese Lasagne

SERVES 8

½ pound lasagne noodles

4 tablespoons butter or margarine

1 large onion, finely chopped

3 garlic cloves, minced

1½ tablespoons chopped fresh green chili pepper

½ cup flour

4 cups milk

3 cups canned crushed tomatoes

1 large zucchini, sliced

½ teaspoon hot red pepper flakes

salt and pepper

3 cups shredded sharp cheddar cheese

1 Preheat the oven to 375°F. Grease a 9- × 13-inch baking dish.

2 Put the lasagne noodles, one at a time, in a bowl of hot water, and let soak for 10–15 minutes.

3 ▲ Melt the butter or margarine in a large saucepan. Add the onion, garlic, and chili pepper and cook until softened, about 5 minutes.

4 Stir in the flour and cook 3 minutes, stirring constantly. Pour in the milk and bring to a boil, stirring. Reduce the heat to low and simmer gently until thickened, about 5 minutes, stirring occasionally.

5 Stir the tomatoes, zucchini, and hot pepper flakes into the sauce. Season with salt and pepper.

6 Spoon a little of the sauce into the prepared baking dish and spread it out evenly over the bottom. Cover with a layer of noodles.

7 ▲ Add one-third of the remaining sauce and one-third of the cheese. Repeat the layers until all the ingredients are used.

8 Bake until the top is golden and bubbling, about 45 minutes. Serve hot, in the dish.

Spaghetti with Sun-Dried Tomato Sauce

SERVES 4

¾ pound spaghetti

4 garlic cloves, minced

10–15 sun-dried tomatoes packed in oil, drained and chopped

1 cup pitted black olives

½ cup extra-virgin olive oil

3 beefsteak tomatoes, peeled, seeded, and chopped

3 tablespoons capers, drained

¼ cup chopped fresh basil, plus leaves for garnishing, or 1 teaspoon dried basil

salt and pepper

1 Cook the spaghetti in a large pan of boiling salted water until just tender to the bite (check package directions for timing). Drain well.

2 ▲ In a food processor or blender, combine the garlic, sun-dried tomatoes, and half the olives. Process until finely chopped.

3 With the motor running, slowly add the olive oil. Continue processing until thickened.

4 ▼ Transfer the mixture to a mixing bowl. Stir in the fresh tomatoes, capers, and basil. Season with salt and pepper to taste.

5 Return the spaghetti to the saucepan and add the tomato sauce. Toss well. Serve immediately, garnished with the remaining olives and fresh basil leaves, if wished.

Spicy Cheese Lasagne (top), Spaghetti with Sun-Dried Tomato Sauce

Pasta with Fresh Pesto Sauce

SERVES 4

1 cup chopped fresh basil, firmly packed

½ cup chopped fresh parsley

½ cup freshly grated Parmesan cheese

2 garlic cloves, peeled

4 tablespoons butter or margarine, at room temperature

¼ cup extra-virgin olive oil

salt

¾ pound mixed green and white fettucine or tagliatelle

½ cup pine nuts, toasted

fresh basil leaves, for garnishing

~ **COOK'S TIP** ~

For the best flavor, use a fruity olive oil in this recipe.

1 ▲ In a food processor or blender, combine the basil, parsley, Parmesan, and garlic. Process until finely chopped.

2 Add the butter or margarine and process to mix well.

3 ▼ With the machine running, slowly add the olive oil. Season with salt to taste.

4 Cook the pasta in a large pan of boiling salted water until just tender to the bite (check package directions for timing). Drain well.

5 Toss the hot pasta with the pesto sauce. Sprinkle with the pine nuts, garnish with basil, and serve.

Penne with Eggplant and Goat Cheese

SERVES 6

1¼ pounds eggplant, cut in ½-inch cubes (about 2 cups)

salt and pepper

3 tablespoons olive oil

1 tablespoon butter or margarine

1 garlic clove, chopped

2 cups canned crushed tomatoes

¾ pound penne (quill-shaped pasta)

¼ pound Montrachet or other firm goat cheese, cubed

3 tablespoons shredded fresh basil, or 1 teaspoon dried basil

1 Put the eggplant cubes in a large colander and sprinkle them lightly with salt. Let drain at least 30 minutes.

2 Rinse the eggplant under cold water and drain well. Dry on paper towels.

3 Heat the oil and butter or margarine in a large saucepan. Add the eggplant cubes and fry until just golden on all sides, stirring frequently.

4 ▲ Stir in the garlic and tomatoes. Simmer until thickened, about 15 minutes. Season with salt and pepper.

5 ▲ Cook the penne in a large pan of boiling salted water until just tender to the bite (check package directions for timing). Drain well and transfer to a warmed serving bowl.

6 Add the eggplant sauce, goat cheese, and basil to the pasta and toss well together. Serve immediately.

Pasta with Fresh Pesto Sauce (top), Penne with Eggplant and Goat Cheese

Farfalle with Chicken and Sausage Sauce

SERVES 4

3 tablespoons olive oil

1 pound skinless boneless chicken breasts, cut in ½-inch pieces

3 Italian sausages, cut diagonally in ¼-inch slices

salt and pepper

6 scallions, cut diagonally in ¼-inch pieces

10 sun-dried tomatoes packed in oil, drained and chopped

1 cup canned crushed tomatoes

1 medium-size zucchini, cut diagonally in ¼-inch slices

¾ pound farfalle (bow-tie pasta)

1 ▼ Heat the olive oil in a skillet. Add the chicken and sausage pieces with a little salt and pepper and cook until browned, about 10 minutes. With a slotted spoon, remove the chicken and sausage pieces from the pan, and drain on paper towels.

2 ▲ Add the scallions and sun-dried tomato pieces to the pan and cook until softened, about 5 minutes.

3 ▲ Stir in the canned tomatoes and cook until thickened, about 5 minutes.

4 ▲ Add the zucchini, and return the chicken and sausage to the pan. Cook 5 minutes longer.

5 Cook the farfalle in a large pan of boiling salted water until just tender to the bite (check package directions for timing). Drain well.

6 Serve the pasta with the chicken and sausage sauce.

Pasta with Spinach, Bacon, and Mushrooms

SERVES 4

6 bacon slices, cut in small pieces
1 shallot, finely chopped
½ pound small mushrooms, quartered
1 pound fresh spinach, coarse stems removed
¼ teaspoon grated nutmeg
salt and pepper
¾ pound shell-shaped pasta
¼ cup freshly grated Parmesan cheese

1 ▼ In a frying pan, cook the bacon until it is browned and the fat is rendered. Drain the bacon on paper towels, then put it in a bowl.

2 Add the shallot to the bacon fat in the pan and cook until softened, about 5 minutes.

3 ▲ Add the mushrooms to the pan and cook until lightly browned, about 5 minutes, stirring frequently. With a slotted spoon, transfer the shallot and mushrooms to the bacon in the bowl. Pour off the bacon fat from the skillet.

4 ▼ Add the spinach to the pan and cook over medium heat until wilted, stirring constantly.

5 Sprinkle with the nutmeg. Raise the heat to high and cook briskly, stirring to evaporate excess liquid from the spinach. Transfer the spinach to a board and chop it coarsely. Return it to the pan.

6 ▲ Return the bacon, mushrooms, and shallot to the pan and stir to mix with the spinach. Season with salt and pepper. Set aside.

7 Cook the pasta in a large pan of boiling salted water until just tender to the bite (check package directions for timing). Just before the pasta is ready, reheat the spinach mixture.

8 Drain the pasta well and return to the saucepan. Add the spinach mixture and toss well to mix. Sprinkle with Parmesan cheese before serving.

Pasta with Chorizo, Corn, and Red Bell Pepper

SERVES 4

3 tablespoons olive oil

1 pound chorizo sausages, cut diagonally in ½-inch slices

1 onion, chopped

1 garlic clove, minced

2 red bell peppers, seeded and sliced

1½ cups fresh corn kernels (cut from 3 ears of corn) or frozen whole-kernel corn, thawed

salt and pepper

¾ pound pasta spirals (fusilli)

1 tablespoon chopped fresh basil, or ½ teaspoon dried basil

fresh basil leaves, for garnishing

1 Heat 1 tablespoon of the oil in a skillet. Add the sausage slices and brown them on both sides.

2 Remove the sausage from the pan with a slotted spoon and drain on paper towels.

3 ▲ Heat the remaining oil in the pan and add the onion, garlic, and bell peppers. Cook until softened, about 5 minutes, stirring frequently.

4 ▲ Stir the sausage and corn into the pepper mixture and heat through, about 5 minutes. Season with salt and pepper.

5 Cook the pasta in boiling salted water until just tender to the bite (check package directions for timing). Drain well and return to the pan.

6 Add the sausage sauce and basil to the pasta. Toss together well, garnish with basil and serve immediately.

Angel Hair Pasta with Tomato-Lime Sauce

SERVES 4

1 pound very ripe tomatoes, peeled and chopped

1 small bunch of tender, young arugula leaves

4 garlic cloves, minced

grated rind of ½ lime

juice of 2 limes

¼ teaspoon hot pepper sauce

¾ pound angel hair pasta (capellini)

¼ cup olive oil

salt and pepper

freshly grated Parmesan cheese, for serving

1 ▼ Combine the tomatoes, arugula, garlic, lime rind and juice, and hot pepper sauce. Stir well to mix. Set aside for 20–30 minutes.

2 Cook the pasta in boiling salted water until just tender to the bite (check package directions for timing). Drain and return to the pan.

3 ▲ Add the olive oil and tomato-lime sauce to the pasta. Toss well together. Season with salt and pepper. Add Parmesan cheese to taste, toss again, and serve.

Pasta with Chorizo, Corn, and Red Bell Pepper (top), Angel Hair Pasta with Tomato-Lime Sauce

Macaroni and Cheese

SERVES 4

1 cup elbow macaroni

4 tablespoons butter or margarine

¼ cup flour

2½ cups milk

1½ cups shredded cheddar cheese

¼ cup finely chopped fresh parsley

salt and pepper

1 cup dry bread crumbs

½ cup freshly grated Parmesan cheese

1 Preheat the oven to 350°F. Grease a 10-inch gratin dish.

2 Cook the macaroni in a large pan of boiling salted water until just tender to the bite (check package directions for timing). Drain well.

3 Melt the butter or margarine in a saucepan. Add the flour and cook 2 minutes, stirring. Stir in the milk. Bring to a boil, stirring constantly, and simmer until thickened, about 5 minutes.

4 ▲ Remove the pan from the heat. Add the macaroni, cheddar cheese, and parsley to the sauce and mix well. Season with salt and pepper.

5 Transfer the mixture to the prepared gratin dish, spreading it out evenly with a spoon.

6 ▲ Toss together the bread crumbs and Parmesan cheese with a fork. Sprinkle over the macaroni.

7 Bake until the top is golden brown and the macaroni mixture is bubbling, 30–35 minutes.

Noodle and Vegetable Casserole

SERVES 10

1 pound egg noodles

6 tablespoons butter or margarine

1 onion, chopped

3 garlic cloves, chopped

3 carrots, shredded

¾ pound small mushrooms, quartered

3 eggs, beaten

1½ cups large-curd cottage cheese

1 cup sour cream

2 zucchini, finely grated in a food processor

3 tablespoons chopped fresh basil or 1 tablespoon dried basil

salt and pepper

fresh basil leaves, for garnishing

1 Preheat the oven to 350°F. Grease a 13- × 9-inch baking dish.

2 Cook the pasta in boiling salted water until just tender to the bite (check package directions for timing). Drain and rinse with cold water. Transfer to a mixing bowl.

3 Melt 4 tablespoons of the butter or margarine in a frying pan. Add the onion, garlic, and carrots and cook until tender, about 10 minutes, stirring frequently.

4 ▲ Stir in the mushrooms and cook 5 minutes longer. Add the vegetables to the noodles in the mixing bowl.

5 In a small bowl, combine the eggs, cottage cheese, sour cream, zucchini, basil, and salt and pepper to taste. Mix well.

6 ▲ Add the cottage cheese mixture to the noodles and mix well. Transfer to the prepared baking dish. Dot the top with the remaining butter or margarine.

7 Cover the dish with foil. Bake until the casserole is set, about 1 hour. Serve hot, in the baking dish, garnished with basil leaves.

Macaroni and Cheese (top), Noodle and Vegetable Casserole

Baked Seafood Pasta

SERVES 6

½ pound egg noodles
5 tablespoons butter or margarine
¼ cup flour
2 cups milk
½ teaspoon mustard powder
1 teaspoon fresh lemon juice
1 tablespoon tomato paste
salt and pepper
2 tablespoons minced onion
½ cup finely diced celery
¼ pound small mushrooms, sliced
½ pound cooked peeled small shrimp
½ pound lump crab meat
1 tablespoon chopped fresh dill
fresh dill sprigs, for garnishing

1 Preheat the oven to 350°F. Generously butter a 2-quart baking dish.

2 Cook the noodles in a large pan of boiling salted water until just tender to the bite (check package directions for timing). Drain well.

3 ▲ While the pasta is cooking, make a white sauce. Melt 3 tablespoons of the butter or margarine in a saucepan. Add the flour and cook 2 minutes, stirring. Stir in the milk. Bring to a boil, stirring constantly, and simmer until thickened, about 5 minutes.

4 ▲ Add the mustard, lemon juice, and tomato paste to the sauce and mix well. Season to taste with salt and pepper. Set aside.

5 ▲ Melt the remaining butter or margarine in a frying pan. Add the onion, celery, and mushrooms. Cook until softened, about 5 minutes.

6 ▲ In a mixing bowl, combine the pasta, sauce, vegetables, shrimp, crab meat, and dill. Stir well to mix.

7 Pour the mixture into the prepared baking dish. Bake until piping hot and the top is lightly browned, 30–40 minutes. Garnish with dill sprigs, if wished.

Pasta-Stuffed Bell Peppers

SERVES 4

6 bacon slices, chopped
1 small onion, chopped
1½ cups canned crushed tomatoes
⅛ teaspoon hot red pepper flakes
½ cup macaroni
1 cup diced mozzarella cheese
12 black olives, pitted and thinly sliced
salt and pepper
2 large red bell peppers
2 large yellow bell peppers
2 tablespoons olive oil

1 Preheat the oven to 350°F. Grease a shallow 8-inch oval or square baking dish.

2 ▲ In a frying pan, cook the bacon until browned and the fat is rendered. Drain the bacon on paper towels.

3 Add the onion to the bacon fat in the pan and cook until softened, about 5 minutes. Pour off excess fat.

4 ▲ Stir in the tomatoes and hot pepper flakes. Cook over high heat until thickened, about 10 minutes.

5 Meanwhile, cook the pasta in a large pan of boiling salted water until just tender to the bite (check package directions for timing). Drain well.

6 ▲ Put the pasta in a mixing bowl and add the bacon, tomato sauce, mozzarella cheese, and olives. Toss well to mix. Season to taste.

7 Cut the stem end off each bell pepper; reserve these "lids". Remove the seeds from inside the peppers and cut out the white ribs.

8 ▲ Divide the pasta mixture evenly among the peppers. Put on the "lids". Brush the peppers all over with the olive oil and set them in the prepared baking dish.

9 Cover the dish with foil and bake 30 minutes. Remove the foil and bake until the peppers are tender, 25–30 minutes longer.

Broccoli and Goat Cheese Pizza

SERVES 2–3

½ pound broccoli florets
2 tablespoons cornmeal
½ cup tomato sauce
6 cherry tomatoes, halved
12 black olives, pitted
¼ pound goat cheese, crumbled
½ cup freshly grated Parmesan cheese
1 tablespoon olive oil
FOR THE PIZZA DOUGH
2–2¼ cups flour
1 package active dry yeast (¼ ounce)
⅛ teaspoon sugar
about ⅔ cup tepid water
2 tablespoons olive oil
½ teaspoon salt

1 For the pizza dough, combine ¾ cup of the flour, the yeast, and sugar in a food processor. With the motor running, pour in the tepid water. Turn the motor off. Add the olive oil, 1¼ cups of the remaining flour, and the salt.

2 ▲ Process until a ball of dough is formed, adding more water, 1 teaspoon at a time, if the dough is too dry, or the remaining flour, 1 tablespoon at a time, if it is too wet.

3 ▲ Put the dough in an oiled bowl and turn it so the ball of dough is oiled all over. Cover the bowl and let the dough rise in a warm place until doubled in bulk, about 1 hour.

4 ▲ Meanwhile, cook the broccoli florets in boiling salted water or steam them until just tender, about 5 minutes. Drain well and set aside.

5 Preheat the oven to 500°F. Oil a 12-inch round pizza pan and sprinkle with the cornmeal.

6 When the dough has risen, turn out onto a lightly floured surface. Punch down the dough to deflate it, and knead it briefly.

~ **COOK'S TIP** ~

If more convenient, the pizza dough can be used as soon as it is made, without any rising.

7 ▲ Roll out the dough to a 12-inch round. Lay the dough on the pizza pan and press it down evenly.

8 ▲ Spread the tomato sauce evenly onto the pizza base, leaving a rim of dough uncovered around the edge about ½ inch wide.

9 ▲ Arrange the broccoli florets, tomatoes, and olives on the tomato sauce and sprinkle with the cheeses. Drizzle the olive oil over the top.

10 Bake until the cheese melts and the edge of the pizza base is puffed and browned, 10–15 minutes.

Pita Pizzas

SERVES 4

4 6-inch round pita breads, split in half
   horizontally

¼ cup olive oil

salt and pepper

1 small red bell pepper, seeded and
   sliced

1 small yellow bell pepper, seeded and
   sliced

½ pound small red potatoes, cooked
   and sliced

1 tablespoon chopped fresh rosemary or
   1 teaspoon dried rosemary

½ cup freshly grated Parmesan cheese

1 Preheat the oven to 350°F.

2 ▼ Place the pita rounds on a
baking sheet. Brush them on both
sides with 2 tablespoons of the oil.
Sprinkle with salt. Bake until pale
golden and crisp, about 10 minutes.

3 ▲ Heat the remaining oil in a
frying pan. Add the bell peppers and
cook until softened, about 5 minutes,
stirring frequently.

4 ▲ Add the potatoes and rosemary
to the peppers. Heat through, about 3
minutes, stirring well. Season with
salt and pepper.

5 Preheat the broiler.

6 ▲ Divide the pepper-potato
mixture among the pita rounds on the
baking sheet. Sprinkle with the
Parmesan cheese.

7 Broil about 3 inches from the heat
until golden, 3–4 minutes.

Onion, Olive, and Anchovy Pizza

SERVES 4

6 tablespoons olive oil

1 pound onions, thinly sliced

3 garlic cloves, minced

1 bay leaf

2 teaspoons dried thyme

salt and pepper

2 cans anchovy fillets, drained and blotted dry on paper towels

12 olives, mixed black and green, pitted

FOR THE PIZZA DOUGH

1 cup whole-wheat flour

¾ cup all-purpose flour

1¼ teaspoons active dry yeast

⅛ teaspoon sugar

⅔ cup tepid water

2 tablespoons olive oil

½ teaspoon salt

1 For the pizza dough, in a food processor combine the flours, yeast, and sugar. With the motor running, pour in the tepid water. Turn the motor off. Add the oil and salt. Process until a ball of dough is formed.

2 Put the dough in an oiled bowl and turn it to coat with oil. Cover and let rise until doubled in bulk.

3 ▲ Heat 3 tablespoons of the oil in a frying pan. Add the onions, garlic, and herbs. Cook over low heat until the onions are very soft and the moisture has evaporated, about 45 minutes. Season with salt and pepper.

4 Preheat the oven to 500°F. Oil a 13- × 9-inch baking sheet.

5 ▼ Transfer the risen dough onto a lightly floured surface. Punch down the dough to deflate it, and knead it briefly. Roll out the dough to a rectangle to fit the baking sheet. Lay the dough on the sheet and press it up to the edges of the pan.

6 Brush the dough with 1 tablespoon olive oil. Discard the bay leaf, and spoon the onion mixture onto the dough. Spread it out evenly, leaving a ½-inch border clear around the edge.

7 ▲ Arrange the anchovies and olives on top of the onions. Drizzle the remaining 2 tablespoons olive oil over the top.

8 Bake the pizza until the edges are puffed and browned, 15–20 minutes.

Pepperoni Pizza

SERVES 2–3

2 tablespoons cornmeal

½ cup tomato sauce

½ pound pepperoni, cut in ⅛-inch slices

2 cups shredded mozzarella cheese

Pizza Dough

1 Make the pizza dough as directed in steps 1–3 of Broccoli and Goat Cheese Pizza.

2 Preheat the oven to 500°F. Oil a 12-inch round pizza pan and sprinkle with the cornmeal.

3 Transfer the risen dough onto a lightly floured surface. Punch down the dough to deflate it, and knead it briefly.

4 ▼ Roll out the dough to a 12-inch round. Lay the dough on the pizza pan and press it down evenly.

5 ▲ Spread the tomato sauce evenly onto the pizza base, leaving a ½-inch rim of dough uncovered around the edge. Arrange the pepperoni slices on top. Sprinkle with the cheese.

6 Bake until the cheese melts and the edge of the pizza base is puffed and browned, 10–15 minutes.

Calzone with Bell Peppers and Eggplant

SERVES 2

3–4 tablespoons olive oil

½ small eggplant, cut in ½-inch-wide sticks

½ red bell pepper, seeded and sliced

½ yellow bell pepper, seeded and sliced

1 small onion, halved and sliced

1 garlic clove, minced

salt and pepper

¼ pound mozzarella cheese, chopped

Pizza Dough

1 Make the pizza dough as directed in steps 1–3 of Broccoli and Goat Cheese Pizza.

2 Heat the olive oil in a frying pan. Add the eggplant and cook until golden, about 6–8 minutes. Add the pepper strips, onion, and garlic, with more oil if necessary. Cook, stirring occasionally, until softened, about 5 minutes longer. Season to taste.

3 Preheat the oven to 475°F.

4 Transfer the risen pizza dough to a lightly floured surface. Punch down the dough to deflate it, and knead it briefly. Divide the dough in half.

5 Roll out each piece of dough into a 7-inch round. With the back of a knife, make an indentation across the center of each round to mark it into halves.

6 ▲ Spoon half of the vegetable mixture onto one side of each dough round. Divide the cheese evenly between them.

7 ▲ Fold the dough over to enclose the filling. Pinch the edges to seal them securely.

8 Set the calzone on an oiled baking sheet. Bake until puffed and browned, 20–25 minutes. To serve, break or cut each calzone in half.

Pepperoni Pizza (top), Calzone with Bell Peppers and Eggplant

Pizza Toasts with Eggplant and Mozzarella

SERVES 4

2 small eggplants, cut across in thin slices (about ½ pound)

1 tablespoon salt

½ cup olive oil

1 garlic clove, crushed with the side of a knife

8 slices French bread, ½-inch thick

½ pound mozzarella cheese, cut in 8 slices

3 tablespoons chopped fresh chives

3 tablespoons chopped fresh basil

1 ▲ Put the eggplant slices in a colander and sprinkle with the salt. Let stand at least 30 minutes to drain. Rinse the eggplant slices under cold water, then blot dry with paper towels.

2 Heat half the olive oil in a frying pan. Add the eggplant slices and fry until golden brown, about 5 minutes on each side. Add more oil if necessary when the slices are turned over. Drain on paper towels.

3 Preheat the oven to 325°F.

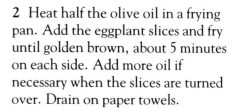

4 ▲ In a small bowl, combine the remaining olive oil and the garlic. Brush both sides of the bread slices with the garlic oil. Place the slices on a baking sheet. Bake until golden brown, about 10 minutes.

5 Preheat the broiler.

6 ▲ Top each slice of garlic bread with a slice of eggplant and a slice of mozzarella. Arrange on a baking sheet.

7 Broil about 3 inches from the heat until the cheese melts, 5–7 minutes. Sprinkle the toasts with the chopped herbs before serving.

Mini Tomato-Phyllo Pizzas

SERVES 6

4 large or 8 small sheets of phyllo pastry, thawed if frozen

¼ cup olive oil

1 pound tomatoes, peeled, seeded, and diced

½ cup freshly grated Parmesan cheese

½ cup crumbled feta cheese

9 black olives, pitted and halved

¼ teaspoon dried oregano

½ teaspoon fresh thyme leaves, or ⅛ teaspoon dried thyme

salt and pepper

fresh thyme or basil, for garnishing

1 Preheat the oven to 350°F. Grease 2 baking sheets.

2 ▲ Stack the phyllo sheets. With a sharp knife, cut into 24 6-inch rounds, using a small plate as a guide.

3 ▲ Lay 3 phyllo rounds on each baking sheet. Brush the rounds lightly with olive oil. Lay another pastry round on top of each oiled round and brush it with oil. Continue layering the pastry rounds, oiling each one, to make 6 stacks of 4 rounds each.

4 Bake the phyllo bases until they are crisp and golden brown, about 5 minutes.

5 ▲ In a bowl, combine the tomatoes, cheeses, olives, and herbs. Mix well. Season with salt and pepper.

6 ▲ Spoon the tomato mixture on top of the phyllo pastry bases, leaving the edges bare. Return to the oven to bake until heated through, about 5 minutes.

7 Serve hot, garnished with fresh herb sprigs.

Couscous with Vegetables

SERVES 4

2 tablespoons olive oil

8 small onions, peeled

1 red bell pepper, seeded and quartered

1 leek, cut across in 1-inch pieces

¼ teaspoon saffron threads

½ teaspoon turmeric

¼ teaspoon cayenne

1 teaspoon ground ginger

1 3-inch cinnamon stick

3 large carrots, cut diagonally in 1-inch pieces

1 rutabaga, peeled and cubed

2 potatoes, peeled and quartered

1 16-ounce can peeled tomatoes

3 cups chicken stock

salt and pepper

2 zucchini, cut across in 1-inch pieces

1 cup whole green beans, trimmed, about ¼ pound

1 15-ounce can chick peas (garbanzo beans), drained

2 tablespoons chopped fresh coriander (cilantro)

2 tablespoons chopped fresh parsley

FOR THE COUSCOUS

2½ cups water

½ teaspoon salt

1½ cups instant couscous

1   Heat the oil in a large saucepan or castiron casserole. Add the onions, red bell pepper, and leek. Cook for 2–3 minutes.

~ **COOK'S TIP** ~

This couscous makes a filling vegetarian meal, and the recipe can be doubled or tripled. When multiplying a recipe, slightly decrease the amount of spices.

2 ▲ Stir in the saffron, turmeric, cayenne, ginger, and cinnamon stick.

3 ▲ Add the carrots, rutabaga, potatoes, tomatoes, and chicken stock. Season with salt. Bring to a boil. Reduce the heat to low, cover, and simmer until the vegetables are nearly tender, about 25 minutes.

4 ▲ Meanwhile, for the couscous, put the water and salt in a saucepan and bring to a boil. Stir in the couscous. Remove the pan from the heat, cover, and set aside until all the liquid is absorbed, about 10 minutes.

5 ▲ Stir the zucchini, green beans, and chick peas into the vegetable mixture. Simmer 5 minutes longer.

6 ▲ Stir in the herbs and add pepper to taste.

7 ▲ Lightly fluff the couscous grains with a fork. Pile the couscous in a mound in the middle of a shallow, round platter. Spoon the vegetables over the couscous and serve.

Bulgur Wheat Salad

SERVES 6

⅔ cup fine bulgur wheat

1 cup water

1½ cups finely chopped fresh parsley

¼ cup chopped fresh mint or 2 tablespoons dried mint

¼ cup finely chopped scallions

¼ cup finely chopped red onion

1 large tomato, chopped

¼ cup olive oil

⅓ cup fresh lemon juice

salt and pepper

½ head of romaine lettuce, leaves separated

1 Place the bulgur wheat in a bowl. Pour the water over the wheat. Let stand until the wheat swells and softens, about 30 minutes.

2 ▲ A handful at a time, squeeze excess water out of the bulgur wheat and put it in a mixing bowl.

3 ▲ Add the parsley, mint, scallions, red onion, and tomato to the bulgur wheat. Stir in the olive oil and lemon juice. Season to taste.

4 Line a large serving platter with romaine leaves. Pile the bulgur wheat salad in the middle.

Hot Cheesy Grits

SERVES 6

3 cups water

¼ teaspoon salt

¾ cup instant grits

1 egg

1½ cups shredded cheddar or Monterey Jack cheese

2 tablespoons butter or margarine

⅛ teaspoon cayenne

1 Preheat the oven to 350°F. Grease a 13- × 9-inch baking dish.

2 Put the water and salt in a medium saucepan and bring to a boil.

~ **COOK'S TIP** ~

Try this Southern specialty for breakfast or brunch, or in place of rice or potatoes to accompany a main course.

3 ▲ Stir in the grits. Reduce the heat to low, cover the pan, and cook the grits until thickened, 5–7 minutes, stirring occasionally.

4 ▲ In a small bowl, beat the egg lightly. Add a large spoonful of the cooked grits and stir well to mix.

5 Stir the egg mixture into the remaining cooked grits in the saucepan. Add 1 cup of the cheese, the butter, and the cayenne. Stir over low heat until the cheese melts.

6 ▲ Transfer the mixture to the prepared dish. Sprinkle the remaining cheese over the top. Bake until the cheesy grits are set and golden on top, 35–40 minutes. Let cool 5 minutes before cutting and serving.

Bulgur Wheat Salad (top), Hot Cheesy Grits

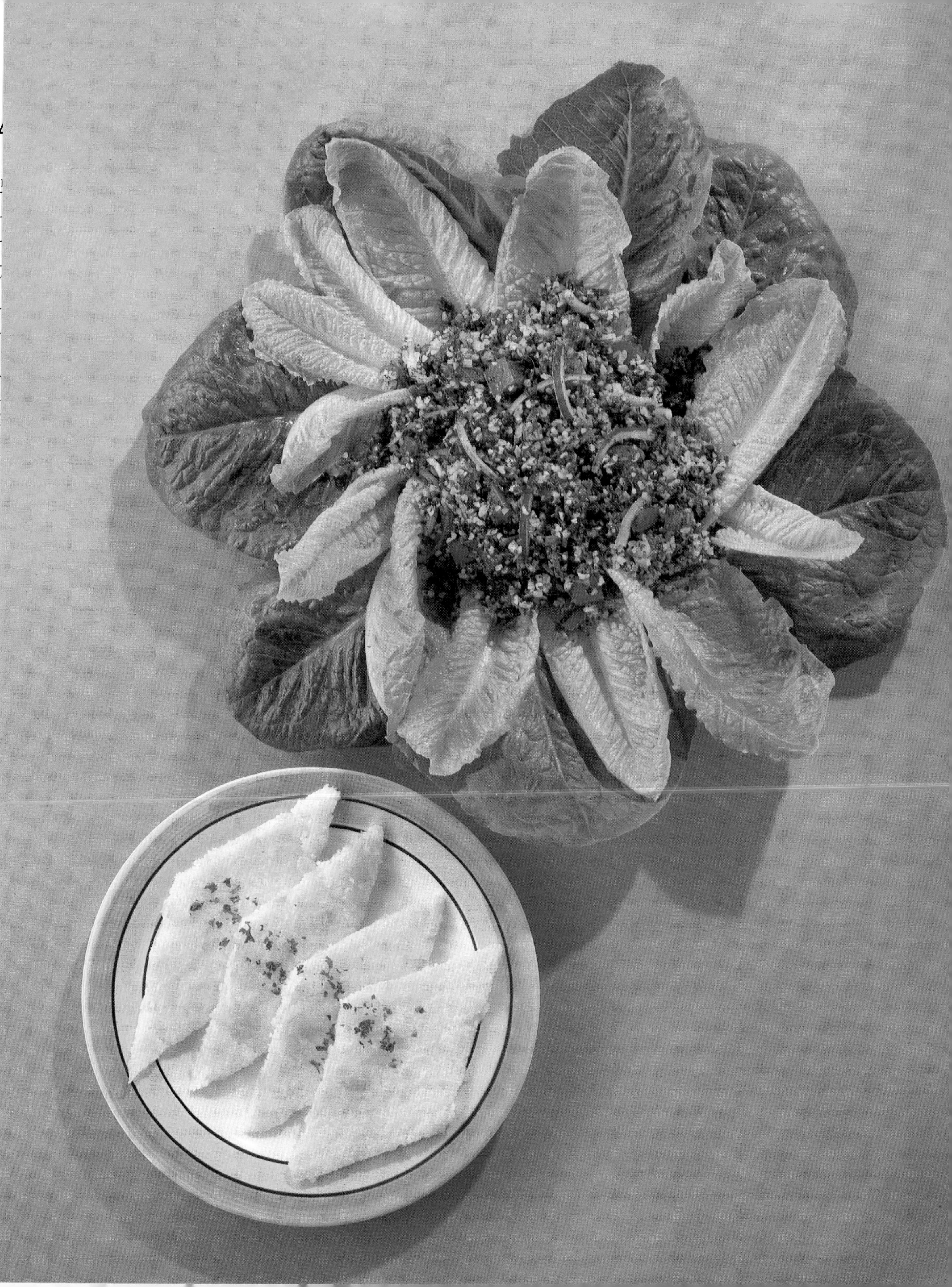

Red Beans and Rice

1 onion, chopped

1 green bell pepper, seeded and chopped

4 bacon slices, chopped

1 garlic clove, chopped

1 cup long-grain rice

2–3 teaspoons chili powder

2 teaspoons fresh thyme leaves or ½
    teaspoon dried thyme

2 cups canned crushed tomatoes

1 cup chicken or beef stock

salt and pepper

1 15-ounce can red kidney beans,
    drained and rinsed

1 ▼ In a medium saucepan, cook the onion, green bell pepper, bacon, and garlic until the vegetables are softened and the bacon has rendered its fat, about 5 minutes.

2 ▲ Add the rice and stir until all the grains are coated with bacon fat. Stir in the chili powder and cook 1 minute.

3 ▲ Add the thyme, crushed tomatoes, and stock and stir well. Season with salt and pepper. Bring to a boil.

4 Reduce the heat to low, cover the pan, and simmer until the rice is nearly tender, about 15 minutes.

5 ▲ Stir in the kidney beans. Cover again and simmer until the rice is tender and all the stock has been absorbed, about 5 minutes longer.

6 Fluff the rice and beans with a fork, then transfer to a warmed serving dish.

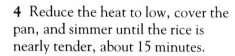

Acorn Squash Risotto

SERVES 4

5 cups chicken stock

3 tablespoons butter or margarine

1 small onion, chopped

½ cup peeled and coarsely grated acorn squash

1½ cups arborio rice

1 zucchini, quartered lengthwise and chopped

1 cup frozen peas, thawed

½ cup freshly grated Parmesan cheese

salt and pepper

1 In a saucepan, bring the stock to a simmer. Keep it simmering gently.

2 Melt 1 tablespoon of the butter or margarine in a heavy saucepan. Add the onion and cook until softened, about 5 minutes.

3 ▲ Add the grated squash to the onion. Cook 1 minute, stirring.

4 ▲ Add the rice and stir to coat all the grains well with butter. Cook 1 minute, stirring.

5 Add about ½ cup of the simmering stock to the rice. Cook, stirring frequently, until the stock is absorbed. Continue adding the stock, about ½ cup at a time, letting each addition be absorbed before adding the next, and stirring frequently.

6 ▲ After about 5 minutes, stir in the zucchini pieces. After about 10 minutes, stir in the peas. The risotto will be cooked in about 20 minutes.

7 ▲ Remove the pan from the heat. Add the remaining butter or margarine and the Parmesan and stir well. Season with salt and pepper. If you like, serve in hollowed-out cooked acorn squash halves.

Red Beans and Rice

1 onion, chopped

1 green bell pepper, seeded and chopped

4 bacon slices, chopped

1 garlic clove, chopped

1 cup long-grain rice

2–3 teaspoons chili powder

2 teaspoons fresh thyme leaves or ½ teaspoon dried thyme

2 cups canned crushed tomatoes

1 cup chicken or beef stock

salt and pepper

1 15-ounce can red kidney beans, drained and rinsed

1 ▼ In a medium saucepan, cook the onion, green bell pepper, bacon, and garlic until the vegetables are softened and the bacon has rendered its fat, about 5 minutes.

2 ▲ Add the rice and stir until all the grains are coated with bacon fat. Stir in the chili powder and cook 1 minute.

3 ▲ Add the thyme, crushed tomatoes, and stock and stir well. Season with salt and pepper. Bring to a boil.

4 Reduce the heat to low, cover the pan, and simmer until the rice is nearly tender, about 15 minutes.

5 ▲ Stir in the kidney beans. Cover again and simmer until the rice is tender and all the stock has been absorbed, about 5 minutes longer.

6 Fluff the rice and beans with a fork, then transfer to a warmed serving dish.

Long-Grain and Wild Rice Ring

2 tablespoons corn oil

1 large onion, chopped

2 cups processed mixed long-grain and wild rice

5 cups chicken stock

½ cup dried currants

salt

6 scallions, cut diagonally into ¼-inch pieces

parsley sprigs, for garnishing

1 Oil a 7-cup ring mold. Set aside.

2 ▼ Heat the oil in a large saucepan. Add the onion and cook until softened, about 5 minutes.

3 ▲ Add the rice to the pan and stir well to coat the rice with the oil.

4 ▲ Stir in the chicken stock and bring to a boil.

5 Reduce the heat to low. Stir the currants into the rice mixture. Add salt to taste. Cover and simmer until the rice is tender and the stock has been absorbed, about 20 minutes.

6 Drain the rice if necessary and transfer it to a mixing bowl. Stir in the scallions.

7 ▲ Pack the rice mixture into the prepared mold. Unmold it onto a warmed serving platter. If you like, put parsley sprigs into the center of the ring before serving.

Pecan and Scallion Pilaf

SERVES 4

2 tablespoons butter or margarine

1 onion, finely chopped

2 cups long-grain brown rice

½ teaspoon finely grated lemon rind

2 cups chicken stock

2 cups water

¼ teaspoon salt

4 scallions, finely chopped

2 tablespoons fresh lemon juice

⅓ cup pecan halves, toasted

1 ▲ Melt the butter or margarine in a medium saucepan. Add the onion and cook until softened, about 5 minutes.

2 ▲ Stir in the rice and cook 1 minute, stirring.

3 ▲ Add the lemon rind, chicken stock, water, and salt and stir well. Bring to a boil. Reduce the heat to low, cover the pan, and simmer until the rice is tender and all the liquid is absorbed, 30–35 minutes.

4 ▼ Remove the pan from the heat and let stand 5 minutes, still covered. Stir in the scallions, lemon juice, and pecan halves. Transfer to a warmed serving dish.

Fried Rice with Asparagus and Shrimp

SERVES 4

3 tablespoons corn oil

¾ pound asparagus, cut diagonally into 1-inch lengths (1½ cups)

1 cup sliced fresh shiitake mushrooms

3 cups cooked rice

1 teaspoon finely grated fresh gingerroot

½ pound cooked peeled shrimp, deveined

½ cup sliced canned water chestnuts, drained

3 tablespoons soy sauce

pepper

~ VARIATION ~

Ingredients for fried rice are infinately variable. Instead of shrimp, try scallops or cubes of firm-fleshed fish. Replace water chestnuts with a crunchy vegetable, such as snow peas.

1 ▲ Heat the oil in a wok over high heat. Add the asparagus and mushrooms and stir-fry, 3–4 minutes.

2 ▲ Stir in the rice and gingerroot. Cook, stirring, until heated through, about 3 minutes.

3 ▲ Add the shrimp and stir-fry for 1 minute.

4 ▲ Add the water chestnuts and soy sauce and stir-fry 1 minute longer. Season with pepper and serve.

Saffron Rice

SERVES 6

4 tablespoons butter or margarine

⅛ teaspoon saffron threads

2½ cups long-grain rice

4 cups chicken stock

½ teaspoon salt

~ COOK'S TIP ~

If preferred, cook the saffron rice in a preheated 375°F oven, in a flameproof casserole. Bring to a boil, then transfer to the oven.

1 Melt the butter or margarine in a large saucepan. Stir in the saffron.

2 ▲ Add the rice and stir to coat all the grains well with the saffron butter.

3 ▼ Stir in the stock and salt. Bring to a boil. Reduce the heat to low, cover, and simmer until the rice is tender and all the stock has been absorbed, about 20 minutes.

4 Fluff the rice grains with a fork before serving.

Fried Rice with Asparagus and Shrimp (top), Saffron Rice

SALADS, VEGETABLES, EGGS & CHEESE

~

Here's a bright selection of tasty vegetable main dishes and accompaniments, colorful salads, and economical and quickly-made egg and cheese dishes, for lunch or supper.

Avocado, Grapefruit, and Canteloupe Salad

SERVES 6

1 pink grapefruit
1 white or yellow grapefruit
1 cantaloupe
2 large, ripe but firm avocados
2 tablespoons fresh lemon juice
2 tablespoons vegetable oil
1 tablespoon clear honey
¼ cup chopped fresh mint
salt and pepper
fresh mint leaves, for garnishing

1 ▲ Peel the grapefruit. Cut out the sections, leaving the membranes. Put the sections in a bowl.

2 Cut the melon in half. Remove the seeds and discard them. With a melon baller, scoop out balls from the melon flesh. Add the melon balls to the grapefruit sections. Chill the fruit at least 30 minutes.

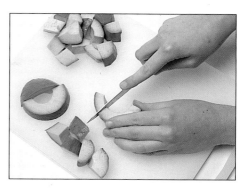

3 ▲ Cut the avocados in half and discard the pits. Cut each half in two. Peel the skin, then cut the flesh into small pieces.

4 ▲ Toss the avocado pieces in the lemon juice. Using a slotted spoon, transfer the avocado to the grapefruit mixture.

5 ▲ For the dressing, whisk the oil into the reserved lemon juice. Stir in the honey, chopped mint, and salt and pepper to taste.

6 Pour the dressing over the fruit mixture and toss gently. Garnish with mint leaves and serve immediately.

Cool and Crunchy Salad

1 medium red onion, thinly sliced into rings
salt and pepper
2 navel oranges, peeled and cut in sections
1 firm jícama, peeled and cut in matchstick strips
2 heads of radicchio, cored, or 1 head of red leaf lettuce, leaves separated
3 tablespoons chopped fresh parsley
3 tablespoons chopped fresh basil
1 tablespoon white wine vinegar
¼ cup walnut oil

1 ▲ Put the onion in a colander and sprinkle with 1 teaspoon salt. Let drain 15 minutes.

2 In a mixing bowl combine the orange sections and jícama strips.

3 Spread out the radicchio or lettuce leaves on a large shallow bowl or serving platter.

5 ▼ Arrange the jícama, orange, and onion mixture on top of the radicchio leaves. Sprinkle with the parsley and basil.

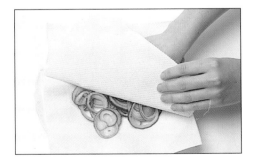

4 ▲ Rinse the onion and dry on paper towels. Toss it with the jícama and orange.

6 ▲ Combine the vinegar, oil, and salt and pepper to taste in a screwtop jar. Shake well to combine. Pour the dressing over the salad and serve immediately.

Creamy Coleslaw

SERVES 6

¾ pound green or white cabbage, cut in wedges and cored

¼ pound red cabbage, cored

3 scallions, finely chopped

2 medium carrots, grated

1 teaspoon sugar

2 tablespoons fresh lemon juice

2 teaspoons distilled white vinegar

½ cup sour cream

½ cup mayonnaise

¾ teaspoon celery seeds

salt and pepper

1 ▼ Slice the green and red cabbage thinly across the leaves.

2 Place the cabbage in a mixing bowl and add the scallions and carrots. Toss to combine.

3 In a small bowl, combine the sugar, lemon juice, vinegar, sour cream, mayonnaise, and celery seeds.

4 ▲ Pour the mayonnaise dressing over the vegetables. Season with salt and pepper. Stir until well coated. Spoon into a serving bowl.

Potato Salad

SERVES 8

3 pounds small new potatoes

2 tablespoons white wine vinegar

1 tablespoon Dijon-style mustard

3 tablespoons vegetable or olive oil

½ cup chopped red onion

salt and pepper

½ cup mayonnaise

2 tablespoons chopped fresh tarragon or 1½ teaspoons dried tarragon

½ cup thinly sliced celery

1 Cook the unpeeled potatoes in boiling salted water until tender, 15–20 minutes. Drain.

2 In a small bowl, mix together the vinegar and mustard until the mustard dissolves. Whisk in the oil.

3 ▲ When the potatoes are cool enough to handle, slice them into a large mixing bowl.

4 ▲ Add the onion to the potatoes and pour the dressing over them. Season, then toss gently to combine. Let stand at least 30 minutes.

5 ▲ Mix together the mayonnaise and tarragon. Gently stir into the potatoes, along with the celery. Taste and adjust the seasoning before serving.

~ **VARIATION** ~

Substitute 3 tablespoons dry white wine for the wine vinegar, if preferred. When available, use small red potatoes to give a nice color to the salad.

Creamy Coleslaw (top), Potato Salad

Caesar Salad

SERVES 4

2 eggs

1 garlic clove, minced

½ teaspoon salt

½ cup olive oil

juice of 1 lemon

¼ teaspoon Worcestershire sauce

1 pound romaine lettuce, torn in bite-size pieces

½ cup freshly grated Parmesan cheese

pepper

8 canned anchovy fillets, drained and blotted dry on paper towels (optional)

FOR THE CROUTONS

1 garlic clove

¼ teaspoon salt

¼ cup olive oil

1½ cups cubed French bread

1 Preheat the oven to 350°F.

2 ▲ For the croûtons, crush the garlic with the salt in a mixing bowl and mix in the oil. Add the bread cubes to the bowl and toss to coat with the garlic oil.

3 Spread the bread cubes on a baking sheet. Bake until golden brown, 20–25 minutes.

4 Meanwhile, put the eggs in a small pan of boiling water and simmer gently for 7 minutes. Transfer the eggs to a bowl of cold water and shell them as soon as they are cool enough to handle.

5 ▼ Mash the garlic clove with the salt in the bottom of a salad bowl. Whisk in the olive oil, lemon juice, and Worcestershire sauce.

6 Add the lettuce to the salad bowl and toss well to coat with the dressing.

7 Add the Parmesan cheese and season with pepper. Add the croûtons and toss well to combine.

8 Cut the hard-cooked eggs in quarters. Arrange on top of the salad with the anchovies, if using. Serve immediately.

Green Salad with Yogurt-Blue Cheese Dressing

SERVES 6

4 cups mixed salad leaves, such as red leaf and Boston lettuce, torn in bite-size pieces

1 small bunch of lamb's lettuce (mâche), arugula, or watercress

FOR THE DRESSING

½ cup plain yogurt

1½ teaspoons white wine vinegar

½ teaspoon sugar

1 tablespoon fresh lemon juice

1 garlic clove, minced

¼ cup crumbled blue cheese

1 ▼ For the dressing, combine the yogurt, wine vinegar, sugar, lemon juice, and garlic in a small bowl and mix well. Fold in the cheese. The dressing should be lumpy.

2 ▲ Put the salad leaves in a salad bowl. Add the dressing and toss until all the leaves are coated. Serve immediately.

Caesar Salad (top), Green Salad with Yogurt-Blue Cheese Dressing

Spinach and Bacon Salad

SERVES 4

1 hard-cooked egg
⅓ cup white wine vinegar
1 teaspoon Dijon-style mustard
2 tablespoons vegetable or olive oil
salt and pepper
1 pound fresh young spinach leaves
1 cup sliced small mushrooms
3 bacon slices
1 medium onion, chopped
2 garlic cloves, minced

1 Separate the egg yolk and white. Chop the egg white and set aside.

2 ▲ To make the dressing, press the egg yolk through a strainer into a bowl. Whisk in the vinegar, mustard, oil, and salt and pepper to taste.

3 Put the spinach in a salad bowl with the mushrooms.

4 In a small frying pan, fry the bacon until crisp. Remove the bacon with tongs and drain on paper towels.

5 ▼ When cool, crumble the bacon over the spinach.

6 Add the onion and garlic to the bacon fat in the frying pan and cook until softened, about 5 minutes, stirring frequently.

7 Pour the onion and garlic over the spinach, with the bacon fat. Add the dressing and toss well to combine. Sprinkle the egg white on top and serve immediately.

Warm Red Cabbage Salad with Spicy Sausage

SERVES 4

1 pound red cabbage, cut in wedges and cored
¼ cup olive oil
2 shallots, chopped
2 garlic cloves, chopped
3 tablespoons cider vinegar
¼ pound chorizo or other cooked spicy sausage, cut diagonally in ¼-inch slices
salt and pepper
2 tablespoons chopped fresh chives
2 tablespoons chopped fresh parsley

1 Slice the cabbage wedges very thinly across the leaves.

2 ▲ Heat the oil in a skillet. Add the shallots and garlic and cook until softened, about 4 minutes. Transfer from the pan to a salad bowl using a slotted spoon.

3 Add the cabbage to the hot oil and cook until wilted, about 10 minutes, stirring occasionally. Add 1 tablespoon of the vinegar and cook 1 minute longer, stirring. Transfer the cabbage and the oil from the pan to the salad bowl.

4 ▼ Add the sausage slices to the pan and fry until well browned. Transfer the sausage to the salad bowl using the slotted spoon.

5 Pour the remaining vinegar over the salad and toss well to combine. Season with salt and pepper. Sprinkle with the chopped herbs and serve.

Spinach and Bacon Salad (top), Warm Red Cabbage Salad with Spicy Sausage

Pasta and Avocado Salad

SERVES 6

3 cups pasta spirals (fusilli) or other small pasta shapes

½ cup drained canned whole-kernel corn or frozen whole-kernel corn, thawed

½ red bell pepper, seeded and diced

8 black olives, pitted and sliced

3 scallions, finely chopped

2 medium avocados

FOR THE DRESSING

2 sun-dried tomato halves, loose-packed (not packed in oil)

1½ tablespoons balsamic vinegar

1½ tablespoons red wine vinegar

½ garlic clove, minced

½ teaspoon salt

5 tablespoons olive oil

1 tablespoon chopped fresh basil

1 ▼ For the dressing, drop the sun-dried tomatoes into a pan containing 1 inch of boiling water and simmer until tender, about 3 minutes. Drain and chop finely.

2 ▲ Combine the tomatoes, vinegars, garlic, and salt in a food processor. With the machine on, add the oil in a stream. Stir in the basil.

3 Cook the pasta in a large pan of boiling salted water until just tender to the bite (check package directions for timing). Drain well.

4 ▲ In a large bowl, combine the pasta, corn, red bell pepper, olives, and scallions. Add the dressing and toss well together.

5 ▲ Just before serving, peel the avocados and cut the flesh into cubes. Mix gently into the pasta salad, and serve at room temperature.

Ham and Black-Eyed Pea Salad

SERVES 8

1 cup dry black-eyed peas

1 onion, peeled

1 carrot, peeled

½ pound smoked ham, diced

3 medium tomatoes, peeled, seeded, and diced (about 1 cup)

salt and pepper

FOR THE DRESSING

2 garlic cloves, minced

3 tablespoons olive oil

3 tablespoons red wine vinegar

2 tablespoons corn oil

1 tablespoon fresh lemon juice

1 tablespoon chopped fresh basil or 1 teaspoon dried basil

1 tablespoon whole-grain mustard

1 teaspoon soy sauce

½ teaspoon dried oregano

½ teaspoon sugar

¼ teaspoon Worcestershire sauce

½ teaspoon hot pepper sauce

1 Soak the black-eyed peas in water to cover overnight. Drain.

2 ▲ Put the peas in a large saucepan and add the onion and carrot. Cover with fresh cold water and bring to a boil. Lower the heat and simmer until the peas are tender, about 1 hour. Drain, reserving the onion and carrot. Transfer the peas to a salad bowl.

3 ▼ Finely chop the onion and carrot. Toss with the peas. Stir in the ham and tomatoes.

4 For the dressing, combine all the ingredients in a small bowl and whisk to mix.

5 ▲ Pour the dressing over the peas. Season with salt and pepper. Toss to combine.

Cobb Salad

SERVES 4

1 large head of romaine lettuce, sliced in strips across the leaves

8 bacon slices, fried until crisp and crumbled

2 large avocados, diced

6 hard-cooked eggs, chopped

2 beefsteak tomatoes, peeled, seeded, and chopped

1½ cups crumbled blue cheese

FOR THE DRESSING

1 garlic clove, minced

1 teaspoon sugar

½ tablespoon fresh lemon juice

1½ tablespoons red wine vinegar

½ cup peanut oil

salt and pepper

1 For the dressing, combine all the ingredients in a screwtop jar and shake well.

2 ▲ On a large rectangular or oval platter, spread out the lettuce to make a bed.

3 ▲ Reserve the bacon, and arrange the remaining ingredients in rows, beginning with the avocados. Sprinkle the bacon on top.

4 Pour the dressing over the salad just before serving.

Spicy Corn Salad

SERVES 4

2 tablespoons vegetable oil

2 cups fresh corn kernels cut from the cob, or frozen whole-kernel corn, thawed

1 green bell pepper, seeded and diced

1 small fresh red chili pepper, seeded and finely diced

4 scallions, cut diagonally in ½-inch pieces

¼ cup chopped fresh parsley

½ pound cherry tomatoes, halved

salt and pepper

FOR THE DRESSING

½ teaspoon sugar

2 tablespoons white wine vinegar

½ teaspoon Dijon-style mustard

1 tablespoon chopped fresh basil or 1 teaspoon dried basil

1 tablespoon mayonnaise

¼ teaspoon hot pepper sauce

1 Heat the oil in a skillet. Add the corn, bell pepper, chili pepper, and scallions. Cook over medium heat until softened, about 5 minutes, stirring frequently.

2 ▲ Transfer the vegetables to a salad bowl. Stir in the parsley and tomatoes.

3 ▲ For the dressing, combine all the ingredients in a small bowl and whisk together. Pour the dressing over the corn mixture. Season with salt and pepper. Toss well to combine, and serve.

Cobb Salad (top), Spicy Corn Salad

Scalloped Potatoes

SERVES 6–8

2½ pounds potatoes, peeled and cut in ⅛-inch slices

salt and pepper

1 large onion, thinly sliced

¼ cup flour

4 tablespoons butter or margarine, cut in small pieces

1½ cups shredded cheddar cheese

1 cup milk

2 cups light cream

1 Preheat the oven to 350°F. Butter a 14-inch oval gratin dish.

2 Layer one-quarter of the potato slices in the prepared dish. Season with salt and pepper.

3 ▼ Layer one-quarter of the sliced onion over the potatoes. Sprinkle with 1 tablespoon of the flour and dot with 2 tablespoons of the butter or margarine. Sprinkle with one-quarter of the cheese.

4 Continue layering these ingredients, making 4 layers.

5 ▲ Heat the milk and light cream in a small saucepan. Pour the mixture evenly over the potatoes.

6 Cover the gratin dish with foil. Place it in the oven and bake for 1 hour. Remove the foil and bake until the potatoes are tender and the top is golden, 15–20 minutes longer.

New Potatoes with Shallot Butter

SERVES 6

1¼ pounds small new potatoes

4 tablespoons butter or margarine

3 shallots, finely chopped

2 garlic cloves, minced

salt and pepper

1 teaspoon chopped fresh tarragon

1 teaspoon chopped fresh chives

1 teaspoon chopped fresh parsley

1 Bring a saucepan of salted water to a boil. Add the potatoes and cook until just tender, 15–20 minutes. Drain well.

2 ▼ Melt the butter or margarine in a skillet. Add the shallots and garlic and cook over low heat until softened, about 5 minutes.

3 ▲ Add the potatoes to the skillet and stir well to mix with the shallot butter. Season with salt and pepper. Cook, stirring, until the potatoes are heated through.

4 Transfer the potatoes to a warmed serving bowl. Sprinkle with the chopped herbs before serving.

Scalloped Potatoes (top), New Potatoes with Shallot Butter

Mashed Potatoes with Garlic

SERVES 6

2–3 heads of garlic, according to taste, cloves separated

4 tablespoons butter or margarine

2½ pounds potatoes, peeled and quartered

salt and pepper

½ cup whipping cream

3 tablespoons chopped fresh chives

1 Drop the garlic cloves into a pan of boiling water and boil 2 minutes. Drain and peel.

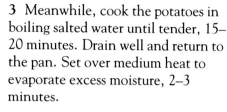

2 ▲ Melt half the butter or margarine in a small saucepan over low heat. Add the peeled garlic. Cover and cook until very soft, 20–25 minutes, stirring frequently.

3 Meanwhile, cook the potatoes in boiling salted water until tender, 15–20 minutes. Drain well and return to the pan. Set over medium heat to evaporate excess moisture, 2–3 minutes.

4 ▲ Push the potatoes through a potato ricer or mash them with a potato masher. Return them to the saucepan and beat in the remaining butter or margarine, 1 tablespoon at a time. Season with salt and pepper.

5 ▲ Remove the pan of garlic from the heat and mash the garlic and butter together with a fork until smooth. Stir in the cream. Return to the heat and bring just to a boil.

6 Beat the garlic cream into the potatoes, 1 tablespoon at a time. Reheat the potatoes if necessary.

7 Fold most of the chives into the potatoes. Transfer the potatoes to a warmed serving bowl and sprinkle the remaining chives on top.

Candied Sweet Potatoes

SERVES 8

3 pounds sweet potatoes, peeled

3 tablespoons butter or margarine

½ cup maple syrup

¾ teaspoon ground ginger

1 tablespoon fresh lemon juice

1 Preheat the oven to 375°F. Grease a large shallow baking dish.

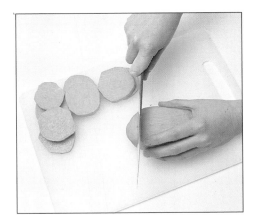

2 ▲ Cut the potatoes in ½-inch slices. Cook them in boiling water for 10 minutes. Drain. Let cool.

3 ▲ Melt the butter or margarine in a small saucepan over medium heat. Stir in the maple syrup until well combined. Stir in the ginger. Simmer 1 minute, then add the lemon juice.

4 ▼ Arrange the potato slices in one layer in the prepared baking dish, overlapping them slightly.

5 ▲ Drizzle the maple syrup mixture evenly over the potatoes. Bake until the potatoes are tender and glazed, 30–35 minutes, spooning the cooking liquid over them once or twice.

Creamed Corn with Bell Peppers

SERVES 4

2 tablespoons butter or margarine

1 small red bell pepper, seeded and finely diced

1 small green bell pepper, seeded and finely diced

4 ears of corn, husks and silk removed

½ cup whipping cream

salt and pepper

1 ▲ Melt the butter or margarine in a saucepan. Add the peppers and cook 5 minutes, stirring occasionally.

2 ▼ Cut the kernels off the ears of corn. Scrape the cobs with the back of a knife to extract the milky liquid. Alternatively, use a corn scraper to remove the kernels and liquid.

~ **VARIATION** ~

2 cups frozen whole-kernel corn, thawed, can be substituted if fresh corn is not available.

3 ▲ Add the corn kernels with the liquid to the saucepan. Stir in the cream. Bring to a boil and simmer until thickened and the corn is tender, 3–4 minutes. Season with salt and pepper.

Fried Okra

SERVES 6

1½ pounds okra

½ cup yellow cornmeal

⅛ teaspoon black pepper

⅓ cup bacon drippings or corn oil

¾ teaspoon salt

~ **COOK'S TIP** ~

When removing the stems of the okra, slice through the point where it joins the vegetable. Cutting into the vegetable allows the release of the viscous insides.

1 Wash the okra well and drain in a colander. Cut off the stems.

2 ▲ Combine the cornmeal and pepper in a mixing bowl. Add the still damp okra and toss to coat evenly with cornmeal.

3 ▼ Heat the bacon drippings or oil in a skillet. Add the okra and fry until tender and golden, 4–5 minutes. Drain on paper towels.

4 Sprinkle the fried okra with the salt just before serving.

Creamed Corn with Bell Peppers (top), Fried Okra

Brussels Sprouts with Chestnuts

SERVES 6

1 pound Brussels sprouts, trimmed

½ cup (1 stick) butter or margarine

3 celery stalks, cut diagonally in ½-inch pieces

1 large onion, thinly sliced

1½–2 cups canned whole chestnuts in brine, drained and rinsed

¼ teaspoon grated nutmeg

salt and pepper

grated rind of 1 lemon

2 ▲ Melt the butter or margarine in a frying pan over low heat. Add the celery and onion and cook until softened, about 5 minutes.

1 ▲ Drop the Brussels sprouts into a pan of boiling salted water and cook 3–4 minutes. Drain well.

3 ▲ Raise the heat to medium and add the chestnuts and Brussels sprouts to the frying pan.

4 Stir in the nutmeg and salt and pepper to taste. Cook until piping hot, about 2 minutes, stirring frequently.

5 ▲ Stir in the grated lemon rind. Transfer to a warmed serving dish.

~ VARIATION ~

For a tasty alternative, substitute grated orange rind for the lemon rind, especially when serving with pork or turkey.

Peas and Pearl Onions

SERVES 6

1 tablespoon butter or margarine

12 pearl onions, peeled

1 small head of Boston lettuce, shredded

2 cups shelled fresh green peas or frozen peas, thawed

1 teaspoon sugar

2 tablespoons water

salt and pepper

2 sprigs fresh mint

1 Melt the butter or margarine in a frying pan. Add the onions and cook over medium heat until they just begin to color, about 10 minutes.

2 ▼ Add the lettuce, peas, sugar, and water. Season with salt and pepper. Bring to a boil. Reduce the heat to low, cover, and simmer until the peas are tender, about 15 minutes for fresh peas and 10 minutes for frozen peas, stirring occasionally.

3 ▲ Strip the mint leaves from the stems. Chop finely with a sharp knife. Stir the mint into the peas. Transfer to a warmed serving dish.

Brussels Sprouts with Chestnuts (top), Peas and Pearl Onions

Broccoli and Cauliflower Mold

Serves 6

1–1½ pounds broccoli, stems trimmed

1–1½ pounds cauliflower, stems trimmed

FOR THE CHEESE SAUCE

3 tablespoons butter or margarine

¼ cup flour

1½ cups milk

¾ cup shredded cheddar cheese

⅛ teaspoon grated nutmeg

salt and pepper

1 Preheat the oven to 300°F. Butter a 1-quart ovenproof bowl or round mold.

2 Break the broccoli into florets. Drop into a pan of boiling salted water and cook 5 minutes. Drain and rinse with cold water to stop the cooking. Drain thoroughly, then spread on paper towels to dry.

3 Break the cauliflower into florets. Drop into a pan of boiling salted water and cook 5 minutes. Drain and rinse with cold water. Drain thoroughly, then spread on paper towels to dry.

4 ▲ Place a cluster of cauliflower on the bottom of the prepared bowl, stems pointing inwards. Add a layer of broccoli, buds against the side and stems pointing inwards. Fill the center with smaller florets.

5 ▲ Add another layer of cauliflower florets. Finish with a layer of broccoli.

6 Cover the mold with buttered foil. Bake until the vegetables are heated through, 10–15 minutes.

7 Meanwhile, for the sauce, melt the butter or margarine in a saucepan. Add the flour and cook 2 minutes, stirring. Stir in the milk. Bring to a boil, stirring constantly, and simmer until thickened, about 5 minutes. Stir in the cheese. Season with the nutmeg and salt and pepper to taste. Keep the sauce warm over very low heat.

8 ▲ Hold a warmed serving plate over the top of the bowl, turn them over together, and lift off the bowl. Serve the molded vegetables with the cheese sauce.

Green Bean and Red Bell Pepper Stir-Fry

Serves 4

1 pound green beans, cut diagonally in 1-inch pieces

2 tablespoons olive oil

1 red bell pepper, seeded and cut in matchstick strips

½ teaspoon soy sauce

1 teaspoon fresh lemon juice

1 Drop the green beans into a pan of boiling salted water and cook 3 minutes. Drain and refresh in cold water. Blot dry with paper towels.

2 ▼ Heat the oil in a frying pan. Add the green beans and red bell pepper and stir-fry until crisp-tender, about 2 minutes.

3 ▲ Remove the pan from the heat and stir in the soy sauce and lemon juice. Transfer the vegetables to a warmed serving dish.

Broccoli and Cauliflower Mold (top), Green Bean and Red Bell Pepper Stir-Fry

Baked Onions with Sun-Dried Tomatoes

SERVES 4

1 pound pearl onions, peeled
2 teaspoons chopped fresh rosemary or ¾ teaspoon dried rosemary
2 garlic cloves, chopped
1 tablespoon chopped fresh parsley
salt and pepper
½ cup sun-dried tomatoes packed in oil, drained and chopped
6 tablespoons olive oil
1 tablespoon white wine vinegar

1 Preheat the oven to 300°F. Grease a shallow baking dish.

2 ▼ Drop the onions into a pan of boiling water and cook 5 minutes. Drain in a colander.

3 ▲ Spread the onions in the bottom of the prepared baking dish.

4 ▲ Combine the rosemary, garlic, parsley, salt, and pepper and sprinkle over the onions.

5 ▲ Scatter the tomatoes over the onions. Drizzle the olive oil and vinegar on top.

6 Cover with a sheet of foil and bake 45 minutes, basting occasionally. Remove the foil and bake until the onions are golden, about 15 minutes longer.

Stewed Tomatoes

SERVES 6

2 pounds very ripe tomatoes, stems removed

2 tablespoons butter or margarine

2 celery stalks, diced

1 small green bell pepper, seeded and diced

2 scallions, finely chopped

salt and pepper

2 tablespoons chopped fresh basil

1 Fill a mixing bowl with boiling water and another bowl with ice water. Three or four at a time, drop the tomatoes into the boiling water and leave them 30 seconds.

2 ▲ Remove the tomatoes with a slotted spoon and transfer to the ice water. When they are cool enough to handle, remove the tomatoes from the ice water.

3 ▲ Peel the tomatoes and cut them into wedges.

4 ▼ Heat the butter or margarine in a flameproof casserole or saucepan. Add the celery, green bell pepper, and scallions and cook until softened, about 5 minutes.

~ **VARIATION** ~

To make stewed tomatoes into a tomato sauce, cook uncovered in a shallow pan such as a skillet until thickened to the desired consistency.

5 ▲ Stir in the tomatoes. Cover and cook until the tomatoes are soft but not mushy, 10–15 minutes, stirring occasionally. Season with salt and pepper.

6 Remove the pan from the heat and stir in the basil.

Braised Red Cabbage with Apples

SERVES 6

2-pound head of red cabbage, quartered and cored

salt and pepper

2 medium red onions, peeled, halved, and thinly sliced

2 Red Delicious apples, peeled, cored, halved, and thinly sliced

1½ teaspoons caraway seeds

3 tablespoons light brown sugar

3 tablespoons red wine vinegar

2 tablespoons butter or margarine, diced

1 Preheat the oven to 400°F.

2 Slice the cabbage quarters thinly across the leaves.

~ **VARIATION** ~

For a sharper flavor, substitute Granny Smith, Greening or other tart varieties for the Red Delicious apples in this recipe.

3 ▲ Make a layer of one-quarter of the cabbage in a large, deep baking dish. Season with salt and pepper.

4 ▲ Layer one-third of the sliced onions and apples on top of the cabbage. Sprinkle with some of the caraway seeds and 1 tablespoon of the brown sugar.

5 Continue layering until all the ingredients have been used, ending with a layer of cabbage on top.

6 ▲ Pour in the vinegar and dot the top with the butter or margarine. Cover and bake 1 hour.

7 Remove the cover and continue baking until the cabbage is very tender and all the liquid has evaporated, about 30 minutes longer.

Glazed Carrots and Scallions

SERVES 6

1 pound baby carrots, trimmed and peeled if necessary

1½ tablespoons butter or margarine

2 tablespoons honey

2 tablespoons fresh orange juice

½ pound scallions, cut diagonally into 1-inch pieces

salt and pepper

1 Cook the carrots in boiling salted water or steam them until just tender, about 10 minutes. Drain if necessary.

2 ▼ In a skillet, melt the butter or margarine with the honey and orange juice, stirring until the mixture is smooth and well combined.

3 ▲ Add the carrots and scallions to the skillet. Cook over medium heat, stirring occasionally, until the vegetables are heated through and glazed, about 5 minutes. Season with salt and pepper before serving.

Braised Red Cabbage with Apples (top), Glazed Carrots and Scallions

Spanish Omelet

SERVES 4

4 bacon slices
3 tablespoons olive oil
1 onion, thinly sliced
½ small red bell pepper, seeded and sliced
½ small green bell pepper, seeded and sliced
1 large garlic clove, minced
¾ pound small round potatoes, cooked and sliced
4 eggs
2 tablespoons light cream
salt and pepper

1 Preheat the oven to 350°F.

2 In a heavy 8-inch skillet with an ovenproof handle, fry the bacon until crisp. Drain on paper towels.

3 Pour off the bacon fat from the skillet. Add 1 tablespoon oil to the pan and cook the onion and bell peppers until softened, about 5 minutes.

4 ▲ Remove the skillet from the heat and stir in the garlic. Crumble in the bacon. Reserve the mixture in a bowl until needed.

5 ▲ Heat the remaining oil in the skillet. Lay the potato slices in the bottom of the pan, slightly overlapping. Spoon the bacon, onion, and bell pepper mixture evenly over the potatoes.

6 In a small bowl, beat together the eggs, cream, and salt and pepper to taste.

7 ▲ Pour the egg mixture into the skillet. Cook over low heat until the egg is set, lifting the edge of the omelette with a knife several times to let the uncooked egg seep down.

8 Transfer the skillet to the oven to finish cooking the omelet, 5–10 minutes longer. Serve hot or warm, cut into wedges.

Spinach and Cheese Pie

3 pounds fresh spinach, coarse stems removed

2 tablespoons olive oil

1 medium onion, finely chopped

2 tablespoons chopped fresh oregano or 1 teaspoon dried oregano

4 eggs

2 cups creamed cottage cheese

6 tablespoons freshly grated Parmesan cheese

grated nutmeg

salt and pepper

12 sheets of phyllo pastry

4 tablespoons butter or margarine, melted

1 Preheat the oven to 375°F.

2 ▲ Stack handfuls of spinach leaves, roll them loosely, and cut across the leaves into thin ribbons.

3 Heat the oil in a large saucepan. Add the onion and cook until softened, about 5 minutes.

4 Add the spinach and oregano and cook over high heat until most of liquid from the spinach evaporates, about 5 minutes, stirring frequently. Remove from the heat and let cool.

5 Break the eggs into a bowl and beat. Stir in the cottage cheese and Parmesan cheese, and season generously with nutmeg, salt, and pepper. Stir in the spinach mixture.

6 ▲ Brush a 13- × 9-inch baking dish with some of the butter or margarine. Arrange half of the phyllo sheets in the bottom of the dish to cover evenly and extend about 1 inch up the sides. Brush with butter.

7 ▲ Ladle in the spinach and cheese filling. Cover with the remaining phyllo pastry, tucking under the edge neatly.

8 Brush the top with the remaining butter. Score the top with diamond shapes using a sharp knife.

9 Bake until the pastry is golden brown, about 30 minutes. Cut into squares and serve hot.

Spinach Flans with Tomato-Thyme Dressing

SERVES 6

1½ pounds frozen chopped spinach, thawed

2 tablespoons butter or margarine

1½ cups fresh bread crumbs

salt and pepper

2 eggs

1 egg yolk

1½ cups milk

3 tablespoons freshly grated Parmesan cheese

fresh thyme sprigs, for garnishing

FOR THE DRESSING

5 teaspoons fresh lemon juice

1 teaspoon sugar

½ teaspoon whole-grain mustard

½ teaspoon fresh thyme leaves or ⅛ teaspoon dried thyme

½ cup olive oil

3 tomatoes, peeled, seeded, and diced

1   Preheat the oven to 350°F. Butter 6 ramekins or custard cups. Place them in a shallow baking dish.

2 ▲ A handful at a time, squeeze the thawed spinach to remove as much water as possible.

3   Melt the butter or margarine in a saucepan. Stir in the spinach and cook 1 minute over high heat, stirring.

4 ▲ Remove the pan from the heat. Stir the bread crumbs into the spinach. Season with salt and pepper.

5   In a small bowl, beat the whole eggs with the egg yolk. Scald the milk in a small saucepan. Lightly beat it into the eggs.

6 ▲ Add the Parmesan cheese to the milk mixture and stir into the spinach mixture.

7 ▲ Spoon the mixture into the ramekins, dividing it evenly. Cover each ramekin tightly with foil.

8 ▲ Add hot water to the baking dish to come halfway up the sides of the ramekins. Bake until a knife inserted in a flan comes out clean, about 35 minutes.

9 ▲ Meanwhile, for the dressing, combine the lemon juice, sugar, mustard, and thyme in a bowl. Whisk in the olive oil. Stir in the tomatoes and salt and pepper to taste.

10   To serve, unmold the flans onto individual plates. Spoon a little dressing over each flan and garnish with a sprig of fresh thyme.

~ COOK'S TIP ~

Fresh bread crumbs are easy to make using a food processor. Remove and discard the crusts from several slices of bread. Tear into smaller pieces and process to obtain fine crumbs.

Corn and Garlic Fritters

SERVES 4

5 garlic cloves

3 eggs, beaten

¾ cup flour

salt and pepper

¾ cup fresh corn kernels, or drained canned corn or frozen corn, thawed

1 cup sour cream

2 tablespoons chopped fresh chives

3 tablespoons corn oil

1 Preheat the broiler.

2 Thread the garlic cloves onto a skewer. Broil close to the heat, turning, until charred and soft. Let cool.

3 ▼ Peel the garlic cloves. Place them in a bowl and mash with a fork. Add the eggs, flour, and salt and pepper to taste and stir until well mixed. Stir in the corn. Set aside for at least 30 minutes.

4 In a small bowl, combine the sour cream and chives. Cover and refrigerate.

5 ▲ To cook the fritters, heat the oil in a frying pan. Drop in spoonfuls of the batter and fry until lightly browned on both sides, about 2 minutes, turning once. Drain on paper towels.

6 Serve the fritters hot with the chive cream.

Cheese and Mushroom Frittata

SERVES 4

2 tablespoons olive oil

2 cups small mushrooms, sliced

3 scallions, finely chopped

6 eggs

1 cup shredded cheddar cheese

1 tablespoon chopped fresh dill or ¼ teaspoon dried dill

salt and pepper

1 Heat the oil in a heavy 8-inch skillet, preferably with an ovenproof handle. Add the mushrooms and scallions and cook over medium heat until wilted, about 3 minutes, stirring occasionally.

2 ▲ Break the eggs into a bowl and beat to mix. Add the cheese, dill, and salt and pepper to taste.

3 Preheat the broiler.

4 ▼ Spread the vegetables evenly in the skillet. Pour the egg mixture into the skillet. Cook until the frittata is set at the edge, and the underside is golden, 5–6 minutes.

5 Place the skillet under the broiler, about 3 inches from the heat. Broil until the top of the frittata has set and is lightly browned, 3–4 minutes. Transfer to a warmed platter for serving.

Corn and Garlic Fritters (top), Cheese and Mushroom Frittata

Baked Goat Cheese with Red Bell Pepper Sauce

SERVES 4

¾-pound log of goat cheese, such as Montrachet, cut in 12 equal slices

1 cup dry bread crumbs

1 tablespoon chopped fresh parsley

⅓ cup freshly grated Parmesan cheese

2 eggs, beaten

fresh parsley, for garnishing

FOR THE SAUCE

4 tablespoons olive oil

4 garlic cloves, chopped

2 red bell peppers, seeded and chopped

1 teaspoon fresh thyme leaves

2 teaspoons tomato paste

salt and pepper

1 Preheat the oven to 450°F.

2 ▼ For the sauce, heat the olive oil in a saucepan. Add the garlic, red bell peppers, and thyme and cook until the vegetables are soft, about 10 minutes, stirring frequently.

3 Pour the pepper mixture into a food processor or blender and purée. Return the puréed mixture to the saucepan. Stir in the tomato paste and salt and pepper to taste. Set aside.

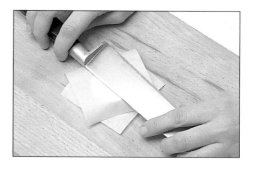

4 ▲ Place each slice of cheese between two pieces of wax paper. With the flat side of a large knife, flatten the cheese slightly.

5 ▲ In a small bowl, combine the bread crumbs, parsley, and Parmesan cheese. Pour the mixture onto a plate.

6 ▲ Dip the cheese rounds in the beaten egg, then in the bread crumb mixture, coating well on all sides. Place on an ungreased baking sheet.

7 Bake the cheese until golden, about 5 minutes. Meanwhile, gently reheat the sauce.

8 To serve, spoon some sauce on 4 heated plates. Place the baked cheese slices on top, and garnish with parsley. Pass the remaining sauce.

Cheese and Dill Soufflés

SERVES 6

2 tablespoons grated Parmesan cheese
4 tablespoons butter or margarine
⅓ cup flour
1¼ cups milk
1 cup grated sharp cheddar cheese
3 eggs, separated
2 tablespoons chopped fresh dill or 1 teaspoon dried dill
salt and pepper

1 Preheat the oven to 400°F. Butter 6 individual soufflé dishes or ramekins, and dust with the Parmesan cheese.

2 ▲ Melt the butter or margarine in a saucepan. Add the flour and cook 2 minutes, stirring. Stir in the milk. Bring to a boil, stirring constantly, and simmer until thickened, about 5 minutes. Remove from the heat and let cool about 10 minutes.

4 In a clean mixing bowl, beat the egg whites with ⅛ teaspoon salt until stiff peaks form.

6 ▲ Divide the mixture evenly among the prepared dishes. Bake until the soufflés are puffed and golden, 15–20 minutes. Serve immediately.

3 ▲ Stir the cheese, egg yolks, and dill into the sauce. Season with salt and pepper. Transfer to a bowl.

5 ▲ Stir one-quarter of the egg whites into the cheese sauce mixture to lighten it. Fold in the remaining egg whites.

Asparagus, Corn, and Red Bell Pepper Quiche

SERVES 6

½ pound fresh asparagus, woody stalks removed

2 tablespoons butter or margarine

1 small onion, finely chopped

1 red bell pepper, seeded and finely chopped

½ cup drained canned corn or frozen corn, thawed

2 eggs

1 cup light cream

½ cup shredded cheddar cheese

salt and pepper

FOR THE CRUST

1⅔ cups flour

½ teaspoon salt

½ cup shortening

2–3 tablespoons ice water

1 Preheat the oven to 400°F.

2 For the crust, sift the flour and salt into a mixing bowl. Using a pastry blender, cut in the shortening until the mixture resembles coarse crumbs. Sprinkle in the water, 1 tablespoon at a time, tossing lightly with your fingertips or a fork until the dough will form a ball.

3 ▲ On a lightly floured surface, roll out the dough. Use it to line a 10-inch quiche dish or loose-bottomed tart pan, easing the dough in and being careful not to stretch it. Trim off excess dough.

4 ▲ Line the pie shell with wax paper and weigh it down with pie weights or dry beans. Bake 10 minutes. Remove the paper and weights or beans and bake until the pastry shell is set and beige in color, about 5 minutes longer. Let cool.

5 Trim the stem ends of 8 of the asparagus spears to make them 4 inches in length. Set aside.

6 ▲ Finely chop the asparagus trimmings and any remaining spears. Place in the bottom of the pie shell.

7 ▲ Melt the butter or margarine in a frying pan. Add the onion and red bell pepper and cook until softened, about 5 minutes. Stir in the corn and cook 2 minutes longer.

8 Spoon the corn mixture over the chopped asparagus in the pie shell.

9 ▲ In a small bowl, beat the eggs with the cream. Stir in the cheese and salt and pepper to taste. Pour into the pie shell.

10 ▲ Arrange the reserved asparagus spears like the spokes of a wheel on top of the filling.

11 Bake until the filling is set, 25–30 minutes.

~ **VARIATION** ~

To make individual tartlets, roll out the dough and use to line 12 3-inch tartlet molds. For the filling, cut off and reserve the asparagus tips and chop the tender part of the stalks. Mix the asparagus and the cooked vegetables into the egg mixture with the cheese. Spoon the filling into the molds and bake as directed, decreasing baking time by about 8–10 minutes.

Cheesy Bread Pudding

SERVES 4

3 tablespoons butter or margarine, at room temperature

2½ cups milk

3 eggs, beaten

½ cup freshly grated Parmesan cheese

⅛ teaspoon cayenne

salt and pepper

5 large, thick slices of crusty white bread

2 cups shredded cheddar cheese

1 Grease an oval baking dish with the butter or margarine.

2 ▼ In a bowl combine the milk, eggs, 3 tablespoons of the Parmesan cheese, the cayenne, and salt and pepper to taste.

3 ▲ Cut the bread slices in half. Arrange 5 of them in the bottom of the prepared dish, overlapping the slices if necessary.

4 ▲ Sprinkle the bread with two-thirds of the cheddar cheese. Top with the remaining bread.

5 Pour the egg mixture evenly over the bread. Press the bread down gently so that it will absorb the egg mixture. Sprinkle the top evenly with the remaining Parmesan and cheddar cheeses. Let stand until the bread has absorbed most of the egg mixture, at least 30 minutes.

6 Preheat the oven to 425°F.

7 Set the baking dish in a roasting pan. Add enough boiling water to the pan to come halfway up the sides of the baking dish.

8 Place in the oven and bake 30 minutes, or until the pudding is lightly set and browned. If the pudding browns too quickly, before setting, cover loosely with foil. Serve hot.

Tomato and Basil Tartlets

MAKES 12–18

2 eggs

3 tablespoons whipping cream

3 tablespoons crumbled feta cheese

salt and pepper

½ pound tomatoes, peeled, seeded, and chopped

12 fresh basil leaves, cut in thin ribbons

FOR THE CRUST

1 ⅔ cups flour

½ teaspoon salt

½ cup shortening

2–3 tablespoons ice water

1 Preheat the oven to 400°F.

2 For the crust, sift the flour and salt into a mixing bowl. Using a pastry blender, cut in the shortening until the mixture resembles coarse crumbs. Sprinkle in the water, 1 tablespoon at a time, tossing lightly with your fingertips or a fork until the dough will form a ball.

3 ▲ On a lightly floured surface, roll out the dough thinly. With a fluted 2½-inch cookie cutter, cut out 18 rounds. Use the rounds to line 18 cups in mini-muffin pans. (Muffin pans vary in size. Cut out larger rounds, if necessary, and make fewer tartlets.)

4 In a bowl, combine the eggs and cream and beat together. Stir in the cheese and salt and pepper to taste.

5 ▼ In a small saucepan, warm the tomatoes with the basil. Drain the tomatoes, then stir them into the egg mixture.

6 ▲ Divide the tomato mixture evenly among the tartlet shells. Bake 10 minutes. Reduce the heat to 350°F and bake until the filling has set and the pastry is golden brown, about 10 minutes longer. Let cool on a wire rack before serving.

BREADS, CAKES, PIES & COOKIES

~

*Both old favorites and lots of new ideas are here, for quick
breads and muffins, simple cakes and layer cakes, fruit pies,
nut pies, cookies and bars – all totally irresistible.*

Zucchini Bread

MAKES 2 LOAVES

2 cups flour
2 teaspoons baking soda
1 teaspoon baking powder
1 teaspoon salt
1 teaspoon ground cinnamon
1 teaspoon grated nutmeg
3 eggs
1½ cups sugar
1¼ cups corn oil
1 teaspoon vanilla extract
2 cups shredded zucchini (about ½ pound)

1 Preheat the oven to 350°F. Grease 2 5½- × 4½-inch loaf pans or a 9- × 5-inch loaf pan.

2 ▼ Sift the flour, baking soda, baking powder, and salt in a mixing bowl. Add the cinnamon and nutmeg, and stir to blend.

3 ▲ With an electric mixer, beat the eggs and sugar together until thick and pale. With a wooden spoon, stir in the oil, vanilla, and zucchini.

4 ▲ Add the flour mixture and stir until just combined. Do not overmix the batter.

5 ▲ Pour the batter into the prepared pan. Bake in the middle of the oven until a cake tester inserted in the center comes out clean, about 1 hour for 2 smaller pans or 1¼ hours for a larger pan.

6 Let cool in the pans on a wire rack for 15 minutes, then unmold onto the wire rack to cool completely.

Zucchini Bread

MAKES 2 LOAVES

2 cups flour

2 teaspoons baking soda

1 teaspoon baking powder

1 teaspoon salt

1 teaspoon ground cinnamon

1 teaspoon grated nutmeg

3 eggs

1½ cups sugar

1¼ cups corn oil

1 teaspoon vanilla extract

2 cups shredded zucchini (about ½ pound)

1 Preheat the oven to 350°F. Grease 2 5½- × 4½-inch loaf pans or a 9- × 5-inch loaf pan.

2 ▼ Sift the flour, baking soda, baking powder, and salt in a mixing bowl. Add the cinnamon and nutmeg, and stir to blend.

3 ▲ With an electric mixer, beat the eggs and sugar together until thick and pale. With a wooden spoon, stir in the oil, vanilla, and zucchini.

4 ▲ Add the flour mixture and stir until just combined. Do not overmix the batter.

5 ▲ Pour the batter into the prepared pan. Bake in the middle of the oven until a cake tester inserted in the center comes out clean, about 1 hour for 2 smaller pans or 1¼ hours for a larger pan.

6 Let cool in the pans on a wire rack for 15 minutes, then unmold onto the wire rack to cool completely.

BREADS, CAKES, PIES & COOKIES

~

*Both old favorites and lots of new ideas are here, for quick
breads and muffins, simple cakes and layer cakes, fruit pies,
nut pies, cookies and bars – all totally irresistible.*

Corn Bread

MAKES 9

2 eggs, lightly beaten

1 cup buttermilk

1 cup flour

1 cup cornmeal

2 teaspoons baking powder

½ teaspoon salt

1 tablespoon sugar

1 cup shredded sharp cheddar cheese

1 cup corn kernels, cut from 2 ears of fresh corn or thawed if frozen

---

~ VARIATION ~

For a spicy cornbread, stir 2 tablespoons chopped jalapeño peppers into the batter after adding the cheese and corn.

---

1 Preheat the oven to 400°F. Grease a 9-inch square baking pan.

2 Combine the eggs and buttermilk in a small bowl and whisk until well combined. Set aside.

3 ▼ In another bowl, stir together the flour, cornmeal, baking powder, salt, and sugar. Pour in the egg mixture and stir with a wooden spoon until just combined. Stir in the cheese and corn.

4 ▲ Pour the batter into the prepared pan. Bake until a cake tester inserted in the center comes out clean, about 25 minutes.

5 Unmold the cornbread onto a wire rack and let cool. Cut into 3-inch squares for serving.

Crunchy Corn Sticks

MAKES 6

1 egg

½ cup milk

1 tablespoon corn oil

1 cup cornmeal

½ cup flour

2 teaspoons baking powder

3 tablespoons sugar

~ VARIATION ~

Fry 3 strips of bacon until crisp. Drain, then crumble and mix into the batter before baking.

---

1 Preheat the oven to 375°F. Grease a castiron corn-stick mold.

2 Beat the egg in a small bowl. Stir in the milk and oil. Set aside.

3 ▼ In a mixing bowl, stir together the cornmeal, flour, baking powder, and sugar. Pour in the egg mixture and stir with a wooden spoon until just combined.

4 ▲ Spoon the batter into the prepared mold. Bake until a cake tester inserted in the center of a corn stick comes out clean, about 25 minutes. Let cool in the mold on a wire rack for 10 minutes before unmolding.

Corn Bread (top), Crunchy Corn Sticks

Sweet Potato and Raisin Bread

MAKES 1 LOAF

2½ cups flour
2 teaspoons baking powder
½ teaspoon salt
1 teaspoon ground cinnamon
½ teaspoon grated nutmeg
2 cups mashed cooked sweet potatoes (about 1 pound)
½ cup light brown sugar, firmly packed
½ cup (1 stick) butter or margarine, melted and cooled
3 eggs, beaten
½ cup raisins

1 ▼ Preheat oven to 350°F. Grease a 9- × 5-inch loaf pan.

2 Sift the flour, baking powder, salt, cinnamon, and nutmeg into a small bowl. Set aside.

3 ▼ With an electric mixer, beat the mashed sweet potatoes with the brown sugar, butter or margarine, and eggs until well mixed.

4 ▼ Add the flour mixture and the raisins. Stir with a wooden spoon until the flour is just mixed in.

5 ▲ Transfer the batter to the prepared pan. Bake until a cake tester inserted in the center comes out clean, 1–1¼ hours.

6 Let cool in the pan on a wire rack for 15 minutes, then unmold the bread from the pan onto the wire rack and let cool completely.

Banana-Pecan Muffins

MAKES 8

1¼ cups flour

1½ teaspoons baking powder

4 tablespoons butter or margarine, at room temperature

¾ cup sugar

1 egg

1 teaspoon vanilla extract

¾ cup mashed bananas (about 3 medium bananas)

½ cup pecans, chopped

⅓ cup milk

~ VARIATION ~

Use an equal quantity of walnuts instead of the pecans.

---

1 Preheat the oven to 375°F. Grease a muffin pan.

2 Sift the flour and baking powder into a small bowl. Set aside.

3 ▲ With an electric mixer, cream the butter or margarine and sugar together. Add the egg and vanilla and beat until fluffy. Mix in the banana.

4 ▼ Add the pecans. With the mixer on low speed, beat in the flour mixture alternately with the milk.

5 Spoon the batter into the prepared muffin cups, filling them two-thirds full. Bake until golden brown and a cake tester inserted into the center of a muffin comes out clean, 20–25 minutes.

6 Let cool in the pan on a wire rack for 10 minutes. To loosen, run a knife gently around each muffin and unmold onto the wire rack. Let cool 10 minutes longer before serving.

Blueberry-Cinnamon Muffins

MAKES 8

1 cup flour

1 tablespoon baking powder

⅛ teaspoon salt

⅓ cup light brown sugar, firmly packed

1 egg

¾ cup milk

3 tablespoons corn oil

2 teaspoons ground cinnamon

1 cup fresh or thawed frozen blueberries

1 Preheat the oven to 375°F. Grease a muffin pan.

2 With an electric mixer, beat the first 8 ingredients together until smooth.

3 ▲ Fold in the blueberries.

4 ▲ Spoon the batter into the muffin cups, filling them two-thirds full. Bake until a cake tester inserted in the center of a muffin comes out clean, about 25 minutes.

5 Let cool in the pan on a wire rack for 10 minutes, then unmold the muffins onto the wire rack and allow to cool completely.

Banana-Pecan Muffins (top), Blueberry-Cinnamon Muffins

Buttermilk Biscuits

~ COOK'S TIP ~

If time is short, drop the biscuit dough onto the baking sheet by heaping tablespoons without kneading or cutting it out.

1 Preheat the oven to 425°F.

2 ▼ Sift the flour, baking powder, baking soda, and salt into a mixing bowl. Cut in the butter or margarine with a fork until the mixture resembles coarse crumbs.

3 ▲ Add the buttermilk and mix until well combined to a soft dough.

4 ▲ Turn the dough onto a lightly floured board and knead 30 seconds.

5 ▲ Roll out the dough to ½-inch thickness. Use a floured 2½-inch cookie cutter to cut out rounds.

6 Transfer the rounds to a baking sheet and bake until golden brown, 10–12 minutes. Serve hot.

Parmesan Popovers

MAKES 6

½ cup freshly grated Parmesan cheese
1 cup flour
¼ teaspoon salt
2 eggs
1 cup milk
1 tablespoon butter or margarine, melted

1 ▼ Preheat the oven to 450°F. Grease six ¾-cup popover pans. Sprinkle each pan with 1 tablespoon of the grated Parmesan. Alternatively, you can use custard cups, in which case, heat them on a baking sheet in the oven, then grease and sprinkle with Parmesan just before filling.

2 Sift the flour and salt into a small bowl. Set aside.

3 ▲ In a mixing bowl, beat together the eggs, milk, and butter or margarine. Add the flour mixture and stir until smoothly blended.

4 ▼ Divide the batter evenly among the pans, filling each one about half full. Bake for 15 minutes, then sprinkle the tops of the popovers with the remaining grated Parmesan cheese. Reduce the heat to 350°F and continue baking until the popovers are firm and golden brown, 20–25 minutes.

5 ▲ Remove the popovers from the oven. To unmold, run a thin knife around the inside of each pan to loosen the popovers. Gently ease out, then transfer to a wire rack to cool.

Devil's Food Cake

SERVES 10

4 1-ounce squares semisweet chocolate

1¼ cups milk

1 cup light brown sugar, firmly packed

1 egg yolk

2¼ cups cake flour

1 teaspoon baking soda

½ teaspoon salt

⅔ cup (10⅔ tablespoons) butter or margarine, at room temperature

1⅓ cups granulated sugar

3 eggs

1 teaspoon vanilla extract

FOR THE FROSTING

8 1-ounce squares semisweet chocolate

¾ cup sour cream

¼ teaspoon salt

1 Preheat the oven to 350°F. Line 2 8- or 9-inch round cake pans with wax paper.

2 ▲ In a heatproof bowl set over a pan of simmering water, or in a double boiler, combine the chocolate, ½ cup of the milk, the brown sugar, and egg yolk. Cook, stirring, until smooth and thickened. Let cool.

3 ▲ Sift the flour, baking soda, and salt into a small bowl. Set aside.

4 ▲ With an electric mixer, cream the butter or margarine with the granulated sugar until light and fluffy. Beat in the whole eggs, one at a time. Mix in the vanilla.

5 On low speed, beat the flour mixture into the butter mixture alternately with the remaining milk, beginning and ending with flour.

6 ▲ Pour in the chocolate mixture and mix until just combined.

7 Divide the batter evenly between the cake pans. Bake until a cake tester inserted in the center comes out clean, 30–40 minutes.

8 Let cool in the pans on wire racks for 10 minutes, then unmold the cakes from the pans onto the wire racks and let cool completely.

9 ▲ For the frosting, melt the chocolate in a heatproof bowl set over a pan of hot, not boiling, water, or in the top of a double boiler. Remove the bowl from the heat and stir in the sour cream and salt. Let cool slightly.

10 ▲ Set 1 cake layer on a serving plate and spread with one-third of the frosting. Place the second cake layer on top. Spread the remaining frosting all over the top and sides of the cake, swirling it to make a decorative finish.

Coconut Angel Food Cake

SERVES 10

1½ cups confectioners' sugar
1 cup cake flour
1½ cups egg whites (about 12 egg whites)
1½ teaspoons cream of tartar
1 cup granulated sugar
¼ teaspoon salt
2 teaspoons almond extract
1 cup flaked coconut
FOR THE FROSTING
2 egg whites
½ cup granulated sugar
¼ teaspoon salt
2 tablespoons cold water
2 teaspoons almond extract
2 cups flaked coconut, toasted

1 ▲ Preheat the oven to 350°F. Sift the confectioners' sugar and flour into a bowl. Set aside.

2 With an electric mixer, beat the egg whites with the cream of tartar on medium speed until very thick. Turn the mixer to high speed and beat in the granulated sugar, 2 tablespoons at a time, reserving 2 tablespoons.

3 ▲ Continue beating until stiff and glossy. Swiftly beat in the reserved 2 tablespoons of sugar, along with the salt and almond extract.

4 ▲ Using a ¼-cup measure, sprinkle the flour mixture over the meringue, quickly folding until just combined. Fold in the flaked coconut in 2 batches.

5 ▲ Transfer the batter to an ungreased 10-inch angel cake pan, and cut gently through the batter with a metal spatula. Bake until the top of the cake springs back when touched lightly, 30–35 minutes.

6 ▲ As soon as the cake is done, turn the pan upside down and suspend its funnel over the neck of a funnel or bottle. Let cool, about 1 hour.

7 ▲ For the frosting, combine the egg whites, sugar, salt, and water in a heatproof bowl. Beat with an electric mixer until blended. Set the bowl over a pan of boiling water and continue beating on medium speed until the frosting is stiff, about 3 minutes. Remove the pan from the heat and stir in the almond extract.

8 ▲ Unmold the cake onto a serving plate. Spread the frosting gently over the top and sides of the cake. Sprinkle with the toasted coconut.

Carrot Cake with Cream Cheese Frosting

SERVES 10

2 cups granulated sugar

1 cup vegetable oil

4 eggs

2 cups finely grated carrots
   (about ½ pound)

2 cups flour

1½ teaspoons baking soda

1½ teaspoons baking powder

1 teaspoon ground allspice

1 teaspoon ground cinnamon

FOR THE FROSTING

2 cups confectioners' sugar

1 8-ounce package cream cheese, at
   room temperature

4 tablespoons butter or margarine, at
   room temperature

2 teaspoons vanilla extract

1½ cups walnut pieces or pecans,
   chopped

1 Preheat the oven to 375°F. Butter and flour 2 9-inch round cake pans.

2 ▲ In a mixing bowl, combine the granulated sugar, vegetable oil, eggs, and carrots.

3 Sift the dry ingredients into another bowl. Add by ½-cup measures to the carrot mixture, mixing well after each addition.

4 ▲ Divide the batter evenly between the prepared cake pans. Bake until a cake tester inserted in the center comes out clean, 35–40 minutes.

5 Let cool in the pans on wire racks for 10 minutes, then unmold the cakes from the pans onto the wire racks and let cool completely.

6 For the frosting, combine everything but the nuts in a bowl and beat until smooth.

7 ▲ To assemble, set 1 cake layer on a serving plate and spread with one-third of the frosting. Place the second cake layer on top. Spread the remaining frosting all over the top and sides of the cake, swirling it to make a decorative finish. Sprinkle the nuts around the top edge.

Apple and Pear Skillet Cake

SERVES 6

1 apple, peeled, cored, and thinly sliced

1 pear, peeled, cored, and thinly sliced

½ cup walnut pieces, chopped

1 teaspoon ground cinnamon

1 teaspoon grated nutmeg

3 eggs

¾ cup flour

2 tablespoons light brown sugar, firmly packed

¾ cup milk

1 teaspoon vanilla extract

4 tablespoons butter or margarine

confectioners' sugar, for sprinkling

1 ▲ Preheat the oven to 375°F. In a mixing bowl, toss together the apple slices, pear slices, walnuts, cinnamon, and nutmeg. Set aside.

2 ▲ With an electric mixer, beat together the eggs, flour, brown sugar, milk, and vanilla.

3 ▼ Melt the butter or margarine in a 9- or 10-inch ovenproof skillet (preferably castiron) over medium heat. Add the apple mixture. Cook until lightly caramelized, about 5 minutes, stirring occasionally.

4 ▲ Pour the batter over the fruit and nuts. Transfer the skillet to the oven and bake until the cake is puffy and pulling away from the sides of the pan, about 30 minutes.

5 Sprinkle the cake lightly with confectioners' sugar and serve hot.

Ginger Cake with Spiced Whipped Cream

SERVES 9

1½ cups flour

2 teaspoons baking powder

½ teaspoon salt

2 teaspoons ground ginger

2 teaspoons ground cinnamon

1 teaspoon ground cloves

¼ teaspoon grated nutmeg

2 eggs

1 cup granulated sugar

1 cup whipping cream

1 teaspoon vanilla extract

confectioners' sugar, for sprinkling

FOR THE SPICED WHIPPED CREAM

¾ cup whipping cream

1 teaspoon confectioners' sugar

¼ teaspoon ground cinnamon

¼ teaspoon ground ginger

⅛ teaspoon grated nutmeg

1 Preheat the oven to 350°F. Grease a 9-inch square baking pan.

2 Sift the flour, baking powder, salt, ginger, cinnamon, cloves, and nutmeg into a bowl. Set aside.

3 ▲ With an electric mixer, beat the eggs on high speed until very thick, about 5 minutes. Gradually beat in the granulated sugar.

4 ▲ With the mixer on low speed, beat in the flour mixture alternately with the cream, beginning and ending with the flour. Stir in the vanilla.

5 ▲ Pour the batter into the prepared pan and bake until the top springs back when touched lightly, 35–40 minutes. Let cool in the pan on a wire rack for 10 minutes.

6 ▲ Meanwhile, to make the spiced whipped cream, combine the ingredients in a bowl and whip until the cream will hold soft peaks.

7 Sprinkle confectioners' sugar over the hot cake, cut in 9 squares, and serve with spiced whipped cream.

Pound Cake

SERVES 12

2 cups flour

1 teaspoon baking powder

1 cup (2 sticks) butter or margarine, at room temperature

1 cup sugar

grated rind of 1 lemon

1 teaspoon vanilla extract

4 eggs

1 Preheat the oven to 325°F. Grease a 9- × 5-inch loaf pan.

2 Sift the flour and baking powder into a small bowl. Set aside.

3 ▲ With an electric mixer, cream the butter or margarine, adding the sugar 2 tablespoons at a time, until light and fluffy. Stir in the lemon rind and vanilla.

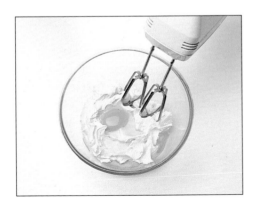

4 ▲ Add the eggs one at a time, beating for 1 minute after each addition.

5 ▼ Add the flour mixture and stir until just combined.

6 ▲ Pour the batter into the pan and tap lightly. Bake until a cake tester inserted in the center comes out clean, about 1¼ hours.

7 Let cool in the pan on a wire rack for 10 minutes, then unmold the cake from the pan onto the wire rack and let cool completely.

Applesauce Cake

SERVES 10

1½ pounds apples, peeled, cored, and quartered

2¼ cups sugar

1 tablespoon water

3 cups flour

1¾ teaspoons baking soda

1 teaspoon ground cinnamon

1 teaspoon ground cloves

1¼ cups walnut pieces, chopped

1 cup raisins

1 cup (2 sticks) butter or margarine, at room temperature

1 teaspoon vanilla extract

FOR THE ICING

1 cup confectioners' sugar

¼ teaspoon vanilla extract

2–3 tablespoons milk

1 ▲ Combine the apples, ¼ cup of the sugar, and the water in a medium saucepan and bring to a boil. Simmer 25 minutes, stirring occasionally with a wooden spoon to break up any lumps. Let cool.

~ **COOK'S TIP** ~

Be sure to grease the cake pan generously and allow this cake to become completely cold before unmolding it.

2 ▲ Preheat the oven to 325°F. Butter and flour a 1½- to 2-quart bundt or tube pan.

3 Sift the flour, baking soda, cinnamon, and cloves into a mixing bowl. Remove ¼ cup of the mixture to a small bowl and toss with 1 cup of the walnuts and the raisins.

4 ▲ With an electric mixer, cream the butter or margarine and remaining sugar together until light and fluffy. Fold in the applesauce gently with a wooden spoon.

5 ▲ Fold the flour mixture into the applesauce mixture. Stir in the vanilla and the raisin-walnut mixture.

6 Pour the batter into the prepared pan. Bake until a cake tester inserted in the center comes out clean, about 1½ hours.

7 Let cool in the pan on a wire rack for 20 minutes, then unmold the cake from the pan onto the wire rack and let cool completely.

8 ▲ For the icing, put the sugar in a bowl and stir in the vanilla and 1 tablespoon of the milk. Add the remaining milk, teaspoon by teaspoon, until the icing is smooth and has a thick pouring consistency.

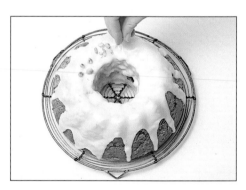

9 ▲ Transfer the cooled cake to a serving plate and drizzle the icing on top. Sprinkle with the remaining nuts. Let the cake stand for 2 hours before slicing, so the icing can set.

Pumpkin Pie

SERVES 8

1½ cups pumpkin purée

2 cups light cream

⅔ cup light brown sugar, firmly packed

¼ teaspoon salt

1 teaspoon ground cinnamon

½ teaspoon ground ginger

¼ teaspoon ground cloves

⅛ teaspoon grated nutmeg

2 eggs

FOR THE CRUST

1⅓ cups flour

½ teaspoon salt

½ cup shortening

2–3 tablespoons ice water

¼ cup pecans, chopped

1 Preheat the oven to 425°F.

2 ▲ For the crust, sift the flour and salt into a mixing bowl. Using a pastry blender, cut in the shortening until the mixture resembles coarse crumbs. Sprinkle in the water, 1 tablespoon at a time, tossing lightly with a fork until the dough will form a ball.

3 ▲ On a lightly floured surface, roll out the dough to ¼-inch thickness. Use it to line a 9-inch pie pan, easing the dough in and being careful not to stretch it. Trim off the excess dough.

4 ▲ If you like, use the dough trimmings to make a decorative rope edge. Cut in strips and twist together in pairs. Dampen the rim of the pie shell and press on the rope edge. Or, with your thumbs, make a fluted edge. Sprinkle the chopped pecans over the bottom of the pie shell.

5 With a whisk or an electric mixer on medium speed, beat together the pumpkin purée, cream, brown sugar, salt, spices, and eggs.

6 Pour the pumpkin mixture into the pie shell. Bake 10 minutes, then reduce the heat to 350°F and continue baking until the filling is set, about 45 minutes. Let the pie cool in the pan, set on a wire rack.

Maple-Pecan Pie

SERVES 8

3 eggs, beaten
½ cup dark brown sugar, firmly packed
⅔ cup corn syrup
⅓ cup maple syrup
½ teaspoon vanilla extract
⅛ teaspoon salt
1 cup pecan halves
FOR THE CRUST
1⅓ cups flour
½ teaspoon salt
1 teaspoon ground cinnamon
½ cup shortening
2–3 tablespoons ice water

1 Preheat the oven to 425°F.

2 For the crust, sift the flour, salt, and cinnamon into a mixing bowl. Using a pastry blender, cut in the shortening until the mixture resembles coarse crumbs. Sprinkle in the water, 1 tablespoon at a time, tossing lightly with your fingertips or a fork until the dough will form a ball.

3 On a lightly floured surface, roll out the dough to a circle 15 inches in diameter. Use it to line a 9-inch pie pan, easing in the dough and being careful not to stretch it.

4 ▲ With your thumbs, make a fluted edge. Using a fork, prick the bottom and sides of the pie shell all over. Bake until lightly browned, 10–15 minutes. Let cool in the pan.

5 ▼ Reduce the oven temperature to 350°F. In a bowl, stir together the eggs, sugar, corn and maple syrups, vanilla, and salt until well mixed.

6 ▲ Sprinkle the pecans evenly over the bottom of the baked pie crust. Pour in the egg mixture. Bake until the filling is set and the pastry is golden brown, about 40 minutes. Let cool in the pan, set on a wire rack.

Apple Pie

SERVES 8

6 cups peeled and sliced tart apples, such as Granny Smith (about 2 pounds)
1 tablespoon fresh lemon juice
1 teaspoon vanilla extract
½ cup sugar
½ teaspoon ground cinnamon
1½ tablespoons butter or margarine
1 egg yolk
2 teaspoons whipping cream
FOR THE CRUST
2 cups flour
1 teaspoon salt
¾ cup shortening
4–5 tablespoons ice water
1 tablespoon quick-cooking tapioca

1 Preheat the oven to 450°F.

2 For the crust, sift the flour and salt into a mixing bowl. Using a pastry blender, cut in the shortening until the mixture resembles coarse crumbs.

3 ▲ Sprinkle in the water, 1 tablespoon at a time, tossing lightly with your fingertips or with a fork until the dough will form a ball.

4 ▲ Divide the dough in half and shape each half into a ball. On a lightly floured surface, roll out one of the balls to a circle about 12 inches in diameter.

5 ▲ Use it to line a 9-inch pie pan, easing the dough in and being careful not to stretch it. Trim off the excess dough and use the trimmings for decorating. Sprinkle the tapioca over the bottom of the pie shell.

6 ▲ Roll out the remaining dough to ⅛-inch thickness. With a sharp knife, cut out 8 large leaf-shapes. Cut the trimmings into small leaf shapes. Score the leaves with the back of the knife to mark veins.

7 ▲ In a bowl, toss the apples with the lemon juice, vanilla, sugar, and cinnamon. Fill the pie shell with the apple mixture and dot with the butter or margarine.

8 ▲ Arrange the large pastry leaves in a decorative pattern on top. Decorate the edge with small leaves.

9 ▲ Mix together the egg yolk and cream and brush over the leaves to glaze them.

10 Bake 10 minutes, then reduce the heat to 350°F and continue baking until the pastry is golden brown, 35–45 minutes. Let the pie cool in the pan, set on a wire rack.

Mississippi Mud Pie

SERVES 8

3 1-ounce squares semisweet chocolate

4 tablespoons butter or margarine

3 tablespoons corn syrup

3 eggs, beaten

⅔ cup sugar

1 teaspoon vanilla extract

4-oz chocolate bar

2 cups whipping cream

FOR THE CRUST

1⅓ cups flour

½ teaspoon salt

½ cup shortening

2–3 tablespoons ice water

1 Preheat the oven to 425°F.

2 For the crust, sift the flour and salt into a mixing bowl. Using a pastry blender, cut in the shortening until the mixture resembles coarse crumbs. Sprinkle in the water, 1 tablespoon at a time. Toss lightly with your fingers or a fork until the dough will form a ball.

3 On a lightly floured surface, roll out the dough. Use to line an 8- or 9-inch pie pan, easing in the dough and being careful not to stretch it. With your thumbs, make a fluted edge.

4 Using a fork, prick the bottom and sides of the pie shell all over. Bake until lightly browned, 10–15 minutes. Let cool, in the pan, on a wire rack.

5 ▲ In a heatproof bowl set over a pan of simmering water, or in a double boiler, melt 3 squares of chocolate, the butter or margarine, and corn syrup. Remove the bowl from the heat and stir in the eggs, sugar, and vanilla.

6 Reduce the oven temperature to 350°F. Pour the chocolate mixture into the baked crust. Bake until the filling is set, 35–40 minutes. Let cool completely in the pan, set on a rack.

7 ▲ For the decoration, use the heat of your hands to slightly soften the chocolate bar. Draw the blade of a swivel-headed vegetable peeler along the side of the chocolate bar to shave off short, wide curls. Chill the chocolate curls until needed.

8 Before serving, lightly whip the cream until soft peaks form. Using a rubber spatula, spread the cream over the surface of the chocolate filling. Decorate with the chocolate curls.

Banana Cream Pie

SERVES 6

2 cups finely crushed gingersnaps

5 tablespoons butter or margarine, melted

½ teaspoon grated nutmeg or ground cinnamon

¾ cup mashed ripe bananas

1½ 8-ounce packages cream cheese, at room temperature

¼ cup thick plain yogurt or sour cream

3 tablespoons dark rum or 1 teaspoon vanilla extract

FOR THE TOPPING

1 cup whipping cream

3–4 bananas

1 Preheat the oven to 375°F.

2 ▲ In a mixing bowl, combine the cookie crumbs, butter or margarine, and spice. Mix thoroughly with a wooden spoon.

3 ▲ Press the cookie mixture into a 9-inch pie pan, building up thick sides with a neat edge. Bake 5 minutes. Let cool, in the pan, on a wire rack.

4 ▼ With an electric mixer, beat the mashed bananas with the cream cheese. Fold in the yogurt or sour cream and rum or vanilla. Spread the filling in the crumb crust. Refrigerate at least 4 hours or overnight.

5 ▲ For the topping, whip the cream until soft peaks form. Spread on the pie filling. Slice the bananas and arrange on top in a decorative pattern.

Lime Meringue Pie

SERVES 8

3 egg yolks

1½ cups sweetened condensed milk

finely grated rind and juice of 4 limes

7 egg whites

⅛ teaspoon salt

squeeze of fresh lemon juice

½ cup sugar

½ teaspoon vanilla extract

FOR THE CRUST

1⅓ cups flour

½ teaspoon salt

½ cup shortening

1 egg yolk

2–3 tablespoons ice water

1 Preheat the oven to 425°F.

2 ▲ For the crust, sift the flour and salt into a mixing bowl. Using a pastry blender, cut in the shortening until the mixture resembles coarse crumbs. Sprinkle in the water, 1 tablespoon at a time, tossing lightly with a fork until the dough will form a ball.

~ COOK'S TIP ~

When beating egg whites with an electric mixer, start slowly, and increase speed after they become frothy. Turn the bowl constantly.

3 ▲ On a lightly floured surface, roll out the dough. Use it to line a 9-inch pie pan, easing in the dough and being careful not to stretch it. With your thumbs, make a fluted edge.

4 Using a fork, prick the bottom and sides of the pie shell all over. Bake until lightly browned, 10–15 minutes. Let cool, in the pan, on a wire rack. Reduce oven temperature to 375°F.

5 ▲ With an electric mixer on high speed, beat the yolks and condensed milk. Stir in the lime rind and juice.

6 ▲ In another clean bowl, beat 3 of the egg whites until stiff. Fold into lime mixture.

7 ▲ Spread the lime filling in the pie crust. Bake 10 minutes.

8 ▲ Meanwhile, beat the remaining egg whites with the salt and lemon juice until soft peaks form. Beat in the sugar, 1 tablespoon at a time, until stiff peaks form. Add the vanilla.

9 ▲ Remove the pie from the oven. Using a metal spatula, spread the meringue over the lime filling, making a swirled design and covering the surface completely.

10 Bake until the meringue is lightly browned and the pastry is golden brown, about 12 minutes longer. Let cool, in the pan, on a wire rack.

Cherry Lattice Pie

SERVES 8

4 cups sour cherries, pitted (2 pounds fresh or 2 16-ounce cans, water-pack, drained)

⅓ cup sugar

¼ cup flour

1½ tablespoons fresh lemon juice

¼ teaspoon almond extract

2 tablespoons butter or margarine

FOR THE CRUST

2 cups flour

1 teaspoon salt

¾ cup shortening

4–5 tablespoons ice water

1 For the crust, sift the flour and salt into a mixing bowl. Using a pastry blender, cut in the shortening until the mixture resembles coarse crumbs.

2 ▲ Sprinkle in the water, 1 tablespoon at a time, tossing lightly with your fingertips or a fork until the dough will form a ball.

3 Divide the dough in half and shape each half into a ball. On a lightly floured surface, roll out one of the balls to a circle about 12 inches in diameter.

4 ▲ Use it to line a 9-inch pie pan, easing the dough in and being careful not to stretch it. With scissors, trim off excess dough, leaving a ½-inch overhang around the pie rim.

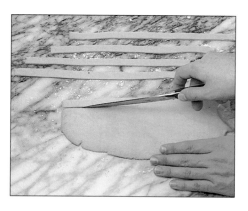

5 ▲ Roll out the remaining dough to ⅛-inch thickness. With a sharp knife, cut out 11 strips ½ inch wide.

6 ▲ In a mixing bowl, combine the cherries, sugar, flour, lemon juice, and almond extract. Spoon the mixture into the pie crust and dot with the butter or margarine.

7 ▲ To make the lattice, place 5 of the pastry-dough strips evenly across the filling. Fold every other strip back. Lay the first strip across in the opposite direction. Continue in this pattern, folding back every other strip each time you add a cross strip.

8 ▲ Trim the ends of the lattice strips even with the crust overhang. Press together so that the edge rests on the pie-pan rim. With your thumbs, flute the edge. Refrigerate 15 minutes.

9 Preheat the oven to 425°F.

10 Bake the pie 30 minutes, covering the edge of the crust with foil, if necessary, to prevent overbrowning. Let cool, in the pan, on a wire rack.

Gingersnaps

MAKES 60

2½ cups flour

1 teaspoon baking soda

1½ teaspoons ground ginger

¼ teaspoon ground cinnamon

¼ teaspoon ground cloves

½ cup (1 stick) butter or margarine, at room temperature

1½ cups sugar

1 egg, beaten

¼ cup molasses

1 teaspoon fresh lemon juice

1 Preheat the oven to 350°F. Grease 3–4 cookie sheets.

2 Sift the flour, baking soda, ginger, cinnamon, and cloves into a small bowl. Set aside.

3 With an electric mixer, cream the butter or margarine and 1 cup of the sugar together.

4 ▲ Stir in the egg, molasses, and lemon juice. Add the flour mixture and mix in thoroughly with a wooden spoon to make a soft dough.

5 ▲ Shape the dough into ¾-inch balls. Roll the balls in the remaining sugar and place about 2 inches apart on the prepared cookie sheets.

6 Bake until the cookies are just firm to the touch, about 12 minutes. With a slotted spatula, transfer the cookies to a wire rack and let cool.

Cowboy Cookies

MAKES 60

1 cup flour

½ teaspoon baking soda

¼ teaspoon baking powder

¼ teaspoon salt

½ cup (1 stick) butter or margarine, at room temperature

½ cup granulated sugar

½ cup light brown sugar, firmly packed

1 egg

½ teaspoon vanilla extract

1 cup rolled oats

1 cup semisweet chocolate chips

1 Preheat the oven to 325°F. Grease 3–4 cookie sheets.

2 Sift the flour, baking soda, baking powder, and salt into a mixing bowl. Set aside.

3 With an electric mixer, cream the butter or margarine and sugars together. Add the egg and vanilla and beat until light and fluffy.

4 ▲ Add the flour mixture and beat on low speed until thoroughly blended. Stir in the rolled oats and chocolate chips, mixing well with a wooden spoon. The dough should be crumbly.

5 ▲ Drop by heaping teaspoonfuls onto the prepared cookie sheets, spacing the cookies about 1 inch apart. Bake until just firm around the edge but still soft to the touch in the center, about 15 minutes. With a slotted spatula, transfer the cookies to a wire rack and let cool.

Gingersnaps (top), Cowboy Cookies

Old-Fashioned Sugar Cookies

MAKES 36

3 cups flour

1 teaspoon baking soda

2 teaspoons baking powder

¼ teaspoon grated nutmeg

½ cup (1 stick) butter or margarine, at room temperature

1 cup sugar

½ teaspoon vanilla extract

1 egg

½ cup milk

colored sugar, for sprinkling

1 Sift the flour, baking soda, baking powder, and nutmeg into a small bowl. Set aside.

2 ▲ With an electric mixer, cream the butter or margarine, sugar, and vanilla together until the mixture is light and fluffy. Add the egg and beat to mix well.

3 ▲ Add the flour mixture alternately with the milk, stirring with a wooden spoon to make a soft dough. Wrap the dough in plastic wrap and refrigerate at least 30 minutes, or overnight.

4 ▲ Preheat the oven to 350°F. Roll out the dough on a lightly floured surface to ⅛-inch thickness. Cut into rounds or other shapes with cookie cutters.

5 ▲ Transfer the cookies to ungreased cookie sheets. Sprinkle each cookie with colored sugar.

6 Bake until golden brown, 10–12 minutes. With a slotted spatula, transfer the cookies to a wire rack and let cool.

Chocolate Chip and Macadamia Nut Cookies

MAKES 36

1 cup flour

1 teaspoon baking powder

¼ teaspoon salt

6 tablespoons butter or margarine, at room temperature

½ cup granulated sugar

¼ cup light brown sugar, firmly packed

1 egg

1 teaspoon vanilla extract

¾ cup chocolate chips

½ cup macadamia nuts, chopped

1 ▲ Preheat the oven to 350°F. Grease 2–3 cookie sheets.

2 Sift the flour, baking powder, and salt into a small bowl. Set aside.

3 ▲ With an electric mixer, cream the butter or margarine and sugars together. Beat in the egg and vanilla.

4 Add the flour mixture and beat well with the mixer on low speed.

5 ▼ Stir in the chocolate chips and ¼ cup of the macadamia nuts using a wooden spoon.

6 Drop the mixture by teaspoons onto the prepared cookie sheets, to form ¾-inch mounds. Space the cookies 1–2 inches apart.

7 ▲ Flatten each cookie lightly with a wet fork. Sprinkle the remaining macadamia nuts on top of the cookies and press lightly into the surface.

8 Bake until golden brown, about 10–12 minutes. With a slotted spatula, transfer the cookies to a wire rack and let cool.

Pepper-Spice Cookies

MAKES 48

1¾ cups flour

½ cup cornstarch

2 teaspoons baking powder

½ teaspoon ground cardamom

½ teaspoon ground cinnamon

½ teaspoon grated nutmeg

½ teaspoon ground ginger

½ teaspoon ground allspice

½ teaspoon salt

½ teaspoon freshly ground black pepper

1 cup (2 sticks) butter or margarine, at
  room temperature

½ cup light brown sugar, firmly packed

½ teaspoon vanilla extract

1 teaspoon finely grated lemon rind

¼ cup whipping cream

⅔ cup finely ground almonds

2 tablespoons confectioners' sugar

1 Preheat the oven to 350°F.

2 Sift the flour, cornstarch, baking
powder, spices, salt, and pepper into a
bowl. Set aside.

3 With an electric mixer, cream the
butter or margarine and brown sugar
together until light and fluffy. Beat in
the vanilla and lemon rind.

4 ▲ With the mixer on low speed,
add the flour mixture alternately with
the cream, beginning and ending with
flour. Stir in the ground almonds.

5 ▲ Shape the dough into ¾-inch
balls. Place them on ungreased cookie
sheets about 1 inch apart. Bake until
the cookies are golden brown
underneath, 15–20 minutes.

6 Let the cookies cool on the cookie
sheets about 1 minute before
transferring them to a wire rack to
cool completely. Before serving,
sprinkle them lightly with
confectioners' sugar.

Five-Layer Bars

MAKES 24

2 cups graham cracker crumbs

¼ cup sugar

⅛ teaspoon salt

½ cup (1 stick) butter or margarine,
  melted

1 cup shredded coconut

1½ cups semisweet chocolate chips

1 cup sweetened condensed milk

1 cup walnut pieces, chopped

1 Preheat the oven to 350°F.

2 ▼ In a bowl, combine the graham-
cracker crumbs, sugar, salt, and butter
or margarine. Press the mixture evenly
over the bottom of an ungreased
13- × 9-inch baking dish.

3 ▲ Sprinkle the coconut over the
crumb crust, then scatter over the
chocolate chips. Pour the condensed
milk evenly over the chocolate.
Sprinkle the walnuts on top.

4 Bake 30 minutes. Unmold onto a
wire rack and let cool, preferably
overnight. When cooled, cut into
bars.

Pepper-Spice Cookies (top), Five-Layer Bars

Lemon Squares

MAKES 12

2 cups flour

½ cup confectioners' sugar

¼ teaspoon salt

¾ cup (1½ sticks) cold butter or margarine

1 teaspoon cold water

FOR THE LEMON LAYER

4 eggs

2 cups granulated sugar

¼ cup flour

½ teaspoon baking powder

1 teaspoon grated lemon rind

¼ cup fresh lemon juice

confectioners' sugar, for sprinkling

1 Preheat the oven to 350°F.

2 ▼ Sift the flour, confectioners' sugar, and salt into a mixing bowl. Using your fingertips or a pastry blender, rub or cut in the butter or margarine until the mixture resembles coarse crumbs. Add the water and toss lightly with a fork until the dough will form a ball.

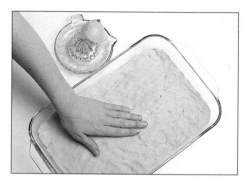

3 ▲ Press the dough evenly over the bottom of an ungreased 13- × 9-inch baking dish. Bake until light golden brown, 15–20 minutes. Remove from oven and let cool slightly.

4 Meanwhile, with an electric mixer, beat together the eggs, granulated sugar, flour, baking powder, and lemon rind and juice.

5 ▲ Pour the lemon mixture over the baked crust. Return to the oven and bake 25 minutes. Let cool, in the baking dish, on a wire rack.

6 ▲ Before serving, sprinkle the top with confectioners' sugar. Cut into squares with a sharp knife.

Hazelnut Brownies

MAKES 9

2 1-ounce squares unsweetened chocolate

5 tablespoons butter or margarine

1 cup sugar

7 tablespoons flour

½ teaspoon baking powder

2 eggs, beaten

½ teaspoon vanilla extract

1 cup skinned hazelnuts, roughly chopped

1 Preheat the oven to 350°F. Grease an 8-inch square baking pan.

2 ▲ In a heatproof bowl set over a pan of barely simmering water, or in a double boiler, melt the chocolate and butter or margarine. Remove the bowl from the heat.

3 ▲ Add the sugar, flour, baking powder, eggs, vanilla, and ½ cup of the hazelnuts to the melted mixture and stir well with a wooden spoon.

4 ▼ Pour the batter into the prepared pan. Bake 10 minutes, then sprinkle the reserved hazelnuts over the top. Return to the oven and continue baking until firm to the touch, about 25 minutes.

5 ▲ Let cool in the pan, set on a wire rack for 10 minutes, then unmold onto the rack and let cool completely. Cut into squares for serving.

HOT & COLD DESSERTS

~

There's always a little space left at the end of a meal for
dessert, particularly if it's rich and creamy, fruity and spiced,
crisp and nutty, icy cold, or, best of all, chocolatey.
You'll find a sweet idea here to meet your requirements.

Hot Spiced Bananas

SERVES 6

6 ripe bananas

1 cup light brown sugar, firmly packed

1 cup unsweetened pineapple juice

½ cup dark rum

2 cinnamon sticks

12 whole cloves

1 ▼ Preheat the oven to 350°F. Grease a 9-inch shallow baking dish.

2 ▲ Peel the bananas and cut them into 1-inch pieces on the diagonal. Arrange the banana pieces evenly over the bottom of the prepared baking dish.

3 ▲ In a saucepan, combine the sugar and pineapple juice. Cook over medium heat until the sugar has dissolved, stirring occasionally.

4 Add the rum, cinnamon sticks, and cloves. Bring to a boil, then remove the pan from the heat.

5 ▲ Pour the pineapple-spice mixture over the bananas. Bake until the bananas are very tender and hot, 25–30 minutes. Serve hot.

Apple-Walnut Crisp

SERVES 6

6 cups peeled and sliced tart apples, such as Granny Smith or Greening (about 2 pounds)

grated rind of ½ lemon

1 tablespoon fresh lemon juice

½ cup light brown sugar, firmly packed

¾ cup flour

¼ teaspoon salt

¼ teaspoon grated nutmeg

½ teaspoon ground cardamom

½ teaspoon ground cinnamon

½ cup (1 stick) butter or margarine, diced

½ cup walnut pieces, chopped

1 Preheat the oven to 350°F. Grease a 9- or 10-inch oval gratin dish or shallow baking dish.

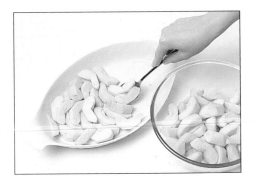

2 ▲ Toss the apples with the lemon rind and juice. Arrange them evenly in the bottom of the prepared dish.

3 In a mixing bowl, combine the brown sugar, flour, salt, nutmeg, cardamom, and cinnamon. With 2 knives, or a pastry blender, cut in the butter or margarine until the mixture resembles coarse crumbs. Mix in the walnuts.

4 ▼ With a spoon, sprinkle the walnut-spice mixture evenly over the apples. Cover with foil and bake for 30 minutes.

5 ▲ Remove the foil and continue baking until the apples are tender and the topping is crisp, about 30 minutes longer. Serve warm.

Baked Apples with Caramel Sauce

SERVES 6

3 Granny Smith apples, cored but not peeled

3 Red Delicious apples, cored but not peeled

¾ cup light brown sugar, firmly packed

¾ cup water

½ teaspoon grated nutmeg

¼ teaspoon freshly ground black pepper

¼ cup walnut pieces

¼ cup golden raisins

4 tablespoons butter or margarine, diced

FOR THE CARAMEL SAUCE

1 tablespoon butter or margarine

½ cup whipping cream

1 Preheat the oven to 375°F. Grease a baking pan just large enough to hold the apples.

2 ▲ With a small knife, cut at an angle to enlarge the core opening at the stem-end of each apple to about 1 inch in diameter. (The opening should resemble a funnel in shape.)

~ VARIATION ~

Use a mixture of firm red and gold pears instead of the apples, preparing them the same way. Cook for 10 minutes longer.

3 ▲ Arrange the apples in the prepared pan, stem-end up.

4 ▲ In a small saucepan, combine the brown sugar, water, nutmeg, and pepper. Bring the mixture to a boil, stirring. Boil for 6 minutes.

5 ▲ Mix together the walnuts and golden raisins. Spoon some of the walnut-raisin mixture into the opening in each apple.

6 ▲ Top each apple with some of the diced butter or margarine.

7 ▲ Spoon the brown sugar sauce over and around the apples. Bake, basting occasionally with the sauce, until the apples are just tender, about 50 minutes. Transfer the apples to a serving dish, reserving the brown sugar sauce in the baking dish. Keep the apples warm.

8 ▲ For the caramel sauce, mix the butter or margarine, cream, and reserved brown sugar sauce in a saucepan. Bring to a boil, stirring occasionally, and simmer until thickened, about 2 minutes. Let the sauce cool slightly before serving.

Upside-Down Pear Brownies

Serves 8

½ cup flour

1 teaspoon baking powder

¼ teaspoon salt

7 1-ounce squares semisweet chocolate

½ cup (1 stick) butter or margarine

2 eggs

½ cup sugar

½ teaspoon vanilla extract

1 tablespoon strong black coffee

¼ cup semisweet chocolate chips

½ cup walnut pieces, chopped

1½ pounds ripe pears, or 2 14-ounce cans pear quarters, drained

1 Preheat the oven to 375°F. Grease a 9-inch round nonstick baking dish.

2 Sift the flour, baking powder, and salt into a small bowl. Set aside.

3 In a heatproof bowl set over a pan of simmering water, or in a double boiler, melt the chocolate and butter or margarine. Remove the bowl from the heat and let cool slightly.

4 ▲ Beat the eggs, sugar, vanilla, and coffee into the melted chocolate mixture. Stir in the flour mixture, chocolate chips, and walnuts.

5 ▲ If using fresh pears, peel, quarter, and core them. Arrange the pear quarters in the prepared baking dish, with the rounded ends against the side of the dish. Pour the batter evenly over the pears.

6 Bake 1 hour, covering with foil after 30 minutes. Let cool 15 minutes, then hold an upturned plate tightly over the top of the baking dish, invert and unmold. Serve hot.

Ginger Baked Pears

Serves 6

6 large firm pears, peeled, cored, and sliced lengthwise

¼ cup honey

¼ cup light brown sugar, firmly packed

1 tablespoon finely grated fresh gingerroot

½ cup whipping cream

~ VARIATION ~

Substitute firm (even underripe) peaches for the pears. To peel, dip the peaches in boiling water for about a minute, then slip off the skins. Cook as for pears.

---

1 ▼ Preheat the oven to 400°F. Butter a 10-inch oval gratin dish or shallow baking dish. Fan the pear slices in a spiral design in the bottom of the baking dish.

2 ▲ In a small bowl, mix together the honey, brown sugar, gingerroot, and cream. Pour this mixture over the pears.

3 Bake until the pears are tender and the top is lightly golden, about 30 minutes. Serve hot.

Upside-Down Pear Brownies (top), Ginger Baked Pears

Blueberry Buckle

SERVES 8

2 cups flour

2 teaspoons baking powder

½ teaspoon salt

½ cup (1 stick) butter or margarine, at room temperature

¾ cup granulated sugar

1 egg

½ teaspoon vanilla extract

¾ cup milk

1 pint fresh blueberries

whipped cream, for serving

FOR THE TOPPING

½ cup light brown sugar, firmly packed

½ cup flour

½ teaspoon salt

½ teaspoon ground allspice

4 tablespoons butter or margarine

2 teaspoons milk

1 teaspoon vanilla extract

1 Preheat the oven to 375°F. Grease a 9-inch round gratin dish or shallow baking dish.

2 Sift the flour, baking powder, and salt into a small bowl. Set aside.

3 ▲ With an electric mixer, or using a wooden spoon, cream together the butter or margarine and granulated sugar. Beat in the egg and vanilla. Add the flour mixture alternately with the milk, beginning and ending with the flour.

4 ▲ Pour the batter into the prepared dish. Sprinkle the blueberries evenly over the batter.

5 ▲ For the topping, combine the brown sugar, flour, salt, and allspice in a bowl. With a pastry blender, cut in the butter or margarine until the mixture resembles coarse crumbs.

6 ▲ Mix together the milk and vanilla. Drizzle over the flour mixture and toss lightly with a fork to mix.

7 Sprinkle the topping over the blueberries. Bake until a cake tester inserted in the center comes out clean, about 45 minutes. Serve warm, with whipped cream if you like.

Peach Cobbler

SERVES 6

5 cups peeled and sliced peaches (about 3 pounds)

3 tablespoons sugar

2 tablespoons peach brandy

1 tablespoon fresh lemon juice

1 tablespoon cornstarch

FOR THE DOUGH

1 cup flour

1½ teaspoons baking powder

¼ teaspoon salt

⅓ cup finely ground almonds

¼ cup plus 1 tablespoon sugar

4 tablespoons butter or margarine

⅓ cup milk

¼ teaspoon almond extract

1 Preheat the oven to 425°F.

2 In a bowl, toss the peaches with the sugar, peach brandy, lemon juice, and cornstarch.

3 Spoon the peach mixture into a 2-quart baking dish.

4 ▲ For the dough, sift the flour, baking powder, and salt into a mixing bowl. Stir in the ground almonds and ¼ cup sugar. With 2 knives, or a pastry blender, cut in the butter or margarine until the mixture resembles coarse crumbs.

5 ▼ Add the milk and almond extract and stir until the dough is just combined.

6 ▲ Drop the dough by spoonfuls onto the peaches. Sprinkle with the remaining tablespoon of sugar.

7 Bake until the cobbler topping is browned, 30–35 minutes. Serve hot, with ice cream, if you like.

Indian Pudding

SERVES 6

4 cups milk
¼ cup cornmeal
½ teaspoon salt
¼ teaspoon ground ginger
¾ teaspoon ground cinnamon
4 tablespoons butter or margarine
¾ cup light molasses
2 eggs, beaten

1 Heat 3 cups of the milk in a saucepan.

2 In a heatproof bowl set over a pan of boiling water, or in a double boiler, combine the cornmeal, salt, ginger, cinnamon, and remaining milk.

3 ▼ Pour in the heated milk, stirring to combine. Cook, stirring constantly, until smooth.

4 Reduce the heat so the water is just simmering, and cook 25 minutes, stirring frequently.

5 Preheat the oven to 350°F. Grease a deep 1-quart earthenware or porcelain baking dish.

6 ▲ Remove the bowl from the heat. Stir in the butter or margarine and molasses until the mixture is smooth. Stir in the eggs.

7 Pour the batter into the prepared baking dish. Bake 1 hour. Serve warm.

Lemon Sponge Pudding

SERVES 6

1 cup flour
1 teaspoon baking powder
¼ + ⅛ teaspoon salt
½ cup (1 stick) butter or margarine, at room temperature
1⅓ cups sugar
finely grated rind and juice of 4 large lemons
4 eggs, separated
1¼ cups milk

1 Preheat the oven to 350°F. Butter a 10-inch shallow oval baking dish.

2 Sift the flour, baking powder, and ¼ teaspoon salt into a small bowl. Set aside.

3 ▼ With an electric mixer, beat together the butter or margarine, sugar, and lemon rind. Beat in the egg yolks, one at a time. Mix in the flour mixture alternately with the milk and lemon juice (reserving a squeeze of juice), beginning and ending with the flour.

4 ▲ In a clean bowl, beat the egg whites with the ⅛ teaspoon salt and squeeze of lemon juice until stiff peaks form. Fold into the lemon batter.

5 Pour into the prepared baking dish. Bake until golden brown, 40–45 minutes. Serve hot.

Indian Pudding (top), Lemon Sponge Pudding

Bread Pudding with Bourbon Sauce

SERVES 8

3 cups stale French bread, in ¾-inch cubes (about 6 ounces)
2 cups milk
2 eggs
1 cup sugar
1 tablespoon vanilla extract
½ teaspoon ground cinnamon
¼ teaspoon grated nutmeg
4 tablespoons butter or margarine, melted and cooled slightly
½ cup raisins
FOR THE SAUCE
2 egg yolks
½ cup (1 stick) butter or margarine
1 cup sugar
⅓ cup bourbon whiskey

1 ▲ Preheat the oven to 350°F. Grease an 8-inch baking dish.

2 ▲ Put the bread cubes in a bowl with the milk and squeeze the bread with your hands until well saturated.

3 ▲ With an electric mixer on high speed, beat the eggs with the sugar until pale and thick. Stir in the vanilla, cinnamon, nutmeg, butter or margarine, and raisins.

4 ▲ Add the soaked bread cube mixture and stir well to mix. Let stand 10 minutes.

5 ▲ Transfer the mixture to the prepared baking dish. Bake until firm and a knife inserted in the middle comes out clean, 45–50 minutes. Let it cool slightly in the dish, set on a wire rack.

6 ▲ Meanwhile, make the sauce. With an electric mixer, beat the egg yolks until thick and pale.

7 ▲ Melt the butter or margarine and sugar in a saucepan. Pour the butter-sugar mixture over the egg yolks, beating constantly, until well thickened. Stir in the whiskey.

8 Serve the warm pudding from its baking dish. Pass the hot whiskey sauce separately.

~ COOK'S TIP ~

It is important to allow enough time for the egg mixture to soak the bread thoroughly; otherwise the bread cubes will float on top, leaving a layer of custard on the bottom when the dish is cooked.

Chocolate Pudding Cake

SERVES 6

¾ cup flour

2 teaspoons baking powder

⅛ teaspoon salt

4 tablespoons butter or margarine

1 1-ounce square unsweetened chocolate

½ cup granulated sugar

6 tablespoons milk

¼ teaspoon vanilla extract

whipped cream, for serving

FOR THE TOPPING

2 tablespoons instant coffee

1¼ cups hot water

½ cup dark brown sugar, firmly packed

⅓ cup granulated sugar

2 tablespoons unsweetened cocoa powder

1 Preheat the oven to 350°F. Grease a 9-inch square baking pan.

2 Sift the flour, baking powder, and salt into a small bowl. Set aside.

3 In a heatproof bowl set over simmering water, or in a double boiler, melt the butter or margarine, chocolate, and granulated sugar, stirring occasionally. Remove the bowl from the heat.

4 ▲ Add the flour mixture and stir well. Stir in the milk and vanilla.

5 ▲ Pour the batter into the prepared baking pan.

6 For the topping, dissolve the coffee in the water. Let cool.

7 ▲ Mix together the sugars and cocoa powder. Sprinkle the mixture over the batter.

8 ▲ Pour the coffee evenly over the surface. Bake 40 minutes. Serve immediately with whipped cream.

Individual Chocolate Soufflés

SERVES 6

5 tablespoons sugar

½ cup plus 1 tablespoon unsweetened cocoa powder

⅓ cup cold water

6 egg whites

confectioners' sugar, for dusting

1 Preheat the oven to 375°F. Lightly butter 6 individual soufflé dishes or ramekins. Mix together 1 tablespoon of sugar and 1 tablespoon of cocoa powder. Sprinkle this mixture over the bottom and sides of the dishes and shake out any excess.

2 ▲ In a saucepan, combine the remaining cocoa powder and the cold water. Bring to a boil over medium heat, whisking constantly. Pour into a mixing bowl.

3 ▲ With an electric mixer, beat the egg whites until soft peaks form. Add the remaining sugar and continue beating until the peaks are stiff.

4 ▼ Add one-quarter of the egg whites to the chocolate mixture and stir well to combine. Add the remaining egg whites and fold gently but thoroughly, until no streaks of white are visible.

5 ▲ Divide the chocolate mixture between the prepared dishes, filling them to the top. Smooth the surface with a metal spatula. Run your thumb around the rim of each dish so the mixture will not stick when rising.

6 Bake until well risen and set, 14–16 minutes. Dust with confectioners' sugar and serve immediately.

Fruit Kabobs with Mango-Yogurt Sauce

SERVES 4

½ pineapple, peeled, cored, and cubed

2 kiwis, peeled and cubed

½ pint strawberries, hulled and cut in half lengthwise, if large

½ mango, peeled, pitted, and cubed

FOR THE SAUCE

½ cup fresh mango purée, from 1–1½ peeled and pitted mangoes

½ cup thick plain yogurt

1 teaspoon sugar

⅛ teaspoon vanilla extract

1 tablespoon finely shredded fresh mint leaves

1 To make the sauce, beat together the mango purée, yogurt, sugar, and vanilla with an electric mixer.

2 ▼ Stir in the mint. Cover the sauce and refrigerate until required.

3 ▲ Thread the fruit onto 12 6-inch wooden skewers, alternating the pineapple, kiwis, strawberries, and mango cubes.

4 Arrange the kabobs on a large serving tray with the mango-yogurt sauce in the center.

Tropical Fruits in Cinnamon Syrup

SERVES 6

2 cups sugar

1 cinnamon stick

1 large or 2 medium papayas (about 1½ pounds), peeled, seeded, and cut lengthwise into thin pieces

1 large or 2 medium mangoes (about 1½ pounds), peeled, pitted, and cut lengthwise into thin pieces

1 large or 2 small starfruit (about ½ pound), thinly sliced

1 Sprinkle ⅔ cup of the sugar over the bottom of a large saucepan. Add the cinnamon stick and half the papaya, mango, and starfruit pieces.

~ **COOK'S TIP** ~

Starfruit is sometimes called carambola.

2 ▼ Sprinkle ⅔ cup of the remaining sugar over the fruit pieces in the pan. Add the remaining fruit and sprinkle with the remaining ⅔ cup sugar.

3 Cover the pan and cook the fruit over medium-low heat until the sugar dissolves completely, 35–45 minutes. Shake the pan occasionally, but do not stir or the fruit will collapse.

4 ▲ Uncover the pan and simmer until the fruit begins to appear translucent, about 10 minutes. Remove the pan from the heat and let stand to cool.

5 Transfer the fruit and syrup to a bowl, cover, and refrigerate overnight.

Fruit Kabobs with Mango-Yogurt Sauce (top), Tropical Fruits in Cinnamon Syrup

Rice Pudding with Mixed Berry Sauce

SERVES 6

2 cups short-grain rice

1⅓ cups milk

⅛ teaspoon salt

½ cup light brown sugar, firmly packed

1 teaspoon vanilla extract

2 eggs, beaten

grated rind of 1 lemon

1 teaspoon fresh lemon juice

2 tablespoons butter or margarine

FOR THE SAUCE

½ pint strawberries, hulled and
   quartered

½ pint raspberries

½ cup granulated sugar

grated rind of 1 lemon

1 Preheat the oven to 325°F. Grease
a deep 2-quart baking dish.

2 ▼ Bring a medium saucepan of
water to a boil. Add the rice and boil
5 minutes. Drain. Transfer the rice to
the prepared baking dish.

3 In a medium bowl, combine the
milk, salt, brown sugar, vanilla, eggs,
and lemon rind and juice. Pour this
mixture over the rice and stir well.

4 ▲ Dot the surface of the rice
mixture with the butter or margarine.
Bake until the rice is cooked and
creamy, about 50 minutes.

5 ▲ Meanwhile, for the sauce,
combine the berries and sugar in a
small saucepan. Stir over low heat
until the sugar dissolves completely
and the fruit is becoming pulpy.
Transfer to a bowl and stir in the
lemon rind. Refrigerate until required.

6 ▲ Remove the rice pudding from
the oven. Let cool completely, and
serve with the berry sauce.

Phyllo Fruit Baskets

SERVES 6

4 large or 8 small sheets of phyllo pastry, thawed if frozen
5 tablespoons butter or margarine, melted
1 cup whipping cream
¼ cup strawberry preserves
1 tablespoon Cointreau or other orange liqueur
1 cup seedless red grapes, halved
1 cup seedless green grapes, halved
1 cup fresh pineapple cubes
½ pint raspberries
2 tablespoons confectioners' sugar
6 small sprigs of fresh mint, for garnishing

1 Preheat the oven to 350°F. Grease 6 cups of a muffin pan.

2 ▲ Stack the phyllo sheets and cut with a sharp knife or scissors into 24 4½-inch squares.

3 ▲ Lay 4 squares of pastry in each of the 6 muffin cups. Press the pastry firmly into the cups, rotating slightly to make star-shaped baskets.

4 ▼ Brush the pastry baskets lightly with butter or margarine. Bake until the pastry is crisp and golden, 5–7 minutes. Let cool on a wire rack.

5 In a bowl, lightly whip the cream until soft peaks form. Gently fold the strawberry preserves and Cointreau into the cream.

6 ▲ Just before serving, spoon a little of the cream mixture into each pastry basket. Top with the fruit. Sprinkle with confectioners' sugar and decorate each basket with a small sprig of mint.

Strawberry Shortcake

SERVES 6

1½ pints strawberries, hulled and halved or quartered, depending on size

3 tablespoons confectioners' sugar

1 cup whipping cream

mint leaves, for garnishing

FOR THE BISCUITS

2 cups flour

6 tablespoons granulated sugar

1 tablespoon baking powder

½ teaspoon salt

1 cup whipping cream

1 Preheat the oven to 400°F. Lightly grease a baking sheet.

2 ▲ For the biscuits, sift the flour into a mixing bowl. Add 4 tablespoons of the granulated sugar, the baking powder, and salt. Stir well.

3 ▲ Gradually add the cream, tossing lightly with a fork until the mixture forms clumps.

4 ▲ Gather the clumps together, but do not knead the dough. Shape the dough into a 6-inch log. Cut into 6 slices and place them on the prepared baking sheet.

5 ▲ Sprinkle with the remaining 2 tablespoons granulated sugar. Bake until light golden brown, about 15 minutes. Let cool on a wire rack.

6 ▲ Meanwhile, combine 1 cup of the strawberries with the confectioners' sugar. Mash with a fork. Stir in the remaining strawberries. Let stand 1 hour at room temperature.

7 ▲ In a bowl, whip the cream until soft peaks form.

8 ▲ To serve, slice each biscuit in half horizontally using a serrated knife. Put the bottom halves on individual dessert plates. Top each biscuit half with some of the whipped cream. Divide the berries among the 6 biscuits. Replace the biscuit tops and garnish with mint. Serve with the remaining whipped cream.

~ **COOK'S TIP** ~

For best results when whipping cream, refrigerate the bowl and beaters until thoroughly chilled. If using an electric mixer, increase speed gradually, and turn the bowl while beating to incorporate as much air as possible.

Individual Tiramisu

SERVES 4

½ pound mascarpone cheese

1½ tablespoons sugar

2 eggs, at room temperature, separated

⅛ teaspoon salt

squeeze of fresh lemon juice

½ cup very strong cold black coffee

2 tablespoons coffee liqueur

1 cup coarsely crumbled butter cookies or pound cake

2 tablespoons unsweetened cocoa powder, sifted

~ **COOK'S TIP** ~

Buying very fresh eggs from a reputable producer is especially important when using them raw.

1 With an electric mixer, beat the cheese, sugar, and egg yolks together until blended and creamy.

2 ▲ In a clean mixing bowl, beat the egg whites with the salt and lemon juice until stiff peaks form. Fold into the cheese mixture.

3 In a small bowl, combine the coffee and liqueur.

4 ▲ Divide half the cookie crumbs among 4 stemmed glasses. Drizzle over 1–1½ tablespoons of the liqueur mixture. Top the moistened crumbs with half the mascarpone mixture. Layer the remaining cookie crumbs, coffee mixture, and mascarpone mixture in the same way.

5 Cover and refrigerate the desserts 1–2 hours. Sprinkle with the sifted cocoa powder before serving.

White Chocolate Mousse

SERVES 8

9 ounces white chocolate

⅓ cup milk

1½ cups whipping cream

1 teaspoon vanilla extract

3 egg whites, at room temperature

⅛ teaspoon salt

squeeze of fresh lemon juice

chocolate covered coffee beans, for decoration

1 In a heatproof bowl set over a pan of barely simmering water, or in a double boiler, melt the chocolate.

2 Scald the milk in a small saucepan. Remove the bowl of chocolate from the heat and whisk in the warm milk until smooth. Let cool.

3 In a mixing bowl, whip the cream with the vanilla until soft peaks form. Refrigerate until needed.

4 ▲ Using an electric mixer and a clean bowl, beat the egg whites with the salt and lemon juice until stiff peaks form (do not overbeat or the mousse will be grainy). Fold into the chocolate mixture.

5 ▲ Gently fold the chocolate-egg white mixture into the vanilla flavored whipped cream.

6 Transfer to a pretty serving bowl or individual stemmed glasses. Cover and refrigerate at least 1 hour. Sprinkle with chocolate covered coffee beans before serving.

Individual Tiramisu (top), White Chocolate Mousse

Chocolate Cheesecake

SERVES 12

1 pound (16 1-ounce squares) semisweet chocolate, broken into pieces

½ cup granulated sugar

2 teaspoons vanilla extract

4 eggs

3 8-ounce packages cream cheese, at room temperature

2–3 tablespoons confectioners' sugar, for decoration

FOR THE CRUST

1 cup graham cracker crumbs

5 tablespoons butter or margarine, melted

2 tablespoons grated semisweet chocolate

2 tablespoons granulated sugar

1 ▲ Preheat the oven to 325°F. Grease a 9- or 10-inch springform pan and line the bottom with wax paper. Grease the wax paper.

~ **VARIATION** ~

For an all-chocolate cheesecake, substitute an equal quantity of finely crushed chocolate wafers for the graham cracker crumbs when preparing the crust.

2 ▲ For the crust, mix together the graham cracker crumbs, melted butter or margarine, grated chocolate, and sugar. Pat evenly over the bottom and up the sides of the prepared pan. (The crust will be thin!)

3 ▲ In a heatproof bowl set over a pan of barely simmering water, or in a double boiler, melt the chocolate with the granulated sugar. Remove the bowl from the heat and stir in the vanilla. Let cool briefly.

4 ▲ In another bowl, beat together the eggs and cream cheese until smooth and homogeneous. Gently stir in the cooled chocolate mixture until completely blended.

5 ▲ Pour the chocolate filling into the crumb crust. Bake until the filling is set, 45 minutes.

6 ▲ Let cool, in the pan, on a wire rack. Refrigerate at least 12 hours.

7 ▲ Remove the side of the pan and transfer the cheesecake to a serving plate. To decorate, lay a paper doily on the surface of the cake and sift the confectioners' sugar evenly over the doily. With two hands, carefully lift off the doily.

Coffee Ice Cream Sandwiches

MAKES 8

½ cup (1 stick) butter or margarine, at room temperature

¼ cup granulated sugar

1 cup flour

2 tablespoons instant coffee

confectioners' sugar, for sprinkling

1 pint coffee ice cream

2 tablespoons unsweetened cocoa powder

1 Lightly grease 2–3 cookie sheets.

2 With an electric mixer or wooden spoon, beat the butter or margarine until soft. Beat in the granulated sugar.

3 ▲ Add the flour and coffee and mix by hand to form an evenly blended dough. Wrap in a plastic bag and refrigerate at least 1 hour.

4 Lightly sprinkle the work surface with confectioners' sugar. Knead the dough on the sugared surface for a few minutes to soften it slightly.

5 ▼ Using a rolling pin dusted with confectioners' sugar, roll out the dough to ⅛-inch thickness. With a 2½-inch fluted cookie cutter, cut out 16 rounds. Transfer the rounds to the prepared cookie sheets. Refrigerate for at least 30 minutes.

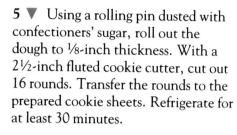

6 Preheat the oven to 300°F. Bake the cookies until they are lightly golden, about 30 minutes. Let the cookies cool and firm up before removing them from the sheets to a wire rack to cool completely.

7 Remove the ice cream from the freezer and let soften 10 minutes at room temperature.

8 ▲ With a metal spatula, spread ¼ cup of the ice cream on the flat side of half of the cookies, leaving the edges clear. Top the ice cream with the remaining cookies, flat-side down.

9 Arrange the cookie sandwiches on a baking sheet. Cover and freeze at least 1 hour, longer if a firmer sandwich is desired. Sift the cocoa powder over the tops before serving.

Chocolate Mint Ice Cream Pie

SERVES 8

⅔ cup semisweet chocolate chips

3 tablespoons butter or margarine

2 cups crisped rice cereal

1 quart mint-chocolate-chip ice cream

3 1-ounce squares semisweet chocolate

1 Line a 9-inch pie pan with foil. Place a round of wax paper over the foil in the bottom of the pan.

2 In a heatproof bowl set over a pan of barely simmering water, or in a double boiler, melt the chocolate chips and butter or margarine.

3 ▲ Remove the bowl from the heat and gently stir in the cereal, ½ cup at a time. Let cool 5 minutes.

4 ▲ Press the chocolate-cereal mixture evenly over the bottom and up the sides of the prepared pan, forming a ½-inch rim. Refrigerate until completely hard.

5 Carefully remove the crust from the pan and peel off the foil and wax paper. Return the crust to the pie pan.

6 Remove the ice cream from the freezer and let soften 10 minutes at room temperature.

7 ▼ Spread the ice cream evenly in the crust. Freeze until firm, about 1 hour.

8 For the decoration, use the heat of your hands to slightly soften the chocolate squares. Draw the blade of a swivel-headed vegetable peeler along the smooth surface of each chocolate square to shave off short, wide curls. Refrigerate the chocolate curls until needed.

9 ▲ Scatter the chocolate curls over the ice cream just before serving.

Hot Fudge Brownie Sundaes

SERVES 8

1 recipe Hazelnut Brownies

1 pint vanilla ice cream

1 pint chocolate ripple ice cream

½ cup walnut pieces, chopped

FOR THE HOT FUDGE SAUCE

3 tablespoons butter or margarine

⅓ cup granulated sugar

⅓ cup dark brown sugar, firmly packed

½ cup unsweetened cocoa powder

⅓ cup whipping cream

⅛ teaspoon salt

1 ▼ For the sauce, combine all the ingredients in a saucepan. Cook gently, stirring, until it is smooth.

2 Cut the brownie cake into squares. Put a brownie in each of 8 bowls.

3 ▼ Top each brownie with a scoop of each ice cream. Spoon the hot fudge sauce on top. Sprinkle with chopped walnuts and serve immediately.

Chocolate Cookie Ice Cream

MAKES 1½ QUARTS

2 cups whipping cream

3 egg yolks

1½ cups sweetened condensed milk

4 teaspoons vanilla extract

1 cup coarsely crushed chocolate sandwich cookies (about 12 cookies)

2 In a mixing bowl, whip the cream until soft peaks form. Set aside.

3 ▼ In another bowl, beat the egg yolks until thick and pale. Stir in the sweetened condensed milk and vanilla. Fold in the cookies and whipped cream.

4 Pour into the prepared loaf pan. Cover with the foil overhang and freeze until firm, about 6 hours.

5 ▲ To serve, remove the ice cream from the pan and peel off the foil. Cut into thin slices with a sharp knife.

1 ▲ Line a 9- × 5-inch loaf pan with foil, leaving enough overhang to cover the top.

~ COOK'S TIP ~

Buying very fresh eggs from a reputable producer is especially important when using them raw.

Hot Fudge Brownie Sundaes (top), Chocolate Cookie Ice Cream

INDEX